# Migration and Agriculture

In recent years, Mediterranean agriculture has experienced important transformations which have led to new forms of labour and production, and in particular to a surge in the recruitment of migrant labour. The Mediterranean Basin represents a very interesting arena that is able to illustrate labour conditions and mobility, the competition among different farming models, and the consequences in terms of the proletarianization process, food crisis and diet changes.

*Migration and Agriculture* brings together international contributors from across several disciplines to describe and analyse labour conditions and international migrations in relation to agri-food restructuring processes. This unique collection of articles connects migration issues with the proletarianization process and agrarian transitions that have affected Southern European as well as some Middle Eastern and Northern African countries in different ways. The chapters present case studies from a range of territories in the Mediterranean Basin, offering empirical data and theoretical analysis in order to grasp the complexity of the processes that are occurring.

This book offers a uniquely comprehensive overview of migrations, territories and agri-food production in this key region, and will be an indispensable resource to scholars in migration studies, rural sociology, social geography and the political economy of agriculture.

**Alessandra Corrado** is assistant professor in the Department of Political and Social Sciences, University of Calabria, and founding member of the Study Center for Rural Development, Italy.

**Carlos de Castro** is lecturer in the Department of Sociology at the Universidad Autónoma of Madrid, Spain.

**Domenico Perrotta** is tenured researcher and lecturer in the Sociology of Cultural Processes at the University of Bergamo, Italy.

**Routledge ISS Studies in Rural Livelihoods**



Routledge and the Institute of Social Studies (ISS) in The Hague, the Netherlands have come together to publish a new book series in rural livelihoods. The series will include themes such as land policies and land rights, water issues, food policy and politics, rural poverty, agrarian transformation, migration, rural-oriented social movements, rural conflict and violence, among others. All books in the series will offer rigorous, empirically grounded, cross-national comparative and inter-regional analysis. The books will be theoretically stimulating, but will also be accessible to policy practitioners and civil society activists.

*For a complete list of titles in this series, please visit* https://www.routledge.com/series/ISSRL

**11 Rural Livelihoods, Regional Economies and Processes of Change**
*Edited by Deborah Sick*

**12 Rural Development and the Construction of New Markets**
*Edited by Paul Hebinck, Jan Douwe van der Ploeg and Sergio Schneider*

**13 The Political Ecology of Agrofuels**
*Edited by Kristina Dietz, Bettina Engels, Oliver Pye and Achim Brunnengräber*

**14 Rural Wage Employment in Developing Countries**
Theory, evidence and policy
*Edited by Carlos Oya and Nicol Pontara*

**15 Migration and Agriculture**
Mobility and change in the Mediterranean area
*Edited by Alessandra Corrado, Carlos de Castro and Domenico Perrotta*

# Migration and Agriculture

## Mobility and change in the Mediterranean area

**Edited by**
**Alessandra Corrado, Carlos de Castro and Domenico Perrotta**

Routledge
Taylor & Francis Group
LONDON AND NEW YORK

First published 2017 by Routledge

2 Park Square, Milton Park, Abingdon, Oxfordshire OX14 4RN
52 Vanderbilt Avenue, New York, NY 10017

*Routledge is an imprint of the Taylor & Francis Group, an informa business*

First issued in paperback 2018



*British Library Cataloguing in Publication Data*
A catalogue record for this book is available from the British Library

*Library of Congress Cataloging in Publication Data*
Names: Corrado, Alessandra, editor.
Title: Migration and agriculture : mobility and change in the Mediterranean Area / edited by Alessandra Corrado, Carlos de Castro, Domenico Perrotta.
Description: New York : Routledge, 2016. | Includes bibliographical references.
Identifiers: LCCN 2016009919| ISBN 9781138962231 (hardback) | ISBN 9781315659558 (ebook)
Subjects: LCSH: Foreign workers—Mediterranean Region. | Agricultural laborers—Mediterranean Region.
Classification: LCC HD8650.7 .M525 2016 | DDC 331.5/44091822—dc23
LC record available at http://lccn.loc.gov/2016009919

ISBN: 978-1-138-96223-1 (hbk)
ISBN: 978-0-367-20012-1 (pbk)

Typeset in Times New Roman
by Book Now Ltd, London

**To the memory of all the people who have died trying to cross the Mediterranean Sea looking for a better life**

# Contents

# Figures



## Maps

# Tables

# Contributors

**Gennaro Avallone** is assistant professor in Sociology of Territory and Environment at the University of Salerno (Italy), and member of FLACSO-España. His research focuses on migration, migrant labour, urban transformations and world-ecology approaches. Over the last years, he has published several articles and books on these topics.

**Vanessa Azzeruoli** obtained a PhD in Sociology at the University of Padova (Italy). Her research interest is focused on the interaction among migration, state policy and the labour market. She currently works as legal operator with asylum seekers in Bologna.

**Mohamed Bouchelkha** is Professor of Rural and Social Geography at the University Ibn Zohr, Agadir, Morocco. His current research interests include the new socio-spatial changes in Moroccan countryside; the impacts of globalization; internal migration dynamics; social management of natural resources.

**Francesco Saverio Caruso** is researcher of the Centre for Rural Development Studies (University of Calabria, Italy) and member of the Centre for the Study of Migration and Intercultural Relations (University of Almerìa, Spain). He is currently Adjunt Professor of Sociology of Environment and Territory at the University 'Magna Graecia' of Catanzaro (Italy).

**Rui F. Carvalho** is a Doctoral student in Sociology at Brown University, USA. He is trained as a geographer and regional planner (BSc, New University of Lisbon, 2009). Before starting his PhD, he worked in various national and international research projects at the University of Lisbon and the New University of Lisbon (Portugal). His present research interests are varied but may overall be framed within the scopes and fields of urban sociology and (international) migration.

**Carlos de Castro** is lecturer at the Department of Sociology at the Universidad Autónoma of Madrid, Spain. His research focuses on the political and institutional configuration of work and workers in the context of global production networks in several sectors.

**Alessandra Corrado** is Assistant Professor of Rural Sociology, and Development and Migrations at the University of Calabria (Italy). She is co-editor of the book series *Sviluppo e Territori / Development and Territories* (Rosenberg & Sellier, Turin) and member of the international editorial committee of the book series *Agrarian Change and Peasant Studies* and editorial board of the journal *Sociologia Urbana e Rurale / Urban and Rural Sociology*. Her research activity revolves around development issues, international migrations, and agri-food systems.

**Chantal Crenn** is lecturer in Social Anthropology, Université Bordeaux Montaigne, and member of Editorial Board of the Journals *Anthropologie au Food* and *Corps*. Her research focuses on the individual and collective processes that contribute to create social and ethnic borders within food areas in the context of a globalized society.

**Frédéric Décosse** is researcher of the Institute of Labour Economics and Industrial Sociology at Centre National de la Recherche Scientifique (CNSR). He holds a doctorate in sociology from the École des Hautes Études en Sciences Sociales (EHESS) in Paris. His thesis focused on Moroccan seasonal workers employed contractually in the agricultural sector by the Office des Migrations Internationales (Office of International Migrations). His research interests include temporary migration programs, workers' health and immigration struggles in the Mediterranean and in Latin America.

**Selma Akay Erturk** (PhD, Istanbul University, 2008; BA, Istanbul University, 2001) is Assistant Professor at the Department of Geography in Istanbul University. Her research focuses on international migration, internal migration, effects of migration on settlements and urban geography.

**Loukia-Maria Fratsea** has studied agricultural economics and geography and currently she is completing her PhD in the Department of Geography at Harokopio University of Athens. She has participated in various research projects as a researcher; her research interests include agricultural transformation, migration and social change, social mobility, civil society and migration and research in rural societies.

**Elena Gadea** is lecturer at the Department of Sociology at University of Murcia. Her research focuses on migrant workers and the impact of global process on agricultural areas. She has published a number of peer-reviewed papers on international workers′ migration and on the role of workers in global agricultural production.

**Alia Gana** is research professor at CNRS (National Centre of Scientific Research, University of Paris-Panthéon Sorbonne) and deputy director of the Research Institute on Contemporary Maghreb (IRMC) in Tunis. Holding a PhD in rural and environmental sociology (Cornell University), she has done extensive research on issues such as social systems of farm production, agricultural policies, rural and farm livelihoods, governance of water resources. Her most recent work focuses on peasants' movements and rural mobilizations in North Africa in the era of 'Arab revolts'.

**Anna Mary Garrapa** obtained a PhD in Urban and Local European Studies at the University of Milano-Bicocca (2015). She is currently post-doctoral research fellow at the Instituto de Investigaciones Economicas of the Universidad Nacional Autonoma de México.

**Emmanuelle Hellio** is lecturer at University of Nice. She holds a PhD in sociology. She is member of the URMIS (Research Unit on International Migration and Society) and works on migration and the agricultural labour market.

**Apostolos G. Papadopoulos** has studied sociology and geography in Greece and the United Kingdom. He is currently Professor of Rural Sociology and Geography at Harokopio University of Athens. He has (co-)edited seven collected volumes (two were published in English) and co-authored one book; he has also published numerous articles in peer-reviewed journals, chapters in books and various papers. His main research interests include: rural development, local food and family farming, rural immigration, the transformation of southern European societies, migrant integration and migrant associations.

**Andrés Pedreño** is Associate Professor of Sociology at the University of Murcia. He has investigated several topics in the areas of agrarian and rural sociology, migration and work. He has published a number of peer-reviewed papers on international workers' migration and on the role of workers in global agricultural production.

**Domenico Perrotta** is Assistant Professor in Sociology of cultural processes at the University of Bergamo (Italy) and co-editor of the journal *Etnografia e ricerca qualitativa / Ethnography and qualitative research*. His research interests include migration processes, ethnography, ethnography of work, the nexus between culture and power, migrant labour and agro-industrial supply chains.

**Valeria Piro** obtained a PhD in Sociology at the University of Milan, with a thesis titled '*Travagghiari a jurnata'. Investigating day labor inside Sicilian tomatoes plastic factories*.

**Alicia Reigada** is lecturer of Social Anthropology at the University of Seville (Spain), and member of the GEISA Research Group. Her studies focus on global agri-food chains, sustainability, social organization of labour, class, migrations and gender relationships. She has participated in several international networks and projects focused on a compared analysis between the Mediterranean and the Latin American intensive agriculture.

**Dora Sampaio** is currently a PhD candidate in Geography at the University of Sussex, UK. Prior to joining Sussex in 2013, she worked at the Centre for Geographical Studies of the University of Lisbon, where she was involved in a number of European projects on national and international migration. Trained as a human geographer at the University of Lisbon (BA, MA), her main research foci lie in international migration and the life course, with particular reference to rural and island contexts.

**Giuliana Sanò** obtained a PhD in Cultural Anthropology at the University of Messina. Currently she is working as a researcher assistant for an ESRC-funded comparative study of the migration crisis in the Mediterranean for the University of Durham.

**Sarah Ruth Sippel** is a geographer and a Senior Researcher at the Centre for Area Studies at the University of Leipzig, Germany. In her past research she has investigated intensive agriculture and livelihood security in the Mediterranean. Within this context she co-edited the volume *Seasonal Workers in Mediterranean Agriculture: The Social Costs of Eating Fresh* (Routledge, 2014). Her current research focuses upon the nexus between food security, financialisation of natural resources, and emerging forms of solidarity within global agrifood systems.

# Acknowledgements

Many of the contributions to this volume were first presented and discussed during the seminar 'Agriculture and Migration in the European Union' held at the University of Bergamo, Italy on 24–25 October 2013. The seminar generated intense discussion and exchange among an interdisciplinary group of scholars. This same network met on two other occasions at the international seminars 'Migrant Labor and Social Sustainability of Global Agri-Food Chains' at the University of Murcia in Spain on 5–7 November 2014, and 'Human Capital, Wage Labour and Innovation in Rural Areas' at the Harokopio University of Athens, Greece on 23–24 October 2015. We would like to thank all the other participants in these seminars for their helpful comments and criticisms.

The preparation of this edited volume presented major obstacles. A key difficulty has been the issue of translation. The contributors are based in universities across the Mediterranean region and are trained in different disciplines (sociology, anthropology and geography); moreover, none of them is a native English speaker. Editing this book has involved the arduous task of translating concepts, arguments and ideas from different national traditions of agrarian research, and of continually crossing academic boundaries. To this end, the language revision carried out by our friend, colleague and excellent scholar Nick Dines has been invaluable. Without his commitment, this book would probably never have seen the light of day. As editors of this volume, we would like to express to him our gratitude.

Another major difficulty facing the completion of this volume has been the dire situation of academic labour in southern Europe over the last few years. Due to austerity policies and public disinvestment in university education and research, especially in Italy, many young, promising scholars after completing their PhD, find themselves employed on extremely precarious contracts that often prevent them from developing further their doctoral research.

We would like to thank Alessandro Bonanno, Jun S. Borras, Luis Camarero, Philip D. McMichael, Dionisio Miranda Ortiz, Antonio Onorati, Germán Quaranta, Apostolos Papadopoulos and Timothy Raeymaekers for their comments on the introduction and on some of the chapter drafts of this volume. We are grateful to Giovanni Salerno for the elaboration of the general map.

Finally, some of the editors and contributors to this volume have collaborated with, or have been directly engaged in organizations of peasants and farm workers: European Coordination of Via Campesina, Confédération Paysanne, Colléctive de Défense des Travailleurs Agricoles, Centro Internazionale Crocevia, Associazione Rurale Italiana, Campi Aperti, Brigate di Solidarietà Attiva, Fuori dal Ghetto, Osservatorio Migranti Basilicata, Funky Tomato, Movimento Migranti e Rifugiati di Caserta, SOS Rosarno, Sindicato de Obreros del Campo. These various initiatives have represented crucial learning moments for many of us. For this reason, we thank all those farm workers, peasants and critical consumers with whom we have shared common experiences, discussions and projects.

# Acronyms

| | |
|---|---|
| AGCM | Autorità Garante della Concorrenza e del Mercato (Italian Antitrust Authority) |
| ANAEM | Agence nationale d'accueil des étrangers and des migrations (National Agency of Reception of Foreigners and of Migration) |
| ANAPEC | Agence Nationale de Promotion de l'Emploi e des Compétences (National Agency for Employment and Competences Promotion) |
| ANGED | Asociación Nacional Grandes de Empresas de Distribución |
| ANICAV | Italian National Canneries Association |
| BBC | British Broadcasting Corporation |
| CAF | Family allowance fund |
| CAP | Common Agricultural Policy |
| CCOO | Comisiones Obreras (Workers' Commissions) |
| CGB | Confédération Générale des Planteurs de Betteraves (General Confederation of Beetroot Planters) |
| CGIL | Confederazione Generale Italiana del Lavoro (Italian General Confederation of Labour) |
| CGT | Confédération Générale du Travail (General Confederation of Work) |
| CMO | Common Market Organization |
| CNSS | Caisse Nationale de Sécurité Sociale (National Bank of Social Security) |
| COAG | Coordinadora de Organizaciones de Agricultores y Ganadero (Coordinator of Farmers' and Livestock Breeders' Organizations) |
| CODETRAS | Collectif de défense des travailleurs agricoles saisonniers (Collective for the Defense of Seasonal Agricultural Workers) |
| COEXPHAL | Almerian Organization of Fruit and Vegetable Producers |
| COSAT | South Africa's Congress of South African Trade Unions |
| CUT | Brazil's Central Unica dos Trabalhadores (Unified Workers Central) |
| DEMP | Disaster & Emergency Management Presidency |

| | |
|---|---|
| EACCE | Etablissement Autonome de Contrôle et de Coordination des Exportations (Authority for the Control and Coordiantion of Exportations) |
| EC | European Commission |
| EEC | European Economic Community |
| ELSTAT | Hellenic Statistical Authority |
| EMDA | Eastern Mediterranean Development Agency |
| EP | European Parliament |
| EU | European Union |
| EUROSTAT | European Statistical Authority |
| FDSEA | Fédérations Départementales des syndicats d'exploitants agricoles (Farmers' local union) |
| FGSTE | General Federation of Trade Unions of Egypt |
| FIDH | Federación Internacional de Derechos Humanos (International Federation of Human Rights) |
| FMO | Fédération Professionnelle Agricole pour la Main-d'Oeuvre Saisonnière (Agricultural Professional Federation for the seasonal work) |
| FMR | French Muslim Return |
| FNSA | Fédération Nationale du Secteur Agricole (Moroccan National Federation of Agricultural Sector) |
| FRCI | French returnee of Islamic Faith |
| GDP | Gross Domestic Product |
| GLOBALGAP | Global Good Agricultural Practices |
| GRASP | GLOBALG.A.P. Risk Assessment on Social Practice |
| GVC | Global value chain |
| HPDA | Hatay Provincial Directorate of Agriculture |
| INAO | National Institute for Denominations of Origin |
| INE | Instituto Nacional de Estadística (Spanish National Institute of Statistics) |
| INEA | Istituto Nazionale Economia Agraria (Italian National Institute of Agricultural Economics) |
| ISMEA | Istituto di Servizi per il Mercato Agricolo Alimentare |
| INTERFRESA | Andalusian Interprofessional Strawberry Growers Association |
| ISTAT | Istituto Nazionale di statistica (Italian National Institute of Statistics) |
| KMU | Philippines' Kilusang Mayo Uno (May First Movement) |
| LMA | Lisbon Metropolitan Area |
| LOA | Leading Organic Alliance |
| MENA | Middle East and North Africa |
| MINAGRI | Ministère de l'agriculture (Ministry of Agriculture) |
| MSA | Agricultural Social Insurance |
| MSSS | Ministry of Solidarity and Social Security |
| NATO | North Atlantic Treaty Organization |
| NGO | Non-governmental organization |

| | |
|---|---|
| OECD | Organisation for Economic Co-operation and Development |
| OFII | French Office for Immigration and Integration |
| OMA | Oporto Metropolitan Area |
| OMI | Office des Migrations Internationales (French Agency for International Migration) |
| ONAGRI | Observatoire National de l'Agriculture, Tunisie (National Observatory of Agriculture) |
| ONI | Office national d'immigration (French National Office for Immigration) |
| ONS-MOI | Ouvriers Non-Spécialisés indochinois de la Main-d'Oeuvre Indigène (Indochinese Semi-Skilled Workers of the Native Workforce) |
| ORMVA/SM | Office Régional de Mise en Valeur Agricole du Souss-Massa (Regional Agency for Registration of Agricultural Value in Souss Massa) |
| PO | Producer Organization |
| REDI | Red Estatal por los Derechos de los Inmigrantes (National Network for Human Rights) |
| RGPH | Haut-Commissariat au Plan du Maroc (High Commisioner for Plan du Maroc) |
| RONA | Returnee of North-African origin |
| SAT | Sindicato Andaluz de los Trabajadores (Andalusian Workers' Union) |
| SE | Southern European |
| SEF | Portuguese Foreign and Borders Service |
| SOC | Sindicato de Obreros del Campo (The Field Workers' Union) |
| SODEA | Société de Développement Agricole (Society for Agricultural Development) |
| SOGETA | Société de Gestion des Terres Agricoles (Society for the Management of Agricultural Lands) |
| SYNAGRI | Union of Tunisian Farmers |
| TNCs | Transnational Companies |
| UGT | Unión General de Trabajadores (General Workers Union) |
| UGTT | General Union of Tunisian Workers |
| UMT | Union Marocaine de Travail (Moroccan Workers Union) |
| UNHCR | United Nations High Commissioner for Refugees |
| US | United States of America |
| UTAP | Tunisian Union for Agriculture and Fisheries |
| WSRW | Western Sahara Resource Watch |
| WTO | World Trade Organization |
| WUAs | Water users' associations |

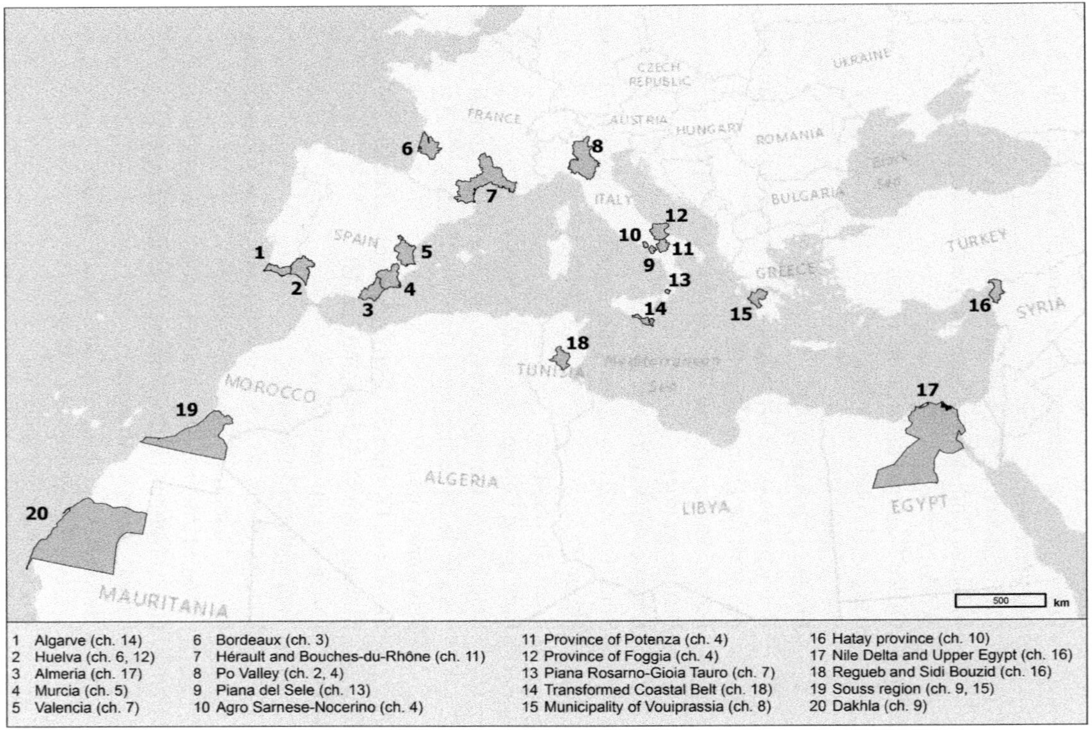

CZECH REPUBLIC
UKRAINE
FRANCE
AUSTRIA
HUNGARY
ROMANIA
BULGARIA
ITALY
SPAIN
TURKEY
GREECE
SYRIA
TUNISIA
MOROCCO
ALGERIA
LIBYA
EGYPT
MAURITANIA
500 km
1 Algarve (ch. 14)
2 Huelva (ch. 6, 12)
3 Almeria (ch. 17)
4 Murcia (ch. 5)
5 Valencia (ch. 7)
6 Bordeaux (ch. 3)
7 Hérault and Bouches-du-Rhône (ch. 11)
8 Po Valley (ch. 2, 4)
9 Piana del Sele (ch. 13)
10 Agro Sarnese-Nocerino (ch. 4)
11 Province of Potenza (ch. 4)
12 Province of Foggia (ch. 4)
13 Piana Rosarno-Gioia Tauro (ch. 7)
14 Transformed Coastal Belt (ch. 18)
15 Municipality of Vouiprassia (ch. 8)
16 Hatay province (ch. 10)
17 Nile Delta and Upper Egypt (ch. 16)
18 Regueb and Sidi Bouzid (ch. 16)
19 Souss region (ch. 9, 15)
20 Dakhla (ch. 9)

*Map 1.1* The Mediterranean area.

# 1 Cheap food, cheap labour, high profits: agriculture and mobility in the Mediterranean

## Introduction

*Alessandra Corrado, Carlos de Castro and Domenico Perrotta*

### 1.1 A history of conflicts

A series of dramatic events in early 2000 in a small town in Andalusia starkly revealed to an international public the dire environmental, social and labour conditions in which fresh food was being produced for Europe's supermarkets. The town in question was El Ejido, the heart of a booming agricultural sector based on intensive greenhouse production that relied on a largely North African and eastern European migrant workforce. The area was already deeply divided by social and racial tensions when in February a young Spanish woman was killed by a mentally ill Moroccan labourer. Her murder sparked a spate of violent attacks against migrants, which led to more than sixty Moroccans being injured and thousands of migrant farm workers going on strike. The events were widely reported by Europe's main newspapers and prompted a host of investigations by NGOs (Forum civique Européen, 2000, 2002), and academic studies (Checa, 2001; Martinez Veiga, 2001, 2014; Potot, 2008; Caruso, this volume).

El Ejido was not an isolated case. Over the following years, rural areas across the Mediterranean region would be shaken by numerous social and labour conflicts. In July 2005, 250 Moroccan, Tunisian and Chinese seasonal workers in the small town of Poscros in the south of France went on strike to demand unpaid wages and better housing and employment conditions. During the same period, migrant workers recruited through the OMI seasonal contracts successfully campaigned for their legal status in France to be made permanent (Décosse, 2011).

Italy would soon 'discover' the dramatic situation of farm workers in its rural areas. In reality, the presence of migrant harvesters in its southern regions had already come to national attention in 1989 after the murder of Jerry Essan Masslo, a South African political refugee employed in the fields of Villa Literno in Campania, who had publicly denounced the apartheid-like conditions in local agriculture. Since this episode, the number of migrant agricultural labourers has steadily grown, but their poor living and working conditions have usually only come to light in similarly dramatic circumstances. In the autumn of 2006, an international scandal broke out over the murder of Polish workers who had been among hundreds of eastern Europeans trafficked for employment in the tomato harvest in Foggia province in northern Puglia. In January 2010, violent riots broke out between migrants and the local population in Rosarno, a small town in Calabria, following the umpteenth attack on sub-Saharan African citrus pickers by local youths. In response, the Italian government sent in the army and 1,500 Sub-Saharan Africans were deported to other regions (Corrado, 2011). In August 2011, around 400 Tunisian and West African watermelon and tomato harvesters went on a two-week strike against their employers and *caporali*, the illegal farm labour contractors, in Nardò, a small town in southern Puglia (Perrotta and Sacchetto, 2013).

In April 2013, the ugly side of Greek agriculture would also come to light. In Manolada, a small town in the Peloponnese region, hundreds of Bangladeshi strawberry pickers had been demanding unpaid wages. Local employers and supervisors responded by opening fire on the workers and wounding 25 of them. As in the other cases, this was by no means the first episode of violence and conflict to have occurred in an area of intensive agricultural production that supplied the markets of the whole of Europe (Papadopoulos and Fratsea, this volume).

In the meantime, the southern shore of the Mediterranean has not been exempt from rural conflicts. Between December 2011 and April 2013, international media reported the struggles of the agricultural trade union FNSA (Fédération National du Secteur Agricole) and thousands of mainly internal migrant farm workers employed in the Moroccan region of Agadir-Souss Massa Drâa, where intensive and export-oriented agriculture had developed during the previous 30 years. The FNSA accused local farms, many owned by European investors or multinational companies, of not respecting Moroccan legislation on labour and denounced the pressures of European retail corporations upon Moroccan producers and the knock-on effects upon farm workers.

Across the Mediterranean, farmers have been just as actively involved in conflicts as agricultural labourers. Southern European fruit and vegetable producers, especially in Spain and Italy, have organized protests against cheap imports from North Africa and the cheap prices paid by retailers, while French farmers have campaigned against the import of Spanish low-cost produce. In 2016, Greek farmers, fishermen and stockbreeders mobilized against austerity measures planned by the government under pressure from the European Union, the International Monetary Fund and the European Central Bank. In a different vein, since 2006 the European Coordination of Via Campesina has organized initiatives in many Mediterranean countries in solidarity with peasants and farm workers involved in struggles against neoliberal policies (Confédération Paysanne, 2011, 2015).

The 2011–12 'Arab Springs' in Tunisia and Egypt have also been analysed in terms of their strong connection with food crises, the restructuring of agriculture, and the marginalization and dispossession of rural populations due to neoliberal policies (Ayeb, 2011, 2012a, 2012b; Bush and Ayeb, 2014; Gana, 2012; similarly, see McMichael, 2009 for an analysis of the 2007–2008 food crises in sub-Saharan Africa). In 2011, following the overthrow of the Ben Alì and Gaddafi regimes, tens of thousands of Tunisians and sub-Saharan Africans crossed the Mediterranean to southern Italy, where many found employment in agriculture and some, in fact, became directly involved in the Nardò strike in the summer of the same year.

As the Via Campesina noted, 'the massive movement of food around the world is forcing the increased movement of people' (Via Campesina, 2000). In other words, neoliberal policies and the consequent conflicts are a major cause for both internal and transnational mobility. A huge number of dispossessed peasants on the southern shore of the Mediterranean – and in the global South more generally – become migrants on the northern shore where many find work in agriculture (Confédération Paysanne, 2004).

## 1.2 Mobility and the restructuring of agri-food production

As the conflicts mentioned above reveal, over the last 30 years Mediterranean countries have experienced important changes in food production, distribution and consumption, agricultural labour and markets. The main hypothesis that underpins the chapters of this volume is that these transformations are intimately related to transnational and internal mobility.

On the one hand, the liberalization of international agri-food trade and intellectual property rights on patents and seeds, the reforms of the EU Common Agricultural Policy (CAP), and the dominance of the EU food industry and retailers on Mediterranean farmers and processors are all factors that have contributed, on both sides of the Mediterranean, to the expansion of export-oriented agri-food production, the crisis, dependence and dispossession of small farmers and peasants, the impoverishment of rural populations, conflicts over resources, and pressures on labour conditions. As well as increasing internal mobility, these processes have fostered transnational migration from the Middle East and North Africa (MENA), but also from eastern European, sub-Saharan and Asian countries, towards the EU. A considerable number of migrants have moved to southern European rural areas, and have often become casual agricultural labourers.

On the other hand, the availability of cheap and flexible migrant labour has represented a fundamental factor in the restructuring the agricultural sector, both in southern Europe and in a number of MENA countries: the compression of labour costs has enabled, to a certain extent, the resilience of a number of southern European small and medium-size farms squeezed by neoliberal globalization and, more important, has contributed to strengthening the power of 'food empires' (Ploeg, 2008) within vertical agri-food supply chains.

This book combines two main research areas in order to analyse the mobility of labourers in relation to agri-food restructuring in the Mediterranean: first, studies of migrant labour in agricultural sector and, second, research on the restructuring of agri-food systems in the context of contemporary capitalism or what has been defined as a 'neoliberal' or 'corporate/environmental food regime' (McMichael, 2005, 2013; Friedmann, 2005; Pechlaner and Otero, 2008).

Since the late 1980s, and with increased attention from the early 2000s, the social sciences have analysed transnational mobility in the Mediterranean area in relation to national and supranational policies and to the restructuring of labour markets. Despite the growing number of studies on the insertion of migrant workers in agriculture (e.g. Cole and Booth, 2007; Michalon and Morice, 2008; Crenn and Tersigni, 2013; Colloca and Corrado, 2013), comparatively little attention has been dedicated to examining how the vulnerable legal status and social condition of migrants have been essential to the restructuring of Mediterranean agri-food production and its integration in global agri-food chains (Lawrence, 2007; Moraes *et al.*, 2012a; Gertel and Sippel, 2014); a process that occurred earlier in other geographical contexts such as the United States.

Conversely, for many years agri-food and rural studies have paid little interest to labour issues, especially to the question of migrant labour.[1] The incorporation of agricultural production in vertical food chains controlled by transnational corporations, the transformation from producer-driven to buyer-driven food chains (Burch and Lawrence, 2007), the consolidation of retailer power through the supermarket revolution (Reardon *et al.,* 2003; McMichael and Friedmann, 2007), and the financialization of agricultural processes have all reshaped the global agri-food system and the connections between the global North and the global South. But, as Bonanno and Cavalcanti note in their introduction to one of the few edited volumes on the topic,

> overall research has moved away from labor as a topic of investigation at a time when the exploitation of labor emerged as one of the primary factors in the restructuring of global agri-food. Also neglected was the topic of labor as an agent of emancipation.
>
> (2014, p. xxv)

The few analyses in this field concentrate on the Americas (e.g. Barndt, 2002; Flora *et al.*, 2011; Harrison and Lloyd, 2011) and, to a lesser extent, northern Europe (Rogaly, 2008).

In Mediterranean agriculture these restructuring processes for the most part have taken place later than in other areas of the world such as the US, northern Europe and Australia (Ortiz-Miranda *et al.*, 2013). Moreover, they have assumed a very specific form, due to the particular structure of agriculture and the history of agrarian relations (Braudel, 1985), as well as a result of the specific role that migration has played in these processes (Corrado, this volume). Through interdisciplinary, empirically based contributions that for the most part draw on ethnographic and other qualitative methods, this book addresses and elaborates this largely missing link between migration studies and agri-food studies, with a specific focus on the Mediterranean region.

Such an analysis needs to consider different forms of regulation: on the one hand, national and supranational politics regarding agri-food production, processing and trade, labour markets and transnational mobility; and, on the other, private standards and certification systems through which transnational corporations of food production, processing and retail claim to regulate issues such as environmental sustainability, food safety and quality, and labour rights. Through this multifaceted regulation, the Mediterranean has become a mobile border, across which capital accumulation occurs through processes of segmentation and 'differential inclusion' (Mezzadra and Nielsen, 2013) and where not only labour but also food products are filtered, selected and channelled. By virtue of selective mobility control, the Mediterranean is crossed by documented and undocumented, EU and non-EU, economic and forced, temporary and permanent, male and female migrants. At the same time, as a result of trade policies, partnership agreements and private standards, there are farmers (and products) more or less coping with quality certification schemes and protocols, and more or less integrated into food chains and free trade mechanisms.

The destinies of both sides of the Mediterranean are connected not only through transnational mobility, but also through new competitive relationships embedded in the neoliberal globalization of agri-food systems. Despite the evident differences that exist between the northern and southern shores of the Mediterranean, but also between areas within each side, the region overall appears as a (semi-) periphery in global food systems. In fact, the central nodes of these networks that control capital accumulation – the seed and biotech corporations, food multinationals, big retailers, and financial actors – are usually headquartered *far away* from the Mediterranean 'enclaves' (Moraes *et al.*, 2012b; Pedreño *et al.*, 2015) of export-oriented and labour-intensive production of fruit and vegetables that compete among themselves and with other regions.

In the next sections, we describe four key issues that are developed further in the chapters of this volume: the restructuring of agriculture; trade liberalization and the growing power of retailers in food chains; mobility patterns and labour in agriculture; and the construction of agricultural wage labour markets. The final section provides an overview of the eighteen contributions to the volume.

## 1.3 Agricultural restructuring

Over the last two centuries, and in contrast to the rest of Europe, southern European agriculture has been characterized by distinctive features with regards to the structure of production and agrarian relations: greater land fragmentation; a higher rate of permanent crops such as olive trees, vineyards and orchards; smaller farms, with low levels of technological development, and, from the 1970s onwards, managed by part-time or elderly farmers. Nevertheless, over the last three decades, the region has undergone significant agrarian change. The number of farms has steadily decreased, as has, to a lesser extent, the utilized agricultural area (UAA), while the average size of farms has grown (Arnalte-Alegre and Ortiz-Miranda, 2013; Papadopulos, 2015).[2]

A few figures can offer a general idea about these transformations. Between 1990 and 2010, average farm size grew from 5.6 ha of UAA to almost 8 ha in Italy, from 4.3 to 7.2 ha in Greece, from 6.7 to 12 ha in Portugal, and from 15.4 to 24 ha in Spain. In comparison, the average UAA in 2010 was 24 ha in the EU-15 countries and 15 ha in the EU-27 countries. Over the same 20-year period, the number of holdings fell from 2,665,000 to 1,621,000 in Italy, from 861,000 to 723,000 in Greece, from 599,000 to 305,000 in Portugal, and from 1,594,000 to 990,000 in Spain. In France, a dramatic decrease in the number of farms had occurred already in previous decades, and remained at around 500,000 between 1990 and 2000

(Eurostat, 2014a, 2014b; see also Arnalte-Alegre and Ortiz-Miranda, 2013). This reduction is largely due to the drop in the number of small farms.

However, a number of strategies have compensated, to a certain extent, the structural limits of southern European agriculture. These include: non-agricultural income diversification in rural households; quality production; multifunctionality; differentiation of the products; and the widening of social networks.[3] Moreover, especially in the coastal plains, numerous farms have been able to specialize in intensive crops of fruit and vegetables and breeding thanks to the growth in plantation density, mechanization and the expansion of irrigated areas. The 'artificialization' of agriculture has profoundly transformed the rural landscape, due to the diffusion of greenhouses and an excessive use of pesticides and fertilizers. Thus, if southern European farms between the 1950s and 1980s were depicted, according to the dominant modernist and productivist paradigms, as traditional and backward in contrast to the agriculture of northern Europe and US, the recent transformations and increased production rates have challenged the idea of a 'delay' in the region's agriculture.[4]

On the other side of the Mediterranean, some of the MENA countries – including Morocco, Tunisia and Egypt as well as Turkey – have recently experimented similar processes of capitalization, commercialization and commoditization of land and agriculture, as well as the integration of farmers in agribusiness commodity chains (Haineh, 2015). Here the changes are mainly due to structural adjustment and trade policies under the pressure of international institutions (IMF, World Bank and WTO), which have favoured transnational agribusiness and financial interests (for Turkey see Aydun, 2010; Ocal, 2014; Yenal, 1999; Keyder and Yenal, 2011; for Egypt see Bush, 2007; Dixon, 2013). Peasant and small farming have been affected by land grabbing linked to private foreign investments and by agrarian counter-reforms that have displaced or exploited agrarian workers, through both dispossession and the intensification of agriculture. The transformation is in fact twofold: on the one hand, major disruption has occurred to rural livelihoods (Sippel, 2014; Mahdi, 2014; Gana, this volume); while, on the other, some rural areas, as in southern Europe, have been profoundly affected by the development of new models of agriculture where production is more closely linked to global markets (Moreno Nieto, 2014), and there is greater dependence on wage labour and internal migration (Bouchelkha, this volume). Here as well, a few figures are helpful in order to grasp these changes: in Morocco, 15 per cent of agricultural land is controlled by 1 per cent of farmers, while less than one-quarter of the land is owned by 70 per cent of farmers; in Tunisia, 1 per cent of farms constitute 26 per cent of the total agricultural land, while 53 per cent of farms are less than 5 ha in size and make up only 11 per cent of the land; and in Egypt, 45 per cent of the smallest farmers own only 10 per cent of the land, while 3 per cent of landholders control a remarkable one-third of the country's entire agricultural area. Indeed, in 2000, a total of 2,281 individuals (0.05 per cent of all landholders) held 11 per cent of Egyptian land (Hanieh, 2015, pp. 285–6).

Across the Mediterranean region, export-oriented enclaves of capitalist agriculture are usually confined to coastal plains. At the same time, internal and mountainous areas that are less suitable for intensive production have been progressively abandoned. In these regions, especially in southern Europe, a huge percentage of holdings have disappeared, despite counterstrategies such as quality production, multifunctionality and, in some cases, the employment of migrants as shepherds (Nori, 2015). This issue is not analysed in this volume and will probably deserve greater attention in future research.

One of the main differences between the northern and southern shores of the Mediterranean concerns the ownership of agricultural businesses. In southern Europe, nearly all businesses are in the hands of national capital, while in countries such as Morocco, Tunisia and Egypt, a higher proportion of large estates are owned by foreign (mainly EU-based) corporations (Bouchelkha, this volume). In several cases, southern European companies have moved part of their production to the Maghreb countries, with the double goal of reducing labour costs and guaranteeing fresh production to supermarkets throughout the year (Gertel and Sippel, 2014).

## 1.4 Trade liberalization and the supermarket revolution

Agricultural production on the opposite sides of the Mediterranean directly competes with each other in international markets. Several factors have contributed to shape this competition. In this section, we will briefly address two of these factors: first, trade policies, in particular the EU's CAP and the partnership agreements between the EU and some MENA countries; and, second, the supermarket revolution, namely the growth of supermarket chains as 'food authorities' (Dixon, 2007) and the imposition of private standards upon agricultural production through retailer-driven agri-food supply chains.

Since its inception, the CAP has largely supported agricultural production in the EU (and especially meat, grain and dairy products), which has strengthened the food industry and developed competitive advantages to penetrate international markets. As in the US, subsidized prices have been dumped on farmers of the global South. At the same time, southern European fruit and vegetable producers have obtained relatively few advantages compared to their northern European counterparts, apart from being in a position to participate in the internal protected common market and to receive income support. Moreover, the CAP reforms implemented since the 1990s have gradually reduced support to farmers, which has especially affected small farmers.

Since the Euro-Mediterranean Conference in 1995, the 'Barcelona process' has been promoted as a means of creating a Euro-Mediterranean Free Trade Area, in which barriers to trade and investment are supposed to be removed. While trade agreements between EU and MENA countries have been signed, the process is still ongoing, and for many reasons remains ambiguous (Boeckler and Berndt, 2014; Sippel, this volume). The mix between subsidized and protected agriculture in the EU and partial trade liberalization has led to the strengthening of the competitive position of large companies on both sides of the Mediterranean.

This partial and unbalanced liberalization is closely linked with what has been called the 'retailing revolution' (McMichael and Friedmann, 2007), which, over the last 30 years, has seen numerous agri-food chains become retailer-driven. Supermarket chains not only control distribution, but also shape decisively the production, processing and consumption of food (Burch and Lawrence, 2007) as a result of their enormous buyer power. These actors are among the monopolistic networks that Jan Douwe van der Ploeg has defined as food empires, arguing that 'it is becoming difficult, if not often impossible, for farmers to sell food ingredients or for consumers to buy food outside of the circuits that they control' (Ploeg, 2010, p. 101). Moreover, European supermarkets have influenced the international policy environment in favour of supermarket investments as well as the liberalization of retail distribution markets in developing countries under the WTO General agreement on trade and services (GATS) negotiations, and they have also accumulated buying power by setting up alliances between retailers, in the form of buying groups (Vorley, 2007). Europe's top 10 retail groups are headquartered in three countries: the UK, France and Germany. For example, in 2010, Carrefour (France) – Europe's largest retailer ahead of the Metro Group (Germany) and Tesco (UK) and second only to US-based Wal-Mart at the global level – employed 475,000 workers and had 15,600 company-operated or franchised stores in 34 countries across the world, with 57 per cent of its turnover coming from outside France (Fritz, 2011).

Supermarket chains can buy (cheap) agricultural products in various parts of the globe, thus exacerbating the competition between farmers in different countries. This is evident, for example, in the production of fresh strawberries and tomatoes on both sides of the Mediterranean, especially in Morocco and Spain. As mentioned, a number of mainly European corporations produce or simply trade in both countries, in order to meet the year-round demand of seasonal and counter-seasonal fresh products among the European supermarket chains (Gertel and Sippel, 2014). This process is favoured by EU trade policies, which displace the EU–Morocco trade barrier southwards on a seasonal basis (Boeckler and Berndt, 2014) in relation to the production of fresh fruit and vegetables.

The power of retailers over suppliers comes mainly from the growing rate of food trade that, at a national and supranational level, passes through corporate supermarkets, at the expense of traditional independent food shops, and from the growing concentration in the sector. A few statistics reflect this development. In Italy, large retailers' share of the food market grew from 44 per cent in 1996 to 71 per cent in 2011 (AGCM, 2013). In Greece, the four largest retailers (three foreign chains and one national company) accounted for 55 per cent of the sales and more than 80 per cent of the profits of the national grocery retail market in 2009 (Skordili, 2013). In Spain, big retailers controlled 63.7 per cent of the food market in 2014 (ANGED, 2014, p. 36). In Morocco, supermarket trade took off in the early 2000s, with the arrival of foreign direct investments, mainly by the French Auchan group. In Tunisia, the market share of the large-scale food retail trade (largely involving French groups) rose from 12 per cent in 2006 to 20 per cent in 2010, and it is set to reach between 40 and 50 per cent by 2016 (Fort, 2012).

In Tunisia, 10 per cent of market capitalization in 2007 was constituted by just one private company, the Poulina group, whose activities are concentrated in agribusiness, banking and retail (Hanieh, 2015). Carrefour was the first large-scale retailer to establish itself in Algeria, opening its first hypermarket in 2006 and thereafter operating in partnership with Arcofino, an Algerian group specializing in insurance and property (Padilla and Abis, 2007).

The role of supermarket own brands also needs to be taken into account. The EU is the world's leading region in terms of the 'private labels' share of the food market, and, according to EU legislation, own brands have turned retailers into 'food business operators' (Vorley, 2007). Thanks to private labels, retailers have been able to impose their own standards[5] on suppliers, covering a wide range of aspects such as quantity, quality, prices, food safety, environmental protection, packaging, as well as the logistics of delivering products, and in doing so have gained a further competitive advantage on other companies, such as processors. In their analysis of the role of supermarkets in global supply chains, Burch *et al.* (2013) and Richards *et al.* (2013) have found that in countries such as UK, Australia and Norway, the introduction of private standards along the food chains has had the secondary effect of marginalizing small and medium-size family farmers. Such farmers, formerly a significant force in agriculture, are often 'unable to meet the stringent requirements of the supermarkets for unblemished, standardized, cheaply produced, high-volume products', while larger suppliers are able to meet the costs of these requirements, and so become 'the allies of the supermarkets in seeking returns to scale in agriculture' (Burch *et al.* 2013, p. 218). The studies presented in this volume confirm this situation, showing how the 'supermarket-induced restructuring of agriculture' and marginalization of small and medium-size farmers has occurred in Mediterranean countries as well, even if one or two decades later than in northern Europe.

Financialization has also played a major role in agri-food restructuring. Some of the retail corporations are among the most important financial actors in contemporary capitalism. Giovanni Arrighi argued that US Wal-Mart, 'the biggest retailer in world history', is the manifestation of the 'monetarist counterrevolution that has facilitated the financialization of US capital'. By driving down workers' wages and benefits 'not just in retailing but in manufacturing and shipping as well', Wal-Mart 'has strengthened the position of the US as the world's financial clearinghouse' (Arrighi, 2007, pp. 171–2). As in the US, suppliers in Europe have also been used as surrogate 'bankers' of the expansion of big supermarkets, contributing to growing amounts of finance through the imposition of back margins or off-invoice discounts, trade credit or demands for cash payments (Vorley, 2007). Moreover, financial actors such as banks, investment finance houses and private equity consortia are interested in manipulating the agri-food sector and in particular the food retail industry. Referring to the case of the acquisition of Somerfeld – once the sixth largest supermarket in the UK – by a group of private equity investors in 2005 (Burch and Lawrence, 2013), Burch *et al.* (2013, p. 218) pose the question of 'whether supermarkets are the new "masters" of the food system' or, rather if it is 'finance capital that has the ability to rework the entire food system'.

The response of many southern European farms to the pressure of vertical food chains has been the growing use of a cheap and flexible labour force. Drawing upon some of the empirical studies presented in this volume, we argue that, especially in the coastal enclaves of fresh fruit and vegetable production, the employment of over-exploited migrant labour represents one of the factors that has allowed the survival of a number of small and medium farms, notwithstanding their incorporation into global supply chains. Thus, the over-exploitation of migrant labour appears to be one of the strategies employed by southern European farmers in resisting the liberalization of international markets and the retailer-driven transformation of supply chains. However, this strategy is at the same time increasingly inadequate as farmers become more dependent and marginal in supply chains. As the data above demonstrate, a huge number of mainly small and medium farms have closed or have been sold to the biggest production units, while corporate supermarkets in the meantime are able to buy (cheap) food where they wish and, ultimately, appear to benefit the most from the lowering of labour costs through the employment of a migrant workforce.

## 1.5 Migrant labour in agriculture

A further relevant feature of the transformation of Mediterranean agriculture is the 'defamilization', or individualization of family farming, the growth of wage labour and the structural dependence on a non-local labour force.[6] In this context, internal and/or transnational migrants not only allow farmers to replace the withdrawal of family labour, but most of all, constitute a reserve of vulnerable, cheap and flexible labour force to meet the downward pressure on costs and the requests of just-in-time production by the agri-food chains.

While, in the US, international migration has been fundamental for the growth and modernization of agriculture since the end of the nineteenth century, as exemplified in the case of California (McWilliams, 1936; Wells, 1996), the agricultural sector in Europe has historically been characterized more by internal migrants (such as the Italian *mondine*: see Gentili Zappi, 1991) than international migration, with some important exceptions, such as the Polish workers (*Landarbeiter*) in Germany analysed in the early writings of Max Weber (1892, 2005) and Italian and Spanish migrants in French viticulture (Noiriel, 1994; Sassen, 1999). France was the first European country where international migration was an important structural factor in the postwar development of intensive agriculture (Berlan, 1986; Décosse, 2011), as a result of its colonial history and the government-led programmes for the recruitment of seasonal agricultural workers in Italy, Spain and Maghreb that were managed by the *Office national d'immigration* after 1945 (Morice, 2008).[7]

The presence of foreign farm workers in southern European countries did not become a significant and noticeable phenomenon until the 1990s, even if the first migrants started to arrive in the 1970s (for example, Albanians and Bulgarians in Greece and Tunisians in Sicily). The number of foreign farm workers in these countries has since grown steadily. They represent 24 per cent of agricultural wage labourers in Spain, 37 per cent in Italy, and 90 per cent in Greece, not counting those who are hired irregularly (Moreno-Perez *et al.*, 2015; Corrado, 2015; Papadopulous, 2015).

In MENA countries, the number of wage farm workers is also rapidly growing. Due to the crisis of rural areas, people have moved to urban areas or abroad, or towards intensive agricultural production areas (Hanieh, 2015; Gana, Bouchelkha, this volume). Some of these countries have also become destination or transit points for migrants from sub-Saharan Africa or South Asia. Both smallholders and landless rural families are increasingly relying on wage labour in response to additional household needs. A significant trend is the increased participation of women in the agricultural wage labour – rising from 34 per cent in 1995 to 45 per cent in 2011 – which sees them also involved in post-harvest activities and agro-processing industries (Bouzidi *et al.*, 2010, 2011; Abdelali-Martini, 2011).

As Bonanno and Cavalcanti (2014) argue, non-market mechanisms (such as feminization and illegalization) play a part in agricultural labour regulation. Agriculture – and especially the southern European enclaves of intensive and export-oriented production – perhaps represents the sector in which Mezzadra and Nielsen's (2013) categories of 'multiplication of labour' and 'differential inclusion of migrants' can be observed most clearly. 'Differential inclusion' refers to the different levels of subordination, command, discrimination and segmentation defined by the current border and migration regimes, which rather than exclude, aim at 'filtering, selecting, and channelling migratory movements', through 'a huge amount of violence' (Mezzadra and Nielsen, 2013, p. 165). Migrant farm workers in southern European countries are segmented by their legal status, nationality, gender, type of work contract and form of recruitment (Potot, 2010; Corrado and Perrotta, 2012). The workers include Maghrebi, eastern European, sub-Saharan African, South Asian and Latin American migrants. These migrants are undocumented or documented, are recruited through seasonal workers programmes, temporary employment agencies, informal networks or brokers, possess different types of permits and may sometimes have even received citizenship in the country of arrival. In extreme cases, they are trafficked and subject to quasi-slavery conditions.

Southern European rural areas can be analysed as places of conflict, entrapment and escape. Farmers require an abundant cheap, flexible and often seasonal workforce, and foreign citizens are usually the best candidates to fill such needs. However, migrants usually consider agriculture only as a source of temporary employment, due to the low salaries, the hard and seasonal work and the difficult housing conditions, and they move away from rural areas as soon as they find better employment opportunities or get a residence permit. Due to the high turnover and increasing cases of resistance and conflict, new labourers are needed to meet the agricultural labour demand. To this end, European governments have supported their farmers in different ways.

## 1.6 The political construction of agricultural labour markets in southern Europe

Informality was one of the main features of the 'Mediterranean model of migration' (King *et al.*, 2000) during its first phase between the 1970s and 1990s, due to the absence of policies on transnational mobility in southern European countries, with the notable exception of France. The situation changed during later years. A number of forms of labour intermediation and recruitment developed and overlapped to assure a cheap and vulnerable workforce for southern European farmers. On the one hand, national and European regulations of transnational mobility and labour markets have been of extreme importance, while on the other, private recruitment services have expanded.

During the 1990s, national and European migratory policies became increasingly restrictive. Rural areas reflected characteristics of what has been termed the 'deportation regime' (De Genova and Peutz, 2010) of migration control. The massive presence of undocumented – 'illegalized' and thus 'deportable' (De Genova, 2002) – migrants in agriculture was one of the main reasons for the vulnerability of the whole migrant workforce. During the 2000s, the situation has slowly and partially changed. National governments have become active brokers, by promoting recruitment programmes for seasonal foreign workers: in addition to the French OFII contracts (Décosse, this volume), Spain launched the *contratacion en origen* in 2000 (Hellio, 2008 and this volume; Márquez Domínguez *et al.*, 2009; Reigada, 2012), while Italy introduced the annual 'flows decrees'.

Since the 1990s, at both national and European level, agricultural labour markets have been liberalized: the role of local public employment offices in recruitment has been reduced and temporary work agencies have been regulated at a national level, while the use of 'posted workers' has been allowed all over Europe (Fudge and Strauss, 2014). These processes have had a huge impact on recruitment practices in agriculture, as reflected by the spread of private formal intermediaries in the agricultural labour market, such as the temporary employment agencies in France (Mésini, 2013, 2014), Spain (Garrapa; Gadea *et al.*, this volume) and, to a lesser extent, Italy, and the private companies and cooperatives offering subcontracting services (Claudon and Rouan, 2013), which sometimes operate in other countries, especially from eastern Europe. Contemporarily, the entry of central-eastern European countries into the EU in 2004 and 2007 has radically changed the legal status of farm workers from Poland, Romania and Bulgaria in Mediterranean rural areas, by allowing them freer mobility in the European space. Since 2011, changes in mobility processes across the Mediterranean have contributed to the growth in the number of asylum seekers and refugees among farm workers, especially in Italy (Dines and Rigo, 2015).

Of course, informal recruiters have not disappeared. The *caporalato* in Southern Italy – a form of labour contracting that was made a criminal offence by the Italian government in 2011 – is perhaps the best-known case (Perrotta and Sacchetto, 2013; Avallone, this volume). Informal intermediaries appear to be an important element even in the management of State recruitment programmes for seasonal workers (Michalon and Potot, 2008). Formal recruitment – run by both public and private actors – does not guarantee better working and housing conditions or longer contracts than informal intermediation. Rather, it appears as a means to 'bridle' and channel the labour force. As Jean-Pierre Berlan argued 30 years ago, it is precisely the overlapping of different sources of the labour force in the same region, and its differentiation by nationality, gender and legal status that has allowed labour to remain cheap and vulnerable (Berlan, 1986). Moreover, racism, processes of ethnicization and the spatial segregation of migrant workers – who often live in the countryside in ghettos, *chabolas* or, in the best cases, in institutional reception centres or on the farms themselves – are key elements in disciplining the migrant workforce, in overcoming instances of resistance and in preserving a well-ordered labour market and social relations in rural areas (Berlan, 2002; Corrado, 2011; Moraes *et al.*, 2012b). Nonetheless, these different forms of labour discipline have not prevented numerous outbreaks of social conflict. As we have shown in the first section of this introduction, the analysis of the restructuring of Mediterranean agriculture cannot leave aside the history of such conflict.

## 1.7 Overview of the volume

The volume is divided into five parts. Parts I to III describe three different patterns of the restructuring of agri-food supply chains in the Mediterranean area. Part IV addresses the construction of agricultural labour markets and different forms of recruitment and organization of the migrant agricultural workforce. Part V is devoted to the issue of conflict in agriculture and rural areas.

The chapters in Part I deal with migrant labour in 'quality' food product chains in what could be defined the North of Mediterranean Europe (France and Northern Italy). Not by chance, these studies concern processed food products (cheese, wine and canned tomatoes). In contemporary food chains, processors are usually more powerful than farmers or fresh food producers in representing their products as quality products and thus managing to sell them at higher prices. The Italian Parmigiano Reggiano and Grana Padano cheeses and the French Bordeaux wines are promoted as 'high-quality' and 'distinctive' products rooted in local territories, brands that are exported and recognized all over the world. However, for many years, migrants have provided much of the manual labour that goes into such production: Indian Punjabi milkers in the stables of the Po valley and 'Arab' workers in the vineyards around Libourne in south-west France. The chapters by Vanessa Azzeruoli and Chantal Crenn highlight the stereotyping of migrant workers, mainly 'positive' in the case of Punjabis in the Po Valley and 'negative' in the case of Arabs in the Bordeaux region. In both cases, the ethnicization of labourers mirrors the construction of the identity of typical 'Italian' and 'French' products. At the same time, Azzeruoli describes how Punjabi migrants have developed a system of informal intermediation through their social networks. Interestingly, she points out that it is precisely this system of brokerage (and the efficient supply of a disciplined, specialized and relatively cheap workforce) that has allowed, on the one hand, the construction of an 'ethnic niche' of Indian workers in the dairy sector in the Po Valley and, on the other, the restructuring of the entire sector of hard cheese production, towards a greater corporate concentration and incorporation within vertical supply chains.

Domenico Perrotta's contribution focuses on another 'typical' food product, heavily subsidized by the CAP: Italian canned tomatoes. He compares the tomato-processing industries in northern and southern Italy and addresses the issue of mechanization of agricultural production as an alternative to the over-exploitation of migrant workers in retailer-driven supply chains. His chapter shows how the same product can be produced in very different ways in the same country: in northern Italy, the harvest has been completely mechanized since the early 1990s; in the South, a large percentage of tomatoes continues to be manually harvested by foreign labourers. Higher wages and better working conditions for migrants in retailer-driven supply chains are essentially unthinkable: in the event that the tomato harvesters in southern Italy were to forcibly demand better working conditions and regular wages, they would most likely be replaced by harvesting machines.

Part II of the book considers the enclaves of export-oriented agriculture in Spain, Italy and Greece that are mostly specialized in fresh production for European markets. The case studies regard Murcia (Elena Gadea, Andres Pedreño and Carlos de Castro); strawberry production in Huelva in Andalusia (Alicia Reigada) and in the Peloponnese region (Apostolos Papadopoulos and Loukia-Maria Fratesa); citrus cultivation in the southern Italian region of Calabria and in the Valencian Community (Anna Mary Garrapa). In these enclaves, local growers and migrant agricultural labourers both experience extreme vulnerability and difficult working conditions. Small and medium producers are in a subordinate position to traders, processors and retailers. It is no coincidence that the most violent social and ethnic conflicts in European rural areas, such as those in Rosarno and Manolada, have occurred in these regions. Gadea, Pedreño and de Castro describe how the continual incorporation and expulsion of vulnerable workers on the basis of gender and ethnicity in the enclave of Murcia has become a central concern in the management of agricultural work. In addition, they address the growing importance of temporary employment agencies in the provision of farm labour. Reigada focuses on the largest area in Europe for the cultivation of strawberries for export, namely Huelva province, and challenges the widespread idea that Andalusia represents the 'California of southern Europe'. In fact, even if there are some similarities between the two cases – such as the fundamental role of migration in agriculture – the Huelva strawberry industry is mainly based on small family farms. As in other Mediterranean regions, the incorporation of intensive agriculture into global agri-food chains has not represented a means of economic and social development: rather it has reaffirmed these areas' subordinate and peripheral economic positions, where endemic unemployment and precarious work prevail.

Garrapa's chapter compares two areas of citrus production: the rural region of Rosarno-Gioia Tauro (Italy) and the metropolitan region of Valencia (Spain). In both cases, she examines the different levels of the supply chain, from the local organization of labour to the supermarkets. By showing that a 'citrus fruit crisis' has not only hit the Gioia Tauro Plain, an area long considered backward, but also Valencia, in contrast usually regarded as very competitive, Garrapa argues that this crisis is largely the upshot of the restructuring of the supply chains, which has led to greater concentration in the commercial and distribution stages and to world-wide competition. In both regions, commercial chains require large quantities of supplies and are heavily dependent on end demand for containing prices as well as ensuring efficiency in delivery schedules. In both cases, 'just-in-time' migrant workers are necessary to reduce production costs and to meet the 'just-in-time' demands of supermarkets. From this perspective, the difference between the formal recruitment of labourers through temporary employment agencies in Valencia and the informal recruitment through the *caporalato* and social networks in Gioia Tauro is negligible, given that salaries and working conditions remain very similar.

The chapter by Papadopoulos and Fratsea provides an account of how the strawberry industry in Greece expanded largely thanks to the availability of a migrant workforce. The authors analyse this expansion in the area of Manolada in the Peloponnese region, which is characterized by a model of migrant labour control based on the precarious legal status of migrants, the ethnic segmentation of the labour market, the informal system of recruitment as well as the use of physical violence by supervisors and growers against labourers. However, this control has not prevented the frequent mobilizations of migrant labourers for higher wages. Together, the chapters of Part II show that the pressures experienced by southern European small and medium farmers and the dramatic working conditions of migrant labourers are currently functional to numerous supply chains. Nevertheless, from a social, economic and environmental perspective, this model of industrial agriculture is not sustainable in the long run.

In Part III, the book crosses the Mediterranean to analyse the restructuring of the agricultural sector in Morocco and Turkey. Sarah Ruth Sippel uses the commodity chain of tomatoes from Morocco to the EU as a lens through which to address the multifaceted aspects that are influencing the trade of agricultural produce across the Mediterranean. The governance of the tomato trade can be seen to be the result of multilayered and often conflicting political goals, interests of EU states and the influence of powerful lobby groups. With the aim of showing how borders are drawn and fixed along commodity chains, Sippel focuses on three issues: first, the discords in the trade regulations set by the EU for the importation of Moroccan tomatoes; second, an analysis of how tomatoes in Morocco are mainly produced by joint ventures of Moroccan and European producers; and, third, the recent relocation of tomato production to the territorially contested Western Sahara, which has been presented as an 'occupation tomato' by the Sahrawi resistance movement. Selma Akay Erturk's chapter offers some considerations on the presence of Syrian refugees in the olive sector in Turkey, and especially in the border region of Hatay Province. Her study shows how forms of forced mobility provoked by geopolitical conflicts and civil wars – in this case the Syrian conflict – can have important effects on the restructuring of agriculture in the Mediterranean basin, which has also occurred in southern Italy with the employment of Tunisian and sub-Saharan African refugees and asylum seekers (Dines and Rigo, 2015).

Part IV focuses on the recruitment of labourers, and analyses how the political construction of agricultural labour markets has become a necessary factor in the restructuring of agriculture. Frédéric Décosse's chapter traces the history of the French OFII contract system, which emerged shortly after the Second World

War, and its relationships with the development of French agriculture. This was Europe's first temporary foreign worker programme and represented a model for intensive agriculture-related migration schemes for the rest of the continent. Emmanuelle Hellio's contribution deals with another programme for the recruitment of seasonal workers, the Spanish *contratación en origen*, in the context of labour market segmentation in the Huelva province. While strawberry farming employs women recruited through the *contratación en origen*, undocumented male workers are preferred for other agricultural products. Similar to Garrapa, Hellio points out that formal recruitment does not necessarily guarantee better labour conditions than informal brokerage: on the contrary, she contends that seasonal recruitment programmes aim to control and to channel – rather than to protect – migrant labour. At the same time, the contributions by Décosse and Hellio both show the influence of labour conflicts upon the transformation of local labour markets and the recruitment of new workers. In the French case, the successful mobilization of thousands of former OMI workers to obtain permanent contracts led French farmers, during the late 2000s, to turn to Spanish temporary employment agencies for recruiting migrant labour. Similarly, Hellio argues that the informal recruitment of Moroccan men in the late 1980s in the Huelva strawberry industry, and the *contratación en origen* in the 2000s were responses to the collective demands and autonomous mobility of first Spanish workers and later Moroccan labourers.

The informal and illegal system of recruitment through the *caporalato* in southern Italy – already mentioned in the chapters of Perrotta and Garrapa – is the central focus of Gennaro Avallone's contribution. This draws on research in the Piana del Sele, which has seen the development of a greenhouse sector over the last 30 years. In this area, the flows decrees – the Italian programme for the recruitment of foreign workers – have often been used by local farmers and illegal brokers to defraud migrants and the State, while the *caporali* have played a fundamental role in providing a cheap and vulnerable labour force to the farmers. Moreover, in the absence of public policies aimed at migrant labourers, these informal intermediaries provide a number of necessary services for documented and undocumented migrants, thus contributing to reproducing their subaltern condition. Dora Sampaio and Rui Carvalho examine the recruitment and labour incorporation of Moroccan agricultural workers in the Portuguese region of the Algarve. Although they focus on a small migrant group, their case is interesting in that it describes the initial formation of a migrant agricultural labour market. While the Moroccan presence in the areas studied by Crenn and Avallone has been well established for decades, it is relatively recent in Algarve agriculture. The authors are therefore able to follow the paths of the 'pioneers' in this region, through the recruitment strategies of companies and the autonomous mobility of workers, some of whom have migrated from the neighbouring enclave of Huelva. Mohamed Bouchelkha's contribution regards the Souss region in Morocco, the most important area of intensive, export-oriented agriculture in the Maghreb, which is also described in Sippel's chapter. He shows how internal mobility has represented a structural factor for both the formation of a local wage labour market and the growth of intensive agriculture in the region, and describes the difficult working and living conditions of agricultural labourers.

Part V of the volume analyses a range of conflicts in Mediterranean rural areas: protests of farmers and peasants in Egypt and Tunisia, the union activity of the *Sindicato de Obreros del Campo* in Andalusia and workplace conflicts in Sicily. Of course, these cases do not cover all types of conflict and resistance in the region. For example, mention should be made of the activity of southern European peasant organizations in building 'alternative' and 'ethical' farming and food networks, at the same time as supporting migrant farm workers or even involving them as co-workers (see Oliveri, 2015 on the case of SOS Rosarno). Alia Gana examines the rural protest movements that were one of the sources of the 'Arab revolts' in Tunisia and Egypt between late 2010 and 2012. This rural unrest was the result of structural adjustment policies and the liberalization of the agricultural sector from the late 1980s onwards, which had caused the progressive marginalization of small farmers. Despite their contribution to the 2011 upheavals, Gana argues that farmers' unions have not been able to influence policy decisions, and the social demands of peasants have had little resonance in political debate. Francesco Caruso's chapter analyses the Andalusian farm workers union *Sindicato de Obreros del Campo* (SOC) through the theoretical lens of Social Movement Unionism. Traditionally based in the northern provinces of Andalusia, which were characterized by the presence of large landed estates, since the race riots in El Ejido in 2000, the SOC has managed to spread to the province of Almería, where thousands of migrant workers are employed in 30,000 hectares of greenhouses that are mostly owned by small farmers. Caruso argues that the SOC was, to a certain degree, successful in 'organizing the unorganizable', namely precarious, vulnerable and invisible migrant farm labourers. Valeria Piro and Giuliana Sanò take us into the 'plastic factory' of the transformed coastal belt in south-eastern Sicily, one of the Mediterranean regions that has seen the development of greenhouse agriculture, alongside the areas analysed by Reigada, Papadopoulos and Fratsea, Sippel, Hellio, Avallone and Bouchelkha. Drawing on workplace ethnography, Piro and Sanò examine the micro-conflicts within greenhouses and packinghouses. Not surprisingly, however, they have more often observed horizontal conflicts – such as competition between farm workers of different nationalities – than vertical conflicts between workers and their employers. The divisions within the workforce are mainly due to the insecurity and precariousness of labour, which encourages competition, accelerates the pace of work and fosters strategies of exploitation and value extraction inside the agri-food system.

In the concluding chapter, Alessandra Corrado reads the history of Mediterranean agriculture from a food regime perspective, focusing in particular on the current neoliberal restructuring. Moreover, building upon the empirical research presented in the volume, she argues that the questions of labour and migration should be considered more seriously in the food regime approach in order to better grasp the transformation of agrarian and geopolitical relations in the global agri-food system.

## Notes

1 In a similar way, labour issues are understudied in fields such as the global value chain and global production network analysis (Coe and Hess, 2013). For a compelling analysis of 'labour mobilization' in 'supply chain capitalism', see Tsing (2009).
2 These transformations are similar to those that have occurred in agriculture across the whole of the EU, which have been recently analysed through the analytical lens of land grabbing (Franco and Borras, 2013; Fritz, 2011; Kay *et al.*, 2015).
3 On these processes, see Salvioni et al. (2013); De Devitiis and Mietta (2013); De Filippis and Henke (2014) for Italy; Kasimis and Papadopoulos (2013) for Greece; Moreno-Pérez *et al.* (2015) for Spain.
4 Moragues-Faus *et al.* (2013) have argued that the 'post-productivist' paradigm that emerged from the 1990s onwards in the CAP was accompanied by a 'new delay' discourse, whereby southern European farms have been considered to be insufficiently 'multifunctional' and lacking in environmental awareness.
5 On the importance of private standards in the neoliberal economy and in global production networks, see Coe and Hess (2013).
6 In any case, it should be noted that family labour still provides the majority of farm labour: in 2010, the agricultural labour input coming from the holder or fellow family members was 77.8 per cent in the EU-28, 80 per cent in Italy, 63 per cent in Spain, 83 per cent in Greece, 81 per cent in Portugal and 44 per cent in France (Eurostat, 2014b).
7 This programme is very similar to the more famous US *Bracero program* that recruited five million Mexican seasonal agricultural workers from 1942 to 1964 (Cohen, 2011). The denomination of this programme has changed over the years in reference to the public agency responsible for it: from 1945 it was known as the *Office national d'immigration* (ONI); in 1988 it became the *Office des migrations internationales* (OMI), in 2005 it was renamed the *Agence nationale d'accueil des étrangers et des migrations* (ANAEM); and in 2009 it became the *Office français de l'immigration and de l'intégration* (OFII).

## References

Abdelali-Martini, M. (2011). 'Empowering women in the rural labor force with a focus on agricultural employment in the Middle East and North Africa (MENA)', in *Expert Group Meeting Enabling Rural Women's Economic Empowerment: Institutions, Opportunities and Participation.* Accra, Guinea: UN Women in cooperation with FAO, IFAD and WFP.

AGCM (Autorità Garante della Concorrenza e del Mercato) (2013). *Indagine conoscitiva sul settore della GDO.* Rome: AGCM. http://www.agcm.it/indagini-conoscitive-db/open/C12564CE0049D161/973E4D42D69C4A11C1257BC60039BBA0.html (last access on 9 June 2015).

ANGED (Asociación Nacional Grandes de Empresas de Distribución) (2014). *Informe annual, 2014.* Madrid: ANGED.

Arnalte-Alegre, E. and Ortiz-Miranda, D. (2013). 'The "Southern Model" of European agriculture revisited: continuities and dynamics', in Ortiz, D., Arnalte, E. and Moragues, A.M. (eds) *Agriculture in Mediterranean Europe Between Old and New Paradigms.* Bingley: Emerald, pp. 37–74.

Arrighi, G. (2007). *Adam Smith in Beijing.* London and New York: Verso.

Aydun, Z. (2010). 'Neo-liberal transformation of Turkish agriculture', *Journal of Agrarian Change* 10 (2), pp. 149–187.

Ayeb, H. (2011). 'Social and political geography of the Tunisian revolution: the alfa grass revolution', *Review of African Political Economy.* 38 (129), pp. 467–479.

Ayeb, H. (2012a). 'Marginalisation of the small peasantry: Egypt and Tunisia' in Bush, R. and Ayeb, H. (eds) *Marginality and Exclusion in Egypt and the Middle East*. London: Zed Book.

Ayeb, H. (2012b). 'Agricultural policies in Tunisia, Egypt, and Morocco: Between food dependency and social marginalization', in *Reversing the Vicious Circle in North Africa's Political Economy, Confronting Rural, Urban, and Youth-Related Challenges*, Mediterranean Paper Series, pp. 5–11. Washington, DC: The German Marshall Fund of the United States (GMF).

Barndt, D. (2002). *Tangled Routes: Women, Work and Globalization on the Tomato Trail*. Aurora, ON: Garamond Press.

Berlan, J.P. (1986). 'Agriculture et migrations', *Revue Européenne des Migrations Internationales*, 2 (3), pp. 9–31.

Berlan, J.P. (2002). 'La longue histoire du modèle californien', *Forum Civique Européen* (2002), pp. 15–22.

Boeckler, M. and Berndt, C. (2014). 'B/ordering the Mediterranean: Free trade, fresh fruit and fluid fixity' in Gertel, J. and Sippel, S.R. (eds) *Seasonal Workers in Mediterranean Agriculture. The Social Costs of Eating Fresh*. London: Routledge, pp. 23–33.

Bonanno, A. and Cavalcanti, J.S.B. (2014). *Labor Relations in Globalized Food*. Bingley: Emerald.

Bouzidi, Z., El Nour, S. and Moumen, W. (2010). 'Invisible actors: Conditions of women work in agriculture'. Paper presented at *Population Council Workshop* in El Cairo, Egypt.

Bouzidi, Z., El Nour, S. and Moumen, W. (2011). 'Le travail des femmes dans le secteur agricole: Entre précarité et empowerment. Cas de trois régions en Egypte, au Maroc et en Tunisie', *Gender and Work in the MENA Region Working Paper Series*, no. 22. El Cairo, Egypt: Population Council.

Burch, D. and Lawrence, G. (eds) (2007). *Supermarkets and Agri-food Supply Chains. Transformations in the Production and Consumption of Foods*. Cheltenham: Edward Elgar.

Burch, D. and Lawrence, G. (2013). 'Financialization in agri-food supply chains: Private equity and the transformation of the retail sector', *Agriculture and Human Values*, 30, pp. 247–258.

Burch, D., Dixon, J., and Lawrence, G., (2013). 'Introduction to symposium on the changing role of supermarkets in global supply chains. From seedling to supermarket: agri-food supply chains in transition', *Agriculture and Human Values*, 30, pp. 215–224.

Braudel, F. (1985). *La Méditerranée*. Paris: Flammarion.

Bush, R. (2007). 'Politics, power and poverty: Twenty years of agricultural reform and market liberalisation in Egypt', *Third World Quarterly*, 28 (8), pp. 1599–1615.

Bush, R. and Ayeb, H., (2014). 'Small farmer uprisings and rural neglect in Egypt and Tunisia', *MERIP*, no. 272.

Checa, F. (2001). *El Ejido: la ciudad cortijo. Claves socioeconómicas del conflicto étnico*. Barcelona: Icaria.

Claudon, H. and Rouan, J. (2013). 'Providing services or subcontracting labour? Two cases of the European trend of private intermediation, in Germany and Italy'. Paper presented at the International Seminar *Agriculture and migration in the European Union*, University of Bergamo, 24–25 October 2013.

Coe, N. and Hess, M., (2013). 'Global production networks, labour and development', *Geoforum*, 44, pp. 4–9.

Cohen, D. (2011). *Braceros: Migrant Citizens and Transnational Subjects in the Postwar United States and Mexico*. Chapel Hill: The University of North Carolina Press.

Cole, J. and Booth, J. (2007). *Dirty Work: Immigrants in Domestic Service, Agriculture, and Prostitution in Sicily*. New York: Lexington Books.

Colloca, C. and Corrado, A. (eds) (2013). *La globalizzazione delle campagne. Migranti e società rurali nel Sud Italia*. Milano: Franco Angeli.

Confédération Paysanne (2004). *Migrations et agriculture: Mondialisation des errances*, Special issue of *Campagnes solidaires*, no. 191.

Confédération Paysanne (2011*). Agriculture industrielle et servitude en Europe*, http://www.confederationpaysanne.fr/sites/1/mots_cles/documents/RAPPORT%20SAISONNIERS%202011.pdf (last access on 20/2/2016).

Confédération Paysanne (2015). *L'agriculture, laboratiore d'exploitation des travailleurs migrants saisonniers*, http://www.confederationpaysanne.fr/sites/1/articles/documents/migrants-brochure_conf-v2_compressed.pdf (last access on 20/2/2016).

Corrado, A. (2011). '*Clandestini* in the orange towns: Migrations and racisms in Calabria's agriculture', *Race/Ethnicity*, 4 (2), pp. 191–201.

Corrado, A. (2015). 'Lavoro straniero e riorganizzazione dell'agricoltura familiare in Italia', *Agriregionieuropa,* 43, pp. 23–27.

Corrado, A. and Perrotta, D. (2012). 'Migranti che contano. Mobilità e confinamenti nell'agricoltura dell'Italia meridionale', *Mondi migranti*, 3, pp. 103–128.

Crenn, C. and Tersigni, S. (eds) (2013). *Migrations et mondes ruraux*, special issue of *Hommes et Migrations*, 1301.

Décosse, F. (2011). *Migrations sous controle. Agriculture intensive et saisonniers marocains sous contrat OMI*, PhD Thesis. Paris: EHESS.

De Filippis, F. and Henke, R. (2014). 'Modernizzazione e multifunzionalità nell'agricoltura del mezzogiorno' *QA Rivista dell'Associazione Rossi-Doria*, 3, pp. 27–58.

De Genova, N. (2002). 'Migrant 'illegality' and deportability in everyday life', *Annual Review of Anthropology*, 31, pp. 419–47.

De Genova, N., and Peutz, N. (eds) (2010). *The Deportation Regime. Sovereignity, Space, and the Freedom of Movement*. Durham, NC and London: Duke UP.

De Devitiis, B. and Maietta, O. W. (2013). 'Regional patterns of structural change in Italian agriculture' in Ortiz, D., Arnalte, E. and Moragues, A.M. (eds) *Agriculture in Mediterranean Europe between Old and New Paradigms*. Bingley: Emerald, pp. 173–205.

Dines, N. and Rigo, E. (2015). 'Postcolonial citizenships between representation, borders and the 'refugeeization' of the workforce: Critical reflections on migrant agricultural labor in the Italian Mezzogiorno' in Ponzanesi, S. and Colpani, G. (eds) *Postcolonial Transitions in Europe: Contexts, Practices and Politics*. London: Rowman and Littlefield.

Dixon, J. (2007) 'Supermarkets as new food authorities', in Burch, D. and Lawrence, G. (eds) *Supermarkets and Agri-food Supply Chains. Transformations in the Production and Consumption of Foods*. Cheltenham: Edward Elgar. pp. 29–50.

Dixon, M. (2013) 'The land grab, finance capital, and food regime restructuring: The case of Egypt', *Review of African Political Economy*, 41 (140), pp. 232–248.

Eurostat (2014a). 'Agriculture statistics – the evolution of farm holdings', Eurostat. http://ec.europa.eu/eurostat/statistics-explained/index.php/Agriculture_statistics_-_the_evolution_of_farm_holdings (last access on 20/2/2016).

Eurostat (2014b). 'Farm structure statistics', Eurostat. http://ec.europa.eu/eurostat/statistics-explained/index.php/Farm_structure_statistics (last access on 20/2/2016).

Flora, J.L., Emery, M., Thompson, D., Prado-Meza, C.-M. and Flora, C-B (2011). 'New immigrants in local food systems: Two Iowa cases', *International Journal of Sociology of Agriculture and Food*, 19, 1, pp. 119–134.

Fort, F. (2012). "Traditional Mediterranean products: Markets and large-scale retail trade" in Mombiela, F. and Abis, S. (eds) *Mediterra 2: The Mediterranean Diet for Sustainable Regional Development*. Paris: Presses de Sciences Po, pp. 305–324.

Forum Civique Européen (2000). *El Ejido, terre de non-droit*. Paris: Golias.

Forum Civique Européen (2002). *Le gout amer de nos fruits et légumes. L'exploitation des migrants dans l'agriculture intensive en Europe*, revue *Informations et Commentaires*, numéro hors série.

Franco, J.C. and Borras, S.M. (eds) (2013). *Land Concentration, Land Grabbing and People's Struggles in Europe*. Amsterdam: Transnational Institute.

Friedmann, H. (2005). 'From colonialism to green capitalism: Social movements and the emergence of food regimes', in, Buttel, F.H. and McMichael, P. (eds) *New Directions in the Sociology of Global Development*. Oxford: Elsevier, pp. 229–267.

Fritz, T. (2011). *Globalising Hunger: Food Security and the EU's Common Agricultural Policy*, Berlin: FDCL-Verlag.

Fudge, J. and Strauss, K. (eds) (2014). *Temporary Work, Agencies and Unfree Labour: Insecurity in the New World of Work*. London: Routledge.

Gana, A. (2012). 'The rural and agricultural roots of the Tunisian revolution: When food security matters', *International Journal of Sociology of Agriculture & Food*, 19 (2), pp. 201–213.

Gentili Zappi, E. (1991). *If Eight Hours Seem Too Few: Mobilization of Women Workers in the Italian Rice Fields*. New York: SUNY Press.

Gertel, J. and Sippel, S.R. (eds) (2014). *Seasonal Workers in Mediterranean Agriculture. The Social Costs of Eating Fresh*. London: Routledge.

Hanieh, A. (2015). 'Mapping the political economy of neoliberalism in Arab World', in Mattei, U. and Haskell, J.D. (eds) *Research Handbook on Political Economy and Law*. Cheltenham: Edward Elgar, pp. 280–297.

Harrison, J.L. and Lloyd, S.E. (2011). 'Illegality at work: Deportability and the productive new era of immigration enforcement', *Antipode*, 44 (2), pp. 365–385.

Hellio, E. (2008). 'Importer des femmes pour exporter des fraises (Huelva)', *Etudes rurales*, 182, pp. 185–200.

Kasimis, C. and Papadopoulos, A.G. (2013). *Rural Transformations and Family Farming in Contemporary Greece*, in Ortiz, D., Arnalte, E. and Moragues, A.M. (eds) *Agriculture in Mediterranean Europe between Old and New Paradigms*. Bingley: Emerald, pp. 263–293.

Kay, S., Peuch, J. and Franco, J. (2015). *Extent of Farmland Grabbing in the EU*. Brussels: DG Agri-European Union.

Keyder, Ç. and Yenal, Z. (2011). 'Agrarian change under globalization: Markets and insecurity in Turkish agriculture', *Journal of Agrarian Change*, 11 (1), pp. 60–86.

King, R., Lazaridis, G. and. Tsardanidis, C. (2000). *Eldorado or Fortress? Migration in Southern Europe*. London: Macmillan.

Lawrence, C.M. (2007). *Blood and Oranges. Immigrant Labor and European Markets in Rural Greece*. New York and Oxford: Berghahn.

Mahdi, M. (2014) 'Between hope and disillusionment. The migration of nomadic pastoralists to Europe', in Gertel, J. and Sippel, S.R. (eds) *Seasonal Workers in Mediterranean Agriculture. The Social Costs of Eating Fresh*. London: Routledge, pp. 211–221.

Márquez Domínguez, J.A., Gordo Márquez, M. and García Delgado, F.J. (2009) 'Temporary "contracts in origin" as policy to control immigration in Spain: The "Huelva model"', *Cahiers de l'Urmis*, 12.

Martinez Veiga, U. (2001). *El Ejido. Discriminacion, exclusion social y racismo*. Catarata: Madrid.

Martinez Veiga, U. (2014). 'The political economy of El Ejido: Genealogy of the 2000 conflict', in Gertel, J. and Sippel, S.R. (eds) *Seasonal Workers in Mediterranean Agriculture. The Social Costs of Eating Fresh*. London: Routledge, pp. 103–111.
McMichael, P. (2005). 'Global development and the corporate food regime', in Buttel, F.H. and McMichael, P. (eds) *New Directions in the Sociology of Global Development*. Oxford: Elsevier, pp. 229–267.
McMichael, P. (2009). 'A food regime analysis of the world food crisis', *Agriculture and Human Values*, 26, pp. 281–295.
McMichael, P. (2013). *Food Regimes and Agrarian Questions*. Halifax and Winnipeg: Fernwood Publishing.
McMichael, P. and Friedmann, H. (2007) 'Situating the 'retailing revolution'', in Burch, D. and Lawrence, G. (eds) *Supermarkets and Agri-food Supply Chains. Transformations in the Production and Consumption of Foods*. Cheltenham: Edward Elgar, pp. 291–319.
McWilliams, C. (1999) [1936]. *Factories in the Field. The Story of Migratory Farm Labor in California*. Berkeley and Los Angeles: University of California Press.
Mésini, B. (2013). 'Mobiles, flexibles et réversibles. Les travailleurs saisonniers latino-américains 'détachés' andins dans les champs de Provence', *Hommes et migrations*, 1301, pp. 67–76.
Mésini, B. (2014). 'The transnational recruitment of temporary Latino workers in European agriculture' in Gertel, J. and Sippel, S.R. (eds) *Seasonal Workers in Mediterranean Agriculture. The Social Costs of Eating Fresh*. London: Routledge, pp. 71–82.
Mezzadra, S. and Nielsen, B. (2013). *Border as Method or the Multiplication of Labor*. Durham, NC and London: Duke University Press.
Michalon, B. and Morice, A. (eds) (2008). *Travailleurs saisonniers dans l'agriculture européenne*, special issue of *Etudes rurales*, 182.
Michalon, B. and Potot, S. (2008). 'Quand la France recrute en Pologne. Réseaux transnationaux et main d'œuvre agricole', *Études rurales*, 182, pp. 87–102.
Moraes, N., Gadea, E., Pedreño, A. and de Castro, C. (2012a) (eds) *Migraciones, trabajo y cadenas globales agrícolas*, special issue of *Politica y Sociedad*, 2012, 49 (1).
Moraes, N., Gadea, E., Pedreño, A. and de Castro, C. (2012b) 'Enclaves globales agrícolas y migraciones de trabajo: convergencias globales y regulaciones transnacionales', in *Política y Sociedad*, 49 (1), pp. 13–34.
Moragues-Faus, A., Ortiz-Miranda, D. and Marsden, T. (2013). 'Bringing Mediterranean agriculture into the theoretical debates', in Ortiz, D., Arnalte, E. and Moragues, A.M. (eds) *Agriculture in Mediterranean Europe between Old and New Paradigms*. Bingley: Emerald, pp. 9–35.
Moreno Nieto, J. (2014). 'Labour and gender relations in Moroccan strawberry culture', in Gertel, J. and Sippel, S.R. (eds) *Seasonal Workers in Mediterranean Agriculture. The Social Costs of Eating Fresh*. London: Routledge, pp. 199–210.
Moreno-Pérez, O., Gallardo-Cobos, R., Sanchez-Zamora, P. and Ceña-Delgado, F. (2015). 'La agricultura familiar en España: pautas de cambio y visibilidad institucional', *Agriregionieuropa*, 43.
Morice, A. (2008). 'Quelques repères sur les contrats OMI et ANAEM', *Études rurales*, 182, pp. 61–67.
Noiriel, G. (1994). 'L'immigration étrangère dans le monde rural pendant l'entre-deux guerres', *Etudes Rurales*, 135–136, pp. 13–35.
Nori, M. (2015). 'Mediterranean Transhumances', Presentation at the International Seminar *Human Capital, Wage Labour and Innovation in Rural Areas*, Athens, 23–24 October.

Ocal, A. (2014). 'La agricultura familiar en Turquía: Respuestas colectivas ante la crisis del modelo agroindustrial', in *Agricultura familiar en España. Anuario 2014*. Madrid: Fundación de Estudios Rurales, pp. 145–151.

Oliveri, F. (2015). 'A network of resistances against a multiple crisis. SOS Rosarno and the experimentation of socio-economic alternative models'. *Partecipazione e Conflitto,* 8 (2), pp. 504–529.

Ortiz-Miranda, D., Arnalte-Alegre, E. V. and Moragues-Faus, A.M. (eds) (2013). *Agriculture in Mediterranean Europe Between Old and New Paradigms*. Bingley: Emerald.

Padilla, M. and Abis, S. (2007). 'La grande distribution au Maghreb'. *Afkar/Idées,* 13 (Spring), pp. 70–73.

Papadopoulos, A. (2015). 'In what way is Greek family farming defying the economic crisis?', *Agriregionieuropa*, 11 (43).

Pechlaner, G. and Otero, G. (2008). 'The third food regime: Neoliberal globalism and agricultural biotechnology in North America', *Sociologia Ruralis*, 48 (4), pp. 351–371.

Pedreño, A., de Castro, C., Gadea, E. and Moraes, N. (2015). 'Sustainability, resilience and agency in intensive agricultural enclaves', *AGER Journal of Depopulation and Rural Development Studies*, no. 18, pp. 139–160.

Perrotta, D., and Sacchetto, D. (2013). 'Les ouvriers agricoles étrangers dans l'Italie méridionale entre 'séclusion' et action collective', *Hommes et Migrations*, 1, pp. 57–66.

Ploeg, J.D. van der (2008). *The New Peasantries. Struggles for Autonomy and Sustainability in an Era of Empire and Globalization*. London: Earthscan.

Ploeg, J.D. van der (2010). 'The food crisis, industrialized farming and the imperial regime', *Journal of Agrarian Change*, 10 (1), pp. 98–106.

Potot, S. (2008). 'Strategies of visibility and invisibility: Rumanians and Moroccans in El Ejido, Spain' in Jansen, S. and Löfving, S. (eds) *Struggles for Home: Violence, Hope and the Movement of People*. Oxford and New York: Berghahn, pp. 109–128.

Potot, S. (2010). 'La précarité sous toutes ses forms: concurrence entre travailleurs étrangers dans l'agriculture francaise' in Morice, A. and Potot, S. (eds) *De l'ouvrier sans-papiers au travailleur détaché: les migrants dans la 'modernisation' du salariat*. Paris: Karthala, pp. 201–224.

Reardon, T., Timmer, C.P., Barrett, C.B. and Berdegue, J. (2003). 'The rise of supermarkets in Africa, Asia and Latin America', *American Journal of Agricultural Economics* 85 (5), pp. 1140–1146.

Reigada, A. (2012). 'Más allá del discurso sobre la 'inmigración ordenada': contratación en origen y feminización del trabajo en el cultivo de la fresa en Andalucía', *Política y sociedad*, 49 (1), pp. 103–122.

Richards, C., Bjørkhaug, H., Lawrence, G. and Hickman, G. (2013). 'Retailer-driven agricultural restructuring – Australia, the UK and Norway in comparison', *Agriculture and Human Values*, 30, pp. 235–245.

Rogaly, B. (2008). 'Intensification of workplace regimes in British horticulture. The role of migrant workers', *Population, Space and Place*, 14, pp. 497–510.

Salvioni, C., Henke, R. and Ascione, E. (2013). 'The emergence of new development trajectories in Italian farms', in Ortiz, D., Arnalte, E. and Moragues, A.M. (eds) *Agriculture in Mediterranean Europe Between Old and New Paradigms*. Bingley: Emerald. pp. 207–232.

Sassen, S. (1999). *Guest and Aliens*. New York: The New Press.

Sippel, S.R. (2014). 'Disrupted livelihoods? Intensive agriculture and labour markets in the Moroccan Souss', in Gertel, J. and Sippel, S.R. (eds) *Seasonal Workers in*

*Mediterranean Agriculture. The Social Costs of Eating Fresh*. London: Routledge, pp. 186–198.

Skordili, S. (2013). 'The sojourn of Aldi in Greece', *Journal of Business and Retail Management Research*, 8 (1), pp. 68–80.

Tsing, A. (2009). 'Supply chains and the human condition', *Rethinking Marxism*, 21 (2), pp. 148–176.

Via Campesina (2000). 'Bangalore declaration of the Via Campesina', *Via Campesina III International Conference*, Bangalore, India. http://viacampesina.org/en/index.php/our-conferences-mainmenu-28/3-bangalore-2000-mainmenu-55/420-bangalore-declaration-of-the-via-campesina (last access on 16 February 2016).

Vorley, B. (2007). 'Supermarkets and agri-food supply chains in Europe: Partnership and protest', in Burch, D. and Lawrence, G. (eds) *Supermarkets and Agri-food Supply Chains. Transformations in the Production and Consumption of Foods*. Cheltenham: Edward Elgar, pp. 245–269.

Weber, M. (1892) 'Die Lage der Landarbeiter im ostelbischen Deutschland', *Schriften des Vereins fur Sozialpolitik*, 55.

Weber, M. (2005). *Dalla terra alla fabbrica. Scritti sui lavoratori agricoli e lo Stato nazionale (1892–1897),* Ferraresi, F. and Mezzadra, S. (eds) Roma-Bari: Laterza.

Wells, M.J. (1996). *Strawberry Fields: Politics, Class, and Work in California Agriculture*. Ithaca, NY: Cornell University Press.

Yenal, N. (1999). 'Food TNCS, intellectual property investments and post-Fordist food consumption: The case of Unilever and Nestlé in Turkey', *International Journal of Sociology of Agriculture and Food*, 8, pp. 21–34.

# Part I

# Migrant labour and 'quality' food products

# 2 The (sacred) cow business

## Narratives and practices of the 'ethnic niche' of Indian Punjab milkers in the Po Valley

*Vanessa Azzeruoli*

### 2.1 Introduction and methodology

This chapter focuses on the supply chains of Grana Padano and Parmigiano Reggiano cheese, food products considered to be of excellent quality and among the most important 'representatives' of the 'Made in Italy' brand around the world. In particular, it analyses the work of milking within the dairy industry of the Po Valley, a sector that in the last 20 years has been characterized by a massive recruitment of workers from the Indian Punjab. Although official data do not exist, experts and breeders estimate that 50 per cent (or more) of milkers come from this small region of India, while a recent BBC news article claims that 60 per cent of the production is currently in the hands of Indians (Mitzman, 2015).

The coexistence of Punjabis and locals in the Po Valley is seemingly peaceful and collaborative; not infrequently, at dusk, families of locals and Indians walk along the country lanes. The news of this Punjabi presence in northern Italy travelled all the way to the *New York Times* (Povoledo, 2011), which maintained that a strike of the Indians could interrupt cheese production. But on the horizon there is no sign of a strike. What lies beneath the apparent calm that reigns in the Po Valley?

This chapter is based on qualitative and ethnographic research conducted between 2011 and 2013.[1] Interviews were carried out with 52 Punjabi migrants and 42 Italians including growers, other actors in the supply chains, and privileged witnesses, while observation was conducted during extended periods living and working in both the Indian Punjab and Italy.

In the analysis of the recruitment of Punjabi workers in dairy production we cannot simply maintain that migrants have replaced local workers. Rather, the contemporaneous processes of transformation of the entire supply chain (and in particular cheesemaking) and the recruitment of a migrant workforce were mutually constitutive. In other words, this chapter aims at showing how Indian Punjab milkers – and their peculiar recruitment system – contributed to the growth of a new and different model of production of Grana Padano and Parmigiano Reggiano. Over the last 20 years, a number of changes in these supply chains can be observed, such as the halving of the number of companies, the expansion in the size of existing farms and the doubling of production. The recruitment system practised by Punjabi migrants has been central in supporting these processes, and has been accepted (or perhaps it is more accurate to say promoted) by local employers and legitimated by the commonplace about the 'good Indian worker' culturally inclined to work with animals, particularly cows.

The employment of Punjabi milkers appears to produce 'positive' effects for all those involved in the recruitment process. For migrant workers, within the framework of Italian legislation which, as we shall see, is based on a restriction (and selection) in the entry of third-country nationals, the chance to work in the stables allows them to regularize their presence in Italy and build, in a short time, an extensive migration chain from the Punjab.[2] For the employers, this system has ensured production 365 days a year, thanks to the constant presence of a disciplined and hierarchized workforce, produced by both the labour broker and the process of 'civic stratification' instigated by migration policies (Morris, 2003).[3] Finally, the labour broker acquires, through the social and economic capital accumulated during recruitment activities, a privileged and powerful position within the migrant network (Krissman, 2005). The practice of informal recruitment produces a hierarchy of migrants in the stables and, more generally, throughout the supply chain, which therefore makes the prospect of a strike of Punjabi milkers currently unlikely.

In the next section I briefly describe the restructuring of the supply chain that has occurred over the last 20 years. The third section then focuses on the development of the 'ethnic niche' of Indian Punjabi milkers and on the cultural constructions that legitimate this niche. The fourth section sketches the life histories of two Indian brokers in order to describe the mechanism of recruitment, while the final section questions why many Punjabi migrants find milking work especially convenient, at least in the first phase of their migratory paths.

## 2.2 The supply chains and the work in the stables

The supply chains of Parmigiano Reggiano and Grana Padano have experienced several radical transformations[4] in recent decades. On the one hand, these changes have been influenced by the inclusion of Punjabi workers; on the other, such changes have rendered the recruitment of Punjabis increasingly necessary. Over the last 20 years, the difficulties of dairy cow breeders have increased, and a huge number of small breeders have disappeared, while in larger farms the Taylorization of the work process and the need for a greater number of employees have become fundamental.

Let us look at the broader picture. Over the past decades the number of farms has fallen by half in all the statistical areas and, at the same time, there has been an expansion in size of the existing farms.[5] The selection of cows has become central to production: the milk produced per head has risen from a few litres produced by the local Friesian species, to 35–40 litres from cows gradually selected, since the 1980s, through artificial insemination with a Dutch breed. Moreover, the cows once stayed in the barn for about 20 years; now they are slaughtered and replaced after two or three gestations. This means a significant expansion in the size of the stables, due to the need to house an increasing number of non-productive animals. In some cases the cows are divided into several structures. In other cases, old stables and properties have been bought by expanding companies with the goal of equipping buildings with the latest technology and using land for forage production.[6] As a result, many farmhouses situated on these lands can be rented or given on lease, which is an important issue, as I will show, in the stabilization of migrants.

Data on dairies (Bonazzi, 2004) reflect the situation in the stables: between 1980 and 2009 the number of production units specializing in Parmigiano Reggiano drastically decreased from 1,178 to 405 dairies. By contrast, production of Parmigiano Reggiano has doubled in the last decade (from 633,329 to 1,114,440 tonnes annually), while between 1994 and 2014 Grana Padano output increased from 2,815,000 to 4,840,000 wheels (CRPA and CFPR, 2010). The transformation of production has led also to Grana Padano overtaking Parmigiano Reggiano: Grana Padano currently amounts to 46.3 per cent of hard cheese produced in Italy, while Parmigiano Reggiano sits at 39.8 per cent. In the 1980s the situation was the reverse with Parmigiano Reggiano accounting for 63.9 per cent of the market and Grana Padano for only 22.6 per cent (Bonazzi, 2004).

In parallel to increased productivity, in recent years there has been a significant increase in the costs of production, which has led to higher prices of the finished product (Callegari and Valentini, 2014), to the extent that, in most cases, revenue fails to cover the total costs of the farmers (CRPA and CFPR, 2010, pp. 15–21). The increase in production costs is mainly due to the dispersed organization of production, the lack of innovation, taxation, energy costs and bureaucratic inefficiency. The increase in prices should also take into account the fact that at least four years elapse between the birth of the cow and the production of cheese ready for consumption and that, over such a prolonged period, it is difficult to forecast the sale price of the product, particularly in the dairy market where prices have been particularly volatile in recent years. Moreover, traditional or high-quality products commanding high consumer prices, such as Parmigiano Reggiano from red cows or organic variants, no longer ensure a higher income for the farmer, because the bulk of the gain is siphoned off by processors and sales agents.

The option of exporting the product abroad does not appear to offer a solution for farmers either. The Consortium of Parmigiano Reggiano, for example, has prioritized exports as a means to ensure greater future stability to the market and in order to avoid a repetition of the large-scale crisis during previous years (CRPA and CFPR, 2010, p. 27) and, indeed, exports have grown exponentially in recent decades (increasing from 47,501 tonnes in 1980 to 354,411 tonnes in 2004). However, the various intermediaries between production sites and sales seem to prevent an increase in direct income to the farmer.

These transformations bear upon the structure of the entire chain, which can be subdivided into three phases: the first regards the farming of cattle and milking; the second includes the transformation of milk into cheese and cheese ripening; the third involves logistics and distribution and, thus, wholesalers and agents.

The supply chain can be structured differently according to the particular players and their relationships within the chain. A first type of chain sees large industrial groups of processors buy milk on the market, without any relationship with the breeder, with the aim to achieve economies of scale. A second type seems to have deeper territorial roots whereby small local companies manage both the farm and the cheese factory. A third type involves a coordinated and integrated relationship that includes forms of historic association between cooperative farmers and privileged relationships with supermarket chains, by virtue of a business-oriented logic aimed at maximizing the efficiency of the supply chain and the quality of milk. The position of farmers is increasingly decentralized in the supply chain. The construction of an integrated supply chain is considered by many producers as a possible means to survive the lower cost of milk imposed by large industrial groups and distribution.

But what have Punjabi milkers to do with all this? To respond to this question it is necessary to briefly describe the work inside the stable. The milking is carried out in double shifts 12 hours apart taking place during the night and day (usually from 4 a.m. to 8 a.m. and from 4 p.m. to 8 p.m.). It is hard work, which requires the ability to independently perform specialized work as milking has become ever more technologically sophisticated. One of the immediate outcomes is that the family of the farm owner is no longer sufficient to cover all the roles of production. There has also been an increase in bureaucracy dictated by the escalation of certifications and inspections, while younger members of the family prefer to work in other industries or carry out office tasks. The historical figure of the *bergamino*, the person who took care of milking and who often lived with his own family in the farm's main property and worked with the farm's owners, has been replaced by a number of workers skilled in one or more tasks, while the farm owner no longer carries out manual labour. In some cases the owners concentrate on managing investments in the company, while the division and organization of labour are handled by an employee. The employer is therefore increasingly less likely to be seen in the stables and so employees have to perform their duties independently. The employers need a workforce 365 days a year, that is reliable, specialized, autonomous and cheap. And, after previously trying with migrants of other nationalities, they found this in Punjabi migrants.

## 2.3 The construction of an ethnic niche between cultural stereotypes and the effectiveness of recruitment

Indian migration to Italy is concentrated in Lombardy (55,171 residents), Emilia-Romagna (18,806), Veneto (17,378) and Lazio (22,870) (UNAR 2013). The first phase of Punjabi migration is concentrated in southern Lazio and consists mostly of single men. The Punjabi presence in the Po Valley, on the contrary, is characterized by a majority of families and is spread over a large area that comprises the provinces of Mantova and Cremona, and the plain areas of the provinces of Brescia and Bergamo (in Lombardy), Piacenza, Reggio Emilia and Modena (in Emilia-Romagna). The geographical distribution of this migrant group is somewhat peculiar, given that it is strongly concentrated in rural areas or in small towns.[7]

Punjabi Indians are mainly employed in agriculture: as farm labourers in Lazio (Omizzolo, 2013) and as skilled workers in the supply chain of Grana Padano and Parmigiano Reggiano in the Po Valley (Compiani and Quassoli, 2005; Cicerchia and Pallara, 2009, p. 39; Lum, 2012; Sahai and Lum, 2013). The data collected by Coldiretti – the principal farmers' union in Italy – also indicate that 27,789 Indian workers were employed in this sector in 2012, one-third of the total number of the workers of both sexes for this national group in Italy, with a positive trend in the years of the economic crisis. The workers of Indian nationality hold the highest proportion of agricultural workers with permanent contracts (6,057), and, as such, far outweigh Romanians (4,824), who are five times more numerous in the agricultural sector but are more often employed on fixed-term contracts. The average wage of Indians is higher than that of other non-EU migrants, while the unemployment rate within this group is in line with that of locals and considerably lower than other migrant nationalities.

The most common form of work for Punjabis in the Po Valley is that of milking in dairy farms, although employment at other levels of the value chain is also possible, either in the transport of milk or in the cheese factories. Other supply chains in which Punjabis are involved include that of buffalo mozzarella in the provinces of Caserta and Salerno (Avallone, 2012; 2013) and there is evidence of their presence in the pastures of the Pre-Alps and the Apennines (Cicerchia and Pallara, 2009, p. 130).

The existence of an ethnic niche[8] in agriculture is the result of processes of segmentation and specialization operated by both the labour market (or, better, by employers) and kinship networks (Bertolani, 2005).[9] In addition to the effective work of the brokers, to which we will return in a moment, an interesting aspect to emphasize, and often underestimated by studies on the agricultural labour market, concerns the construction of stereotypes that influence the different networks in allocating people to various productive sectors (Light *et al.*, 1993). In the case analysed here, these stereotypes seem to have been decisive: the main elements of the representation of the Punjabi 'good worker' include a disposition towards agricultural work, community organization and the tendency to respect authority (see also Jacobsen and Myrvold, 2011, p. 5). The list of stereotypes culminates with the religious devotion to some animals considered sacred, particularly the cow, thus *naturalizing* a predisposition to work in agriculture (Bertolani, 2003). This is demonstrated in the following excerpt from an interview with a farmer from Parma:

> They learn very quickly, it seems they were born in the barn. The cow is sacred . . . and *they have this Hindu mentality* that in our line of work is great because Hindus have this education . . . the Indian has a different kind of reasoning . . . 'I must maintain my social rank in the most dignified way possible . . . doing the best of what is given to me to do . . .'
>
> (Farmer, Province of Parma, Interview, 01/10/2012)

The stereotype is apparent even in a report by the National Institute of Agricultural Economics (INEA),

> Indian and Eastern European immigrants are highly appreciated by our farmers, especially in the livestock sector in the Centre-North, for the care and management of the animals in the stable but also in semi-free grazing zones in the central Apennines. [. . .]. Indians and Pakistani – *by virtue of a religious vocation* – are employed in the care of livestock.
>
> (Cicerchia and Pallara, 2009, p. 118, emphasis added)

Obviously, these stereotypes and preconceptions are part of the process of production of differences that some authors (Grappi, 2012) define as institutional racism, and that affects all the social relations in which 'racialized' actors find themselves. The branding, in this case, is widely used by the Punjabi migrants themselves, who contribute to the consolidation of preconceptions (Bertolani, 2012). These together form a kind of symbolic and social capital for migrants that is constantly reinforced in their dealings with Italian society, at both the individual and collective level, in what appears to be a 'game of mirrors': I am as you see me, I am as you want me (Bertolani *et al.,* 2011).

The cultural stereotypes cultivated by employers and local society about the alleged vocational propensity for milking dictated by the sacredness of the cow does not stand up even to shallow analysis. First and foremost, most of the milkers are Sikh or Ravidassia, religions in which cows are not sacred. Indian migrants, therefore, are able to find a better position than other nationalities within the segmentation of the Italian labour market by combining the game of mirrors and the power of 'positive stigma' with an efficient system of labour mediation and recruitment in networks where access is controlled by those who have contacts with a previous Italian employer.

In other words, the stereotype hides the fact that employers, after having 'tested' workers of different backgrounds, have consciously selected Indian migrants because their system of labour replacement is particularly effective in assuring the continuity of production. At the same time, the migrants themselves 'culturalize' this selection, and as such conceal the power of the broker to choose the workers to be hired, which usually implies excluding whoever is not within his network of influence.

It is crucial then to analyse the system of recruitment of Indian migrants in the stables; I propose such an analysis in the next section. The following excerpt from an interview with a farmer provides an entry point as well as a general historical overview:

> The Indians are a positive phenomenon of globalization. In the 1980s no one wanted to work in the stable and it was impossible to find guys who would wake up at 4 am. [. . .] They'd ask if their Saturday was free and how much you'd pay them if they worked Sunday. Saturdays and Sundays don't exist on a farm. In the 1980s the Filipinos and Vietnamese arrived. We never kept them on. People told us they were unreliable and it was true. They came and went the next day . . . then the blacks came and that was a leap into the unknown . . . we've had some incompetent ones: that happens. Whites, blacks

> . . . if someone doesn't want to work, the skin color doesn't matter! We had one from the Congo, one from Senegal, and another from the Ivory Coast who certainly didn't work badly . . . They were good but the next day a friend of theirs turned up saying that TNT would pay them 10 euros more and so off they went. Then the Indians began to offer themselves . . . look how good they are! We had one at the beginning who was really good, this was around 1997, 1998, he worked for four years! Then they recommended another . . . he also worked really well . . . he also decided to become a night courier, this was 2004–2005 . . . *But the Indians are more farsighted than the other ethnic groups... they worry about the place they leave* . . . it's a characteristic the other farmers told me about: *they worry about their employer: 'I'm changing jobs but if you want I have a guy who could take my place'* . . . *you see a worker who works well, who tells you: 'I recommend him'* . . . *'Obviously if he's as good as you are, bring him.'* This guy had two brothers, one very good who worked with us, who found a replacement for when he wasn't at the farm or went on vacation. We got the daughter a job: she is an adult, she said she would come willingly . . . she's an amazing girl. She works with her dad.
>
> (Farmer, Province of Parma, Interview 01/10/2012)

## 2.4 The Punjabi recruitment system

Before describing the system of recruitment it is necessary to add an additional element to the analysis. The Punjabi workers possess intimate knowledge of farming activities because they themselves were often farmers in their country of origin and, in some cases, continue to conduct their own business transnationally.[10] For this reason they are well aware of the employer's needs and are careful to respond to them. For example, workers are trained for free by the labour broker before being allocated to a barn.

The organization of mediation and recruitment is quite complex and it is possible to identify various types of brokers. A first distinction exists between occasional and professional intermediaries. In the former case, a Punjabi worker performs brokerage activities on one or more occasions, often 'placing' a relative or friend and accumulating, as we shall see, social capital in the Bourdieuian sense (Bourdieu, 1980). In the latter case, brokerage is a real profession, whereby the Punjabi broker recruits labourers for one or more employers and, in addition to social capital, he also gains economic capital.

A second distinction concerns the position of the broker in the relationship with the employer. In the first case the broker is an employee, usually the first Punjabi hired on the farm, who acts as a supervisor for the (potential) workers subsequently recruited and assumes responsibility for the quality of new employees (and therefore also of their training), or he manages the temporary replacements, in other words by providing the name of a substitute in the case of illness or holidays; in other cases he provides the name of his successor at the time of his dismissal. In the second case, the broker is not formally employed by the companies for which he is working as an intermediary.

The work contract provided by the intermediary has a different cost depending on the function it performs. A contract that allows for the regularization of undocumented migrants already resident in Italy[11] is always followed by a payment, even in the case of mediation by relatives. For direct arrival in Italy using the 'flows-decrees' (*decreti flussi*) of the Italian government[12] the amount to be paid sometimes surpasses 20,000 euros and necessarily involves a connection with an agent in India and the agreement of the employer and other figures in Italy.

In short, the stratification among workers produces a dense network of asymmetrical ties between migrants at the centre of which is positioned the broker. The broker manages the work of subordinates and, in the eyes of the employer, is responsible for the same people. The fact that the workers are related to each other allows the employer to hire even those who have a limited knowledge of the Italian language. In many cases only the supervisor knows Italian and is therefore the only person who talks to the employer. As such, employers find themselves with both a hierarchized and specialized workforce. Moreover, the continuity and quality of production are guaranteed, and the workforce is subject to the disciplining role of the broker who carries the burden of dealing with the employers' expectations concerning the new employees.

In order to better understand the (peaceful) operation of this system of recruitment, it is worth recounting the stories of two brokers.

Amandeep arrived in Italy in 1990 at the age of 22 with a tourist visa to watch the World Cup football tournament. He became an overstayer and found a job as an (undocumented) seasonal worker near Latina in central Italy. He worked for five years without a contract as a labourer in the area and then moved to Rome, where he worked as a waiter. Fed up with precarious work, and after learning a bit of Italian, he decided to try his fortune in northern Italy. It was at this point that he arrived at Mario's stable with only a plastic bag in hand. Mario's father had had some health problems, so the family decided to hire Amandeep as a milker. The business was growing: it had acquired a new property where the stable was modernized and Amandeep was given the nearby house on lease. The number of cows quickly rose from 150 to 350. Through the amnesty of 1996 Amandeep obtained a residence permit and, thanks to the house and support from Mario's family, in 1998 he was able to bring his wife and daughter to Italy through family reunification. Other local farmers were interested in hiring new workers and asked Mario and his family to find them other 'Indians.' Mario, in this way, recruited tens of workers.

Franco is one of these farmers. Amandeep was hosting a fellow villager, Darshan, who for some years had been living in Rome without documents. Amandeep trained him as a milker and recommended him to Franco. Darshan obtained his documents in 1998 thanks to another amnesty. Franco then decided to enlarge his stable from 80 to 300 head of cattle and asked Darshan to recruit other milkers. Darshan called a brother from India through the 'sponsorship' of the employer, a mode of entry into Italy introduced by Law 40 in 1998 and later abolished by the so-called Bossi-Fini Law (Law 189/2002). Soon, both Darshan and his brother brought over their wives and children through family reunification.

In 2009, they called another brother through an amnesty for domestic work,[13] who was hired on the same farm. Darshan now no longer has to get up at 3 a.m., and only organizes the supply of animal food and supervises the work in the barn, while his brothers do the milking.

Mario, in the meantime, decided to set up a labour replacement cooperative. He did not collaborate with Amandeep in this activity: Amandeep quitted the farm without prior warning in 2012, and continues his activity as a broker for new arrivals, thanks to the contacts he built up over the last 20 years.

These two stories demonstrate, among other things, the strong links between the business decision of expanding stables and the need for reliable recruitment mechanisms in order to provide disciplined workers trained for the range of associated tasks.

Amandeep and Darshan are two very different figures: one becomes a professional broker and is remunerated in both economic and social capital. The second is an occasional broker who only accumulates social capital.

The social capital obtained by the broker allows him to gain power within the network by being 'reinvested' to improve his own position. One example is the ability to negotiate a marriage with a bride from a family of higher status. Hence, by recruiting an older member of a prominent family as a milker, Baljeet (31 years old, interviewed in the province of Mantova) was able to marry this man's daughter, even though Baljeet's family had 'fallen from grace' after the arrest and death of his father. Similarly, Amandeep (46 years old, interviewed in the province of Mantova) arranged a wedding between his own daughter and heir to the largest landowner in his city of origin, reversing the tradition and imposing the transfer of the groom to the bride's home. But why do the workers need – and legitimize – the figure of the broker?

## 2.5 Why do they do it? A strategic job in the times of Bossi-Fini Law

The work in the stables is strategic for Punjabis because, through the amnesties, decrees on immigration and family reunification of the last two decades, it has allowed for the arrival and/or regularization of migrants. Three factors constitute a major advantage for these migrants: the work is regular and permanent; the wages are comparatively high (although they have fallen in recent years); and the availability of a house on lease adjacent to the barn.

The legislation on transnational mobility that is currently in force – Law 286/1998, as amended by the Bossi-Fini Law (189/2002)[14] – inextricably links the renewal of a residence permit to the possession of an employment contract and to residence in suitable accommodation. The work in the stables in the Po Valley is usually contract employment, and the monthly wage varies between 1,800 and 2,500 euros. This is a rare case among the jobs available to migrants in Italy, and not only in the agricultural sector. The significance of contract employment is not limited to obtaining a residence permit: the requirements for obtaining Italian citizenship, according to Law 91/92, include a minimum income threshold to be proven for three years preceding the application. Moreover, stable employment and income is linked to the request for the reunification of spouses, relatives (parents) and descendants (children), in other words to the particular migratory strategy pursued by migrants themselves but also encouraged by governmental institutions. For the migrant, a job and a *regular* salary of a certain amount thus become central in order to access the rights of citizenship.[15]

The houses that are rented out to migrants are often large enough to host several people, even though they are unheated and often dilapidated. The reunified families include the wife, children, parents/in-law and sometimes brothers and sisters, relatives and acquaintances recruited by the same farm or simply accommodated for the short period during which work is sought.

However, if the rented home is fundamental to the first phase of stabilization in the area, it can also turn into a sort of cage, which is how one Punjabi female migrant described the sense of 'seclusion' that came with living in the property of her boss:[16]

> [It's] like being a chick under the eyes of the eagle. Living on property rented from the farm turns you into a slave. Because if you want to leave the job you're faced with two problems: if you don't want to accept everything, you have to find another job and another house at the same time.
>
> (Sunny, 49 years, Province of Reggio Emilia, Interview 09–04-2012)

Changing jobs therefore simultaneously means becoming homeless. In the meantime, the replacement system manages the transfer of the outgoing family and guarantees that the job position and the house are filled by a fellow national.

As already stated, the brokerage system is beneficial for all parties involved. However, in the years of economic crisis the situation has changed, in particular due to the lowering of wages of dairy workers. In some cases, new brokers propose workers to employers at a lower price in order to get a foothold in the recruitment market; in other cases, farmers force brokers into a downward competition with other brokers. Workers are often obliged to accept lower wages, because of the link between labour contract and renewal of the residence permit, or more generally, in order to keep open their access to citizenship rights. At the time of writing, monthly wages are often below 1,000 euros per month, compared to the 1,800 to 2,500 euros previously earned. In other cases, only a proportion of the time worked is paid (e.g. 6 hours instead of the 8–10 hours actually worked) or the work load is greater, due to the increased number of animals to be milked.

> When the new owners of the farm arrived from Brescia, they wanted to pay me six hours. They said: 'we've got 300 cows. Our daughter's computer says it takes this amount of time to milk them.' Then there was an increase in the number of cows and there were also the calves, but the computer didn't say anything . . . and we were left there . . . Then there's one cow who gets ill, so you lose time, you have to cure him . . . I gave injections, I was doing everything . . . After my husband died they wanted to take advantage a bit

> because now the world works like that. They had helped me a lot, they had always been good. But then they wanted more work for the same pay, and I said no because I had to leave my children at home. I do my job, but I don't work for free. Before, I didn't do Sundays, then they wanted me to work on Sunday, and for me there was no problem . . . But when I finish my work you can't give me a piece of cheese and 10 eggs. No, you give me what I deserve and I'll go to buy eggs.
>
> (Sunny, cited interview)

Nevertheless, having a stable job and a leased home still appears to outweigh the lowering of wages. But how far can one be pushed?

## 2.6 Conclusions: entrepreneurs in the mirror

It is difficult to understand the presence of Punjabi milkers in the Po Valley in terms of the conflict between workers and employers. First of all, the employers are only one link in the supply chain, and are very often subordinate to the pressures of processors and big retailers. Second, the system of recruitment of Punjabis highlights the mutual connections between the restructuring of the chain and the growing importance of migrant labour. Through the Punjabi brokerage system and their provision of a cheap, disciplined, specialized and hierarchized workforce, a huge number of employers have been able to endure the transformations of the supply chain, in both the stables and the dairies.

The three actors in the recruitment and mediation process – employer, worker and broker – benefit from the system and its continuation. At the same time the three actors do not have equal power within negotiations. Obviously, the workers are in the least powerful position: however, they see this kind of employment as a possibility to stabilize themselves in Italy and reunify with their families, and, as such, they endure the lowering of wages and their subalternity to conational brokers. Through their intermediation, the brokers gain the social capital to be spent within the transnational network: in this way they are able to arrange favourable marriages or to subvert family hierarchies, as exemplified by the case of a man who through reunification with his older brother is able to take over his place in decisions concerning the family. At the same time, the broker can acquire a negative reputation depending on the worker he recommends and can subsequently lose the trust of an employer. The employers are the ones who gain the most from the intermediation with Punjabis, for this enables them to have a hierarchical and specialized workforce available 365 days a year.

The brokerage of Punjabi labour works as a temporary employment agency. The service is often free and is sometimes paid for by the worker, but this should not obscure the fact that it falls squarely into a capitalist exchange. In fact, the employee pays the broker through social and sometimes economic capital, especially if the employment contract is essential for the regularization of the worker. It is through this service, combined with the containment of labour costs, that farmers can remain in the market. Once more, this process shows how the 'civic stratification' of migrants is useful for global capitalist economy. At the same time, migrants accept low labour standards with the aim of obtaining the much coveted rights of citizenship.

## Notes

1 The study was undertaken during doctoral research in social sciences at the University of Padua (Azzeruoli, 2014).

2 Punjabi migration to Italy, and more generally its various diasporas around the world, often follows a common migratory pattern: the man migrates, stabilizes himself and obtains his documents, gets married and is joined by his wife and children (if any). In the following years he facilitates the migration of relatives and friends. The number of Indian residents during the past seven years has increased faster than the average rate of + 48 per cent for non-EU residents in Italy, rising 84.4 per cent from about 87,000 in 2008 to 160,000 in 2014 (MLPS, 2014). It should be noted that only 4,137 Indians resided in Italy in 1991, while this figure had climbed to 35,000 in 2001 (Istat, 1991, 2001).

3 Morris (2003) revised the notion of civic stratification (Lockwood, 1996) as the inequality in the access to formal citizenship and proposed a broader discourse on rights as an instrument of *governance* applied to migration. She thus shows how European policies segment the migrant population into long-term residents, short-term and undocumented migrants. This hierarchization of migrants (Bertolani *et al.*, 2014), also enters migrant families (Fix and Zimmermann, 2001). For an analysis of the concept see Rinaldini (2011) and for an application to the case considered here see Bertolani *et al.* (2014).

4 On 1 April 2015 the 'milk quotas' were abolished by the European Union. Milk quotas imposed a financial levy on European farmers for every kilogram of milk they produced above a certain threshold (the milk quota). EU Regulation 856/84 had fixed the total quantity of milk for each member state. In 1983, the value for Italy was 8.823 million tonnes and had been obtained by adding the quantities of milk delivered by producers to processors. The figure was, according to producer associations, underestimated and many farmers have been fined by the EU for producing higher quantities than officially stated (Borroni, 2001). A study on the possible impact of the elimination of milk quotas tends to reduce their importance in the supply chain: the production cannot be simply increased in a complex supply chain like that of milk in Italy (Callegari and Valentini, 2014).

5 In comparison to farms in the Netherlands or the US, farms that produce Parmigiano Reggiano producing are still small to medium in size, with 70 per cent of them possessing less than 100 head of cattle (CRPA and CFPR, 2010, p. 8). This said, the larger dairies, that constitute 20 per cent of all the farms, produce 50 per cent of the cheese (Ivi, p. 13).

6 It should be specified that the new protocol of the Parmigiano Reggiano consortium allocates land for on-site fodder production.

7 In terms of the total residential population, three of the five areas of highest concentration are small towns: Suzzara (in the province of Mantova) with 1,158 Indian residents out of a total population of 21,049; Arzignano (province of Vicenza), with 1,140 Indian residents out of a population of 25,996; and Sabaudia (province of Latina) with 1,083 Indian residents out of a population of 20,252 (data relating to 2013, available at demo.istat.it, last access on 25/07/2014).

8 Regarding the definitions of ethnic economy and the distinctions between 'enclave' and 'niche' see the contributions of Portes (1995), Waldinger (1994), Wilson and Portes (1980) and Wilson and Martin (1982). On the application of these concepts in agriculture see Portes (1998) and Ambrosini (2001).

9 It is worth underlining that although the situation is more diversified in other productive sectors, the Punjabis tend to build ethnic niches comparable to those in the livestock sector. The main cases that have been observed are transport, tanneries (such as the tanning district in the province of Vicenza, Tommasini, 2005b), construction and factories. The case of the logistics company GFE in Campegine (Reggio Emilia) is particularly significant, where more than two-thirds of the 400 workers were of Punjabi origin (Bertolani, 2012).

10 Punjabi migration is characterized by a strong propensity towards entrepreneurship (Allen *et al.*, 1977; Aldrich *et al.*, 1981): many of the migrants come from families of farmers for whom the ultimate goal of migration is to open their own business (Sahai and Lum, 2013, p. 20). In Italy one can therefore hypothesize that, within the livestock and trade sectors, the Punjabis are transforming the ethnic niche into an ethnic economy (Gold and Light, 2000), i.e. in which the employer and the workers are of the same nationality.

11 Over the last 25 years, 'amnesties' have been the tool most used by the Italian government to resolve administrative irregularity.

12 The 'flows decrees' (*decreti flussi*) – established by Law 40/1998 – is the Act by which the Italian government determines each year how many non-EU foreign citizens can enter Italy for work. There is a section devoted to people from certain countries that is set through bilateral agreements, while a second part concerns specific types of jobs.

13 Improper use of the amnesty for domestic work in order to regularize a brother or sister highlights, on the one hand, the inability to join adult relatives through legal channels, and, on the other, the irreducibility of migrations that force through state constraints (Mezzadra, 2006) and in this case redefine the concept of family imposed by regulations (Kofman, 2004).

14 The residence permit has a duration of two years if the employment contract is open-ended and one year if the employment contract is for a fixed period. The situation changes when the foreign citizen obtains a long-term residence permit (after five years of stay on Italian territory) as the labour contract is no longer required for renewal.

15 The only cases where there is no link with the employment contract are the possession of Italian citizenship, possession of a residence permit for family purposes and the request for international protection.

16 Ferruccio Gambino uses the concept of 'seclusion' (2003, pp. 104–107) to refer to a spatial arrangement that reinforces the overlap of the workplace, leisure space, resting place and more generally, the reproduction of daily life of an individual or a group. It differs from imprisonment in that they are formally free to leave this spatial arrangement.

## References

Aldrich, H.E., Cater, C.J., Jones, T.P. and McEvoy, D. (1981). 'Business development and self segregation: Asian enterprise in three British cities' in Peach, C., Robinson, V. and Smith, S. (eds). *Ethnic Segregation in Cities.* London: Croom Helm.

Allen, S., Bentley, S. and Bornat, J. (1977). *Work, Race, and Immigration.* Bradford: University of Bradford.

Ambrosini, M. (2001). *La fatica di integrarsi. Immigrazione e lavoro in Italia.* Bologna: Il Mulino.

Avallone, G. (2012). 'Dimensioni della fragilità territoriale. Gli immigrati nelle aree agricole della Piana del Sele' in Osti, G. and Ventura, F. (eds). *Vivere da stranieri in aree fragili L'immigrazione internazionale nei comuni rurali italiani.* Napoli: Liguori, pp. 89–104.

Avallone, G. (2013). 'Making history. Labour market and migrant workers in Piana del Sele's agriculture (Campania, Italy)'. Paper presented at the seminary '*Agriculture and migration in the European Union*', University of Bergamo (Italy), 24–25 October.

Azzeruoli, V. (2014). *Legami tra pianure. Gli intermediari nella migrazione dei panjabi indiani in Italia.* Unpublished PhD thesis. Padova: University of Padova. http://paduaresearch.cab.unipd.it/7004/1/Azzeruoli_Vanessa_Tesi.pdf (last access on 09/08/2015).

Bertolani, B. (2003). 'Capitale sociale e intermediazione etnica: il caso degli indiani Punjabi inseriti in agricoltura in provincia di Reggio Emilia', *Sociologia del lavoro,* no. 91, pp. 92–102.

Bertolani, B. (2005). 'Gli indiani in Emilia: tra reti di relazioni e specializzazione del mercato del lavoro' in Denti, D., Ferrari, M. and Perocco, F. (eds). *I Sikh, storia e immigrazione*. Milano: Franco Angeli, pp. 163–176.

Bertolani, B. (2012). 'Emilia 'rossa': una terra solidale? Riflessioni a margine di uno studio di caso' in Osti, G. and Ventura, F. (eds). *Vivere da stranieri in aree fragili L'immigrazione internazionale nei comuni rurali italiani.* Napoli: Liguori, pp. 23–41.

Bertolani, B., Ferraris, F. and Perocco, F. (2011). 'Mirror games: A fresco of Sikh settlements among Italian local societies' in Jacobsen, K.A. and Myrvold, K. (eds). *Sikh in Europe. Migration, Identities and Representations.* Farnham–Burlington, VT: Ashgate, pp. 133–161.

Bertolani, B., Rinaldini, M., and Tognetti, M. (2014). 'Combining civic stratification and transnational approaches for reunited families: The case of Moroccans, Indians and Pakistanis in Reggio Emilia', *Journal of Ethnic and Migration Studies*, 40(9), pp. 1470–1487.

Bonazzi, G. (2004). 'Il formaggio parmigiano reggiano nel sistema agroalimentare europeo', *Atti della società italiana di Buiatria,* Vol. XXXVI. Bologna: Editografica.

Borroni, R. (2001). *Le quote latte in Italia.* Milano: Franco Angeli.

Bourdieu, P. (1980). 'Le capital social: notes provisoires' *Actes de la recherche en sicences sociales*, 31, pp. 2–3.

Callegari, F. and Valentini, M. (2014). *Filiere d'Italia: produzioni e reti dell'agroalimentare*, Roma: Donzelli.

Cicerchia, M. and Pallara, P. (eds) (2009). *Gli immigrati nell'agricoltura italiana.* Roma: Istituto Nazionale di Economia Agraria (INEA). http://www.inea.it/ap/bollettini/docs/Rapp_immigrazione.pdf (last access on 25/07/2014).

Compiani, M.J. and Quassoli, F. (2005). 'The milk way to labour market insertion. The Sikh community in Lombardy' in Spaan, E., Illmann, F. and Van Naerssen, T. (eds). *Asian Migrant and European Labour Market.* London: Routledge, pp. 138–158.

CRPA (Centro Ricerche Produzioni Animali) and CFPR (Consorzio del Formaggio Parmigiano-Reggiano) (2010). *Parmigiano-Reggiano. Viaggio lungo la filiera.* Bologna: CRPA.

Fix, M., and Zimmermann, W. (2001). 'All under one roof: Mixed-status families in an era of reform', *International Migration Review*, 35(2), pp. 397–419.

Gambino, F. (2003). *Migranti nella tempesta- Avvistamenti per l'inizio del nuovo millennio*. Verona: Ombre corte.

Gold, S.J. and Light, I.H. (2000). *Ethnic Economies*. New York: Academic Press.

Grappi, G. (2012). 'Lungo la linea del lavoro. Migranti e razzismo istituzionale' in Curcio, A. (ed). *La razza al lavoro*, Roma: Manifestolibri.

Istat (Istituto nazionale di statistica) (1991). *Censimento popolazione 1991,* Roma: Istat.

Istat (Istituto nazionale di statistica) (2001). *Censimento popolazione 2001,* Roma: Istat.

Jacobsen, K. and Myrvold, K. (2011). *Sikh in Europe. Migration, Identities and Representations*. Burlington, VT: Ashgate.

Kofman, E. (2004). 'Family-related migration: A critical review of European studies', *Journal of Ethnic and Migration Studies*, 30(2), pp. 243–262.

Krissman, F. (2005). 'Sin coyote ni patrón: Why the 'migrant network' fails to explain international migration', *International Migration Review*, 39(1), pp. 4–44.

Light, I., Bhachu, P. and Karageorgis, S. (1993). 'Migration networks and immigrant entrepreneurship' in I. Light and P. Bhachu (eds) *Immigration and Entrepreneurship. Culture, Capital, and Ethnic Networks*. New Brunswick, NJ–London: Transaction, pp. 25–49.

Lockwood, D. (1996). 'Civic Integration and class formation', *British Journal of Sociology*, 47, 531–550.

Lum, K. (2012). *The Quiet Indian Revolution in Italy's Dairy Industries*. CARIM-India RR RR2012/08, Robert Schuman Centre for Advanced Studies, European University Institute, San Domenico di Fiesole (FI). http://cadmus.eui.eu/handle/1814/23486 (last access on 25/07/2014).

Mezzadra, S. (2006). *Diritto di fuga: migrazioni, cittadinanza, globalizzazione*. Verona: Ombre Corte.

Ministero del lavoro e delle politiche sociali (MLPS) (2014). *La Comunità Indiana in Italia. Rapporto annuale sulla presenza degli immigrati*. http:www.italialavoro.it (last access on 10/04/2014). http://www.integrazionemigranti.gov.it/Attualita/IlPunto/Documents/rapporti_comunita_2014/rapporti per cent20integrali/ComunitaIndiana.pdf (last access on 20/2/2016).

Mitzman, D. (2015). 'The Sikhs who saved Parmesan', *BBC news*, 25/06/2015. http://www.bbc.com/news/magazine-33149580 (last access on 20/07/2015).

Morris, L. (2003). *Managing Migration: Civic Stratification and Migrants Rights*. London: Routledge.

Omizzolo, M. (2013). 'La formazione dello spazio sociale transurbano e il caso della comunità sikh della provincia di Latina' in Corrado, A. and Colloca, C. (eds). *La globalizzazione delle campagne. Migranti e società rurali nel Sud Italia*. Milano: Franco Angeli, pp. 159–171.

Portes, A. (1998). 'Social capital: Its origins and applications in modern sociology', *Annual Review of Sociology*, 24, 1–24.

Portes, A. (ed.) (1995). *The Economic Sociology of Immigration. Essay on Networks, Ethnicity and Entrepreneurship*. New York: Russell Sage Foundation.

Povoledo, E. (2011). 'In Italian heartland, Indians keep the cheese coming', *New York Times*, 07–09–2011, http://www.nytimes.com/2011/09/08/world/europe/08iht-italy08.html?pagewanted=all&_r=0 (last access on 06/11/2013).

Rinaldini, M. (2011). 'Stratificazione civica e famiglie migranti' in Tognetti-Bordogna, M. (ed.). *Famiglie ricongiunge. Esperienze di Ricongiungimento di Famiglie del Marocco, Pakistan e India*. Torino: UTET, pp. 63–88.

Sahai, P. and Lum, K.D. (2013). *Migration from Punjab to Italy in the Dairy Sector: The Quiet Indian Revolution*. CARIM-India RR 2013/10, Robert Schuman Centre for Advanced Studies, European University Institute, San Domenico di Fiesole (FI).

Ufficio Nazionale Antidiscriminazioni Razziali (UNAR) (2013). *Immigrazione. Dossier Statistico 2013. Dalle discriminazioni ai diritti*. Roma: Centro studi e Ricerche IDOS.

Waldinger, R. (1994). 'The making of an immigrant niche', *International Migration Review*, 28(1), pp. 3–30.

Wilson, K.L. and Martin, W. A. (1982). 'Ethnic enclaves: A comparison of the Cuban and black economies in Miami', *The American Journal of Sociology*, 88(1), pp. 135–160.

Wilson, K.L. and Portes, A. (1980). 'Immigrant enclaves: An analysis of the labor market experiences of Cubans in Miami', *The American Journal of Sociology*, 86(2), pp. 295–319.

# 3 Wine heritage and the ethnicization of labour

## Arab workers in the Bordeaux vineyards

*Chantal Crenn*

### 3.1 Introduction

This chapter is based on ethnographic fieldwork in the region of Aquitaine in south-west France, and especially in the area east of Bordeaux, between Saint-Emilion, Sainte-Foy-La-Grande, Bergerac and Duras. Over the past decade, as both an anthropologist and a resident in this area, I have observed the so-called 'inter-ethnic relations' and social hierarchies in the vineyards, paying particular attention to farm workers of North African origin.

In French sociological and anthropological research, the issue of migrant labour in wine production appears to be somewhat neglected, particularly in the Aquitaine region, despite the economic and cultural relevance of this production.[1] In south-west France, scholars have mainly analysed the economy and governance of agriculture in general and of wine in particular (Bélis-Bergouignan and Corade, 2008; Hinnewinckel, 2010). As for research on migrant labour in agriculture, over the last 30 years a number of studies have been conducted in south-east France, largely due to the widespread presence of migrant seasonal labour and the relations that have been built between social researchers, agricultural unions and organizations for the defence of migrants' rights (Berlan, 1986, 1994; Noiriel, 1994; Morice 2005; Michalon and Potot, 2008; Lamanthe, 2008; Mésini, 2013; Décosse 2013; Gertel and Sippel, 2014). A similar degree of attention has not been paid to migrant agricultural labour in south-west France. Moreover, available research is limited to the fresh produce sector, while Bordeaux vineyards remain underrepresented (Roudié, 1987; Crenn, 2006, 2013).

France is the most studied country in Europe regarding migrant labour in agriculture. Nonetheless, a majority of French social researchers[2] still tend to view urban areas as the most conducive setting in which to study changes in international migration. The rural world is sometimes considered as if it was unaffected by migration processes. Wine production, in particular, is usually associated with 'whiteness', '*terroir*', French identity and the origins of the French nation. How could this symbolic world be studied in relation to something so *un-French*? Moreover, as Berlan (1994) and Noiriel (1994) have indicated, this neglect is also due to the significance of family farming, which is still heavily promoted by farmers' unions. Migrant farm workers are often seen as a transient labour force even if they have increasingly settled in the area on a more permanent basis.

This chapter analyses the construction of the category of 'Arab' worker in the vineyard (as produced by employers, the local population and workers themselves), and describes how this category has, over time, been shaped by a number of processes: the transformation of migrants' legal statuses; changes in the agricultural sector; generational changes, as well as the arrival of workers from other countries who compete in the labour market with the 'first' 'Arabs' arrived from North Africa. My argument is that the violence of social relations that derives from competition in the labour market and precarious employment, finds its justification in the racist and commonsensical representations of local workers and elites. In other words, racism has become a consensual means of regulating social relations. On the one hand, one can observe the construction of a 'French white rural world', with its famous *châteaux* (castles) producing excellent wines, and a vineyard landscape recognized as world heritage by UNESCO (as in the case of the Jurisdiction of Saint-Émilion) and valued for its tourist appeal. On the other hand, there exists the parallel (racist) construction of the category of 'Arab' workers.

The chapter is structured as follows. After a short description of the fieldwork, I provide a historical overview of both wine production and labour migration in agriculture in Aquitaine. The analysis then focuses its attention on three topics: first, I describe the labour experiences of the first generation of so-called Arab vineyard workers who arrived in this region in the 1970s, through a collection of life histories; second, I analyse how racism structures labour relations in places renown for producing 'high quality' wines; third, I describe acts of resistance (mostly of an individual nature) carried out by farm labourers of North African origin.

## 3.2 Anthropology in the vineyards

As opposed to numerous monographs on urban 'ethnic' neighbourhoods, my research on winemaking *milieux* (I use the plural because the areas of production are highly diverse from a sociological and economic point of view[3]) did not set out to consider a specific post-colonial 'ethnic community' at a micro-local level, isolated from the rest of the host society. On the contrary, since 2002, I have examined the wine industry as a whole, including all the actors in the region:[4] from vineyard owners, non-Arab farm workers, salespeople, traders and customers to members of brotherhoods (*confréries*), social workers for the Family Allowance Fund (*Caisse d'Allocations Familiales,* CAF) and the Agricultural Social Insurance (*Mutualité Sociale Agricole*, MSA), and other privileged observers such as teachers and medical doctors. I collected 20 life histories, conducted more than 50 interviews and spent ten years as a participant observer, which was made possible as a result of living in the local area.

The goal of my research over the last decade, therefore, was neither to focus on a specific cultural group (the so-called Arabs or Moroccans), nor to concentrate on a specific place (in the sense that I have examined local winemaking in relation to processes affecting the industry at a global level). The areas of study, variously situated at around 70 kilometres from the city of Bordeaux, are famed for their local wine culture and participation in French national history, but they have also recently experienced the growth of an 'urban' culture (Althabe and Selim, 1998). In addition, they have all been reshaped by processes of cultural and economic globalization. Ten years ago, few in the region were interested in the topic of migrant labour. However, due to the general impoverishment[5] of wine regions (particularly those producing mid-range wines) and the arrival of people in search of work from the Bordeaux urban area (parts of which had experienced displacement of inhabitants due to gentrification and economic crisis) as well as from other French regions and Spain, the issue of foreign farm workers has recently emerged in daily conversation as well as media and political discourse.[6]

## 3.3 Workers from Maghreb and the longstanding history of migration in Aquitaine

Vineyards occupy much of Aquitaine, with the exception of the great Landes Forest and the Pyrenees mountains. The large vineyards between Garonne and Dordogne in the north of the region form a continuum that cover more than 50 per cent of the land in some areas. The *terroir* of the Bordeaux vineyards has been materially, socially and historically constructed over the course of history and during the 1930s was granted a Controlled Designation of Origin (*Appellation d'Origine Contrôlée*, AOC).[7] Since the Middle Ages and up to the creation of the AOC, the legal framework of wine production had always been the preoccupation of the local elites. Moreover, from the late Middle Ages onwards, the need for a labour force in the vineyards had always attracted seasonal migration from the Pyrenees, particularly during harvest time (*Aquitains d'ici et d'ailleurs*, 2013, p. 31).

Aquitaine, like three other French Regions (Rhône-Alpes, Provence-Alpes-Côte-d'Azur and Midi-Pyrénées), has long employed foreign labour to meet agricultural needs due to the low birth rate in the local area and a rural exodus that began as early as the industrial revolution between 1850 and 1870 (Crenn and Tersigni, 2014) and which continued until after the First World War. In many French departments, the population had been continually decreasing since the middle of the nineteenth century; the south-west lost about 235,000 inhabitants between the 1911 and 1921 census; Laurence Teulières (2002), in fact, describes the central role of landlords and local elites in managing the arrival of foreign seasonal workers. They personally organized recruitment in a number of regions in France and Spain (see also Hubscher, 1996). Spanish workers in France were a sizeable presence as early as the nineteenth century and worked mainly in the vineyards, in spraying, priming and harvesting. From the start of the twentieth century, and more consistently after the First World War and during Fascism, workers from Italy also arrived in the region. These Italians were mostly experienced farmers (salaried workers, sharecroppers and small farmers) who were escaping the economic difficulties at home and, in doing so, answered the ongoing needs of French farmers. In the Libourne and Bergerac polyculture areas,[8] they soon became landowners, and contributed to the modernization of agriculture, and, to a lesser extent, of viticulture (Crenn, 2013; Drot, 2007). In the second half of the 1930s, despite the hostility of local populations, migration from Italy remained constant, while new migratory movements from Spain took place, with the arrival of numerous republican refugees in Sainte-Foy-La-Grande, Eymet and other towns of the region (*Langage Pluriel*, 2013). Following the Second World War, Spanish and Portuguese migrants, fleeing poverty or the Franco and Salazar regimes, continued to settle in Aquitaine and found seasonal employment in the vineyards.

By the end of the 1960s, decolonization in North Africa had led to the mass arrival of returnees (known as *Pieds-Noirs* and *Harkis*[9]). A number of them found employment in the vineyards or bought acres of land and set up farms, at a time when locals continued to leave the rural region for urban centres, especially Bordeaux.

The independence of the former colonies, and in particular the bilateral agreements signed with Algeria, triggered the arrival of the so-called Arabs, who found employment on farms – still in great need of labour – through contracts organized by the *Office National d'Immigration* (ONI, see Décosse, this volume). In addition to specific winemaking tasks, such as spraying, priming, harvesting and bottling, these migrants worked in livestock activities, horticulture, and fruit-canning factories and were therefore employed all year round. The Algerians were soon followed by Moroccans and Tunisians. These Maghrebis replaced Spanish farm workers who either returned to Spain after the end of Franco's regime, moved to the city, or simply retired. From a population of 6,000 in 1968, by the mid-1970s there were 15,000 North Africans in Aquitaine (Drot, 2007).

Many of the Moroccan and Tunisian farm workers I met during my research arrived at the end of the 1970s. In most cases, they arrived alone from rural areas. Most Moroccans arrived from the wine-producing region of Gharb. Some of them were recruited through ONI contracts, while others arrived irregularly via south-east France and were regularized in 1981.[10] Those who arrived between the end of the 1980s and the beginning of the 1990s had either an OMI (*Office Migrations Internationales*, as the ONI had been renamed in 1988) contract or a tourist visa and found employment through personal or family networks (Morice, 2008; Décosse, 2012 and this volume). Since the end of the 1990s, others have come with the aim of working and getting married to 'French' cousins.

In the 1990s, as indicated by Michalon and Potot (2008, p. 88), two new processes affected migrant farm labour in France:

> On the one hand, French legislation on labour, particularly concerning the employment of foreign workers, has undergone major changes over the past few years as a result of European enlargement and French and European migration policies. On the other hand, the origin of workers has diversified.

The arrival of Polish migrants (who would become EU citizens after 2004) in the vineyards in the Libourne area to the east of Bordeaux has to be read in this context and meets the need for cheap farm labour. The historic Arab farm workers have seen their situation change: their once secure and permanent employment contracts are now challenged by harvesting machines and by other workers recruited through OMI contracts, such as Polish and Moroccans resident in either Spain or Morocco. Moreover, new forms of recruitment have emerged in the Bordeaux vineyards, such as temporary employment agencies and international subcontracting. This has led to illicit labour practices (Décosse and Duntze, 2007; Mésini, 2013) and has seen also a number of undocumented workers being hired in the sector.

## 3.4 Wine worlds in the Bordeaux region

The wine world of the Libourne area studied in this chapter is experiencing many changes: the modernization of production structures, mechanization, financialization, the growing hegemony of supermarket chains, standardization and economic globalization, which coexist with the 'staging' of traditional production processes (with the aid of props such as wooden barrels and stainless-steel vats), the 'return to traditional taste' and the quest for absolute 'quality'.

These processes of patrimonialization and distinction (Bourdieu, 1979) stand in sharp contrast with another identity referred to variously as Muslim, Arab or Maghrebi and perceived (or represented) by 'natives' to be more or less incapable of integration. In the face of the dramatic changes that have affected the wine community, racism is exacerbated and used as a means to regulate social and economic interactions. 'Here, a good Moroccan is a Moroccan who doesn't speak French and doesn't know his rights as a worker' (interview with Roger, 55, winegrower). The figure of the migrant vineyard labourer, at the beck and call of his employers, ignorant of his rights, or uninterested in benefiting from them, is still prevalent in the wine industry. However, today, the Moroccans (or so-called Moroccans, because most of them have French nationality), who settled in the region 30 years ago, represent a population that no longer meets these criteria. The legitimacy of their presence was questioned by local elected representatives during the official meetings of the Municipality councils as well as during informal conversations at the Saturday morning street market, particularly in the areas where they live[11] and work, although less intensively now than before the general use of machines (Crenn, 2013). As indicated earlier, they are now in competition with a number of other migrants: Polish workers, the so-called 'Sahrawi Moroccans',[12] 'Moroccans from Andalusia' and 'Portuguese Moroccans', as well as Russians and Ukrainians.

Many of the workers that I met have worked in several vineyards between Saint-Emilion and Monbazillac over the last 20–30 years. Particularly in recent years, their jobs have become increasingly dispersed and sporadic: 'one season here and the next there; this employer never called me back'; 'I did grafting one year on this property'; 'they call me less and less'. Some of these workers had been employed previously on a permanent basis, and were dismissed in the 1990s because of economic problems, very often to be replaced by the farmer's own unemployed brother or son-in-law. Others have been laid off more recently, only to be replaced by seasonal workers from a service supply agency. Very few still have a permanent work contract. Permanent workers are then called 'the Arab of this or that farmer':

> I was the first person in my village to really employ a Maghrebi, and everybody said: "you are invading us with your Moroccans ..." And when I sold them a piece of land so that they could build their house, there was a revolution!
>
> (Interview with Bernard, winegrower, 57 years old)

Mohamed, a former employee of this grower, remembers being called 'the Arab from the Courret' (Courret being the name of a wine *chateau* and surrounding area). Among older workers who brought over their wives in the 1970s, there is a perceptible degree of distress. Their living conditions are difficult: they often have to seek welfare support[13] and suffer variously from diabetes, respiratory pathologies and carpal tunnel syndrome. They often tell the history of the vineyard farm in which they used to work, and, paradoxically, of their 'love for the vines, as if they were our own children'. All life histories betray an ambiguous mixture of love and repulsion towards the farmers, who provide wages, the opportunity for their real participation in the local economy, a professional identity and the hope for permanent integration, but who also offer precarious working conditions and discrimination. As Karim, a 57-year-old seasonal worker, noted: 'Many of us go from being seasonal workers to being unemployed; some years I work for two months, in others I work seven'. Then there were those who lost their job because of a work accident that was never officially recognized, although these same individuals believed their employer 'liked them', because they were good pruners, recruited other workers, or were simply obedient.

> He considered me like his son. My wife and I had our own lodgings, I was given responsibilities. I don't know why, but he treated me better than my fellow countrymen who lived in the dormitories with earth-beaten floors. Maybe it is because I worked well. But when my fingers got cut off, I had to go to court, and I lost, because he knew all the judges. He won and all I now have is a small disability pension... I cannot work anymore.
>
> (Interview with Brahim, 57 years old)

Others discovered that, after being dismissed or reaching retirement age, their employer had not officially declared them during the early years of their contract, and so they were prevented from receiving their full monetary entitlements.[14] It should be emphasized that many native vineyard workers have also experienced similar setbacks.

The management of these labourers is also laced with contempt. Halema (50) recalls with bitterness waiting for phone calls from her employers during seasonal peaks: 'Last year I worked in a vineyard in Saint-Emilion; they were quite satisfied with my work and told me: 'we'll call you next year', but they never called me back ... They employed a Moroccan woman from Morocco instead!'. For some Moroccans, like Halema's husband, the situation is not perceived to be precarious since he is re-employed every year by the same employer, but he is also invariably dismissed at the end of the season. However, he can still claim unemployment benefit.

These workers have not always been subject to such precarious conditions. For example, Ahmed (who first arrived with an OMI contract) remembers with nostalgia the time when he obtained a permanent permit of stay and took part in all the stages of winemaking and accompanied the 'boss' from the grapes to the wine cellar. He eventually obtained what he had long striven for: a permanent contract. However, this did not last long:

> When I used to work for Gilles, a Protestant organic wine producer, I worked in both the vineyard and the cellar, so I knew what was going on ... The office was next to the cellar ... I sometimes attended wine fairs ... or else Gilles would tell us about them. Now, with my new employer, I only work in the vineyard and I have no idea about what is going on.
>
> (Ahmed)

Ahmed explained to me how his OMI contract bound his right to stay in the country to his work contract. 'My employer didn't want to keep me, so I had to find another farm'. This type of contract accentuates the subordinate relationship between migrant workers and their employers. If the worker demands his rights, or simply the farmer does not like him, he probably will not be employed the following year.

Brahim recounts how his daily life was totally dedicated to work and expresses what Abdelmalek Sayad (2004) referred to as the 'truth of immigration':

> After I got married in Morocco I moved here with my wife. We had a clear idea in our minds: to work and earn money. There was nothing for us in Morocco: I couldn't live on my uncle's farm or my father-in-law's farm. So we came here. I introduced my wife to my employer and he hired her right away. We used to have lunch on the job. I remember we didn't have to cook as much as we do nowadays. When our children were born, we had them looked after by a French lady, so that Djéma could carry on with her job. All our lives were organized around our jobs. But in the end, the day I had a work accident, my boss let me down.
>
> (Brahim)

According to Brahim, they would have accepted and endured anything just to obtain a permanent status, a fixed salary and recognition from the natives. Because of a longstanding lack of recognition, their words now express distrust, as well as a negative opinion about their employers, which extends to the French in general.

## 3.5 Racism as a means of structuring employment relations

Even though they have gained an in-depth knowledge of the vineyards, the workers and their families realize that they cannot move beyond their original status as immigrants; a position that is compounded by the ethnic division of labour and their residential segregation in towns. They are also aware that their 'integration into the local wine community' is now more difficult than in the past, because they have to compete with other migrants, who are cheaper and more obedient, such as Poles (Michalon and Potot, 2008) or, more recently, Sahrawi-Moroccans.

According to the children of the early arrivals from the Maghreb (who are now themselves adults and parents), employers still maintain, thirty years on, 'unacceptable levels of exploitation' (Yassine, 37 years old). This same informant believes that they will always remain Arabs and *ratons* (young rats).[15] The demand for moral integrity weighs heavily upon the younger generation of Arabs ('they loiter in the streets, they're not at work in the vineyards, they are Muslims'). The younger generation responds by accusing the French and the employers of not respecting their parents, of being 'bandits' and 'thieves', and outlaws in terms of human rights. They bitterly observe that their parents were not protected during the chemical spraying of vines and so now suffer from respiratory problems. In addition to bad working conditions, their children denounce the practice of undeclared work, which prevents them from obtaining their full pension entitlements. They also question the competition between their parents and other foreign workers.

While acknowledging humiliating situations in the workplace, the parents describe being subject to more threatening behaviour away from the vineyards. For instance, Haléma (55 years old) notes: 'we were free in the vineyards: there was nobody to stare at us. But in the street or at school, you can read on people's faces that we shouldn't be here! It is very hard!' Their employment in the vineyards justified their presence in France, but the more recent changes to the wine industry and the subsequent lay-offs of workers have occurred in a climate of growing racism across French society. Although racism against Maghrebis greatly increased after the New York attacks of 11 September 2001, this has become quite unbearable since the Paris attack of 7 January 2015. In fact, in many rural wine towns, people demonstrated under the '*je suis Charlie*' banner, while many migrants felt themselves excluded from such initiatives.

Regarding the lack of respect of the workers' rights as citizens, as pointed out by their children, it should be noted that the local labour office (*Direction Départementale du Travail*) and the trade union CGT have long condemned employers' lack of adherence to labour regulations. Indeed, as Jean-Pierre Berlan has argued (in reference to the murder of two labour inspectors in the region in 2004), flexibility masks the extreme violence in the management of the agricultural labour force.[16] The farmers are wary[17] of not being competitive and this makes collective resistance by farm workers difficult. This reticence in turn perpetuates a climate of silent domination: 'anything that might threaten the harvest, in particular any form of union action, is like a death threat to the farmer; which explains the violence of social relations that are ideologically justified by racism' (Berlan, 2008, p. 222).

A code of silence prevails. Serious threats hang over those who might wish to reveal the hidden mechanisms in the vineyards. Everyone involved in the industry adheres to this code of silence, as demonstrated by a rare article in the local media in 2003[18] which reported how the elected representatives of a local administration were relatives of one farmer and expressed total ignorance about the fact that he employed workers illegally. The local labour office and the trade union denounced the exploitation of Moroccan-Andalusian seasonal field workers; the general secretary of the local branch of the union commented:

> For some employees in this vineyard, the season starts in February and ends in November. According to the documents provided, four seasonal workers worked 12 to 15 hours per day, 7 days a week, and did not get paid a monthly salary. They were only given pocket money to buy their groceries. They only got paid at the end of the season as stipulated in their work contract, which was backdated, and extra hours were not paid. [...] The employer explained that benefits in kind compensated extra hours, which is difficult to believe if you consider the poor standard of accommodation.

The journalist who wrote the 2003 article added that, while visiting the estate, the mayor and local councillors were appalled: 'they know the landlord well, who is also a local councillor. If the workers had denounced this before, things would not have gone so far'. The small talk of mutual acquaintanceship works to euphemize the violence and to hide the real constraints that foreign labourers endure.

Considering such resistances, some farmers claim that they prefer to employ 'real French workers', who are considered to be more efficient, and moreover can contribute to revive the 'lost tradition' of conviviality that once characterized grape-picking: 'at least they eat pâté and drink wine!' (interview with Roger, cit.).

Most of all, the absenteeism of the early Arab settlers is frequently singled out as a handicap. One farm supervisor affirms:

> North-Africans? You can't depend on them, they are always absent. If they have a doctor's appointment ... they don't go to work! They usually live some distance from the pick-up places and they do not want to drive all the way to the Médoc area, so they are impossible to deal with!

Nevertheless, in spite of the popular rhetoric about needing to take on French workers, most people employed for the harvesting season are Sahrawi-Moroccans, Ukrainians, or Portuguese.

This said, the overt racism on the part of some French farm workers towards Moroccan workers in particular, is often endorsed by employers through their decision to exclude Moroccans from their workforce. Mr B., a winemaker in the Sainte-Foy-Bordeaux AOC area who is involved in local politics, confirms such a state of affairs: 'Moroccans? I don't employ them anymore. They tend to create loads of problems with the other [non-Moroccan] workers. They mistreat their wives, they don't eat the things we do, they have their own religion, they can't integrate'. The 'integration' of Moroccans is considered something that is entirely their own responsibility. Integration is usually talked about in the fields of education and culture but never in the sphere of work, which, as in fact observed in almost all vineyards, relegates them to subordinate seasonal tasks and prevents them from any career advancement. The division of labour assigns them manual tasks, but when they are promoted to mechanical work, they often face overt racism. Consider, for example, the following comment made during a conversation at a village service station between farm workers who consider themselves 'local' and 'native': 'there was an accident between a tractor and a car at la Grand'Croix. Of course, the *raton* with his trailer was to blame ... They shouldn't give a driving licence to a *raton*, you're sure to have accidents!' (Georges, 49-year-old farm worker who calls himself 'French').

These sorts of discriminatory discourses are reinforced by the ethnic division of labour, in turn compounded by the spatial and temporal segregation on the farm, which means that Maghrebis perform the most unrewarding tasks among themselves, without any contact with other workers. Some employers consider the exchange of racist comments as friendly banter among workers that helps guarantee the successful completion of tasks. With a rare frankness, Mr B., farmer, explains: 'The diverse groups – native French, Arabs, Gypsies – tend to compete in the vineyards; which is good because they are paid by piece rate, therefore it costs me less!'.

Discriminatory practices have become just another component of labour organization. The emergence of a sort of 'agricultural fascism' – an expression used by Carey McWilliams (1939, pp. 230–263) to refer to the situation in California in the 1930s – is evident in regions where the party of the extreme right, the National Front, has been obtaining unprecedented electoral results (Baqué, 2014). The violence in social relations induced by competition in the labour market finds its ideological justification through racism, which prevents any kind of organized resistance.

Contemporary forms of discrimination that are tacitly accepted (or barely condemned) by employers are linked to the continual goal of increasing production in winemaking. This accepted racism cannot be regarded simply as a manifestation of chauvinistic xenophobia. One needs to also consider the key role of employers and the social hierarchy within the organization of labour in shaping labour management (De Rudder *et al.*, 2000, p. 40). The so-called Arabs who settled in the region 20 or 30 years ago are not the only ones to have suffered a deterioration of employment conditions: French workers are also subject to poor working conditions in the vineyards. Nonetheless, popular racism has just become a consensual means of regulation, which makes it possible to endure precarious employment in the face of mechanization, pressures to increase productivity and flexibility.

## 3.6 Body and soul: individual forms of resistance

Over recent years, I have paid close attention to the sharp increase in workers' demands and refusal of certain labour conditions. These are mostly carried out on an individual basis and in a disorganized manner. For instance, the older generation of labourers from North Africa now refuses to be employed on task-based contracts after being dismissed from their permanent positions. Some of them have even dared to sue their employers in administrative courts. They refuse to work in places that are too far from home and swap their job with their nephews and nieces arriving from Morocco.

In some cases, they demand that their religious calendar (*Ramadan, Eïd*, pilgrimage to Mecca as well as diverse religious gatherings in Bordeaux or Paris) be respected. In other cases, they spend increasingly more time in their country of origin, where they assist nephews and nieces in their migration to France, by marrying them to their own children or procuring them illegal employment (through the use of tourist visas) in the vineyards of former employers. In yet other cases, they open their own businesses, often in the food retail sector (butchers, catering, fast-food, fruit and vegetable stalls at markets, ritual slaughter of animals, meat storage, etc.).

They reclaim the free time that is imposed on them by employers who offer them fewer and sporadic working hours. Their body becomes the centre of attention through the treatment of various maladies such diabetes, hypertension, back pain and carpal tunnel syndrome. Some spend more time at the mosques of Port-Sainte-Foy and Castillon-La-Bataille (built during the 1990s), which have become places where power relations are constructed and negotiated both among Muslims and between the mosques and other social actors in the area (Juteau, 1999). The first-generation workers strive to differentiate themselves from the 'troublemakers' who tarnish their image as 'good, respectable Muslims'. Their children's success at school is also seen as a form of resistance, even though it is not recognized as such by the majority society.

Forms of collective and organized resistance to racism and poor labour conditions are rarer than individual ones. In 2015, a group of associations and unions was set up in the Libourne area and publicly denounced the unacceptable living conditions of foreign seasonal workers;[19] they wrote a letter to the local public authorities. The objective was to improve the standard of accommodation for seasonal workers (around 2,000 seasonal labourers work in the vineyards in the Libourne area). The Sahrawi-Moroccan asylum-seekers squatting under the Saint-Jean bridge in Bordeaux aroused public solidarity and the mobilization of community-based organizations. As job-seekers or employees in the vineyards, the squatters used their Bordeaux network and the CGT trade union to denounce their situation.[20] At the same time, 'old' Moroccans have accused them of accepting low wages and irregular employment. These disputes among workers convinced unions and migrant rights organizations to compel the local authority to set up a Resource Centre for seasonal workers.

## 3.7 Conclusion

Whether poor or rich, the bodies of Arabs and Muslims are not welcome in town. Indeed the bodies of farm labourers who arrived in the 1970s came to work the land or cook 'Moroccan' dishes in the châteaux, away from the public eye (Crenn, 2006). 'Young' bodies are all too visible in the small towns of the wine region. They are subjected to processes of differentiation and categorization on the basis of presumed hereditary, somatic and psychological characteristics and a representation of Islam as a dangerous religion. The majority society interprets their presence as a provocative act of refusal to fit the role of the obedient farm labourer, as a contestation of the existing social order, and even the expression of their ungratefulness for the employment that they might be offered (Crenn, 2008).

In the world of winemaking, 'the acceptance of racism' requires us to move beyond the issue of xenophobia and consider its instrumental role in current choices to increase productivity in the context of neoliberal globalization, irrespective of the claims made by wine elites about authenticity, quality, the purity of *terroir*, organic methods and well-being. Racism has become a means of regulating social and labour relations, which enables all protagonists to manage labour precarity. In explaining this racism, local residents, journalists and elected representatives rarely take into account either the all-powerful wine *chateaux* that impose such a regulation of social and labour relations, or the structural economic logics of the winemaking industry.

This absence can be explained by a number of reasons. A first reason is that few of the migrant (or indeed national) farm workers are unionized. Moreover, trade union denunciations of racism and labour exploitation do not raise the interest of the local or national press (and one should not forget the threats against some journalists and the murder of two labour inspectors in the region in 2004). A second and deeper reason is connected with the issue of identity. In the French imaginary, this wine world is seen to occupy a central role in the construction of the French nation, thanks to its associations with purity, peasantry and family farming. It is precisely the strength of such symbols that presents an obstacle to a true public debate about the place of old and new migrants in local and national society. It should also be remembered that all this is happening at a moment when winemakers struggle to survive in the face of a general economic downturn and increasing competition in global markets which has seen a decline in the dominance of French wine world and some local producers being bought by Chinese or Argentinian entrepreneurs. These difficulties partly explain why the National Front has managed to greatly increase its share of the local vote.

In the context of the Bordeaux vineyards, where 'differences' are contemporaneously hidden and produced, the racism and ethnicization of Arab labour is constitutive of the patrimonial construction of French wine. Beyond the economic dimension, one can interpret the enthusiasm for the celebration of national history and the rejection of Arab workers by the majority society (both in rural and urban contexts) as a means to conjure the threat of losing the significance of the continuity of this history, and to ensure its sovereignty. In sum, this established asymmetric relationship between *us* and *them* appears to resurrect the classic, colonial vision in which everyone keeps to their own time and place; a process of social hierarchization that is deeply inscribed in the very history of the French Republic.

## Notes

1 A recent book on the global winemaking industry does not even tackle the issue of wage labour in the vineyards (Black and Ulin, 2013).
2 A notable exception is represented by Bourdieu and Sayad (1964).
3 As noted by Roudié (1988, p. 358):

> from the 1970s onward, the range of *crus* [vineyards, especially those of recognized quality] has been increasing in the Bordeaux region. Good wines produced under the *Bordeaux* label or even with other regional denominations, which were produced in large quantities, were set in opposition to the famous Saint-Emilion and Medoc wines that were produced in limited quantities, not to mention more common wines that were priced according to alcoholic content, produced in neighbouring areas and whose yield kept increasing.

4 I refer to Di Méo's definition of the *territoire* (2010, p. 86) as 'the voluntary appropriation of a geographical space by local social groups which is at once ideological, political and economic. These social groups tend to display a particular picture of themselves, of their history and of their identity'.
5 According to the survey Caf, MSA and Insee (2011), the small towns of Castillon-La-Bataille and Sainte-Foy-La-Grande are part of the well-known and somewhat caricatured 'poverty belt' that extends from the Medoc region to city of Agen. In both towns 29 per cent of the total population depend on welfare benefits.
6 In July 2015 the local government of Sainte-Foy-La-Grande launched a feasibility study to establish a resource centre for seasonal workers so that they could access information about decent housing, transportation services, employment offers, etc.
7 The AOC system came about as the result of the reorganization of French vineyards in 1935 and the law on the production of so-called 'quality' wines (Hinnewinckel, 2004). The AOC designation attributes a product with the features of 'authenticity' and 'typicalness'.
8 Besides winemaking, the agricultural activities between Sainte-Foy-La-Grande and Duras and Bergerac include the production of grains and fresh fruit, as well as the rearing of livestock.
9 *Pied-Noirs* are European who settled in the Maghreb area during the period of French colonization. They were often referred to as Arabs or colonists (cf. Roudié, 1988, pp. 352–5). *Harki* is often used as a synonym for a 'French Muslim returnee' after 1962 (the year of Algerian independence), a 'French returnee of Islamic faith' in the 1970s or a 'returnee of North-African origin' in the 1980s.
10 On 20 November 1981, in addition to President Mitterrand's main regularization package, a special circular was issued called 'Permanent Regularization of Seasonal Workers'. The aim of this act was to regularize seasonal workers employed on long-term contracts, in the cases in which they had worked at least 21 months over the previous three years. Subsequently, a seasonal worker who had worked at least four months per year over the five previous years could obtain a residence permit, as long as he could present an employment contract and was living in France at the time of regularization.
11 Due to the high price of land, farm workers cannot live in Saint-Emilion itself.
12 Many 'Sahrawi-Moroccans' have acquired Spanish nationality since the War in the Western Sahara. Their presence in Aquitaine has been in the spotlight since altercations with Franco-Moroccans broke out in October 2012 in the Médoc area. The latter accused the Sahrawi-Moroccans of being employed without a contract or of being under the minimum wage, and thus of breaking national labour regulations. In 2015 they again became the subject of media attention after a group of Sahrawi asylum-seekers squatted under bridges in Bordeaux.

13 The French welfare support scheme called *Revenu de solidarité active* ensures a minimum income to destitute people, and varies according to people's situations. Officially, in 2015, the minimum amount is 513 euros per month for a single, workless, incomeless and homeless person.
14 In the 1990s, delegates from the trade union Confédération Générale du Travail (CGT) tried in vain to convince these workers to sue their former employer. In some cases, the farmer had hired other members of these workers' families; in other cases, they were afraid of retaliation, or simply wary of losing the case.
15 Words such as 'dirty Arabs', 'goat dicks' and 'dirty *ratons*' are often painted on road signs (Crenn, 2013).
16 Similar to what Jean-Pierre Berlan has recounted (2008), it has been difficult for me as a researcher to reconcile the contradictory positions of officials in the ministries of agriculture and social affairs. In the former case they were trying, with the help of the farmers' local union (FDSEA, *Fédération départementale des syndicats d'exploitants agricoles*), to facilitate employment flexibility and profitability, while in the latter case they were trying to promote human and particularly workers' rights.
17 During my field research, several civil servants (such as social workers, doctors for agricultural insurance, and labour inspectors) told me that they were accused by 'French people' of taking the 'side of the Moroccans' and of even giving them an unfair advantage.
18 'Conditions de travail critiquées', *Le Résistant du Libournais,* 14 November 2003, p. 18.
19 'Libourne area: A collective to support seasonal workers in the vineyards', *Sud-Ouest,* 11 August 2015.
20 'Clandestine employment: The court will initiate an investigation', *Sud-Ouest,* 10 September 2015.

## References


Althabe, G. and Selim, M. (eds) (1998). *Démarches ethnologiques au présent.* Paris: L'Harmattan.

Aquitains d'ici et d'ailleurs (eds) (2013). *Apports et enjeux des immigrations pour le développement de l'Aquitaine.* Bordeaux: Ceser Aquitaine.

Baqué, P. (2014). 'On veut des Polonais et des Marocains!' *Le Monde Diplomatique,* September, pp. 20–21. www.monde-diplomatique.fr/2014/09/BAQUE/50768 (last access on 20/2/2016).

Berlan, J-P. (1986). 'Agriculture et migrations'. *Revue Européenne de Migrations Internationales,* 2(3), pp. 9–32.

Berlan, J.P. (1994). 'Dynamique d'intégration dans l'agriculture Provençale'. *Études rurales,* nos. 135–136, pp. 151–160.

Berlan, J.P. (2008). 'L'immigré agricole comme modèle sociétal?'. *Études rurales,* no. 182, pp. 219–225.

Bélis-Bergouignan, M.-C. and Corade, N. (2008). 'Fusions des coopératives vinicoles et ancrage territorial'. *Revue d'Economie Régionale et Urbaine,* 1, pp. 43–68.

Black, E.R. and Ulin, R.C. (eds) (2013). *Wine and Culture: Vineyard to Glass.* New York and London: Bloomsbury Academic.

Bourdieu, P. (1979). *La distinction. Critique sociale du judgement.* Paris: Minuit.

Bourdieu, P. and Sayad, A. (1964). *Le déracinement: La crise de l'agriculture traditionnelle en Algérie.* Paris: Minuit.

Caf, MSA and Insee (2011). 'Pauvreté en ville et à la campagne: plus intense de la pointe du Médoc à Agen'. *Insee Aquitanie,* no. 194. www.insee.fr/fr/insee_regions/aquitaine/themes/4pages/ia194_0611/ia194.pdf (last access on 20/2/2016).

Crenn, C. (2006). 'Normes alimentaires et minorisation ethnique: discours et pratiques de femmes originaires du Maroc (vignobles bordelais)'. *Journal des anthropologues*, nos. 106–107, pp. 123–144.

Crenn, C. (2008). ''Chez nous c'est Marrakech' ou l'animation en territoire rural prise dans les toiles de la mondialisation' in Jakob, M.-C. and Reichmuth, J. (eds). *Community Development: Local and Global Challenges.* Lucerne: Interact, pp. 177–185.

Crenn, C. (2013). 'Des invisibles trop visibles? Les ouvriers agricoles marocains dans les vignobles du bordelaise' in Crenn, C. and Tersigni, S. (eds). *Migrations et Mondes ruraux. Hommes et Migrations*, 1301, pp. 99–108.

Crenn, C. and Tersigni, S. (2014). 'Milieux ruraux et immigrations' in Blum Le Coat, J.Y. and Eberhard, M. (eds). *Les immigrés en France.* Paris: La documentation française, pp. 59–76.

Décosse, F. (2012). 'Les contrats OMI et l'action du CODETRAS'. *Actes de la réunion technique sur la traite des êtres humains et le travail forcé en France*. Paris: CNCDH/BIT, pp. 170–185.

Décosse, F. (2013). 'Immigrés, solidarité! Histoire d'une lutte, envers d'un slogan' in Crenn, C. and Tersigni, S. (eds). *Migrations et Mondes ruraux. Hommes et Migrations,* 1301, pp. 93–101.

Decosse, F. and Duntze N. (2007). 'Ni vu, ni connu, je t'empoisonne'. *Mouvements,* 22. http://www.mouvements.info/Ni-vu-ni-connu-je-t- empoisonne.html

De Rudder, V., Poiret, C. and Vourc'h, F. (eds) (2000). *L'inégalité raciste: l'universalité républicaine à l'épreuve*. Paris: PUF.

Di Méo, G. (2010). 'A propos de la qualité des productions agricoles et de sa relation aux territoires', in Hinnewinkel, J.C. (ed.), *La gouvernance des terroirs du vin.* Bordeaux: Editions Féret, pp. 73–88.

Drot, C. (ed.) (2007). *Histoire et mémoires des immigrations en Aquitaine*. La Charre: Kynos. http://www.goutdesautres.fr/pdf/ImmigrationsAquitaineSyntheseAcse.pdf (last access on 20/2/2016).

Gertel, J. and Sippel, S.R. (eds) (2014). *Seasonal Workers in Mediterranean Agriculture. The Social Costs of Eating Fresh.* London: Routledge.

Hinnewinkel, J.C. (2004). 'Les AOC dans la mondialisation'. *Anthropology of food* [online], http://aof.revues.org/247 (last access on 20/2/2016).

Hinnewinkel, J.C. (eds) (2010). *La gouvernance des terroirs du vin*, Bordeaux: Editions Féret.

Hubscher, R. (eds) (1996). *La moisson des autres. Les salariés agricoles aux 19e–20e siècles*. Paris: Éditions Créaphis.

Juteau, D. (eds) (1999). *L'ethnicité et ses frontières*, Montréal: Presses universitaires de Montréal.

Lamanthe, A. (2008). 'Les paradoxes de la formalisation de la relation salariale en milieu rurale (Briançonnais)', *Etudes rurales,* no. 182, pp. 29–44.

Langage Pluriel (ed.) (2013). *D'un pays à l'autre, de l'Espagne à l'Aquitaine*. Bourdeaux: Editions Parole.

McWilliams, C. (ed.) (1969 [1935]). *Factories in the Field. The Story of Migratory Farm Labor in California*. Los Angeles: Hamden Archon Books.

Mésini, B. (2013). 'Les travailleurs saisonniers latino-américains détachés Andins dans les champs de Provence' in Crenn, C. and Tersigni, S. (eds). *Migrations et Mondes ruraux. Hommes et Migrations,* no. 1301, pp. 67–76.

Michalon, B., and Potot, S. (2008). 'Réseaux transnationaux et main-d'œuvre agricole: quand la France recrute en Pologne'. *Études rurales,* no. 182, pp. 87–102.

Morice, A. (2005). 'Les saisonniers agricoles en Provence: un système de main-d'œuvre' in Gisti, A. (ed.). *Immigration et travail en Europe Les politiques migratoires au service des besoins économiques*. Rapport interne, pp. 17–26.

Morice, A. (2008). 'Quelques repères sur les contrats OMI et ANAEM'. *Etudes rurales*, no. 182, pp. 61–68.

Noiriel, G. (1994). 'L'immigration étrangère dans le monde rural pendant l'entre-deux-guerres'. *Études rurales*, nos. 135–136, pp. 13–35.

Roudié, P. (ed.) (1987). *Les Salariés saisonniers étrangers en Aquitaine septentrionale*. Talence: MSHA.

Roudié, P. (ed.) (1988). *Vignobles et vignerons du Bordelais (1850–1980)*. Bordeaux: Editions Féret.

Sayad, A. (2004). *The Suffering of the Immigrant*. Cambridge: Polity Press.

Teulières, L. (eds) (2002). *Immigrés d'Italie et paysans de France, 1920–1944*. Toulouse: Presses universitaires du Mirail.

# 4 Processing tomatoes in the era of the retailing revolution

## Mechanization and migrant labour in northern and southern Italy

*Domenico Perrotta*[1]

### 4.1 Introduction

In the early 1960s, Californian growers of industrial tomatoes were faced with a major problem: the proposals to close the 'Bracero Program' were becoming increasingly insistent. Through this programme, the US federal government had been recruiting Mexican migrants to work in US agriculture,[2] and its closure would have deprived growers of the labour force that manually harvested tomatoes. The Bracero Program ended in 1964, and the lack of this essential labour pool prompted the development of harvesting machines, which teams of California researchers had been developing for many years despite being generally ignored by the farmers. The transformation was rapid: in 1963, 66 machines harvested 1.5 per cent of California's tomato crops, but by 1970 1,521 machines were harvesting 99.9 per cent; and between 1964 and 1972 the number of labourers dropped from 50,000 to 18,000. The mechanization of harvesting also led to a structural transformation of California's tomato production: a new composition of the workforce, the selection of tomato varieties that were more suitable for mechanical harvesting, a geographical switch in tomato production locations, a drastic reduction in the number of producers (from 4,000 in 1962 to 597 in 1973), and an increase in total production and the average size of farms. This 'revolution' – analysed by Friedland and Barton (1975) and Pritchard and Burch (2003, pp. 41–58) – helped California become the world's largest producer of tomatoes.

Around twenty years later, Italy – the world's second largest producer of industrial tomatoes and the principal producer in Europe – started to mechanize its harvest. This process, however, was very different in Italy than in the US. First, mechanization did not occur due to a sudden lack of migrant workers. In fact, the move towards mechanization in the 1980s coincided with the arrival of first migrant populations. Second, mechanization was uneven across the two main areas of industrial tomato production. In northern Italy, manual harvesting had virtually disappeared by the early 1990s; in the South, a large percentage of tomatoes – difficult to estimate but probably close to 50 per cent – continues to be manually harvested by foreign labourers from sub-Saharan Africa and Eastern Europe. What occurred in southern Italy at the end of the twentieth century is in some ways the opposite to the transformation of California's tomato industry in the 1960s. The increased presence of a vulnerable, inexpensive and flexible migrant labour force formed a viable alternative to mechanical harvesting, preventing (or possibly delaying) the use of harvesting machines by the growers. The living and working conditions for these agricultural labourers are among the worst in Europe: they inhabit abandoned houses or large 'ghettos' and slums in rural areas; they are unable to work without the mediation of farm labour contractors known as *caporali*; and they are paid mostly cash-in-hand on a piece rate basis. This situation has been denounced repeatedly by the media, trade unions and NGOs and has been described in detail in academic research (e.g. Brovia, 2008; Perrotta, 2015). The images of slums self-built by labourers in Puglia, and the allegations of illegal practices such as the *caporalato* and piece rate payment cause significant reputational damage to these tomato producers, who in turn employ the rhetoric of gastronomic traditions and 'Made in Italy' as leverage to compete in international markets.

How can it be that the cultivation of the exact same product within the same country is developed in such different ways? Many studies have shown that migrants represent a pool of cheap and flexible labour that is rendered vulnerable by restrictive laws on transnational mobility. Agriculture is one of the economic sectors where the irregular work of migrants is widespread, especially in southern Italy, where housing segregation in rural areas exacerbates the conditions of exploitation (Perrotta and Sacchetto, 2013; Dines and Rigo, 2015). However, the vulnerability of migrant labour does not sufficiently explain what has happened in the production chains of the Italian tomato industry. In fact, in northern Italy there are many foreign workers who are subject to the same legislative restrictions, and the employment of migrants has become a structural component of many agri-food chains (see Azzeruoli, this volume), with features in some areas resembling the situations in other parts of southern Europe (Brovia, 2014). However, in the North we find no trace of migrants engaged in the manual harvesting of industrial tomatoes.

It is therefore necessary to analyse in depth the restructuring processes of this sector during the last three decades and how these have diverged in the two areas. This chapter is structured as follows. First, I briefly outline the geography and history of industrial tomato production in Italy. Second, I describe the role played in the past two decades by big retailers and, in doing so, I argue that the production chains of both North and South have become *retailer-driven* (Burch and Lawrence, 2005; Burch *et al.*, 2013). Third, I show how the production chains in the two areas have responded to retailer power in very different ways. The final section is devoted to examining the competition between harvesting machines and crews of migrant harvesters in southern Italy.

What are the consequences of the persistence of manual harvesting in the South? My argument is that the use of migrant workers in exploitative conditions has contributed to delaying the disappearance of small tomato growers and processors in southern Italy. Much research on buyer-driven agri-food chains (e.g. Burch *et al.*, 2013) indicates the disappearance of small producers vis-à-vis a growing corporate concentration in these chains. This trend is confirmed with regard to the production of processing tomatoes in northern Italy, although here it has undergone a process of 'districtualization', which has sought to coordinate the interests of farmers and canneries. Diversely, we find much less of this corporate concentration in southern Italy, where the processing plants unload the retailers' pressures onto the farms, which, in turn, offload them onto migrant labourers.

The data that underpin this chapter were collected between 2010 and 2015 using qualitative methods; in particular 75 in-depth interviews with agricultural workers, *caporali*, farmers, managers of producer organizations (POs) and canning factories, agronomists, union officials, academic researchers and institutional representatives, both in the Italian South and in the northern region of Emilia-Romagna. In addition, the transformation of production and company structure are reconstructed here using the annual reports of the National Institute of Agricultural Economics (INEA) and the Censuses of Agriculture conducted by the Italian National Institute of Statistics (Istat).

## 4.2 The geography and history of the Italian canned tomato

Today, Italy is the largest producer of industrial tomatoes in Europe and third in the world, after the US and China. Canned tomatoes (peeled, stewed, pureed) are considered among the products most representative of 'Made in Italy'. Italy transforms more than 50 per cent of the approximately 10 million tonnes of tomatoes processed in Europe. Sixty percent of the production is destined for foreign markets, in particular northern Europe (Germany, UK, France), the US and Japan.[3] Production has declined in recent years, after growing continuously over the past decades (see Table 4.1).

Since the beginning of the twentieth century there have existed two main areas of production: the provinces of Salerno and Naples in the Campania region in the South, which is the production area for the *San Marzano* variety and for canned peeled whole tomatoes (*pomodori pelati*), and the provinces of Parma and Piacenza in Emilia-Romagna in the North. On the one hand we have Campania, a region long considered 'marginal' in the Italian economy and lacking the necessary capital to complete its development (Bonazzi *et al.*, 1972); on the other,

*Table 4.1* Production of tomatoes for processing by year in Italy and selected regions (thousands of tonnes)

| *Year* | *Total Italy* | *Emilia-Romagna* | *Lombardia* | *Campania* | *Puglia* | *Basilicata* |
|---|---|---|---|---|---|---|
| 1970 | 3,617.9 | 521.0 | | 1,046.0 | 277.0 | 30.9 |
| 1980 | 4,818.5 | 701.8 | | 1,403.7 | 625.4 | 238.0 |
| 1985 | 5,934.2 | 833.2 | | 1,079.8 | 1,563.5 | 190.3 |
| 1990 | 5,576.7 | 989.8 | | 701.4 | 1,879.3 | 123.1 |
| 1995 | 5,196.8 | 956.0 | | 340.9 | 2,034.1 | 200.0 |
| 2000 | 7,838.2 | 2,114.6 | 346.4 | 559.7 | 2,643.3 | 282.1 |
| 2005 | 7,186.9 | 1,645.4 | 503.8 | 464.9 | 2,235.4 | 270.4 |
| 2010 | 6,019.0 | 1,666.5 | 570.1 | 366.7 | 1,524.3 | 227.2 |
| 2013 | 5,322.0 | 1,480.0 | 330.9 | 340.5 | 1,461.1 | 162.3 |

Source: Numbers based on INEA data.

we have Emilia-Romagna, a region characterized for many decades by industrial agriculture and rich in capital (Brusco, 1979).[4]

During the last quarter century, in both areas, the production chains have undergone similar structural pressures and processes: subsidies from the EU Common Agricultural Policy (CAP) have been received for the production of tomatoes;[5] international competition has increased because of greater trade liberalization in food products; retailers have gained more power at the expense of processing companies by setting prices and production standards along the chain. Furthermore, there has been a notable – although uneven – rise in the concentration process within the canning sector. Despite these similarities, there are many differences between the two areas (see also Pritchard and Burch, 2003, pp. 183–190).

The first difference concerns the distance between the farms and canneries. In northern Italy, the production and processing of tomatoes take place in the same area: the tomatoes in the provinces of Parma, Piacenza, Ferrara, Cremona, Mantova and Modena, are processed only a few kilometres away from the fields. This proximity has favoured, as I explain below, a process of districtualization,[6] formalized in 2007 by the creation of the *Distretto del pomodoro da industria del Nord Italia* (Tomato Processing District of Northern Italy) which is based in Parma (Canali, 2012).

In southern Italy, on the other hand, much of the agricultural production was relocated, between the 1970s and 1980s, from Campania to Puglia (200 kilometres away, on the other side of the Apennines); particularly to Capitanata in the province of Foggia (which is Italy's second largest plain after the Po Valley) and to a lesser extent to the province of Potenza in Basilicata (see Table 4.1). The causes of this shift are complex and include: the impact of a virus that struck Campania during the 1970s and 1980s that infected the *San Marzano* and hybrid varieties that had partially replaced it; the reconstruction and speculation following the 1980 earthquake which led to the urbanization of farmland around Salerno; and above all the need for vast, flat tracts of land that could greatly increase the yield produced by the small plots in Campania. The goal was to increase production and enable the mechanization of farming activities.

> In Campania plots were rather small, they were all on different levels because the Campania landscape is very rugged; and so the harvesting had to be done manually. This is what characterized Campanian quality; when you pick by hand, you select exactly what should be picked, and then leave the rest to ripen on the plant until the next harvest. Conversely, Puglia had its *Tavoliere* [literally tableland], a huge expanse of land, so by the time these mechanical harvesting techniques came on the market, Puglia became a sort of breeding ground for these machines, and slowly production grew in Puglia and decreased in Campania. [. . .] The Agro Sarnese Nocerino [in Campania] provided the best quality, the famous *San Marzano*, and all the production areas were comprised of small holders, manual harvesting such great quality, low quantity. The moment that industrial production became important, all this became less interesting.
>
> (Interview with Emanuele,[7] owner of a company that provides equipment to canneries, Naples, April 2014)

The tomato-processing industries, however, remained in Campania, due to both the difficulty of relocating related industrial sectors and skilled workers and technicians, and the opposition by politicians and local workers to the delocalization of the industry that would have resulted in the loss of thousands of (largely seasonal) jobs. There are still only a few canneries in Puglia and Basilicata, the largest of which are managed by big Campanian or Emilian groups. In 2009, AR, one of the largest groups in Campania, opened a cannery near Foggia, which is among the largest in Europe. Sold in 2012 to Princes, a multinational agri-food company based in the UK (but owned by the Japanese Mitsubishi), this cannery can process about 20 per cent of Capitanata's tomatoes; the rest of the production, therefore, continues to be transported to Campania. As I explain below, the relocation of agricultural production in Puglia, which aimed to promote the mechanization of harvesting, instead led, paradoxically, to the deterioration of relations between farmers and the canning companies, and indirectly contributed to the persistence of manual harvesting.

A second important element concerns the number and size of canning companies. In Campania, although a process of concentration has been underway for years and the sector has become dominated by four or five large groups, there are now almost one hundred mostly small canneries (in the early 2000s they were 144; Pritchard and Burch, 2003, p. 185). This large number of small companies, along with their significant distance from the farms, makes negotiations between factories and farmers and the organization of chain chaotic and complicated. Particularly striking is the difference between this situation and the tomato production chain of the North, where there are around 25 (mostly large) canneries, fifteen of which are located in Emilia-Romagna.

A third element relates to the dimensions of the farms. In Emilia-Romagna, tomato-producing farms grow on average 16.8 hectares of processing tomatoes (with some up to 26 hectares in Piacenza, 18.3 in Parma and 17.5 in Ferrara). In Puglia, the average size is 8.75 hectares (with some up to 10 hectares in Foggia province), roughly half of those in the North; the average size in the province of Potenza is about 7 hectares, while in Campania it is 2.6 hectares. In Puglia there are 407 tomato-producing farms with less than 5 hectares of Utilized Agricultural Area (UAA) and 96 farms with more than 100 hectares of UAA. In Emilia-Romagna the opposite is the case: 127 farms with less than 5 hectares and 245 larger than 100 hectares produce industrial tomatoes (see Table 4.2).[8]

Although historical data are not available for industrial tomatoes within the census of agriculture conducted by Istat, we can refer to aggregate data relative to the production of vegetable crops in open fields, of which industrial tomatoes are a significant part. Table 4.3 illustrates that the number of farms producing vegetable crops in open fields has decreased across Italy, and that the average size grew steadily between 1982 and 2010. The *timing* of this process, however, differs in the two areas considered here. In the provinces of Parma and Piacenza the concentration began in the 1980s, probably due to the mechanization of harvesting, as occurred in California. In the province of Foggia, on the other hand, the increase in the average size of vegetable production per farm underwent a surge after 2000, which confirms a contemporaneous trend across the whole of Italy. Likely to affect this trend in corporate concentration, alongside the (partial) mechanization of harvesting, is the transition from a producer-driven supply chain to a buyer-driven supply chain. This transition is the subject of the next section.

*Table 4.2* Number of farms by agricultural area utilized for growing industrial tomatoes (hectares) in selected Italian regions and provinces

| | *Less than 5 ha* | *5–20 ha* | *20–50 ha* | *50–100 ha* | *More than 100 ha* | *Total* | *Average area utilized* |
|---|---|---|---|---|---|---|---|
| Puglia | 407 | 849 | 758 | 244 | 96 | 2,354 | 8.75 |
| Province of Foggia | 140 | 758 | 688 | 225 | 90 | 1,901 | 10.07 |
| Basilicata | 46 | 135 | 106 | 44 | 16 | 347 | 6.9 |
| Campania | 745 | 373 | 86 | 8 | 4 | 1,216 | 2.62 |
| Emilia-Romagna | 127 | 386 | 465 | 368 | 245 | 1,591 | 16.79 |
| Province of Parma | 10 | 50 | 76 | 78 | 42 | 256 | 18.34 |
| Province of Piacenza | 7 | 51 | 153 | 138 | 90 | 439 | 25.9 |
| Province of Ferrara | 4 | 90 | 148 | 86 | 55 | 383 | 17.52 |
| Lombardia | 23 | 134 | 253 | 173 | 89 | 672 | 11.64 |

Source: Numbers based on Istat Census of Agriculture (2010).

*Table 4.3* Horticultural vegetable crops in open fields: number of farms and average utilized agricultural area per farm (hectares), in selected Italian regions and provinces

| | *1982* | | *1990* | | *2000* | | *2010* | |
|---|---|---|---|---|---|---|---|---|
| | *No.* | *Area (ha)* | *No.* | *Area (ha)* | *No.* | *Area (ha)* | *No.* | *Area (ha)* |
| Puglia | 38,695 | 1.08 | 38,031 | 1.51 | 27,991 | 1.55 | 14,336 | 3.98 |
| Province of Foggia | 6,284 | 2.18 | 6,964 | 3.57 | 4,930 | 4.23 | 3,791 | 8.77 |
| Basilicata | 16,331 | 0.52 | 10,498 | 0.87 | 7,879 | 0.90 | 2,197 | 3.06 |
| Campania | 97,809 | 0.42 | 73,821 | 0.44 | 55,177 | 0.41 | 12,470 | 1.40 |
| Emilia Romagna | 25,777 | 1.16 | 16,405 | 2.31 | 11,285 | 3.78 | 7,112 | 6.91 |
| Province of Parma | 2,246 | 1.91 | 753 | 4.07 | 535 | 9.71 | 420 | 13.03 |
| Province of Piacenza | 1,946 | 2.74 | 1,602 | 5.85 | 1,135 | 14.13 | 804 | 19.15 |
| Province of Ferrara | 4,460 | 1.85 | 3,613 | 3.74 | 1,991 | 4.71 | 1,119 | 10.85 |
| Lombardia | 11,617 | 0.75 | 4,850 | 1.92 | 3,187 | 3.32 | 2,507 | 5.43 |
| Italy | 550,509 | 0.52 | 376,705 | 0.80 | 251,514 | 0.94 | 99,130 | 2.69 |

Source: Numbers based on Istat Censuses of Agriculture.

## 4.3 Canneries and supermarket (own-brand)s

The international debate on agri-food chains has repeatedly stressed that over the last three to four decades, big retailers have assumed a dominant position in the global chains of food production (e.g. Burch and Lawrence, 2005; McMichael and Friedmann, 2007; Ploeg, 2008). In Mediterranean Europe and Italy specifically this process has also occurred, although some years later[9]. In 2003, Pritchard and Burch argued that Europe's processing tomato sector did not conform to the ideal-types of either producer-driven or buyer-driven supply chain; nonetheless, they noted that 'retail consolidation in northern Europe has narrowed supply channels and for suppliers, has heightened the importance to economies of scale and quality assurance' (p. 182). They concluded that 'retail restructuring in Europe, with its demands for larger volume, lower priced purchases, will reinforce these pressures' on Italian tomato processors' (p. 190). About fifteen years later, my research shows that canned tomato production has become in many ways retailer-driven, both in northern and in southern Italy.

The actors I interviewed are well aware of the strength of the large retailers. Gabriele Canali, a professor of agri-food economics at the University of Piacenza, and one of the creators of the Tomato Processing District of Northern Italy, describes the restructuring of the production chain as follows:

> The principal opponent – the principal 'enemy' – of the farmer used to be the processor. Basically, the canning plant; and the cannery owner used to say: 'ok, I have negotiating power especially over the farmer.' This is the refrain that was repeated for decades. This is no longer the case, because *now the real bargaining power is not in the hands of the canneries, it is more in the hands of the retailers.* So, this industrial system is a link stronger than the farmers, but it is no longer a strong link [...] *The power dynamic within the different phases of production has changed radically in Italy since the early 1990s, with the development of modern distribution.* In the rest of Europe and the western world, the dynamics of the retail market were far more advanced. In the early 1990s, when we [in Italy] changed our legislation, we began to see shopping malls and large retail chains spring up and increase their share in the market as well as their negotiating power.
>
> (Interview, Piacenza, July 2013)

On the other hand, these producers have some strength in relation to buyers. First, unlike fresh produce (Friedland, 1994), processed tomatoes are not perishable (see on the same theme Lee *et al.*, 2012). Second, 60 per cent of the production is exported, and although there is international competition, this mainly affects the canneries that produce chopped tomatoes or tomato concentrate, which are lower-quality products compared to pureed and peeled tomatoes.

The label has a relevant function. Some companies produce their own brands, and others produce for private labels.[10] In the first case, the possession of a recognized and 'quality' brand lends some bargaining power to the canning company.

Examples are trademarks like Mutti (considered the best cannery of Emilia-Romagna), Cirio and Valfrutta, the last two owned by Conserve Italia, a leading European canning company based in Emilia-Romagna, which owns four major plants in Italy as well as others in various foreign countries. Nonetheless, the massive presence of private-label tomato products on supermarket shelves is a big challenge for even the strongest brands, which not only have to compete with other producers, but also with the retail giants, as explained by the administrator of an Emilia cannery that produces only for supermarket own-brands:

> My clients are six big players, who account for my entire turnover and allow me to have effective, high-performance machines. On the other hand, there is Mr Mutti: his products are sold in supermarkets [under its own brand name], but he has competitors such as Coop and Esselunga [two of the major Italian supermarket chains], which have their own brands. Mutti has much higher prices than ours, and he does its own advertising [. . .] Today he is in the market, but honestly he doesn't gross much, about 52 million [euros], which is not a small thing of course, but he has to compete with the big retailers, Carrefour for example . . . if they want to get rid of him, they can do so. But they won't because it is good for them that there is a higher-priced branded product called Mutti, because they can sell theirs at a lower price without having to advertise.
>
> (Interview with Camillo, CEO of a cannery, Parma, July 2013)

If Mutti can find itself under threat, many small and medium-sized canning companies in Campania are at far greater risk. Those that have not developed their own brand strategy are vulnerable to retail chains that simply 'buy at the prices they want', as one witness who knows the sector well explained. These canning companies produce on a seasonal basis, which exposes them to pressure from banks and often forces them to sell below cost. This is why many fail.

> For many years these large retailers have been a powerful force; the small or medium-sized industries in particular are under their sway. [. . .] Large retailers buy at the prices they want, and for this reason many companies have closed down. [. . .] When the discount retail chain arrives and wants to buy a lot of goods at a very low price; and you have a warehouse, but you need a flow of cash income to pay for the electricity, for this and that, you end up selling at prices that do not justify your costs. Sometimes the amount is so great – you might see 400 to 500,000 euros in one lump sum – that you sell. Many companies do it one year, then do it again the next year, then the next, and they come to a bad end. [. . .] On the other hand, these small producers cannot even find another retail channel because even the grocer downstairs cannot sell a product for much more than those in the supermarket or discount stores.
>
> (Interview with Emanuele, cit.).

In the case of production for private labels, the buyer (a supermarket chain) sets all the standards of quality, quantity, food security and price, thus weakening the bargaining power of the cannery, unless it produces for other brands at the same time, or has its own recognized brand.

Those who work in the canning industry describe the pressure surrounding production standards:

> Today many of these canneries are virtual slaves to large retailers, and many have closed down for this reason. [. . .] Large retailers want service, big volumes, and a uniformity of quality [. . .] They want all the things that only a big company can provide: the service, the guarantee that on day X the product will be delivered because of course it will be ready, and there will be no defects in the labels, etc. Small canneries now struggle to do this, and this is one more reason for the concentration of business.
>
> (Interview with Emanuele, cit.).

The cannery owners' counterparts in the retail chains make similar points. In the following excerpt, the person responsible for controlling cannery production for one of Italy's largest supermarket chains explains how suppliers for this chain's private label are selected:

> The *pelato* branded *** comes about after a series of selective evaluations. If there is a new supplier we have not yet seen, I go to the supplier and evaluate whether it meets our standards, according to a list of complex criteria [...] I assess the supplier's overall compliance with our standards, and if it passes, then my colleagues can go ahead. [. . .] Of course, the price is important. But alongside the price, there are all the other values. [. . .] We do random checks on incoming raw materials and even do field visits to see if the pesticides are acceptable. Then, there's the whole SA8000 part [regarding working conditions within the factory] and the organoleptic issues, in other words, if the product tastes good and is good looking, if the tomatoes are peeled, if they are damaged. There's also the merchandise testing, which is done later [. . .] Then the specific question of quantity is discussed, which is when we try to get all the quantity that we need. All of this is a pretty long process.
>
> *If I understand correctly, there are three controls: food safety, the organoleptic quality and the price . . .*
>
> It is actually much more complex. Depending on the product, there may be many more checks.
>
> (Interview with Renzo, March 2014)

The checks on quality standards and food security lead to a final selection of both the direct suppliers (the canneries) ...

> We have one supplier who works almost exclusively for us, which is very good and so we hold on tightly to this relationship. There are other suppliers

> that work for virtually everyone. In one particular cannery, you may see the private labels of all the major national chains, as well as many international labels, especially English ones.
>
> (Interview with Renzo, cit.)

... and the farms that produce for the canneries:

> If a check on a day of production [in a cannery] reveals too many pesticides [in the delivered tomatoes], then this is not a good day for us [and the products are discarded]. [. . .] Let's be clear that this has generated a virtuous circle, [because] we have the power to cancel a day's work. It does not happen very often, but it has happened. The suppliers themselves [the canneries] are on high alert, and they urge the farmers not to over-treat the crop and to respect the timetable [for the use of chemicals]. Then they discard those that are not deemed reliable. Over the years this has generated a great selection of suppliers [. . .] Let's say that our tomato producers are trustworthy.
>
> (Interview with Renzo, cit.)

These practices for selecting suppliers do have some contradictory aspects. According to the interviewee above, they have the positive effect of improving product quality, at least in terms of food safety (thanks to the reduced use of chemicals in production), and offering convenient prices for consumers. At the same time, scholars (for example McMichael and Friedmann, 2007; Burch *et al.*, 2013), as well as the Italian Antitrust Authority, point out that the dominance of a few large retail groups and the asymmetrical power relationship between buyers and suppliers (*buyer power*) can 'exclude certain small operators, even when these are efficient, due to the rising costs of the access to distribution channels' (AGCM, 2013, p. 140), and this situation ultimately harms the consumer because it decreases the variety of offers.[11]

As well as production standards, there is pressure on the price at which the retailer will agree to buy a product from a cannery, as the same witness above admits:

> This is the only way we can do it. Our competitors, the retail store on the other side of the street, all the supermarket chains ... they all work on the price, so we have no choice but to do it this way.
>
> (Interview with Renzo, cit.)

Renzo is aware that the pressure exerted by retailers on canneries is passed down to the farms, and then, in southern Italy, onto the farm workers. He estimates that a tomato farmer receives between 1 and 2 per cent of the consumer price for a can of *pomodori pelati*. However, he says, if the farmer (even the one he considers to be *the best supplier*) increases his price, 'nobody's going to buy tomatoes from them', and the farmer would go 'out of business'.

> A very good supplier [farmer] I know in the zone of Lesina [Foggia], connected with a very good cooperative, who only once in ten years, maybe

> twenty years, made a mistake [in production], could say to me: 'Do you want our tomatoes? Well, we want twenty per cent more because, we know how to grow them organically and we've never cheated you'. But if you do that, you're out: no one's going to buy tomatoes from you.
>
> *Not even if you've been buying from them for twenty years?*
>
> That makes no difference. But, note: I don't buy directly from the farmer . . . so I've got a clear conscience. It is the cannery that doesn't buy from him any more. [. . .] Now, I cannot deny that there is pressure on the price. [. . .] We don't make agreements with farmers, only with the canneries [. . .] I realize that these nevertheless affect the farmers. If we pay a small price to the supplier [cannery], it is clear that the supplier cannot [pay more to the farmer] but if we were to pay a higher price, that's not a sufficient enough reason for the supplier to pay the farmer more as well. We must agree on the entire supply chain, with real controls throughout, but this is extremely difficult [. . .] Raising prices across the supply chain is very difficult. If only one of us does it, we go out of business.
>
> (Interview with Renzo, cit.)

To summarize the findings in this section, it can be said that even the supply chains of the Italian industrial tomatoes are in many ways retailer-driven. The buyer power, exercised by big retailers through pressure on production standards and prices, seems to have had two major effects on the production chain. First, it has contributed to an ongoing concentration process in the tomato-processing industry. Second, this pressure, albeit indirect, is offloaded onto farms. The reactions of the production chains in the two areas, however, have been very different.

## 4.4 Between growers and processing plants

Producers in the two areas reacted to similar structural pressures in very different ways. A fundamental issue that needs to be analysed, in this regard, is the traditionally complicated relationship between the farmers and canneries.

In the case of Emilia-Romagna, this relationship has brought about a process of districtualization. The Tomato Processing District of Northern Italy was formally established in Parma in 2007; in 2011 it became, in the terminology of the EU's common organization of the market, an 'interbranch organization'. Here all the economic players in the northern tomato production chain are represented, primarily the POs and the organizations of the processors, together with the University and local institutions (Canali, 2012). According to Canali, the birth of this *Distretto* directly addresses the difficulties faced by processing companies in their dealings with the big retailers who, not surprisingly, decided not to enter the organization:

> The power clearly belongs to the big retailers, which have weakened the position of the processing industry and created, perhaps, more reasons for forming strong partnerships with actors in the agricultural phase of production.

> Together, the agricultural producers and the processing industry can collaborate more effectively and function as a single competitive system that exerts extra leverage over the retailers, and also ultimately over the final customer.
> (Interview with Canali, cit.)

Thus, the tomato producers in northern Italy, thanks to a strong tradition of cooperation between farmers and the support of local institutions, have aimed to coordinate the interests of farmers and canning companies in an efficient organized chain, in order to cope with the pressures of retailers, both from the point of view of costs and product quality. Within this process, harvest mechanization has been a fact of life for more than twenty years. Despite this organization, however, many canning factories are still in great economic difficulty and, according to some respondents, the process of concentration is not yet over.

The interviews carried out in the South tell a very different story. Here the relationships between farmers and canneries are much more tense and confrontational.[12] All the farmers interviewed in Puglia and Basilicata claim that canning factories in Campania adopt unfair practices in relation to the purchase of tomatoes, especially in years of overproduction. Such unfair practices concern: negotiations on the price of tomatoes, sending trucks from factories to farms the days of harvest, the weight of the product on arrival in the cannery, and the payment.

> You cannot have a serious relationship with these factories because [. . .] they do whatever they like. We are at their mercy. If there is a small volume of product, they do what was agreed in the contract because they rarely compete with each other. However, when there is too much volume, they don't consider you [. . .] they use every possible excuse not to respect the contract. Sometimes they do not send the vehicles to pick up the product and therefore force you to throw it away [. . .] These companies speculate on tomatoes, if they have contracted 8 cents [per kilogram] in the end they pay you only 5 cents [. . .] It was at that point that I stopped producing tomatoes.
> (Interview with Giovanni, farmer, province of Barletta, Andria and Trani, August 2010)

In the North the price of tomatoes is fixed each year before the planting. This process is initiated through negotiations between the POs and the factories, formalized within the *Distretto*, and is valid for all players. This often does not happen in the South: instead, the price is often fixed by one single factory and one single PO; in these cases, the negotiating power of growers is much lower. As is well known (Berlan, 1986), the farmer is in a difficult position: when the product is mature it has to be harvested; any delay of even a few days or hours can destroy the work and economic investment of an entire year.

The characteristics of POs are very interesting to analyse. These organizations were set up by the CAP of the EU to regulate the marketing of agricultural products (EC Regulations no. 2200/96 and 1234/2007) with the objective of concentrating supply (thus increasing the bargaining power of farmers) and stabilizing the relationship between supply and demand. Farmers were practically obliged to participate because CAP subsidies were paid through POs. From a formal point of view, these organizations are supposed to be the same everywhere in Europe. However, research shows that the 'interpretations' of these organizations are very different in southern Italy compared with the North.

First of all, there is a quantitative issue. In the North there are only twelve POs for processing tomatoes, and the three largest account for two-thirds of production. In the South it is not possible to find accurate figures, but according to individuals interviewed, there are dozens of POs and they are generally much smaller. In short, producers in northern Italy have come together to create POs that truly represent their needs, while in the South the supply of processing tomatoes is less organized.

Second, southern POs often were not formed on the initiative of farmers; rather, some were set up by 'old traders', who used to broker between farmers and processors, while others were created by the processors with the aim to secure direct control of the agricultural product.

> [Our PO] is the biggest [in Puglia]. It is the only one managed by growers. What differentiates our situation from the other area [in northern Italy] is that [up there] it's the growers or representatives of growers who form the POs. There are less of them compared to what we have here. There are too many of them here, and many have been set up by the old brokers, who mediated between the farmers and the canneries, who organized the transportation, and anticipated the money and generally profited from the whole situation [. . .] If one goes to view the list of POs, very few have been registered with the offices in Foggia. Others have their headquarters elsewhere, for example in Caserta [in Campania].
>
> (Interview with Mario, farmer and representative of PO, Foggia, August 2010)

Some of the farmers interviewed in Emilia-Romagna even expressed suspicions about the fairness of the canneries and of their own POs. Nonetheless, most consider themselves sufficiently protected by their POs, which can use their weight in negotiations on price and, during the harvest, are able to control the delivery of the product to the processing plants.

> In the North we have strong growers' associations and we're able to make contracts with the industry. In the South, on the contrary, they have sold tomatoes at one third of the price we earn. [. . .] The problem is always the balance of power. We have POs that are consistent, that contract with the processor, and control waste. [. . .] It is important that our PO has sufficient credibility to avoid getting shafted.
>
> (Interview with Atos, farmer, province of Ferrara, July 2011)

The POs in the North, especially the largest ones, have a major technical role in planning the harvest and the delivery of the product (which is facilitated by the shorter distance between the farms and the canneries). The logistics are agreed from the time of planting. Moreover, the biggest POs are among the key players in the *Distretto*.

Finally, it is important to note that many large canneries in Emilia-Romagna are themselves owned, at least formally, by farmer cooperatives. By processing about 40 per cent of tomato products in the area, their presence affects the behaviour of the entire canning industry.

## 4.5 Manual harvesters versus harvesting machines

What connection is there between what as has been said thus far and the persistence of manual harvesting in the South? As noted, the pressure of big retailers affects the entire production chain. In the case of Emilia-Romagna, producers have responded by bringing about a process of districtualization, which has been in place for many years. The *Distretto del pomodoro da industria del Nord Italia* is at once a place to coordinate the interests of canneries, cooperatives and farms, and also an important tool for improving the organization and logistics of production. The larger size of individual companies (both canning factories, and farms and POs) and the higher availability of capital have also been instrumental in this process.[13]

In southern Italy, conversely, a number of factors have made both the creation of a well-organized supply chain and the completion of the process of mechanization difficult. The long distance between the production and processing of tomatoes, as well as the larger number of (mostly small) canning factories and POs, have so far frustrated attempts to create an organization like the *Distretto* in the North. The pressure of retailers and the relative scarcity of capital have exacerbated the already difficult relationship between the processing industry and agricultural producers. The canneries aim at buying raw material at low costs, thus passing the pressure of the retailers down to the farms. For their part, the farmers of Puglia and Basilicata often refer to a lack of trust and failed coordination with the canning factories as key reasons why they (especially the very numerous small farms) continue to use manual harvesting methods, which allows them to save the costs involved with mechanical harvesting.

During several visits to these farms, I observed that many producers have harvesting machines, but it is not uncommon to leave them in the shed while manual labourers work in the fields. One rationale may be the fear, often well founded, that processing plants are not sending the agreed number of trucks to pick up their product.[14]

> This year, the industries are not fulfilling the contracts. If you have agreed to load ten trucks a day, they send four, and so the rest of the product just rots in the ground. This also triggers problems among the farmers [in the cooperative], for example, who will get these trucks?
>
> (Interview with Mauro, technical manager of a farmers' cooperative, province of Potenza, August 2010)

The foreign labourers, then, have found themselves competing with the harvesting machines. They practice a harvesting technique that Italian farmworkers, especially women who worked on the tomato fields until the early 1990s, had never done before: crews of harvesters pass through the field once, ripping out the plants and shaking the tomatoes into 300 kg crates – exactly what the machines do.

A manual harvest, however, can be done at a lower cost than mechanical harvesting only by resorting to practices that are illegal and extremely oppressive for labourers: the pay is piece rate and the labour mediation is carried out by the *caporali*. Piece rate payments in the absence of regular employment contracts allows the farmer more control over the cost of harvesting (Berlan, 1986): he may, for example, compare the cost per ton of product harvested by a team of labourers to the cost of a harvesting machine provided by a contractor. This would not be possible if he paid workers an hourly wage with regular contracts. The *caporalato* system is therefore essential in that it ensures farms rapid and efficient delivery of extremely disciplined labourers (Perrotta, 2014; Garrapa, Avallone, this volume).

## 4.6 Conclusion

What are the consequences of the persistence of manual harvest in southern Italy? First I contend that the presence of a flexible and affordable migrant workforce has enabled the southern Italian tomato production chain to avoid, to a certain extent, the process of corporate concentration at the agricultural and industrial levels.

Many studies on the retailer-driven agri-food chains have shown that the dominance assumed by large retailers decisively influences the production. This often results in the closure of small agricultural producers because only the biggest producers can meet the standards imposed by supermarket chains (Burch *et al.*, 2013). It is possible to speculate that this is what has happened and is happening in the two areas examined in this chapter: the big retailers select their suppliers and, in doing so, contribute to the closure of small and medium-sized companies (both canneries and farms) and to a higher corporate concentration.

Nonetheless, this is occurring with varying speed and intensity. The strategies of resistance put in place by the two production chains discussed here are in fact very different. Through the *Distretto*, the production chain of northern Italy has focused on organizational improvements, logistics and technology, which are favoured by both the proximity of agricultural production to the processing plants, and the greater availability of capital. Thanks to cooperative structures and efficient POs, a number of small farms still produce industrial tomatoes. However, the concentration process started earlier than in the South and it is at a more advanced stage.

The southern production chain has aimed more towards reducing labour costs, using, where possible, teams of labourers in lieu of harvesting machines, and thus avoiding seemingly necessary investments. This approach, coupled with the CAP subsidies for tomato production, has enabled the survival of a much larger number of small farms and small canning factories, at the expense of migrant workers.

This balance, however, seems extremely precarious. The lower cost of labour guaranteed by the crews of migrant workers often does not generate enough savings to allow these small farms to continue producing. An increasing number of these farms therefore close down or stop producing industrial tomatoes, unless, of course, they are able to mechanize the harvest. In recent years, a number of campaigns have called on supermarkets in northern Europe to boycott the *pomodori pelati* from (southern) Italy until improvements are made to the living and working conditions of migrant labourers (e.g., see Joint Ethical Trade Initiatives, 2015). However, this chapter has illustrated how, *under the current production chain conditions*, this improvement is unlikely. In the event that the migrant harvesters forcibly demanded better working conditions and regular wages, they would most likely be replaced by harvesting machines, just as what occurred in California during the 1960s and in Emilia-Romagna during the 1980s. Such a process, in turn, would lead to the disappearance of Puglia's small tomato producers and Campania's small processors.

## Notes

1 For comments, criticisms and suggestions on earlier versions of this chapter, I thank Vanessa Azzeruoli, Wolf Bukowski, Alessandra Corrado, Franco Cossentino, Carlos De Castro, Enrico Gabrielli, Arturo Lavorato, Valeria Piro, Timothy Raeymaekers, Isacco Turina, the participants in the seminar 'Agriculture and migration in the EU' (Bergamo, 24–25 October 2013) and the social sciences seminar at the University of Bergamo (5 March 2014).

2 The Bracero Program recruited around 5 million Mexican workers between 1942 and 1964 (Cohen, 2011).

3 Data provided by the National Canneries Association (ANICAV) in reference to 2014: http://www.anicav.it/news/2015/5/19/406, last accessed on 2 October 2015.

4 The province of Parma is considered the Italian 'food valley': in addition to canning, it is home to Barilla, the largest Italian pasta maker, and Parmalat, a powerful multinational milk distributer until its bankruptcy in 2003, and is also the production area for Parmigiano Reggiano cheese (see Azzeruoli, this volume) and the famous Parma ham.

5 These subsidies were awarded in proportion to the quantities produced, through a system of national and factory-based quotas, at first for the canning industry (1978–2000), and later directly to farms. Since 2011, the subsidies are no longer 'coupled' with production, but are increasingly subject to 'conditionality'. They have favored large farms more than small farmers and they also induced years of overproduction and consequent price compression within the tomato chain (Pritchard and Burch, 2003, pp. 161–178). In order to concentrate the offer of agricultural products and pay the subsidies, and as a means to establish the common organization of agricultural markets, the EU has set up the POs, which I discuss in greater detail in Section 4.4.

6 Industrial districts are clusters of small and medium-sized enterprises that specialize in particular products and are connected by their common geographical location. According to many scholars, this production model, structured around internal competition and cooperation, was fundamental after the 1960s, for rapid economic growth in the regions of the so-called 'Third Italy', including Emilia-Romagna (Becattini *et al.*, 1990; for a critique see Harrison, 1994). Although the majority of the districts have an industrial connotation, the agro-industrial tomato district in Parma was already cited by Brusco (1982) as one of the Emilian districts.

7 The names of those interviewed are fictitious, except Gabriele Canali.

8 These figures are calculated using data from the Census of Agriculture that was conducted by Istat in 2010. It is important to note that the average size of Italian farms is much smaller than those in the US or Australia. In 2004, 32 farms were producing all of Australia's 360,000 tonnes of processing tomatoes (Pritchard *et al.*, 2007). In Italy in 2010, the total production was about 6 million tonnes, and the number of farms producing tomatoes was 9,564.
9 According to the Italian Antitrust Authority, from 1996 to 2011 the big retailers' share of the food market in Italy grew from 44 to 71 per cent (AGCM, 2013).
10 Many studies have focused on the conflict between trademark canneries and supermarket own- brands. In relation to the production of tomatoes in Europe, see Harvey *et al.* (2002), specifically in relation to the 'battle of tomato identities'.
11 Other adverse effects reported by the Antitrust Authority include the need for producers to access public funds (AGCM, 2013, p. 117). It is exactly what happened with CAP subsidies for tomato producers.
12 The establishment of a Tomato Processing District of Southern Italy, based on the model of the North, was recently announced (www.anicav.it/news/2014/4/26/349, last accessed on 2 October 2015). However, it is too early to tell whether a real process of districtualization is taking place also in the South.
13 It is also no coincidence that the two major Italian retail corporations – Coop Italia and Conad – have their headquarters in Emilia-Romagna, while none is based in the South.
14 Other justifications provided by farmers regard their inability to use harvesting machines after the rain, and the greater sensitivity required to harvest the 'long' tomatoes that are destined to become canned whole peeled tomatoes (*pomodori pelati*), and which are grown exclusively in southern Italy.

## References


AGCM [Autorità Garante della Concorrenza e del Mercato – Antitrust Authority] (2013). *Indagine conoscitiva sul settore della GDO.* Rome, www.agcm.it/indagini-conoscitive-db/open/C12564CE0049D161/973E4D42D69C4A11C1257BC60039BBA0.html (last accessed on 9 June 2015).

Becattini, G., Pyke, F. and Sengenberger, W. (eds) (1990). *Industrial Districts and Inter-firm Co-operation in Italy*. Geneva: International Institute for Labour Studies.

Berlan, J.-P. (1986). 'Agriculture et migrations', *Revue européenne des migrations internationales*, 2(3), pp. 9–31.

Bonazzi, G., Bagnasco, A. and Casillo, S. (1972). *L'organizzazione della marginalità. Industria e potere politico in una provincia meridionale*. Torino: L'impresa.

Brovia, C. (2008). 'Sous la férule des *caporali*. Les saisonniers de la tomate dans les Pouilles'. *Études rurales*, 182, pp. 153–168.

Brovia, C. (2014). 'The camp of "Guantanamò". Migrant seasonal workers in the agricultural area of Saluzzo (Piedmont, Italy)', presentation at the conference '*Migrant Labor and Social Sustainability of Global agri-food Chains*', University of Murcia, 5–7 November 2014.

Brusco, S. (1979). *Agricoltura ricca e classi sociali*. Milano: Feltrinelli.

Brusco, S. (1982). 'The Emilian model: productive decentralisation and social integration'. *Cambridge Journal of Economics*, 6, pp. 167–184.

Burch, D. and Lawrence, G. (2005). 'Supermarket own brands, supply chains and the transformation of the agri-food system'. *International Journal of Sociology of Agriculture and Food*, 13(1), pp. 1–28.

Burch, D., Dixon, J. and Lawrence, G. (2013). 'Introduction to symposium on the changing role of supermarkets in global supply chains'. *Agriculture and Human Values*, 30, pp. 215–224.

Canali, G. (2012). 'Il pomodoro da industria nel Nord Italia: l'innovazione organizzativa per migliorare la competitività'. *AgriRegioniEuropa*, 8, 30.

Cohen, D. (2011). *Braceros. Migrant Citizens and Transnational Subjects in the Postwar United States and Mexico*. Chapel Hill, NC: The University of North Carolina Press.

Dines, N. and Rigo, E. (2015). 'Postcolonial citizenships between representation, borders and the "refugeeization" of the workforce: critical reflections on migrant agricultural labor in the Italian Mezzogiorno' in Ponzanesi, S. and Colpani, G. (eds.). *Postcolonial Transitions in Europe*. London: Rowman and Littlefield.

Friedland, W.H. (1994). 'The new globalization: The case of fresh produce', in Bonanno, A. *et al.* (eds). *From Columbus to ConAgra. The Globalization of Agriculture and Food*. Lawrence: University Press of Kansas, pp. 210–231.

Friedland, W.H. and Barton, A. (1975). *Destalking the Wily Tomato. A Case Study in Social Consequences in California Agricultural Research*. Research Monograph No. 15, Santa Cruz: University of California.

Harrison, B. (1994). *Lean and Mean. The Changing Landscape of Corporate Power in the Age of Flexibility*. New York–London: The Guildford Press.

Harvey, M., Quilley, S. and Beynon, H. (2002). *Exploring the Tomato. Transformations of Nature, Society and Economy*. Cheltenham (UK)-Northampton (USA): Edward Elgar.

Joint Ethical Trade Initiatives (2015). *Counteracting Exploitation of Migrant Workers in Italian Tomato Production. Due Diligence in Agricultural Supply Chains*, www.ethicaltrade.org.files/resources/italian_tomato_production_report.pdf, (last accessed on 2 February 2016).

Lee, J., Gereffi, G. and Beauvais, J. (2012). 'Global value chains and agrifood standards: Challenges and possibilities for smallholders in developing countries', *PNAS*, 109, 31, pp. 12326–31.

McMichael, P. and Friedmann, H. (2007). 'Situating the "Retailing Revolution"', in Lawrence, G. and Burch, D. (eds.). *Supermarkets and Agri-Food Supply Chains*, Cheltenham/Northampton: Edward Elgar, pp. 291–319.

Perrotta, D. (2014). 'Vecchi e nuovi mediatori. Storia, geografia ed etnografia del caporalato in agricoltura'. *Meridiana*, 79, pp. 193–220.

Perrotta, D. (2015). 'Agricultural day laborers in southern Italy: Forms of mobility and resistance'. *South Atlantic Quarterly*, 114, 1, pp. 195–203.

Perrotta, D. and Sacchetto, D. (2013). 'Les ouvriers agricoles étrangers dans l'Italie méridionale'. *Hommes et migrations*, 1301, pp. 57–66.

Ploeg, J.D. van der (2008). *The New Peasantries. Struggles for Authonomy and Sustainability in an Era of Empire and Globalization*. London: Earthscan Routledge.

Pritchard, B. and Burch, D. (2003). *Agri-food Globalization in Perspective. International restructuring in the Processing Tomato Industry*. Aldershot: Asghate.

Pritchard, B., Burch, D. and Lawrence, G. (2007). 'Neither 'family' nor 'corporate' farming: Australian tomato growers as farm family entrepreneurs', *Journal of Rural Studies*, 23, pp. 75–87.

# Part II

# Social (un)sustainability of intensive agriculture

## Migrant labour in supply chains 'under pressure' in Southern Europe

# 5 Producing and mobilizing vulnerable workers

## The agribusiness of the region of Murcia (Spain)

*Elena Gadea, Andrés Pedreño and Carlos de Castro*

### 5.1 Introduction

The development of global agricultural enclaves goes hand-in-hand with processes of labour mobility due to the insufficient capacity of local workforces in meeting the intense labour demands generated by industrial scale agricultural production. Consequently, the effective functioning of global supply chains depends increasingly on an ability to recruit workers from other regions or countries. The way that these enclaves respond to the challenge of mobilizing workers and situating them in the production process, in the right quantity and at the right time, is key to understanding the operation and configuration of these productive territories. In this chapter we contemplate the linkages between restructured agricultural production, labour mobility and the construction of a vulnerable labour force. In doing so, we focus on the processes of incorporation and expulsion of workers that constitute a major feature of global production chains (Bair and Werner, 2011; Bair *et al.*, 2013). To do this, the analysis presented in this chapter is based on extensive research conducted in the region of Murcia, one of the principal agriculture enclaves of the Spanish Mediterranean.[1]

Located in southeast Spain, the region of Murcia, since the late 1970s, has been configuring and positioning itself as one of these new agricultural exporting regions, specialized in the production of fruit and fresh vegetables for supply to the markets of northern Europe. Operating annual production cycles and a business structure dominated by large companies and exporting agricultural cooperatives, these regions integrate cultivation with the processing and preparation of foodstuffs (Pedreño, 1999). The development of this business model has its origins in the period after the Spanish civil war, when the region developed vegetable-canning plants that had their golden age in the 1960s. It was after the transition to democratic government in the late 1970s and early 1980s that the region began to develop the current agri-food business model (Pedreño et al, 2014).

By narrating this process from an historical perspective it is possible to map how the current Murcian agri-food industry was constituted by strategies deployed by different social actors in response to the need to produce and reproduce an available, vulnerable and cheap labour force. This history can be considered from the perspective of three principal groups of workers: women in the processing plants, immigrants in the fields and temporary third-party contracted workers. This text considers the history of these groups in three parts. Section 5.2 outlines the social, political and economic contexts in which workers were mobilized and strategies were employed by businesses to integrate Murcia into the global agri-food supply chains. Section 5.3 proceeds to analyse the processes of incorporation, expulsion and substitution of different groups of workers, while Section 5.4 considers the social implications of the creation of a reserve army of workers.

## 5.2 Mobility, incorporation and expulsion of workers in the Murcian agri-food industry

Murcia is one of many intensive-farming enclaves that have emerged in southern Europe and generally in the south of the world economy. The incorporation of Spain into the European Union in 1986 and the subsequent access to its vast markets allowed the horticultural sector of Murcia to rapidly expand its scale of production. Since then, about 70 per cent of agricultural production has been exported, mainly to supply the varieties of fruit and vegetables most in demand by European consumers (peaches, saturn peaches, table grapes, plums, etc.), with an important market being the extra-early season fruits. This export orientation has been accompanied by the development of new business strategies propelled by consumer preferences and controlled by the large retail chains. As such, the large commercial distribution chains, which control the marketing channels, exert powerful pressure on local producers (Gereffi *et al.*, 2005). As they need year-round supply, their strategy is to use local producers from different parts of the world, known as the counter-seasonal market.

In order to maintain and improve their position in the global agri-food supply chain, local producers have been forced to develop innovative production and commercial strategies, such as the flexibilization of the workforce, to deal with the seasonal production cycles and the perishability of the produce. Therefore, these intensive agricultural enclaves have become highly dependent on large quantities of discontinuous wage labour, especially during harvest periods; hence, the importance of business and institutional strategies in the management of flexible work.

In the case of Murcia, since the late 1980s increased demand for wage labour in agriculture has been met by migrant workers and local women, which has led to a labour market segmented on the basis of gender and ethnicity. In general, these groups have coexisted peacefully in the fields and in the processing warehouses, although clearly there have been substitution processes that have prioritized the incorporation of certain types of workers and the expulsion of others. This continual process has existed throughout the agri-food labour history of Murcia, and it is a process that has reproduced vulnerability. The only change has been the incorporation and expulsion of different groups, which, over the last 40 to 50 years, have included: Andalusian day labourers, local women, and immigrant workers from Morocco, Ecuador, Bolivia and sub-Saharan Africa. Under this model, the management of flexible work depends on the reproduction of the vulnerable social positions of these temporary workers within the existing social structure of the region.

As such, the processes of incorporation and expulsion of workers are constitutive of global production chains. In order to develop this point, this chapter draws on the disarticulations perspective of Jennifer Bair and Marion Werner (2011, 2013). In their critical discussion of literature on commodity chains, they argue that inclusion in the global supply and production networks is a complex process that can lead to disruptions, dislocations, friction or expulsions.

Bair and Werner are also critical of the emphasis that the majority of studies in this field place on how a region (understood as the totality of inputs, including labour) inserts itself into a global production chain and the subsequent impact on local actors. From their disarticulations perspective, they propose that processes of expulsion should also be included, which is to say a more holistic view of the supply chain and the territory is required to understand the role of both incorporation and expulsion in how the chain is constituted.

Such a view obliges us to take a historical-analytical perspective of the development of social conditions that permit the incorporation and expulsion of different subjects and productive factors. As such, this chapter follows the approach initiated by other studies dedicated to exploring the conflicting processes of incorporation and expulsion in the labour markets of different global production chains (Brendt, 2013; Brown, 2013; Goger, 2013; Wilson, 2013).

## 5.3 Producing and reproducing vulnerable workers for the agri-food industry

### *5.3.1 Women in the processing plants*

The presence of women employed in the processing and handling of agricultural produce goes back to the early development of intensive agriculture in Murcia in the 1960s, with the launch of the canning industry and the production of fresh fruit for export. The canning industry emerged as a sector made up of small and medium-sized family businesses, characterized by a low level of mechanization, a reliance on intensive labour and a largely informal, self-regulated or paternalistic type of organization of labour. This model of productive organization was geared towards seasonal production and a female-dominated workforce, originally sourced from local rural families. Two key factors help explain the feminization of the labour market during this period: first, the strong interrelationship between production and the local community, and second, the survival strategies adopted by households. The seasonal and intermittent work of women in the canning plants and warehouses reflects a strategy of multiple labour activities within the family unit, as a means of earning additional income. The position of these women in the agricultural labour market was based, therefore, on a continuation of their traditional position in the agricultural social order, which linked women to the home, saw them as having a periodic presence in the productive sector, and constructed their work as supplementary rather than central. In addition, the lack of employment alternatives in these territories also favoured the feminization of the workforce. This area has traditionally been characterized by seasonal agricultural activity, which means that workers have to implement strategies such as sector and territorial mobility. For these rural women, responsible for the reproduction of domestic life, mobility was not always an option and the proximity of the canning and processing plants compensated for the inferior working conditions and allowed them to balance work inside and outside the home. A labour force with these features proved very attractive to the requirements of flexibility and wage restraint of agricultural enterprises, as the social position of women legitimized the temporary and precarious nature of the work.

Family and community organization, therefore, favoured the establishment of a reserve army of women, highly functional to the needs of companies and a labour market segmented along gender lines. However, the increasing modernization of the canning industry and warehousing in the 1970s and the social transformation of the local community gave rise to a process of estrangement. The growth of large companies, the arrival of workers from other towns in Murcia and Andalusia, along with the development of trade unions, would permanently change the way in which agricultural work was carried out. The unions undertook intense negotiations to replace the informal self-regulated and paternalistic labour relations with formal regulations that would bring working conditions closer to those of other industrial sectors. With the introduction of these regulations, the unions tried to influence the recruitment processes in order to contain the companies' substitution strategies and the formation of a reserve army of idle workers. The business owners eventually accepted the need to negotiate with union representatives, although they tried to limit the agreements to improve the work and wage conditions to salaried employees, so as to stop them being extended to casual labourers, who constituted the majority of the sector's workforce (Manzanares, 2006). By this means another logic of segmentation was reinforced: the temporality of work.

Another factor that challenged the labour organization model of the canning and warehousing plants, from the 1980s, was the growing importance of a younger generation of women workers who had superior education levels and even came from non-agricultural social classes. These women no longer saw their work as a supplementary household income, and their demands for recognition challenged the gender division of labour in the fields and in the processing plants.

> The women [. . .] who joined the labour market during the early years of the food and agricultural industry, believed that the contribution of their work to the household economy was supplementary. They didn't assume that they were workers in their own right [. . .] We had to take that job because it was the only one available, but that meant it was socially less worthy, we weren't respected in terms of pay or we might have started to demand the same rights and the same type of employment relationship as the rest of the workers.
>
> (Spanish union official)

As local women left the agricultural industry labour force, the growing presence of non-EU migrant workers provided a new source of labour for the agricultural enterprises. Thus, day labourers and immigrant day labourers were incorporated into a labour force already segmented by gender, and from now on ethnicity became a new differentiating factor.

### *5.3.2 Immigrants in the fields*

In the late 1980s, as the processing of fresh fruit and vegetables became increasingly important in the local economy, a series of significant events occurred that preceded the first wave of immigrant workers and the imminent diversification of the workforce. During this same period, the unions made a series of labour demands in an attempt to transfer established conditions in the canning plants to the new processing and warehousing plants, which initiated a series of demonstrations and strikes at the start of the 1990s. These demands, along with a loss of day workers to other sectors, meant that the agri-food industry was faced with a labour shortage soon after Spain joined the European Economic Community in 1986 and just as the Single European Market was established in 1991.

In this context, towards the end of the 1980s, young male immigrant workers began to arrive in Murcia from the Maghreb region of northern Africa and would become the primary source of labour until the late 1990s. Subsequently, the ethnic makeup of the labour force would diversify to include Ecuadorians, Bolivians and Romanians, amongst others, and an increased presence of women workers, as processes of reunification of migrant families and the formation of new families took hold (Torres, 2007). From the 1980s and 1990s onwards the patterns of workforce mobility would also be transformed. The workers now migrated in a circular and pendular fashion as they followed the harvests or returned to their countries of origin when work was scarce or the need for intense manual labour stopped due to production cycles. Currently, however, it is more common for workers to settle in the region, as the new intensive agricultural processes allows them to work almost year round (Gadea, Ramírez and Sánchez, 2014).

Agriculture, as such, served as a gateway to work for the recently arrived immigrants, not just because it was a sector with an intense need for manual work, but also because it was possible to work without the necessary permits. Most of the immigrants who arrived in the area without the required documentation could find work on small agricultural holdings, in the informal economy, with working conditions characterized by precariousness and extreme flexibilization. This meant that many of these workers remained on these holdings until they could regularize their work permits and then would leave to find more formal employment in agriculture or other sectors (Pedreño *et al.*, 2013). This process of informal entry into the labour market, followed by "flight" once formalized/legalized, has typified the employment histories of many immigrant workers. However, it has also functioned as a mechanism to sustain the informal economy and the reproduction of a reserve army of workers that serves the strategic replacement of ethnic groups and, in turn, perpetuates vulnerability. Social security registration data in Table 5.1 shows the proportion of foreign agricultural worker registrations in comparison to the total.

*Table 5.1* Foreign workers registered for social security and in employment, according to industry sector, Murcia, 2001–2013

| | *Total* | *Non-agricultural sector* | *% non-agricultural sector* | *Agricultural sector* | *% agricultural sector* | *Other* |
|---|---|---|---|---|---|---|
| 2001 | 33,447 | 8,507 | 25.4 | 23,082 | 69.0 | 1,858 |
| 2002 | 51,815 | 16,305 | 31.5 | 32,572 | 62.9 | 2,938 |
| 2003 | 56,279 | 20,439 | 36.3 | 32,791 | 58.3 | 3,049 |
| 2004 | 58,568 | 25,720 | 43.9 | 29,269 | 50.0 | 3,579 |
| 2005 | 94,568 | 42,703 | 45.2 | 41,423 | 43.8 | 10,442 |
| 2006 | 97,059 | 49,942 | 51.5 | 37,936 | 39.1 | 9,181 |
| 2007 | 97,484 | 51,367 | 52.7 | 36,466 | 37.4 | 9,651 |
| 2008 | 91,154 | 38,737 | 42.5 | 42,359 | 46.5 | 10,058 |
| 2009 | 89,848 | 35,713 | 39.7 | 44,211 | 49.2 | 9,924 |
| 2010 | 86,224 | 31,898 | 37.0 | 44,012 | 51.0 | 10,314 |
| 2011 | 82,754 | 29,431 | 35.6 | 43,107 | 52.1 | 10,216 |
| 2012 | 79,473 | 25,978 | 32.7 | 42,546 | 53.5 | 10,949 |
| 2013 | 74,121 | 30,494 | 41.1 | 32,684 | 44.1 | 10,943 |

Source: Ministry of Employment and Social Security.

At the start of the 2000s, 69 per cent of foreign worker registrations were in the agricultural sector. However, with the development of other sectors, such as construction and services, the number of non-agricultural foreign workers in the region increased dramatically until 2007, when the economic crisis decimated the local economy and employment. The way that the agricultural sector operates as a refuge for foreign workers expelled from other sectors, is evident in the data from 2008 onwards, when the employment of foreign workers in the agricultural sector started to grow in real terms and, later, as a proportion of all foreign workers. From 2010 there is a decrease in the total number of registered foreign workers, which as we shall see, signals a return of the autochthonous worker to the agricultural sector.

If the temporary and precarious status of women workers in the agricultural sector has been legitimated by their position in the domestic setting, in the case of immigrant workers it is necessary to pay attention to two factors that have reinforced their status as a vulnerable group within the labour force: first, immigration policy, and second, ethnic replacement as a business employment strategy.

Spanish immigration legislation is an important source of vulnerability for migrant workers, which limits their chances of integration and labour mobility: first, because migrant integration and mobility depends on the legal status of the foreign worker is linked to employment and the possession a work contract; second, because migrant integration and mobility depends on the circumstances of the 'national employment' situation, such that work permits are only granted for those occupations where the supply of local labour is insufficient. Thus, the immigrant is constructed as a stopgap solution in sectors where Spanish or foreign resident workers have abandoned employment.

*Table 5.2* Foreign worker permissions by sector, region of Murcia, 1995–2013

| | *Agriculture* | *Industry* | *Construction* | *Services* | *Not classified* | *Total* | *% agriculture* |
|---|---|---|---|---|---|---|---|
| 1995 | 4,567 | 105 | 50 | 574 | 162 | 5,458 | 83.7 |
| 1996 | 6,489 | 157 | 56 | 650 | 78 | 7,430 | 87.3 |
| 1997 | 3,778 | 102 | 41 | 556 | 7 | 4,484 | 84.3 |
| 1998 | 1,743 | 73 | 33 | 460 | 7 | 2,316 | 75.3 |
| 1999 | 7,320 | 303 | 183 | 1,382 | 41 | 9,229 | 79.3 |
| 2000 | 5,722 | 400 | 359 | 1,531 | 7,320 | 15,332 | 37.3 |
| 2001 | 8,421 | 1,149 | 1,378 | 2,432 | 3,980 | 17,360 | 48.5 |
| 2002 | 12,738 | 1,961 | 2,586 | 3,974 | 147 | 21,406 | 59.5 |
| 2003 | 3,910 | 846 | 1,229 | 2,046 | 194 | 8,225 | 47.5 |
| 2004 | 21,691 | 3,359 | 6,681 | 6,829 | 3,861 | 42,421 | 51.1 |
| 2005 | 24,444 | 3,845 | 10,746 | 14,857 | 4,602 | 58,494 | 41.8 |
| 2006 | 18,980 | 2,756 | 9,267 | 13,054 | 3,107 | 47,164 | 40.2 |
| 2007 | 5,455 | 1,285 | 3,329 | 5,491 | 1,249 | 16,809 | 32.5 |
| 2008 | 14,946 | 2,615 | 7,283 | 13,267 | 3,652 | 41,763 | 35.8 |
| 2009 | 7,326 | 747 | 1,363 | 6,203 | 1,513 | 17,152 | 42.7 |
| 2010 | 5,362 | 606 | 778 | 6,067 | 437 | 13,250 | 40.5 |
| 2011 | 4,985 | 440 | 545 | 6,064 | 468 | 12,502 | 39.9 |
| 2012 | 3,426 | 281 | 242 | 4,678 | 279 | 8,906 | 38.5 |
| 2013 | 1,969 | 195 | 115 | 3,665 | 192 | 6,136 | 32.1 |

Source: Ministry of Employment and Social Security. Quota managed registrations not included.

The statistics on foreign worker permits by activity demonstrate the fundamental role that legislation has played in the ethnic segmentation of the Murcian labour market (Table 5.2). At the end of the 1990s, permits issued for the agriculture sector accounted for more than 80 per cent of all permits granted. In the following decade, with the development of other industrial sectors, such as construction and services, the importance of the agricultural sector diminished.

A second factor to bear in mind is the way that ethnic substitution strategies are employed by businesses. The employment of the first Moroccan workers in agriculture towards the end of the 1980s represented a segmentation strategy in response to the demands of the local workforce for better working conditions. These Moroccan day labourers, many of whom were working illegally, constituted a particularly vulnerable workforce. However, following the process of regularization in the 1990s, it was these workers who would demand improvements to working conditions, which would lead businesses to implement new segmentation strategies, substituting Moroccans for workers from other countries, mostly Ecuadorians, sub-Saharan Africans and eastern Europeans (Segura, Pedreño and de Juana, 2002). These processes of ethnic segmentation and substitution are also legitimated by cultural factors, although it is evident that the underlying logic for such strategies is the continual search for a submissive workforce.

> The Moroccans arrived and there was this saying that the Moroccans were better than the gypsies, because the gypsies would get drunk, they'd fight, steal, threaten others, etc. At that time the Moroccans didn't have papers, and not having papers meant that you earned much less than you should have earned. You worked because you had to, in order to live, and because above all, if you've come to a country it's to improve your circumstances [...]. When the Ecuadorians came [. . .] they changed the saying: the Moroccans are no good, they fight and whatever else, and the Ecuadorians are better, they speak Spanish as well and they go to church [. . .]. Then the sub-Saharan Africans came: the sub-Saharans are coming, they're strong, tall, they can do everything, and then it was they who were better. We don't want Ecuadorians because the Ecuadorians get drunk, etc., when they get their papers they leave, [. . .]. And now, more recently, as everyone has papers [. . .], they want the ones who don't speak up. If you know how to stand up for yourself and you speak Spanish, you're a smart ass.
>
> (Moroccan worker)

Employers are conscious that the vulnerability of these immigrant workers is greater at the start of the migratory project, when many of these workers find themselves in a legally precarious situation and the pressures of migrating are considerable. Along with the mobilization of vulnerable social groups, employers have developed business strategies that produce and reproduce the vulnerabilities of these workers: informal employment of undocumented migrants, keeping workers for years with temporary contracts, etc.:

> They pay them only half of what they earn, or they don't pay them at all … and so they don't give them their papers, they don't recognize collective agreements and their contract should be permanent or permanent part-time, but it's still temporary after ten years working in the same company [. . .]. If a person has been in the company for a certain length of time, what most companies do is let them go, send them to register for unemployment benefits [. . .] and then rehire them three months later, so that you don't have the right to change your contract due to the length of service.
>
> (Spanish union official)

The use of such practices is a way to contain labour costs, while maintaining the worker in labour conditions that allow businesses to employ and dispense with them at will.

> They favour rotation, as they can't change nationalities like they did in the beginning because now they have different nationalities and many stable workers. What they do now is to rotate the workers, which means keeping them temporary and not making them permanent or permanent part-time [. . .] because if they become more stable they are going to demand more rights and they are more likely to argue back when they're spoken to in a way they don't like.
>
> (Spanish union official)

In this last case, temporary contracts have become a central characteristic of employment in the Murcian agricultural sector, reproducing the traditional figure of the seasonal worker in a labour market that has effectively reduced seasonality as a factor in production. As such, they have initiated a new phase in the mobilization of vulnerable workers, whereby the temporary worker takes centre stage, in other words, workers who are contracted through employment agencies.

### *5.3.3 Workers contracted through temporary employment agencies*

As the demand for seasonal workers has increased, employment agencies have played an increasingly central role in the restructuring of work practices and labour intermediation (Sánchez, 2006; Avallone, this volume). The increased emphasis on temporary workers means that their influence now extends far beyond recruitment to include the control and discipline of workers.

In the Murcian agri-food industry there are two important periods in the organization of labour intermediation:[2] the 1990s, which saw the expansion of the *furgonetero* (literally meaning a person who drives a van, i.e. the recruiter-transporter), and the period since 2000 which has seen the growing role of temporary employment agencies (TEAs). The *furgonetero* is the person responsible for recruiting and transporting the day workers and who often takes charge of monitoring the crew's work and of paying them.

As Castellanos and Pedreño (2001) point out, the *furgonetero* is a mode of intermediation that implies a great deal of control over the labour market and recruitment networks.[3] On the one hand, they control the contact information with the agricultural holdings, and on the other, they know the local workforce and who is available for agricultural work (Castellanos and Pedreño, 2001). They are generally migrant workers who have been working in agriculture for a longer period than others and who possess good relationships with the business owners. The expansion of the system of informal intermediation in the 1990s was related to an increased need for labourers and the progressive specialization of the territory in different fruit and vegetable crops, which favoured the mobility of workers from one crop type to another. Out of this context, the situation evolved between the late 1990s and early 2000s towards "greater organizational complexity and a more formal, regulated system, which saw the introduction of agricultural service companies and, later, temporary employment agencies" (Castellanos and Pedreño, 2001, p. 22–23).

The temporary employment agencies were created in 1994,[4] as part of a framework of institutional reforms that permitted the business sector to develop flexibilization strategies for the organization of work (Ortiz, 2013):

> We draw up a contract for the worker who is with us. He's contracted with us at the temporary work agency and not with the client company or with the warehouse, as in this case. We have a commercial relationship with the company and are under contract to make workers available but we organize the work contract. We have to sort out the prevention of occupational risks.

> [. . .] All the worker's expenses, wages and everything go through our accounts [. . .]. The company doesn't have to do anything, because we're responsible for everything. We have to monitor the worker: that's why I have to be in the warehouse, because if anything happens, any kind of accident, it is me and not the company who has to deal with it.
>
> (Spanish employee in a temporary contract agency)

In Murcia the speed at which the temporary employment agencies have assumed a central role in the labour market reflects the fact that they have taken over the function previously provided by the *furgonetero*, and before that by the *enganchadores* (literally meaning the one who hooks, i.e. recruiter). However, this does not represent the substitution of a mode of intermediation, but rather its integration into the workplace and division of labour. Just as the agricultural enterprises had done in the 1990s, the employment agencies continue to use the *furgoneteros* to fulfil their role of intermediating and controlling workers. For its part, the employment agency handles all the administrative aspects of the work relationship: drawing up contracts, payroll, registration with social security, etc. It is apparent, therefore, that the employment relationships are extremely blurred, not just between the worker and the final employer, but also with the employment agency. In the region of Murcia the importance of temporary employment agencies has continued to grow over recent years, rising from 67.3 per cent of all occupational contracts in the agricultural sector in 2006 to 85.9 per cent in 2014. As such, the employment agencies have become the most important actor in the supply of day labourers to the agri-food industry, moving workers across the whole region and nearby provinces such as Albacete, Almeria and Alicante.

The employment agencies have played a fundamental role, not just in the ethnic segmentation of the agri-food labour force but in the increased use of temporary work and the recruitment and rotation of foreign workers, a phenomenon that was already highlighted by some authors during the mid 2000s (Andreo *et al.*, 2005; Andreo, 2007), and which has intensified since the economic crisis. As is evident from the data in Table 5.3, the contracting of agricultural workers through employment agencies is greater for foreign workers, even though it has increased in recent years for Spanish day labourers as well. This leads to greater seasonality and rotation in hiring foreigners and, therefore, greater job insecurity.

### *5.3.4 Border intermediaries: the migrant industry*

The activity of the TEAs may be pointing to a new scale in the recruitment and mobilization of workers. By specializing in the recruitment and mobilization of agricultural workers, TEAs from Murcia not only supply labour to firms in the region but also provide services to agricultural firms in other European countries as well as services to mobilized workers themselves. The case of Terra Fecundis provides interesting insights into the new management of agricultural work in the current agri-food system.

*Table 5.3* Contracts in agricultural occupations and contracts in employment agencies by nationality, region of Murcia, 2006–2014 (% of all contracts)

| | *Contracts in agricultural occupations* | | *Contracts through employment agencies in agricultural occupations* | |
|---|---|---|---|---|
| | *Spanish Nationals* | *Foreigners* | *Spanish Nationals* | *Foreigners* |
| 2006 | 12.5 | 87.5 | 3.0 | 97.0 |
| 2007 | 11.7 | 88.3 | 3.0 | 97.0 |
| 2008 | 12.2 | 87.8 | 3.3 | 96.7 |
| 2009 | 18.5 | 81.5 | 6.7 | 93.3 |
| 2010 | 16.0 | 84.0 | 6.1 | 93.9 |
| 2011 | 16.0 | 84.0 | 6.2 | 93.8 |
| 2012 | 18.2 | 81.8 | 8.8 | 91.2 |
| 2013 | 21.1 | 78.9 | 12.0 | 88.0 |
| 2014 | 22.3 | 77.7 | 13.6 | 86.4 |

Source: SEFCARM Observatory.

In Murcia, Terra Fecundis is the most important company in the supply of agricultural labourers. But Terra Fecundis is much more than a TEA. On the one hand, unlike other companies, it not only hires temporary workers out to farms or processing warehouses, but also maintains a large number of labourers on permanent part-time contracts who, like boxes of fruit, can be moved around the European countryside in a few hours, ready to be consumed.

> [In France] there are areas where they have difficulty getting local workers, or stable workers during the season . . . at which point, of course, they need to go to an employment agency. The fact is that someone who travels is someone who wants to work, and not someone who will go one day and then leave.
>
> (TEA Worker)

> Last year we had an average of 4,000 to 4,500 [employees] . . . These are people who work in Spain and across Europe [. . .]. We work in southern France, even in Paris for the strawberry picking . . . in the Rhone and several other regions. [. . .] When our workers finish a job in one place, then they can be sent to somewhere else in France or Italy. In Italy we have also done grapes and tomatoes.
>
> (TEA Worker)

Agricultural work is considered low-level and low-paid work, but that does not mean anybody can do agricultural work. Farmers and labour brokers are always looking for workers with specific qualities. The ideal agricultural worker should not only know how to prune and thin out trees or to handle fruit quickly and carefully but, above all, should be someone who is willing to make sacrifices, to obey and to endure hard work. Perhaps the most sought-after and valued quality in these workers is their disposition to mobility. Judging by the composition of the workforce, ethnicity and immigration appear to have become warranties of suitability.

> Yes it is true that most immigrants repeat [the mobilization to France] every year [. . .] There is everything. When we offer work in the field to the Spanish, they're not interested. Agricultural work is still not very popular in Spain [. . .], especially if you tell someone that they have to go to work in France for three months to pick lettuce or nectarines . . . This is why out of about 3,000 workers only 300 or 400 are Spanish. The rest are people from North Africa and South America. As they have left their country they don't mind working in Spain or anywhere else. All they want is to earn money.
>
> (Male TEA partner).

The other novelty is that Terra Fecundis not only supplies workers to agricultural firms but also organizes and coordinates multiple aspects of mobility, both those related to the work itself (such as transportation or accommodation in agricultural enclaves) as well as those linked to the political status of migrant workers. Legal representation in immigration matters, money transfer services, financial support for air travel and even the selling of homes in countries of origin are just some of the services that the company offers its workers. Services are reinvented, as are the narratives.

> Our employees are our customers and we treat them as such. You try to do your best for your customers, and our workers are our customers. Not only are they hired and driven to France, Italy or wherever we go . . . but we always give them housing, electricity, water, all the usual services except food. At the same time, the worker is always a potential client because we have a number of auxiliary companies that deal with money transfer, selling and financing flight tickets, and offer Real Estate services – we sell houses in Ecuador . . .
>
> (Male TEA partner)

Terra Fecundis represents a new kind of labour market intermediary which could be defined as a genuine "migration industry" operating in a frontier economy (Hernández, 2012: 41–42); a migration industry that uses European directives on the free movement of workers and national differences in labour regulations to build an infrastructure for supplying cheap and docile labour. For example, seasonal agricultural labour in French intensive agriculture used to be provided by workers from southern Europe, including many Spaniards, and by non-EU workers from Morocco and Tunisia (Crenn, this volume). Over the last several years, and since the enlargement of the European Union towards Central and Eastern Europe, these workers have been replaced by workers from new member states, but also by non-EU workers who are employed by TEAs in other countries of the European Union (Mesini, 2014).

> When we arrived in France in 2000, there was still a large group of Spaniards who had moved there during previous years . . . Between 2000 and 2001, Spaniards stopped going to France but are now returning, although now the foreign client does not want them because they left back in 2000. Now they have been replaced by people from North Africa through the OMI contracts, workers from Eastern European countries, and those working for Terra Fecundis or similar businesses.
>
> (Male TEA partner)

The EU regulation of the TEAs has operated, therefore, as the basis for a process of ethnic replacement. The supply of workers through TEAs has also allowed employers to avoid national labour regulations, according to reports from several French farmers' unions. These unions criticize the transnational hiring practices and point to violations of labour law and to the construction of a "state of emergency" in French labour camps. The replacement of some workers who are entitled to labour rights by more precarious and docile workers is not a new situation in southern European agriculture. What seems to be new are the intermediary mechanisms of bringing this about.

## 5.4 Restructuring agricultural production and labour mobility: the establishment of a reserve army of workers

As we have seen, the forms of social relations mobilized in the export-oriented agri-food economy to lower labour costs are based on gender inequalities, ethnicity and citizenship. These inequalities, continuously reconstituted over time and which allow for the creation and reproduction of a differentiated and segmented reserve army of labour, are a fundamental prerequisite to disciplining worker relations and the social organization of work as a means to adjust to the seasonal discontinuities and supply chain management in agricultural food production.

At the outset of the development of intensive agriculture in Murcia, women constituted a fundamental part of this reserve army of workers. The construction of their work as an exceptional activity and as a form of extra-family support was consistent with the requirements of flexibility following the productive restructuring of agri-food processing companies. This configuration justified the labour flexibility as well as their subordinate position in the occupational structure, a position that was defined by lower wages and lower positions (Pedreño, 1999). In the 1980s and 1990s, Murcian agribusinesses experienced substantial growth and the need to recruit a significant number of workers as a result of an exodus of labourers to other industrial sectors. The reserve army in the fields began to source migrant workers in the informal economy, incorporating Moroccans, sub-Saharan Africans, Ecuadorians and Bolivians gradually into its ranks. These were groups that were particularly vulnerable to the wage containment strategies of agricultural enterprises. As Martin (2006) notes, the demand for labour in agriculture has been subjected to a continuous process of cost inflation, so a key strategy in minimizing production costs is to establish a triple segmentation (ethnic, gender and legal) process that incorporates and expels groups to create a workforce more willing to bend to the industry's demands for labour flexibility. Although these processes of substitution have been legitimated by cultural and gender stereotypes, it is evident that it is the constant search for submissive workers that underscores the logic of these strategies. Business owners are conscious that the vulnerability of immigrant workers is greater when they are in the initial stages of the migratory process. Furthermore, Spanish legislation positions foreign workers in a situation of vulnerability and dependence on their employers, just as their legal stability depends on them obtaining and maintaining employment. We are faced with a regime that constrains the mobility of immigrant workers (Mezzadra, 2005) and limits their chances of integration and of finding better jobs.

Along with the mobilization of fragile social categories, the agri-food firms have developed business strategies that produce and reproduce the vulnerabilities of these workers and prevent them from gaining bargaining power. The casualization of work represents a major source of vulnerability, while labour intermediaries, headed by employment agencies, are the main instruments in the implementation of this business strategy. Hence, temporary workers, recruited through employment agencies and already segmented along gender and ethnicity lines, are configured as the main actors in this third wave of labour force mobilization and vulnerability.

In the context of the current economic crisis, insecurity constitutes a principal disciplinary mechanism in a labour market that, more than ever, is defined by temporariness, sectoral and territorial mobility, and the combination of formal and informal market activities. The collapse of the construction sector, which previously employed a significant portion of the men of the area, has flooded the fields with both Spanish and foreign day workers, in search of employment, which, in turn, is used by employers to exert downward pressure on working conditions. With the reserve army of labourers increasing more and more in size, the structural organization of labour lies less in the mobilization of vulnerable categories than in the flexibilization of these workers. It is here that the employment agencies take a leading role given their capacity to restructure the agri-food labour market.

The institutional and corporate management of worker mobility simultaneously administers the twin phenomena of incorporation and expulsion of different social groups in order to ensure a disciplined labour force and reduced labour costs, illustrating how these processes are constitutive of global food chains.

## Notes

1 The empirical basis of this work derives from a series of mostly qualitative studies on agricultural employment and international migration that have been coordinated by the Region of Murcia since the late 2000s. This chapter is specifically based on interviews with field and warehouse workers, agri-food businesses, union representatives and

labour intermediaries, carried out between November 2012 and March 2015, within the framework of the Social Sustainability Project on New Agricultural Enclaves: Spain and Mexico (CSO2011-28511).

2 This system is not new in rural Murcia and is a deeply ingrained practice during the citrus fruit harvesting period in the interior parts of the region. The system is organised on a completely informal basis, with all agreements being verbal (Castellanos and Pedreño, 2001, p. 22). A different system can be found in the Valencia area (see Garrapa, this volume).

3 In Italy this informal system of intermediation is called *caporalato* (see Avallone, this volume).

4 Law 14/1994 regulates the temporary employment industry.

## References


Andreo, J. C. (2007). *Inmigración extranjera y empresas de trabajo temporal en la Región de Murcia.* Madrid: Doble J. Colección Ciencias Sociales.

Andreo, J. C., Guerrero, Mª J., Arcos, B. and Gálvez, D. (2005). 'Intermediación en el mercado laboral de mano de obra inmigrante extranjera en la Región de Murcia: el caso de las empresas de trabajo temporal'. *Papeles de geografía*, 41–42, pp. 51–70.

Bair, J. and Werner, M. (2011). 'Commodity chains and the uneven geographies of global capitalism: a disarticulation perspective'. *Environment and Planning A*, 43(5), pp. 988–997.

Bair, J., Werner, M., Berndt, C. and Broecker, T. (2013). 'Dis/articulating producers, markets, and regions: new directions in critical studies of commodity chains'. *Environment and Planning A*, 45, pp. 2544–2552.

Berndt, C. (2013). 'Assembling market b/orders: violence, dispossession, and economic development in Ciudad Juárez, Mexico'. *Environment and Planning A,* 45(11), pp. 2646–2662.

Brown, S. (2013). 'One hundred years of labor control: violence, militancy, and the Fairtrade banana commodity chain in Colombia'. *Environment and Planning A,* 45(11), 2572–2591.

Castellanos, Mª L. and Pedreño, A. (2001). 'Desde el Ejido al accidente de Lorca. Las amargas cosechas de los trabajadores inmigrantes en los milagrosos vergeles de la agricultura mediterránea'. *Sociología del Trabajo*, 42, pp. 3–31.

Gadea, E; Ramírez, A. and Sánchez, J. (2014). 'Estrategias de reproducción social y circulaciones migratorias de los trabajadores en los enclaves globales', in Pedreño, A. (coord.). *De cadenas, migrantes y jornaleros. Los territorios rurales en las cadenas globales agroalimentarias.* Madrid: Talasa, pp. 134–149.

Gereffi, G., Humphrey, J. and Sturgeon, T. (2005). 'The governance of global value chains'. *Review of International Political Economy*, 12(1), p. 78–104.

Goger, A. (2013). 'From disposable to empowered: rearticulating labor in Sri Lankan apparel factories'. *Environment and Planning A*, 45(11) 2628–2645.

Hernández, R. (2012). 'La industria de la migración en el sistema migratorio México-Estados Unidos'. *Travaux et Recherches dans les Amériques du Centre,* 61, pp. 41–61.

Manzanares, D. (2006). 'Determinación de los salarios de hombres y mujeres en la industria de conservas vegetales, 1939–1975'. *Trabajo*, 17, pp. 31–54.

Martín, E. (2006). 'Mercado de trabajo, género e inmigración' in *Mujeres migrantes, viajeras incansables.* Monográfico sobre Género e Inmigración. Bilbao: Harresiak Apurtuz, Coordinadora de ONGs de Euskadi de Apoyo a Inmigrantes.

Mésini, B. (2014). 'The transnational recruitment of temporary Latino workers in European agriculture' in J. Gertel, and S. R. Sippel (eds) *Seasonal Workers in Mediterranean Agriculture: The Social Costs of Eating Fresh*. London: Routledge, pp. 71–82.

Mezzadra, S. (2005). *Derecho de fuga: Migraciones, ciudadanía y globalización*. Madrid: Traficantes de Sueños.

Ortiz, P. (2013). 'Flexibilidad laboral en el mercado de trabajo español'. *AREAS Revista Internacional de Ciencias Sociales*, no. 32.

Pedreño, A. (1999). 'Taylor y Ford en los campos: trabajo, género y etnia en el cambio tecnológico y organizacional de la agricultura industrial murciana'. *Sociología del Trabajo*, 35, pp. 25–56.

Pedreño, A., Gadea, E. and García, A. (2013). 'Jornaleras de la globalización en el campo murciano' in M. J. Sánchez and I. Serra (coords.) *Ellas se van, Mujeres migrantes en Estados Unidos y España*. México: Instituto de Investigaciones Sociales, UNAM.

Pedreño, A., Gadea, E. and de Castro, C. (2014). 'Labor, gender and political conflicts in the global agri-food system. The case of agri-export model of Murcia, Spain' in A. Bonanno and J. Salete Cavalcanti (eds) *Labor Relations in Globalized Food*. Bingley: Emerald, pp. 193–214.

Sánchez, K. (2006). *Los capitanes de Tenextepango. Un estudio sobre intermediación cultural*. México: Plaza y Valdés/UAEM.

Segura, P., Pedreño, A. and de Juana, S. (2002). 'Configurando la Región Murciana para las frutas y hortalizas: racionalización productiva, agricultura salarial y nueva estructura social del trabajo jornalero'. *Areas*, 22, pp. 71–93.

Torres, F. (dir.) (2007). *Los nuevos vecinos de la mancomunidad del sureste, los inmigrantes y su inserción en Torre Pacheco, Fuente Álamo y La Unión (Murcia)*. Murcia: Universidad de Murcia.

Wilson B. R. (2013). 'Breaking the chains: coffee, crisis, and farmworker struggle in Nicaragua'. *Environment and Planning A* 45(11), 2592–2609.

# 6 Family farms, migrant labourers and regional imbalance in global agri-food systems

## On the social (un)sustainability of intensive strawberry production in Huelva (Spain)

*Alicia Reigada*

### 6.1 Introduction

Since the expansion of so-called 'new agriculture' in the coastal areas of Andalusia, in southern Spain, numerous scholars (Berlan, 1987; Martín, 1995; Lacomba, 1997; Delgado, 2002, 2012) have called into question the idea of Andalusia as the 'California of Europe' and have queried the sustainability and quality of its agricultural production. Among other questions, these studies highlight the problems derived from the intensification of agricultural techniques and the overuse of natural resources. They also draw attention to employment issues such as the feminization and ethnic segmentation of the labour force and highlight the role played by family farms within global capitalism. By refraining from decontextualized comparisons, they focus their analysis on the centrality of the 'Californian model' (Carter *et al.*, 1992) in the development of agricultural sector in Andalusia. In this chapter, I show that, even if there are some similarities between California and Andalusia – for example, the political construction of an ethnicized and segmented labour market (Berlan, 1987; Thomas, 1985; Martin, 1995; Wells, 1996) – the case of Andalusia is different in that agricultural production in this region can be considered both peripheral in and dependent on the global agri-food system.

This chapter undertakes to evaluate the appropriateness of using the Californian model to understand the situation of agriculture in Andalusia, particularly in relation to labour and migration. To do so, it discusses the results of empirical research carried out between 2005 and 2009 in one of the principal agri-exporting enclaves[1] of Mediterranean agriculture: strawberry cultivation in Huelva.[2] Based on small-scale farming, this area has become the largest exporter of strawberries in Europe, and second in the world after California.

This chapter provides a general overview of the development and current implications of Andalusian industrial agriculture and addresses the problem of social sustainability in the region. The first section commences with a summary of the history of Andalusian strawberry production before focusing on the role assumed by small family farms. The second section proceeds to describe the tensions that result from the subordinate insertion of this agricultural production into the global supply chains of the agri-food industry. The third section considers the fundamental role of (domestic and international) migration in the historical formation of capitalist agriculture in the region. I argue that intensive agricultural production in Huelva is sustained by a highly segmented labour market and by the precarious conditions of migrant labourers. These socially unsustainable practices form the structural basis of this global agricultural enclave.

On the basis of this analysis the chapter sets out to show how the social history of food production can illuminate a wider analysis of the social and cultural transformations that are taking place in the current phase of capitalism (Rosberry, 1996), which implicate, inter alia, labour, production, migration, space, consumer trends and social identities.

## 6.2 The formation of a global agricultural enclave: regional imbalance, family agriculture and migration

During the last four decades, the focus of the new political economy of agriculture (Friedland *et al.,* 1978; Bonanno *et al.,* 1994; McMichael, 1996; Friedland, 2004) has been on, amongst other things, the regional dimension as an explanatory variable of international relations of food production and consumption that shape capital accumulation (Friedmann and McMichael, 1989). This topic has been recently considered in rural sociology, which emphasizes the need to rethink the central role of regions in the reconstitution of agri-food relations and to opt for a more integrated spatially oriented approach (Marsden, 2012).

A long history of regional analysis in Andalusia confirms that its system of intensive agriculture has a very different point of departure to that of California (Carter *et al.,* 1992; Lacomba, 1997).[3] Andalusia now occupies a peripheral position in the spatial division of labour, which was crystallized by a number of factors during the first and second food regimes (Friedmann and McMichael, 1989[4]): the specialization in activities closely related to the exploitation of its natural resources, the sustaining of an abundant and cheap labour force, its role as a supplier of raw materials and certain agri-food goods, and the conversion to a market for capital goods and inputs that required the industrialization of agriculture (Delgado, 2002).

The beginning of the third phase of the world food system coincides with the expansion and consolidation of so-called 'new agriculture',[5] based on the intensification of capitalist forms of production. As established by numerous empirical studies, new agriculture develops on the basis of intense industrialization, externalization and specialization (Delgado, 2002), which translates to a process of vigorous depletion of natural resources with important environmental effects (Carpintero and Naredo, 2006).

Regional analysis also connects with another of the primary pillars of this model of agriculture that endows it with certain degree of uniqueness: the role of small family farm holdings and the tensions arising from their inclusion in global agricultural chains. As in other areas of southern Europe, labour migrations are a structural element in the historical formation of these agricultural enclaves, though with their own peculiarities and characteristics.

The first phase of agrarian capitalism in Andalusia (from the mid-nineteenth century to the Second World War) had already witnessed an intensification of social tensions, after it led many impoverished and landless peasants to migrate first to the major cities and regional capitals and then abroad, while many more became day labourers for large properties (Lacomba, 1997). This workforce, often settled in colonies on these agricultural estates, was managed and controlled through an organizational work system that combined characteristics of an organizational work system that was both disciplinary and paternalistic (Gavira, 2002). These temporary internal migrations became a key part of the social history of the large agricultural estates of Andalusia, and a foundational element that is often invisible in the agricultural development model.

In the following phase, identifiable by the processes of industrialization, urbanization and agricultural modernization, various authors highlight the importance that the migratory phenomenon played in the collapse of traditional agriculture. This emigration, which took place between the 1950s and 1970s, played a fundamental role in the economic and industrial growth of northern European countries such as France, Germany and Switzerland, and converted Andalusia into an exporter of human resources, not just natural ones. Therefore, somewhat paradoxically, along with the grave social consequences of this rural exodus, the modernization and mechanization of Andalusian agriculture was precipitated, at least in part, by an increasingly scarce and therefore more expensive labour force (Delgado, 2002; Naredo, 2004). As such, the new demand for specialization and skills of a small group of salaried employees would have as a counterpart the expulsion of a large number of casual workers and the mass disqualification of a labour force doomed to live and work in increasingly unstable and precarious conditions (Gavira, 2002).

If foreign migration had come to be a reality of traditional agriculture, internal migration would come to be a decisive factor in shaping the enclaves of intensive agriculture in Andalusia. However, first it is necessary to look at the role of the State in agricultural development and the experience of a new wave of small family farms. Through land settlement policy, the Franco regime promoted a model of agriculture sustained by the labour of the members of the household, and then later by wage-earning employees and migrants hired as casual day workers, during peak season. This model started in western Almeria in 1958 following an initiative by the National Institute of State Settlement. In this period, more than 50 per cent of the land in the province of Huelva was in the hands of the State and Local Government. The weight of public policy is of special relevance in that it established the concession of small lots of between one and two hectares, in the form of tenant farming, to those neighbours who had nothing more than their workforce (Martín, 1995). However, this tenant farming was accompanied, especially in the 1970s and 1980s, by the aggressive, disorganized and illegal occupation of lands designated for communal use.

Consequently, in a short period of time, many former day labourers, peasants or workers from other sectors (fishing, industry, construction and commerce) became the 'new cultivators' of Andalusian agriculture and would go on to experience unexpected success with their crops. As such, the expansion of the agri-food industry, at this time, did not occur due to the consolidation of large properties but by an exponential increase in the number of small strawberry growers, commonly known as *freseros*. Their life stories, often defined by internal and international migration, provide access to their experience and collective memory. Their recollections reinforce the idea that they are people of humble social origins who have made themselves into the (small) owners of the garden of Europe. As we will see later, the origins of the social identity of these small holders goes on to play an important role in the dynamic of their relationships with the foreign migrant workers in their employ. The biography of this 38-year-old small farmer is representative of the history of greenhouse agriculture in Andalusia:

> I started working . . . I think I was born working. As before there wasn't any childcare, when I was one or two my mother took me with her to the field, because my family has always had strawberries. My father worked for the companies and my mother would carry me on her back along with the strawberries. Before the strawberries weren't grown under plastic, so not so many were produced, maybe a woman would collect ten crates of strawberries a day. Before they were only small farms and the family did everything. There weren't any day labourers, nor any social security. There was nothing at all. Men and women and everyone in the family worked. My mother always worked on the strawberries, she got the meals ready, she cleaned ... A slave of life. [. . .] We started working on my grandparents' land and then we inherited some ourselves. We had a hectare and you couldn't even plant it all, my father combined the field with construction work or going out to sea, and maybe my father was working at sea and my mother, my grandfather or an uncle of mine harvested the strawberries, the following year it would be the opposite, my uncle would be working in another sector and my father would collect the strawberries, and they went splits on it. The strawberries, in any case, in those years were cultivated between March and May, and the rest of the year they worked elsewhere. Agriculture at that time was a great help. Then later we got more land and got it ready little by little, we got some of the land from the State. [. . .] You started as a tenant farmer, without any rights or anything, you could mortgage it, you could only plant. [. . .] And then we started to buy what we could and now we've got three and a half (hectares).

As expansion and intensive agriculture created too much labour for family members, farmers resorted to wage labour to fulfil the shortfall. At first, this workforce was sourced through internal migrations of Andalusian day labourers, and then, from the middle of the 1990s onwards, from transnational migrations. The convergence of these transformations and trends in the labour market, such as the decreased importance of family work (defamilization), increased numbers of salaried workers (salarization) and foreign labourers, has led Camarero (2014) to call into question the very definition of the category 'family farms' for this type of productive activity.

Even though this strategy conforms to business logic, the ultimate objective is generally not the accumulation of capital and the creation of large capitalist properties. Rather, these smallholdings respond to the need to sustain the viability of the farm, and the family, by reproducing the social structures of this productive model. Therefore, the debate cannot be limited to the questions raised by the progressive 'defamiliarization' of this model, but it also needs to consider the problem of the conditions established by the structure of the global agri-food chain.

## 6.3 Small family farms in global agri-food chains

This section will show the main conditions that small family farms need to create in the context of global agri-food chains. First, as agricultural production is subject to the demands of technology and the market, there is an important change in the traditional labour culture (Camarero *et al.,* 2002) that breaks with the framework of accumulated knowledge at the same time as degrading agricultural work (Ploeg, 2009). Second, it is evident that the control exerted by the large agri-food supply chains (Mercadona, Carrefour, Eroski, Dia, Alcampo, Lidl, Hipercor) corresponds to a loss of profitability for producers, due to downward pressure on prices, at the same time as an increase in production costs (land, inputs, labour).[6] For example, in the first decade of this century strawberry growers received 3.8 per cent less for their product than in 1989 (Verdier, 2006). Exacerbating this pressure is the intense competition from countries such as Morocco, favoured for lower production costs and the agreements established in the CAP framework:

> Before, ten or fifteen years ago, everyone with just a few hectares made some money, first because the workforce wasn't as expensive as it is now, second because there weren't as many strawberries and so the sector was more competitive. [. . .] Today a kilo of strawberries is worth the same as ten years ago, however labour costs, materials, plastic and pesticides have all gone up by 100%.
>
> (Paco Serrano, manager of one of the largest cooperatives in the strawberry cultivation zone[7])

In this context, demands by Andalusian farmers for a fair price make sense. Spanish farmers clearly and explicitly identify the large supermarket chains as the agents responsible for the fall in prices and the consequent loss of profitability. Farmers' grievances against retail corporations such as Carrefour, Lidl or Mercadona, amongst others, are frequently mentioned in their discourses and accounts. It is also indicative that these farmers have chosen the entrances to supermarkets as a major space of protest, evidenced in the series of demonstrations throughout the late 1990s and 2000s, which has made the conflict more publically visible, unlike in other countries.[8] They consider that these chains expropriate the value added by their efforts to improve the production. As expressed by the Organizational Secretary of the growers' association COAG-Huelva:[9] 'sometimes they say: "it is not because of the added value of the fruit ...", but the only one who adds value to the fruit is the farmer'. Paradoxically, the strategy of intensive agriculture to increasingly invest in inputs has corresponded to a decrease in participation by the sector in adding value. And, at the same time as modern agriculture increases the profits of the added value of the industrial and retail sector, it also conceals the increasing environmental costs of producing this added value (Carpintero and Naredo, 2006).

Demands and proposals to alter the imbalance of power of the global agri-food chain are varied. Among them are those that request the intervention of public institutions – the government and the European Union – to support greenhouse cultivators. On the one hand, they demand a reform of the CAP, which until now excludes horticultural crops from subsidies. But while some authors consider that the EU must protect fruit and vegetable farming in the Mediterranean and control price distortions between the producer and retailer (Larrubia, 2008), others argue that competitiveness should not rely on CAP subsidies. Following the guidelines set by the World Bank and the OECD, they argue that agricultural activity should be seen as competitively viable when it is able to sustain itself without external support (Galdeano-Gómez *et al.*, 2013).[10]

Third, the intensification of production is often the only strategy available to the production sector to try to recuperate the added value lost due to their subordinate position in the supply chain. However, the hidden social costs generated by a strategy of intensification are evident in the need to intensify labour that ultimately translates to self-exploitation or exploitation of the workforce, or both. Furthermore, it requires a deeper exploitation of natural resources. Taking into account an approach that defends social, economic and ecological sustainability, it can only be concluded that the current situation in Andalusia most closely resembles what Marsden (2012) has called a 'chaotic neo-productivism'. In the face of a food security crisis, this trend is being created under the 'bio-economic model' and the new, highly contradictory, political rhetoric of 'sustainable intensification' (Marsden, 2012). As Marsden obverses, if sustainable intensification is supported by the argument that environmental costs can be reduced by the control of nature through science, in practice what is produced is an 'illusion of control' (Stuart, 2008). Crises such as the *E. coli 0157: H7* outbreak in 2006 in the Californian spinach crop illustrate the fallacy of attempts to control nature in these systems of intensive industrial food production (Stuart, 2008).

The increasingly prominent campaigns by the horticultural sector and public institutions, in which agricultural intensification is presented through discourses about scientific research, ecological cultivation and biological control, create the notion that intensive agriculture in Andalusia is increasingly safe and sustainable. Examples of how such discourses promote economic health values of the cultivation of fruit in greenhouses is evident in such activities as the 'Interstrawberry against Cancer' campaign, started in 2015 by the Andalusian Interprofessional Strawberry Growers Association (Interfresa) and the Spanish Association Against Cancer, or the research carried out in the Coexphal (Almerian Organization of Fruit and Vegetable Producers) laboratory under the headings 'taste and health' and 'food safety'.

On the other hand, although the specialization of quality products can be considered as a way to increase the profitability of growers, numerous studies show how supply chains use certification, quality and food safety standards as a strategy to exert increased control over the market and producers (Konefal *et al.*, 2005; Bonanno and Cavalcanti, 2012; Ransom *et al.*, 2013). It is within this reality that the cultivators of Andalusia find themselves trapped.

## 6.4 Transnational migrations, globalization of capital and localization of work

In her analysis of the political construction of the labour market in the California strawberry fields, Wells (1996) connects global dynamics with a micro-social perspective. Through her analysis, she explains how, within a capitalist structure, politics, industry and local context exercise influence over the labour market. Californian model has come to occupy a central role in agricultural development in the rest of world and it has been evident in Europe since the 1980s. Related practices include the increased flexibilization, temporality and diversification of recruitment channels, the internationalization and fragmentation of the workforce and the contracting of migrant labour (Pugliese, 1991). Similar to the Californian case (Thomas, 1985), gender and the legal status of labourers are particularly important in the social organization of work in the intensive agricultural industry of Southern Europe. As explained below, and as demonstrated by other studies (Berlan, 1987), this political construction of labour market is accompanied by a proliferation of socially unsustainable conditions.

A brief look at the evolution and substitution of the labour force in intensive agriculture in Andalusia reveals that the labour market is structured through processes of internationalization, fragmentation, ethnicization and feminization. With the expansion of production in the 1970s and the 1980s and subsequent inadequacy of the family-based workforce, it was the Andalusian day labourer that offset labour requirements in the strawberry fields. This period was mostly characterized by temporary migrations. The Andalusian day labourer families recall the difficulties and the terrible living and working conditions that they suffered during these migrations. The lack of decent lodging and places in schools, the absence of labour regulation and collective bargaining agreements and the payment of low wages were just some of problems that they had to face every season. These issues were the primary motivations behind some of biggest ever demonstrations and strikes in this agricultural sector in the 1980s. The members of the *Sindicato de Obreros del Campo* (Field Workers' Union), without doubt the largest union in Andalusian agriculture during the final third of the last century, have often identified the precariousness of work and life as the main reasons why the Andalusian day labourer families began to abandon agricultural work.

On the other hand, growers and farm managers usually offer a different explanation about why a huge number of Andalusian day labourers preferred to abandon agricultural labour. They usually link this mobility to the economic growth and development that Andalusia was experiencing at the time. In their descriptions, they compare the previous generations of local labourers that left to occupy the jobs that Swiss, German and French nationals would not do in their own countries, because they were too hard or poorly paid, with the foreign migrants that arrive in the region nowadays: 'Fortunately, the lack of Andalusian workers gives the impression that the country is improving' (President of the Organization of Strawberry Producers, Freshuelva). This type of argument coincides with the discourse of 'Andalusian modernization' disseminated by the regional government, which maintains that it has gone from being a land of emigration to a territory that receives immigrants. This change is interpreted in terms of progress.

The arrival of the first foreign migrants in the strawberry fields of Huelva dates to around the middle of the 1990s. They were largely from the Maghreb region, principally from Morocco. At the end of the 1990s, new migrants from Mauritania and sub-Saharan Africa, specifically Senegal, Mali, Nigeria and the Ivory Coast began to work in the sector. In both cases, these migrants were largely young males, with and without work permits, and with a high degree of geographical and occupational mobility. The migrations of male African workers would later be accompanied by waves of female workers from Eastern Europe and Morocco.

In the 2000s, a new recruitment practice was adopted, based on a Seasonal Agricultural Workers Programme known as *contratacion en origen* (literally: 'Contracting labourers in [the country of] origin'; see Hellio, this volume).[11] Following a number of pilot programs, this was fully implemented in 2002 and soon became one of the largest seasonal workers programmes in Europe, deploying on average 35,000 migrant women per season during its peak period. The demand for women (middle-aged with children) from Eastern Europe and Morocco – through the *contratos en origen* – reflects the rapid feminization of migration and labour in the region, in addition to segmentation on the basis of class, ethnicity and nationality:

> Why women and not men? Well it's very simple. First the women have more resistance than the men. Women have more capacity to suffer than men. Women are more submissive than men. Women are more selective than men, more curious. You're just better than us!'
>
> (Francisco López, strawberry grower)

According to the producers, the labourers recruited through the seasonal programme are 'poor people who only come to work and do not complain'. Thus, 'they give us fewer problems completing the strawberry harvest':

> Thanks to the *contratos en origen* things are working out. If all the foreigners in Palos now had their papers the season might as well stop right away, because they would say 'Antonio, there's little fruit here, I'm going to go to Lerida for the oranges, or to Murcia for the tomatoes or to Almeria'. If they have their papers you can't stop them. What can you do? You have to get the strawberries going. Instead, with the *contratos en origen* they know that they can't leave until the boss says that the harvest is over. That's the

advantage. [. . .] It's like an insurance policy, it's worth it, especially when the year is good.

(Antonio Fernández, strawberry grower)

For example, if there is no work tomorrow, Antonio tells us that there is no work tomorrow. He tells us in the afternoon when the work finishes, or, for example, yesterday we finished this parcel of land and Antonio says, ′ok, go home`, at one o'clock, we worked four hours.

(Dorina Craciunescu, Romanian woman worker)

In her analysis of the work of female migrants in the agricultural industry of South Africa, Johnston (2007) notes how the demands of the employers structure opportunities for migrants and how they shape the systems that regulate the 'fluxes' in labour market demand. These preferences cannot be explained simply by cost reduction (Johnston, 2007). In a similar way, the demand by Andalusian producers for a migrant labour force with particular profiles is based on a complex set of social, economic and cultural dynamics, which include the need for an available and flexible labour force of temporary and casual workers, work performance and capacity, vulnerability resulting from life circumstances and the constraints of legal, social and labour rights, the degree of conflict with trade unions as well as stereotypes and cultural values. In the strawberry fields, large numbers of migrant women are subject to the conditions imposed by the system of *contratacion en origen.* This prevents their organization in trade unions to claim labour rights. Middle-aged women with children who guarantee hard work, discipline and a return to their countries of origin at the end of the contract are favoured. Similarly, racism, prejudice and cultural distance mean that Eastern Europeans are often favoured over the supposedly problematic Moroccan men.

The racialization and ethnicization of the global workforce supply channels has become, therefore, a fundamental instrument in the development of a fragmented, hierarchical group of workers (Preibisch and Binford, 2007). Of course, the *contratos en origen* are not the only means of recruiting the workforce. Within the intensive agriculture industry in Andalusia a number of different workforce and recruitment management models coexist: traditional forms of recruitment based on verbal agreements or contracts signed on arrival, where the migratory networks (families, friends and neighbours) play a fundamental role; recruitment of migrants in their country of origin via quotas, established within the bilateral migratory framework; informal methods of recruiting undocumented workers through contacts or in the public spaces near the holdings or in nearby towns.

The use of different recruitment strategies and the trend to feminization and ethnicization of the workforce should be understood as strategies on the part of farmers to be competitive in the global agri-food markets and to guarantee the social reproduction of this productive model. As different empirical studies have shown, these strategies for increasing production, besides representing an added cost for producers, have substantial social and labour costs for the female workers and temporary migrant workers (Barrientos *et al.*, 1999; Deere, 2005; Carton de Grammont and Lara, 2010; Reigada, 2011; Pedreño *et al.*, 2014; Gertel and Sippel, 2014). In this regard, the work of women in the packaging plants (native and migrant) and in the fields (migrant day labourers) stands out. Working days without fixed hours and a necessity to be constantly available to work become the daily norm during the peak production periods:

> Depending on the production that comes in, the senior women would tell us, 'right, today you're on until seven', 'today until eight'. But you go at whatever time and you don't know when you'll be back. During the peak period, we spend sometimes three weeks working between 12 and 15 hours a day. I can't do that much, I can't do 12 hours, so I had to leave, I had to give up the work. It's a lot of hours, with back pain, then my legs started to hurt a lot. I had one month of the season left, of course I wanted to stay, but it was too much. You can work for 12 hours if you know that the next day you can rest, or that you're only going to do 6 hours, but if the company needs it . . .. But today 12 hours, you get home completely worn-out, you just feel like lying down. However early you get up, you have your food and then you're off again doing twelve hours. For me it was very hard. That's why these people prefer immigrants, because they get no food, no home, nothing at all.
>
> (Carmen Moreno, Andalusian packaging plant woman worker)

The variability of prices and the commitment to a differentiated product offer (such as a wide range of varieties, formats and brands) goes hand in hand with an increase in labour flexibility that manifests itself at two levels: the type of work, on one hand, and the hours, rhythm and volume of work, on the other. This results in pressure on wage labourers to intensify the pace of work and to increase productivity in order to compensate for lower prices:

> Some orders, like the heart-shaped strawberry boxes for Valentine's day, aren't worth it. You have to pack and cushion them very carefully, although it's true that they pay you one euro extra. But there are people who say it's not worth it. The same goes for the ones you have to pick with a little stalk, for the English market [. . .] If you're able to collect 20 crates with the other crops, then with this way you do 15 or less. There is another very small tub that you use to collect all the strawberries of the same size. There are some women who do this quickly, others who don't . . . There are women who sort the strawberries correctly; they pick the right ones from the bush. There are others, however, who have to spend time afterwards sorting them out.
>
> (Andrés Vázquez, strawberry grower)

> Last year the big European companies bought a lot of industrial strawberries from China, Huelva and Morocco. They overloaded the market with industrial strawberries. They had all the cold storage warehouses full, so the price of the industrial strawberry fell so much that I said that at that price I wouldn't harvest them on my farm, because it wasn't worth it. Because I have to get

tough on the workers, 'how many crates have you filled? Well you haven't earned even part of your wage'. [. . .] In the end, the only thing I managed to get was stress and I didn't earn anything.

(Francisco López, strawberry grower)

When discussing the reasons for the feminization of these 'non-traditional' agricultural sectors, Barrientos (1999) notes that to the extent that it is insecure and unstable work, employers use this temporary female workforce engaged in insecure and unstable work as a 'buffer' against the risks presented by the sector. As such, it is the women who have to adapt to the varying intensity and volume of work, depending on the fluctuations in production or the market.

Moreover, we have to take into consideration the effects that strategies based on competing through quality have on the work. As different studies have revealed, quality certification programmes, that promote 'best practices' in production, have negative consequences for the workforce, particularly concerning the work and production schedule, pay, conditions, labour controls, increased levels of temporary work and sub-contracting (Konefal *et al.*, 2005; Carton de Grammont and Lara, 2010; Bonanno and Cavalcanti, 2012; Moraes and Cutillas, 2014).

Such an approach encourages us to view labour migration as a phenomenon conditioned by the internal dynamics of intensive agriculture, which, in turn, is framed by the network of interdependencies generated by the socioeconomic system of the receiving country.

## 6.5 Conclusions: an unsustainable model

The features of intensive agriculture that have been addressed in this chapter show how the idea that Andalusia represents the 'California of Southern Europe' is inaccurate. On the contrary, they reinforce the notion that this region of southern Spain is an 'enclave economy' (Delgado, 2012). The contemporary situation supports the studies conducted more than two decades ago, which argued that the agricultural specialization that triggered the growth of regional economies, such as California, was not comparable to the Andalusian case (Lacomba, 1997). Rather, it is evident that far from being a means of economic and social development of the Mediterranean regions, such specialization has reaffirmed these areas' subordinate economic positions, where endemic unemployment and precarious work now prevail.

The unbalanced relationships established between agri-food systems, the environment and different regions are reflected in the role played by family farms in the development of modern agriculture and, in particular, their ongoing function within the capitalist system. In this sense, a series of contradictions stand out, namely, those that arise out of the integration of this model in the global supply chains, which impose crop varieties, packaging formats and quality certifications, production and working methods, commercial and financial partners, input and product prices.

However, the confrontation between small agricultural producers and large multinational retail chains should be considered in light of the complexities of structural hierarchies in the global food chain. The small producer's self-identity when faced with the large capitalist company, and the strength of grievance against the power of distribution chains, has contributed to a diminish the asymmetric relationship between work and capital, in the collective imaginary of these communities. Here resides one of the great paradoxes and tensions of this model: although these small producers use the term 'employer', they often see themselves less as business people and identify more with their subordinate position as small farmers. As such, the perception of landowning Andalusians as socially distinct from the day labourers they employ acquires certain degree of opacity. The emphasis they place on hard work and commitment to the farm, at all cost, has led to an almost total undervaluing of one of the most fundamental pillars that supports these enterprises: migrant wage labour.

Along with these above points, the analysis has noted the need to consider the relationship that has been established between capital mobility, agricultural products and the movement of workers. Within a framework of the spatial reconfiguration of production and the spatial division of labour, the acknowledgement of these relationships can help us to properly understand the social dynamics of globally subordinate agricultural enclaves. Hence, we are obliged to look at the confluence of internal and international migrations in the intensive agriculture of Andalusia, which have generated a multiplicity of unsustainable social and regional issues over the last 40 to 50 years.

The chapter has shown that these problems are not only to be found in the dysfunctional elements of the system, and which can be resolved simply by implementing best practice in production, work and land management. Instead, changes in the structural foundations of the model are required. A reordering of priorities that situates sustainability and dignified living and working standards for all social groups at the centre of the model would require that the agri-food system address the fundamental incompatibility between sustainable social reproduction and the accumulation of capital. This contradiction reveals how the neoliberal agri-food regime is based on a process of 'accumulation by dispossession' (McMichael, 2011).

A critical assessment of intensive agriculture in Andalusia must not lose sight, however, of the double dimension that Marsden (2012) observed – the problem of the present lack of sustainability vis-à-vis the potential for agriculture to achieve overall sustainability at a local and regional level. This point of view connects agriculture within a global framework of economics, ecology and communities. As such, this localized view of agriculture must be understood in relation to the principle of food sovereignty, which is substantially reformulated by local applications of rights, in line with social and ecological requirements (Patel, 2009; McMichael, 2011).

## Notes

1 The concept of 'enclave' is used to refer to agricultural regions connected with global production networks. This global scale drives legal, political, economic and cultural transformations in the region. These transformations are promoted and oriented not only by 'global' companies and institutions, but also by economic and political actors in the region itself (see Moraes *et al.*, 2012).

2 This study (2005–2009), financed by the Andalusia regional government, draws on a total of 83 in-depth interviews and participant observation. In order to conduct fieldwork, the researcher lived in the strawberry-growing region for a period of one year and nine months (2006–2007). The analysis does not contemplate the changes in the composition of the labour market that took place after these dates, and therefore does not consider the current phase of economic recession. The study of intensive agriculture in Andalusia was part of the research project 'Social sustainability of the new agricultural enclaves: Spain and Mexico (ENCLAVES), directed by Andrés Pedreño and financed by the Spanish Ministry of Science and Innovation (2012–2014, CSO2011-28511). This study was also made possible thanks to the programme 'Contrato Postdoctoral del V Plan Propio de la Universidad de Sevilla'.

3 Apart from similarities in geography and climate, a comparative study has noted that the economic trajectories of both territories are clearly divergent, from the point of view of access to credit and to an integrated market and the existence of a developed transport network (Carter *et al.*, 1992).

4 The concept of a food regime makes reference to the whole set of international relations that configure the accumulation of capital in the system of food production and consumption (Friedmann and McMichael, 1989). The first food regime includes the period from the eighteenth century until the Second World War. The second one includes the period up to the economic crisis of 1973 and the third food regime corresponds with the subsequent development of a globalized agrifood system (see Corrado in this volume).

5 During this period, that ran from the 1960s to the 1980s, four main areas in southern Spain were focused on greenhouse cultivation: western Almeria, which is known for growing vegetables; the coastal area of Huelva, dedicated to the cultivation of strawberries; the coast of Granada, which is largely focused on tropical fruits; and Cádiz, oriented toward the growth and export of flowers.

6 In addition, finance has become in recent years another means to exert vertical control over production (Burch and Lawrence, 2009; Iakson, 2014).

7 In order to guarantee confidentiality pseudonyms have been used for all informants.

8 In contrast, brokers in the north of Brazil have assumed the role of intermediary between the supermarkets and the producer, notionally guaranteeing quality and protecting companies such as Tesco, Carrefour or WallMart from direct interactions with local actors and hence concealing the concentration of power (Bonanno and Cavalcanti, 2012).

9 Coordinator of Farmers' and Livestock Breeders' Organizations (*Coordinadora de Organizaciones de Agricultores y Ganaderos*).

10 The critique that the protectionist measures of the CAP constitute effectively subsidized dumping (McMichael, 2011) with a consequent impact on the agriculture of the South, points to a very different perspective, similar to the food sovereignty proposal and in opposition to the guidelines of the OECD and the World Bank.

11 The third major shift in migration flows, not contemplated in this chapter, has occurred during the current economic crisis, which has seen the return of Andalusian day labourers from other sectors.

## References

Barrientos, S. (1999). 'Ethical trade and gender: Exports of non-traditional horticultural products', in *United Nations Conference on Trade and Development*. New York/Genova.

Barrientos, S., Bee, A., Matear, A., and Vogel, I. (1999). *Women and Agribusiness. Working Miracles in the Chilean Fruit Export Sector*. Basingstoke: Macmillan Press.

Berlan, J.P. (1987). 'La agricultura mediterránea y el mercado del trabajo: ¿Una California para Europa?' *Agricultura y Sociedad* 42: 233–245.

Bonanno, A. and Cavalcanti, J.S. (2012). 'Globalization, food quality and labor: The case of grape production in North-Eastern Brazil', *International Journal of Sociology of Agriculture and Food* 19(1): 37–55.

Bonanno, A., Busch, L., Firedland, W., Gouveia, L. and Mingione, E. (1994). *From Columbus to ConAgra: The Globalisation of Food and Agriculture.* Lawrence: University Press of Kansas.

Burch, D. and Lawrence, G. (2009). 'Towards a third food regime: Behind the transformation', *Agriculture and Human Values* 26: 267–279.

Camarero, L. (2014). 'Trabajadores del campo y familias de la tierra: Instantáneas del tránsito agrario', *International Seminar Migrant Labor and Social Sustainability of Global Agri-food Chain,* 5–7 November. University of Murcia.

Camarero, L., Sampedro, R., and Vicente-Mazariegos, J.L. (2002). 'Los horticultores: Una identidad en transición', *AREAS. Revista de Ciencias Sociales* 22: 43–69.

Carpintero, O. and Naredo, J.M. (2006). 'Sobre la evolución de los balances energéticos de la agricultura española, 1950–2000', *Historia Agraria* 40: 531–554.

Carter, S.B., Ranson, R.L. and Sutch, R. (1992). *Agriculture, Savings, and Growth: Conjunctures on the California and Mediterranean Experiences.* Riverside: University of California.

Carton de Grammont, H. and Lara, S. (2010). 'Productive restructuring and 'standardization' in Mexican horticulture: Consequences for labour', *Journal of Agrarian Change* 10(2): 228–250.

Deere, C.D. (2005). The feminization of agriculture? Economic restructuring in rural Latin America. Geneva: *United Nations Research-Institute for Social Development (UNRISD).*

Delgado, M. (2002). *Andalucía en la otra cara de la globalización.* Sevilla: Mergablum.

Delgado, M. (2012). 'La economía andaluza durante las tres últimas décadas. 1981–2011', in C. Jiménez and J. Hurtado (eds) *Andalucía: identidades culturales y dinámicas sociales,* pp. 87–122. Sevilla: Aconcagua.

Friedland, W. (2004). 'Agrifood globalization and commodity systems', *International Journal of Sociology of Agriculture and Food* 12: 1–12.

Friedland, W. Barton, A. and Thomas, R. (1978). *Manufacturing Green Gold. The Conditions and Social Consequences of Lettuce Harvest Mechanization.* Davis: University of California.

Friedmann, H. and McMichael, P. (1989). 'Agriculture and the state system: The rise and decline of national agricultures, 1870 to the present', *Sociologia Ruralis* 29(2): 93–117.

Galdeano-Gómez, E., Aznar-Sánchez, J.A. and Pérez-Mesa, J.C. (2013). 'Sustainability dimensions related to agricultural-based development: The experience of 50 years of intensive farming in Almería, Spain', *International Journal of Agricultural Sustainability* 11(2): 125–143.

Gavira, L. (2002). *Andalucía sobreviviendo en la globalización.* Sevilla: Mergablum.

Gertel, J. and Sippel, S.R. (eds) (2014). *Seasonal Workers in Mediterranean Agriculture. The Social Costs of Eating Fresh.* London: Routledge.

Iakson, S.R. (2014). 'Food and finance: the financial transformation of agro-food supply chains', *Journal of Peasant Studies* 41(5): 749–775.

Johnston, D. (2007). 'Who needs immigrant farm workers? A South African case study', *Journal of Agrarian Change* 7(4): 494–525.

Konefal, J., Mascarenhas, M. and Hatanaka, M. (2005). 'Governance in the global agro-food system: Backlighting the role of transnational supermarket chains', *Agriculture and Human Values* 22: 291–302.

Lacomba, J.A. (1997). 'La agricultura mediterránea andaluza y California, de finales del XIX a principios del XX: permanencias y cambios en una fase de transformaciones', in J. Morilla *et al.* (eds) *Impactos exteriores sobre el mundo rural mediterráneo: del Imperio Romano a nuestros días*, pp. 473–494. Madrid: Ministerio de Agricultura, Alimentación y Medio Ambiente.

Larrubia, R. (2008). 'El sudeste andaluz: incertidumbres comerciales de una agricultura productivista'. *Estudios Geográficos*, LXIX: 265, 577–607.

Marsden, T. (2012). 'Third natures? Reconstituting space through placemaking strategies for sustainability', *International Journal of Sociology of Agriculture and Food* 19(2):, 257–274.

Martín, E. (1995). 'El cultivo del fresón en la zona de Palos y Moguer: Cambios socioeconómicos y sectores sociales implicados', *AESTUARIA. Revista de Investigación*, 3, 31–55.

McMichael, P. (1996). 'Globalization: myths and realities'. *Rural Sociology*, 61(1): 25–55.

McMichael, P. (2011). 'Food system sustainability: Questions of environmental governance in the new world (dis)order', *Global Environmental Change* 21: 804–812.

Moraes, N. and Cutillas, I. (2014). 'Nuevos dispositivos de regulación transnacional: un análisis sobre los estándares de calidad y responsabilidad social y su impacto en los enclaves globales agrícolas', in Pedreño, A. (dir.) *De cadenas, migrantes y jornaleros. Los territorios rurales en las cadenas globales agroalimentarias*, pp. 195–218. Madrid: Talasa.

Moraes, N., Gadea, E., Pedreño, A., and de Castro, C. (2012). 'Enclaves globales agrícolas y migraciones de trabajo: convergencias globales y regulaciones transnacionales', *Política y Sociedad* 49(1): 13–34.

Naredo, J.M. (2004). *La evolución de la agricultura en España (1940–2000)*. Granada: Universidad de Granada.

Patel, R. (2009). 'Food sovereignty', *Journal of Peasant Studies* 36(3): 663–706

Pedreño, A., Gadea, E. and Castro, C. (2014). 'Labor, gender and political conflicts in the global agri-food system: The case of agri-export model in Murcia, Spain', in A. Bonanno and J.S. Cavalcanti (eds) *Labor Relations in Global Food*, pp. 193–214. Bingley, UK: Emerald Publishing.

Ploeg, J.D. van der (2009). *The New Peasantries: Struggles for Autonomy and Sustainability in an Era of Empire and Globalization*. London: Earthscan.

Preibisch, K. and Binford, L. (2007). 'Interrogating racialized global labour supply: An exploration of the racial/national replacement of foreign agricultural workers in Canada', *Canadian Review of Sociology and Anthropology* 44(1): 5–36.

Pugliese, E. (1991). 'Agriculture and the new division of labor', in W. Friedland (ed.) *Towards a New Political Economy of Agriculture*, pp. 137–150. Boulder, CO: Westview Press.

Ransom, E., C. Bain, and V. Higgins (2013). 'Private agri-food standards: Supply chains and the governance of standards', *International Journal of Sociology of Agriculture and Food* 20(2): 147–154.

Reigada, A. (2011). 'Agrarian restructuring, labor migration and feminization of labor in Andalucía (Spain)', *Agricultura, Sociedad y Desarrollo* 8(1): 19–43.

Rosberry, W. (1996). 'The rise of yuppie coffees and the reimagination of class in the United States', *American Anthropologist* 98(4): 762–775.

Stuart, D. (2008). 'The illusion of control: Industrialized agriculture, nature, and food safety', *Agriculture and Human Values* 25: 177–181.

Thomas, R.J. (1985). *Citizenship, Gender and Work. Social Organization of Industrial Agriculture.* Los Angeles: University of California Press.

Verdier, M. (2006). *Reflexiones en torno a la situación actual del sector fresero de Huelva.* Huelva: Freshuelva (unpublished).

Wells, M. (1996). *Strawberry Fields. Politics, Class, and Work in California Agriculture.* Ithaca, NY: Cornell University Press.

# 7 The citrus fruit crisis

## Value chains and 'just in time' migrants in Rosarno (Italy) and Valencia (Spain)

*Anna Mary Garrapa*

### 7.1 Introduction

This chapter analyses and compares two rural areas in two different countries in Mediterranean Europe, the Gioia Tauro Plain in the region of Calabria in southern Italy and the autonomous community of Valencia in Spain. These two areas share a number of similarities with regards their agricultural production: they both possess intensive fruit and vegetable cultivations targeted at large agri-food distribution chains, and extensive use is made of low-skilled and seasonal immigrant labour. Rosarno[1] is a small town in the Gioia Tauro Plain, which appeared in the national and international press following a revolt in 2010. This brought to light the degrading living and working conditions of African migrant labourers, employed in local farms mainly as citrus fruit pickers during the winter period (Corrado, 2011; Pugliese, 2012). Since this event, thousands of mostly sub-Saharan Africans continue to spend the winter season in emergency tents erected by local administrations and religious institutions, shanty towns and dilapidated farm buildings. From November to December they pick clementines, informally or semi-formally; in other words either with false contracts or contracts which, for tax evasion purposes, declare a smaller number of days than those actually worked. January and February are orange-picking months, although there is less work and many are left unemployed. In the Gioia Tauro Plain there has been, in fact a continuous reduction in the harvesting of citrus fruit for industrial processing, a general lowering of prices for citrus fruit directed at fresh produce markets and the consequent abandonment, in some cases, of cultivated land.

Since the late 1990s, numerous authors have analysed the crisis of citrus fruit production in the Gioia Tauro Plain, in comparison with the same industry in Spain, pointing out how the economic problems were 'entirely Italian, and caused by protectionist and welfare policies, which applied European regulations in such a way as to provoke paradoxical structural distortions' (Cavazzani and Sivini, 1997a, pp. 7–8). However, recently the crisis in the sector has also appeared to affect citrus growing in Valencia, which has been long perceived to be a 'virtuous' example and an important competitor of the Gioia Tauro Plain. It is for this reason that it is particularly appropriate and useful to carry out a detailed comparison of the organization and labour relations in the production chains of the two areas.

Many recent sociological contributions on the questions of migration and agricultural labour in Mediterranean Europe and Latin America refer to the global dynamics of goods and capital markets, and include analyses of labour relations, social and political forms of discrimination and the poor standard living conditions in different local areas (Morice and Michalon, 2008; Colloca and Corrado, 2013; Pedreño Cánovas, 2014a). Inspired by the world-systems approach (Hopkins and Wallerstein, 1994), research on global commodity chains (Gereffi and Korzeniewicz, 1994), global value chains (Gereffi *et al.*, 2005) and global production networks (Henderson *et al.*, 2002), and specifically in relation to agri-food chains (Callegari and Valentini, 2014; Cesaretti and Green, 2006), all tend to focus their analysis on the circulation and exchange of goods, the latest changes in distribution models and the spread of quality standards of production (Lee *et al.*, 2012). Some studies and debates refer to the concept of 'food empire' (Ploeg, 2008) and outline the periodization of 'food regimes' (McMichael, 2005), thus contributing to updating the analysis of current forms of accumulation and mobility of agri-food capital (Friedland, 2001).

However, to date, relatively few studies have attempted to analyse the interconnected changes in agri-food chains and labour relations (Barndt, 2002; Bonanno and Cavalcanti, 2014); and fewer still have directly looked at rural areas in Mediterranean Europe (Gertel and Sippel, 2014; Pedreño Cánovas, 2014b).

In this chapter I will draw on the analytical concepts of global commodity chains and global value chains in order to observe the distribution of power among the various protagonists of each economic transaction and market deal. With the aim of combining a focus on capital and labour, I will examine the various stages of the citrus fruit chain (Figure 7.1), starting from local production and leading up to the final distribution of the fruit on the world market. In particular, I will consider the fresh food market, and how this sits in relation to the considerable decline of fruit production for industrial processing and the closure of processing plants in Calabria, and to the specialization of the Valencian Community in producing citrus fruit for export. I will reconstruct the main processes that have contributed to a citrus fruit crisis in both areas. In doing so, I will observe how the transformation of agri-food capital, symptomatic of a more general reorganization of capital, has influenced changes in the citrus fruit chain with regards the processes of capital circulation and the social relations of production that take place specifically in rural areas.

The two areas of study are markedly different in terms of area size, population and degree of urbanization. The Gioia Tauro Plain is made up of 33 municipalities, which are similar from a geographical, social and productive point of view. The Plain extends for 20 kilometres at its widest point and 30 kilometres at its longest point running north to south. Olive groves predominate in the area, but along the coastal zone there are large tracts of land devoted to citrus fruit. The main orange-growing areas are located around the towns of Taurianova, Rosarno, Laureana di Borrello and Rizziconi, while clementine orchards are found principally in the municipalities of Rosarno, Candidoni and San Ferdinando (Facoltà di Agraria di Reggio Calabria, 2012).

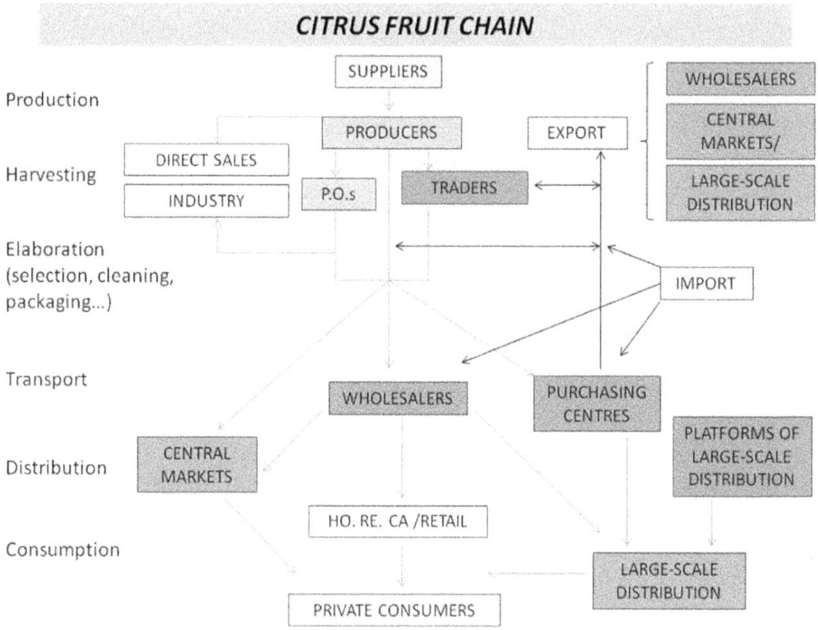


*Figure 7.1* Citrus fruit chain.

Source: own elaboration of data, 2014.

The autonomous community of Valencia (also known locally as País Valenciá) includes the provinces of Castellón, Alicante and Valencia, and is composed of a total of 34 sub-regions *(comarcas)*. This area stretches for 400 kilometres along the Mediterranean coast and extends inland for about 60 to 70 kilometres. The selected area for this study includes the city of Valencia and a series of surrounding towns and villages belonging to the region's citrus belt that spreads along the coast.

According to data of the Italian National Institute of Statistics (Istat) for 2011, the area of the Gioia Tauro Plain had an overall resident population of 164,098 people. The Spanish study area includes the regional capital of Valencia, which, according to the latest official statistics on 1 January 2013, had 794,228 inhabitants, while the surrounding *comarcas* of the *Horta Nord, Horta Oest* and *Horta Sud* have a combined population of 749,325 (Ajuntament de Valencia, 2013; Facoltà di Agraria di Reggio Calabria, 2012; Generalitat Valenciana, 2012).

This comparison between the Gioia Tauro Plain and the Valencian Community is based primarily upon qualitative analysis conducted in the two areas between January 2013 and January 2014, which included extended periods of observation, semi-structured interviews (about 80 in total), focus groups among employers and workers, and participation in the activities of local associations, in order to reconstruct, on the one hand, social and labour relations and market exchanges within the agri-food chain, and, on the other, the living and working conditions of migrant agricultural labourers.

## 7.2 The organization of production

In both areas, citrus production is fragmented: there is a prevalence of small farms measuring on average one hectare of Utilized Agricultural Area (UAA). In the Gioia Tauro Plain, farms under 5 hectares constitute 86 per cent of the total number of farms and account for 45 per cent of the area planted with citrus fruit (Istat, 2012). Similarly, in the Valencian Community, 86 per cent of farms are under this size and cover 41 per cent of the citrus-growing area (INE, 2009).[2] Meanwhile, in both cases, there are very few farms with more than 50 hectares: 0.4 per cent of all farms in the Gioia Tauro Plain (corresponding to 8.2 per cent of the total area dedicated to citrus fruit), and 1 per cent of farms in the Valencian Community (which account for 16 per cent of the citrus-growing area).

There are two common groups of actors involved in agriculture in the two areas. The first group is made up of small farmers: elderly retired owners, who were once full-time farmers, and younger generations of owners involved in other sectors, who dedicate only part of their time to citrus growing. The second group is composed of medium and large farmers who are often members of producer organizations (POs).

In both areas the small farmer has traditionally held the double role of day labourer and owner of a small plot of land. This small property has been pieced together over the years through successive acquisitions, and sometimes has been subdivided later through inheritance. During the 1980s and 1990s, increasing numbers of people abandoned agriculture to study or to look for work in other sectors. In Italy this movement took the form of migration towards central and northern Italy or to other countries, while in the case of the Valencian Community, this mainly took place within the region itself, especially following the construction and tourism boom along the coastal areas. In the Valencian Community the figure of the small landowner employed in various types of paid work still partly exists, especially in cooperatives and in certain skilled jobs, such as pruning or chemical treatment. Over recent years, in both countries there has been a growing return to agricultural work among the local autochthonous population: in the face of economic recession and subsequent redundancies in other sectors, agriculture has represented a safe-haven asset for those who have always maintained a contact with the land.

On the whole, however, there are relatively few professional farmers among the small and medium landowners. In both areas, the majority of this group comprises people who continue to own land but are no longer directly involved in cultivation, or individuals for whom agriculture is more of a leisure activity, since their main job is in other sectors. The reasons for keeping land are similar in both areas: either because it is considered a safe-haven asset or due to a sentimental attachment to family property. Occasionally, landowners strategically plant a particular variety of citrus fruit with the hope of ensuring a margin of profit or in anticipation of a general upturn in the market.

The situations in Calabria and Valencia start to significantly diverge when we turn our attention to the production strategy adopted for the selling of fruit, which is evident in the organization of fruit picking. In the Gioia Tauro Plain there are two principal ways in which business deals are made and harvests are managed: either the fruit is sold to private traders when it is still on the tree, according to what is called 'in block', or else the producer undertakes to directly deliver the harvested product to private warehouses of the producer organizations, where it is paid for 'by weight'. In the case of Valencia, on the other hand, the fruit is sold strictly when it is still on the tree and the harvest is traditionally the responsibility of the trader, who arranges for the necessary seasonal workforce. Moreover, where the citrus fruit grower is a member of a cooperative, it is this organization that is responsible for the picking stage.

As far as the larger producers are concerned, their roles are less clearly defined and more closely connected to the selling stage. In both areas, the large producers are also owners of large warehouses where fruit is packed, thus their agricultural activity is combined with packaging and commerce. These producers act as private companies or as part of a PO where they often have a majority voice.

According to the findings from my fieldwork, the POs very often represent formal instruments for satisfying bureaucratic regulations set out by the Common Agricultural Policy (CAP), rather than true associations of farmers who have grouped together to concentrate the offer and lower costs. In reality these are private organizations that have grown around large traders and farmers and who get smaller producers to join; this way they can receive its benefits and manage the funding received, for example, for modernizing infrastructure, refurbishing warehouses and purchasing the very costly machinery needed to meet the requirements of the big supermarket chains (ISMEA, 2008, 2011). In such cases, the fruit picking is organized according to economy of scale criteria, which I discuss in greater depth below. We can see a process of aggregation of the offer, which is not brought about by the farmers themselves, but is rather caused by the growing presence of large traders in local agricultural production. In fact, both areas have witnessed an emerging trend of delocalized cultivation, whereby producers seek to extend the trading calendar through out of season harvests and to produce in areas that offer lower costs or possess land better suited to the productive facilities of a large landowner. Such companies have invested in other parts of Italy and Spain, for example Basilicata and Andalusia respectively, or even in other producing countries.

## 7.3 The commercial stage and its intermediaries

The citrus chain follows a number of intermediate stages, from harvest through to cleaning, selection, packaging and delivery. The operators involved in these processes are many and include private traders, wholesalers, producers organized in cooperatives, POs and intermediaries who take part in different commercial operations. These various operators are in constant contact with each other, exchanging services and goods, so in reality their roles are less clearly defined than the above categories suggest.

The gradual shift towards distribution techniques based on the North American large store model, which began to take hold in Spain and Italy from the 1990s onwards, has brought about a structural change in the business stage in both citrus-growing areas. Local traders are now distinguished by a new boundary line: some make agreements with the big national and multinational chains of supermarkets, while others deal with wholesalers and intermediaries of general markets, in the same country or abroad.

In the Gioia Tauro Plain, traders can be divided into three basic categories: 'small', 'medium' and 'large'. In the case of the small and medium dealers, the search for products for purchase takes place through informal contacts and sometimes through an intermediary who, for a fee, helps conclude the deal between producer and trader. In the Italian literature on agricultural production, this prominent figure is often referred to as a *sensale* (Piselli, 1990), which is similar to the *corredor* in the citrus-growing area in Valencia. The biggest dealers in Calabria, as noted earlier, are also large producers, who, together with other small farmers, have formed associations, sometimes dubbed producer organizations. Due to the extreme fragmentation of local production and the need to meet big supermarket chain orders, producers have inevitably resorted to the aforementioned purchasing and harvesting methods, with a prevalence towards delivering 'by weight'. Where dealers are part of a PO, the organization employs a certain number of workers, mostly on a temporary basis, to do the picking for all members, in addition to other workers who are employed in packing the fruit. Member producers can choose either to use PO workers or organize the picking themselves. Usually, member producers prefer the second option, as described in the previous section, and the corresponding sum is paid according to the quantity delivered. In addition, an extra quantity of fruit is bought from the warehouse by third parties, mainly 'by weight'.

As far as the sale is concerned, many small dealers still trade in modest quantities of citrus fruit: between two and three hundred tonnes per season are bought, prepared in small warehouses and then transported with their own vehicles straight to wholesale markets in southern Italy or to other intermediaries. According to the research findings, increasingly these small traders set up business only to go bankrupt after a short time. Those who manage to keep their business solvent are only able to do so because their firm is entirely family-based, which avoids outgoings in wages and in any case their profit margin remains low.

The number of medium traders has also gradually decreased in recent years and across the Plain today there are no more than a dozen traders who deal with quantities of between 2,000 and 5,000 tonnes per season. Some of these traders resort to foreign dealers, mainly in Eastern Europe, others sell to local intermediaries, while only a few manage to make deals with supermarket chains. The handful of large traders active in the Plain, who, as noted earlier, sometimes also operate as large producers, deal mainly with supermarket chains and sell smaller quantities of poorer quality fruit to other traders in Eastern Europe.

Private traders are also present in the Valencian Community but, in contrast to the Gioia Tauro Plain, there also exists a widespread cooperative system, which in reality was set up by the farmers themselves. At present the citrus cooperative is in charge of organizing fruit picking in the orchards of member farmers, and owns warehouses, where its members' products are prepared (i.e. selected, cleaned and packed) to be sold. On the whole, there does not appear to be a clear distinction between the market outlets for cooperatives and for private dealers: produce may be sent to big supermarket chains, wholesalers or central markets, in Spain or abroad, although both groups tend much more towards foreign exports.

Cooperatives have a long history in Spanish agriculture and often have grass-roots origins, especially in the more inland and poorer areas in the country (Abad, 1984; Hermet, 1999). The cooperative system in Valencia has been cited as a virtuous example of collective participation and a key element in the success of local agriculture. In other words, this was not something imposed artificially from above with the sole purpose of accessing financial resources, which is what has occurred in Calabria (Cavazzani and Sivini, 1997a, 1997b). Nevertheless, the current crisis in citrus fruit production has also affected the cooperatives in Valencia, which demonstrates how the cooperative system of production is no longer able to protect farmers from the general lowering of prices and the erosion of earnings. The findings from fieldwork indicate a very complex situation in Valencia, with internal competition between cooperatives and low profit margins for farmers.

In both areas, the phase that follows the harvest takes place in what are generically referred to as 'warehouses'. The dimensions of these buildings, the variety of mechanical and electrical equipment and the presence of storage refrigerators all depend on the investment capacity of individual dealers and members of POs. This phase of production usually follows the same stages: the fruit is first washed, it is then selected according to size and appearance, rejects are eliminated and sometimes the fruit is covered in wax before it finally gets packed. The timing, method of preparation and the type of packaging depend on the destination of the product.

## 7.4 End markets: from the wholesale market to the big supermarket chains

A number of common elements in both areas explain the changes that have occurred in the citrus fruit industry, despite the fact that cultivation in Valencia is mainly for export, while production in the Gioia Tauro Plain is presently aimed at domestic consumption (Cesaretti and Green, 2006; FAO, 2012; Generalitat Valenciana, 2012; ISMEA, 2011; Mostaccio, 2012; Callegari and Valentini, 2014).

Wholesale markets in Italy have become increasingly inaccessible and unfavourable for citrus fruit dealers in the Gioia Tauro Plain, both for the change in local production and trading, and as the result of global factors, that have been equally significant in the case of Valencia. Global factors include the progressive increase in productive areas and circulation of goods, both at a national and worldwide level, and the opening of EU markets to fruit and vegetables from non-EU countries. Problems related to the history of production in the Gioia Tauro Plain include the fraudulent way in which CAP funding was managed (Cavazzani and Sivini, 1997b; Chirico and Magro, 2010), the 'protectionist' system used against dealers from other areas (Arlacchi, 1980, 1983; Piselli and

Arrighi, 1987) and the infiltration of organized crime in the running of some wholesale markets in Italy. The general delay among producers in the Gioia Tauro Plain to convert to growing varieties considered more suited to the fresh food market and to processing fruit in more modern structures represents an additional disadvantage in the face of growing competition in terms of quality, quantity and price. Moreover, a very short growing season, concentrated between November and January during the months of maximum saturation of the market, finds itself having to fit into a global market geared to the purchase and consumption of citrus fruit all the year round.

Although the two areas in question operate at different scales – national in the case of the Gioia Tauro Plain and international in the case of the Valencian Community – in both cases two key processes over the last two decades have contributed to the development of the citrus fruit crisis and the decline of the model of distribution of wholesale markets. On the one hand, there has been an overall increase in the offer of citrus fruit and the global circulation of agricultural produce; on the other, there has been a concentration of distribution dealers and a reduction in the number of buyers and in the volume exchanged in wholesale markets. Importing countries are mainly in northern Europe: Germany, France, the Netherlands and the United Kingdom. Since the opening of the EU market to agricultural products from 'third' (non-EU) countries, there has been a continual increase in the amount of fresh citrus fruit exported to the EU from these countries.[3] Exporting countries of the Mediterranean area have the leadership in the volume of *fresh* citrus fruit marketed in the world and reach the market during the same season, from September–October to May–June. The main exporter by far is Spain, followed by Egypt and Turkey, both of which during the 2000s saw an exponential increase in their production and exports, and by Greece and Morocco, with lower volumes that have remained more stable over the period. Fresh citrus fruit from the southern hemisphere, mainly from South Africa, enters the EU market during the summer months, which adds to out-of-season consumption and sometimes overlaps with the production in the northern hemisphere (FAO, 2012; Mostaccio, 2012).

Overall, the globalization of the citrus trade has dramatically increased the level of competition. The modest cost incurred by buyers when replacing suppliers ultimately increases the bargaining power of the big supermarket chains over fixing prices and requesting additional services. Initially, even the largest groups bought their supplies from wholesale markets; however, with the evolution of distribution methods and new forms of consumer behaviour, the retail supply system has changed. The main development has been the transition from a situation in which local and regional retail outlets were supplied with fruit bought from central markets and wholesalers and importers were located in areas near the retail points, to one in which produce is bought directly from source through agreements with the large producers, dealers and exporters, individually or as members of an association. These are suppliers who are able to select, prepare and pack fresh produce to order and deliver it from the area of production to the logistic platforms of the big chains, from which they are then distributed to the retail outlets (Castro and Alfonso, 2008). The big supermarket chains have gradually managed to detach themselves from logistic and transport costs, as well as the organization of labour during the different stages of the chain, through a long succession of sub-contracts with various suppliers of products and services.

Specifically in the case of the citrus chain in Valencia, some of the bigger retail names have set up a supply system that has, in fact, replaced all the intermediaries along the chain by strategically placing their purchase centres in the vicinity of production (Cesaretti and Green, 2006). These are private agencies which are responsible for calling the suppliers, defining agreements, making orders and managing, through further sub-contracts, the logistic aspects and quality control of the flow of products ordered by their own clients (Castro and Arevalo, 2008; ISMEA, 2011).

The establishment of quality standards for own-brand products within a controlled supply chain allows the major companies to achieve two fundamental outcomes, which have been outlined in the sociological and economic literature on the subject (Cesaretti and Green, 2006; Lee *et al.*, 2012; Burch *et al.*, 2013; Callegari and Valentini, 2014) and were confirmed in the research interviews with operators in the sector. The first result is the elimination of the designation of origin of the product that enables buyers to substitute suppliers more easily; the second is the enforced compliance of production rules on the part of suppliers, which allows for greater intervention by the purchasing centre at all points in the supply chain. It is thus the end market which approaches the production areas and not vice versa.

Orders for products can be made at various intervals (fortnightly, weekly or daily) depending on the distance to be covered, the logistic capacity of the various traders and on the degree of 'freshness' promoted by the distribution brand. Quantity and price are settled for each order and, as similarly occurs for delivery dates, these are adjusted according to consumption trends. Through a systematic combination of marketing strategies, the contracting out of various activities and the practice of charging suppliers for logistic costs, the big brands in distribution manage to raise profit margins from sales and make major savings in production costs. The operators interviewed also point out the advantages offered by the supermarket chains to the supplier, which consist principally in the large quantities of fruit purchased, the amount of payment (which is made after 60 to 90 days) and the fluctuations in prices, which are high in season, although they tend to be lower than those in wholesale markets.

Access to the group of suppliers of the big supermarket chains is inevitably selective and there are a number of similar criteria in the two production areas: direct personal relations with the management of the purchasing company, the size and organization of the production unit that allows it to guarantee large quantities, a broad selection of fruit, continuity, punctuality and standardization of supplies. Only producers that are able to supply large quantities of goods, offer a wide range of products, and handle and package them using modern machinery and technology can work with the large retail chains. Moreover, only those that command large quantities of capital for investment and risk cover (i.e. they are able to buy large supplies or face failed payments) or those who own logistical infrastructure and are able to offer additional services other than supplying the produce, can ultimately survive the conditions and standards imposed by today's supermarkets. This large-scale economy is self-sustaining and the selection process and economic concentration occur at different points of the supply chain, spreading back from the big supermarkets to influence the production stage, through all the different traders.

## 7.5 Citrus fruit supply chain and the value chain

By tracing the citrus fruit supply chain, it is possible to reconstruct the trends that spread from the end market back through the various stages and commercial operations, until they influence the choice of production made by the farmers and determine the ways in which picking is organized. In the face of growing energy and production costs, there has been a general downturn in the price at origin and considerable inconsistency between the time and volume of production.

The distribution of the margins in the supply chain, calculated in euros per kilogram in Italy and Spain,[4] shows higher profits for traders (local wholesalers or associated producers who deal with both the commercial handling and sale of the product) and for retailers (local shops or supermarkets) when compared with the share for farmers. The fluctuation in prices is not shared out proportionally at the different stages of the chain: any reduction in price is carried mainly by those involved at the productive stage; moreover these same actors still receive relatively lower percentages of profit margins when consumer prices increase. Traditional and modern retail outlets maintain a greater stability in the net benefits compared to wholesalers and traders at the production stage.

Furthermore, despite the direct agreements between retail brands and local operators, the drop in the number of intermediaries in the modern distribution channels controlled by supermarkets, compared with traditional supply chains led by wholesale markets, is more apparent than real. As observed particularly in the case of purchasing centres 'integrated' into the supermarket chains in Valencia, the modern supply chain is intertwined with a series of sub-contracts with private agencies, who are either independent or controlled by the big names (Castro and Arevalo, 2008; ISMEA, 2008). Such 'integrated channels' appear shorter than the traditional ones, usually characterized by the intervention of many intermediaries, but the substantial difference consists rather in a control by retailers over operators in other stages, with the resulting appropriation of an increasing share of the surplus generated along the entire chain (Figure 7.2).

Even when the activities along the supply chain are not directly incorporated by the big brands in distribution, due to action by integrated purchasing centres, there nevertheless still exists in both areas a process of natural selection in favour of those operators with a greater capacity for logistics and for supplying a larger quantity of goods and services and who possess more capital for investment and risk. The processes described thus far have caused such a fall in earnings from agricultural products in comparison with the final price of goods that the supply of food produce

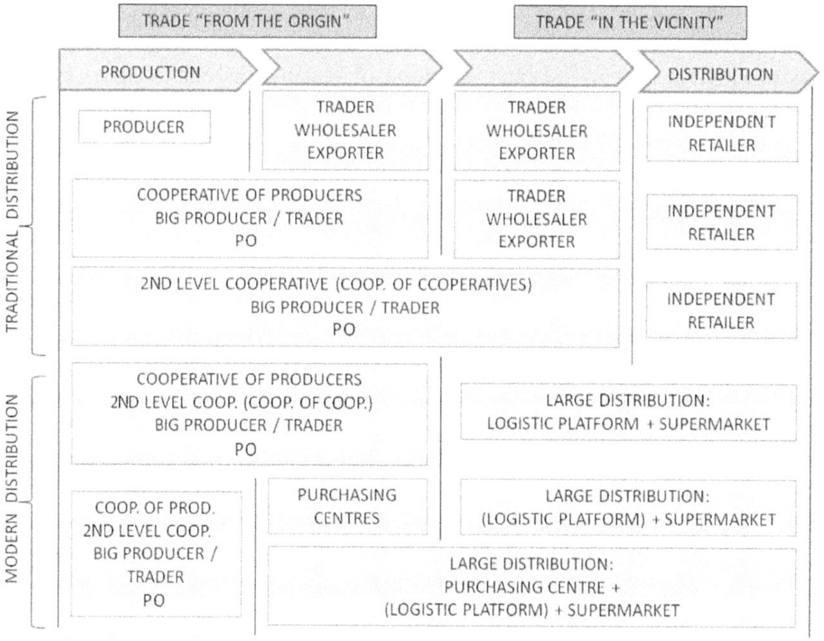


*Figure 7.2* Traditional and modern distribution.
Source: own elaboration of data, 2014.

is in fact being transformed into a series of multiple services, which only some of the bigger and more structured operators are able to provide (ISMEA, 2011).

## 7.6 'Just in time' labourers

In the two areas of study, small and medium citrus fruit farmers have responded to the shrinking of profit margins and the tightening of market conditions with a range of similar actions: they abandon the cultivations; they plant new varieties of citrus fruit or change type of cultivation altogether; or they continue to sell the same product attempting to cope with the lowering of prices by containing labour and maintenance costs. However, regarding the organization of harvesting, producers in the two areas appear to have developed different strategies and methods.

Citrus fruit growers in the Valencian Community outsource the management of the harvest to traders or to cooperatives of which they are members. Traders and a certain number of cooperatives, in turn, outsource the organization of the picking stage by resorting to an extremely flexible workforce supplied by so-called ETTs (*Empresas de Trabajo Temporal*, regulated by Law No. 14/1994): private agencies that offer temporary and affordable work in agriculture and other sectors, and which also supply and manage teams of mainly foreign pickers. Alternatively, to increase the number of pickers when necessary, producers make use of informal contacts with labourers who were members of core teams during previous seasons, and who are put in charge of recruiting additional labour to meet orders and peak production times. The intermediation of seasonal labour in Spain is legal and the pay and responsibilities of the team leader are regulated by the collective agreement stipulated with the Valencian Community.[5]

Differently, in the Gioia Tauro Plain a number of small and medium farmers take charge of the picking themselves. They resort mainly to foreign labourers for brief periods of picking, sometimes only for a few days. In such cases, the traditional custom of recruiting informal and occasional workers directly from the street or through other farmers still exists. Producers usually contact previous employees or rely on word of mouth among labourers, who often alternate jobs between several farmers. Otherwise, farmers recruit a small number of day labourers off the street and although they usually only offer a few, discontinuous days of informal work, they often establish a closer relationship with these workers. The result of this personal relationship between worker and employer is ambivalent: more humane compared to the labour relations mediated by a gangmaster, but at the same time paternalistic and masking the reality of precarious and badly paid work. When traders take charge of organizing harvest labour, just like in Valencia, they utilize core teams for longer periods, composed of labourers who have been employed repeatedly over the years. Additional labourers are brought in, usually through existing contacts, in order to cope with extra picking that arises with an increase in seasonal productivity, adverse weather conditions or the unexpected arrival of an order. Various types of informal intermediaries are responsible for forming the teams, substituting absent pickers, organizing transport, managing the work and translating information into the language of the migrant labourers. They also resolve misunderstandings between workers and employers or any failure on the part of the labourers in conducting jobs, count up the total days worked, hand out wages, and sometimes even find accommodation for labourers. In this area, however, the brokerage of the workforce, often for profit, known locally as *caporalato*, is carried out informally, since it is illegal according to Italian law (the Decree of 13 August 2011).[6]

The widespread outsourcing of the harvest, especially in the Valencian Community, creates a clear division between the productive structure and the organization of work. The size of the farms in fact loses its explanatory value, while the relevant scale for the analysis of the organization of the picking becomes that of the traders and big producers, which in turn sub-contract to private temporary employment agencies or to formal or informal intermediaries. The different roles in the citrus-growing chain are filled by many types of intermediaries. They broadly range from, on the one hand, more formal and internally complex agencies that supply a temporary workforce to medium and large operators, requiring a large turnover of regular employee, to, on the other hand, more informal organizations, which answer to small and medium operators, with fewer and discontinuous requirements and a lower spending capacity. More than just representing an economic saving, the ETTs offer the client firms a series of advantages, such as guaranteeing the workforce's almost complete adherence to the needs of production and, as various union representatives have complained, preventing any kind of claim or formal protest on the part of the workers.

The comparison between the Gioia Tauro Plain and the Valencian Community shows how the organization of seasonal work typical of large-scale capitalist agriculture can also develop in a rural area with a productive structure based around small farms. This type of labour organization has been described in sociological and historical studies of various rural areas in Italy (Arlacchi, 1980; Piselli and Arrighi, 1987; Piselli, 1990). Moreover, the issue of labour flexibility, which has always been a feature of seasonal agricultural work, is today exacerbated by the demands of the market and recent developments in the citrus chain, which requires the supply of large quantities and is heavily dependent on end consumption, both in terms of containing prices and maintaining efficiency in delivery times. In both areas, alongside the core teams that work during the fruit-picking months, there is a need for a 'just in time' workforce (Ohno, 1988); in other words, labourers who during short peak periods are recruited quickly and at a low cost according to the needs of the market. Entrepreneurs, regardless of whether they are producers or traders, prefer to employ migrant labour, because it allows them to lower production costs considerably.

The research indicates, in both cases, a fragmented picture of the workforce in which competition between different national groups is deliberately manipulated by intermediaries and employers. In Calabria, overall, men and women from new member countries of the EU (Bulgaria and Romania) are more likely to be employed in core teams for longer and more continuous work, while sub-Saharan Africans, especially young men, represent an agricultural 'reserve army' (Marx, 2015 [1867]) that is more often recruited informally for short and occasional periods during the harvests. It is evident that these preferences respond to an urgent need to maintain a semblance of legality, which also, as in the case of Valencia, reflects the most recent changes in the citrus fruit chain with regards to the organization and mediation of seasonal agricultural labour.

In both areas similar work conditions exist: transport is at the expense of the labourer, which usually costs between 5 and 7 euros per person in Valencia and between 3 and 4 euros in the Gioia Tauro Plain; the collective agreement of agricultural work, which in any case stipulates very low pay, tends to be ignored by employers and the wage, which is mainly paid by piecework, is lower than the minimum union pay. Labourers are either employed entirely informally or with fixed-term contracts (although with the latter they receive false pay slips where, for tax evasion purposes, only a few of the days worked are declared). Even when the mediation is carried out by ETTs, the transport, brokerage and work organization costs are at the expense of the labourer, just like with the most informal recruiting systems; in the same way, wages are very low and official contributions do not correspond to established regulations. The differences between the roles and the organization of ETTs and the *caporalato* are negligible. The spread of ETTs is a formal evolution of the informal gangmaster system, which has developed in parallel to the partial regularization of the legal and employment status of migrants. The development of the organization and the progressive legalization of the pyramidal system of labour mediation have done little to alleviate the system of exploitation. The *caporalato* in the Gioia Tauro Plain, although showing the early stages of organization, follows a similar logic of adapting to the changes in the agricultural food chain and to the requirements of employers: on the one hand, centralizing the supply management and providing flexible labour in order to maximize large-scale profit; on the other, creating an appearance of a regularization in labour relations.

It is clear that the cases of the two areas represent different points along a continuum of possible arrangements in the citrus sector. They also reflect similar developments, both in the demand and the offer of seasonal agricultural work, and therefore in the dynamics and systems which govern the relationship between worker and employer.

## 7.7 Conclusions

In this chapter I have examined the process of circulation of capital alongside the social relations of production, indicating the importance of developing an analysis of a chain that connects capital to work. Examining the different levels of the chain, I have sought to demonstrate how the recent global reorganization of agri-food capital is connected to changes in the relations between farmer and labourer at the local level. In both cases studied, producers and traders resort to a 'just in time' workforce.

The frequent outsourcing during harvests results in a clear division between the productive system and the organization of labour, which takes place during the stages of commercialization and distribution of the product and is unrelated to the size of the farm. This division determines a contradictory coexistence between the small property productive system and the labour relations in large-scale farm production: there is a need for a big workforce to be concentrated territorially over a period of time, as similarly occurs in other regions with extensive monoculture such as Puglia in Italy or Huelva province in Spain.

The citrus fruit crisis that has beset the Gioia Tauro plain is not just the corollary of a backward and uncompetitive agricultural sector, but in reality is an advanced symptom of a long-term global transformation that has also hit a traditionally very competitive area, namely Valencia. The crisis can be traced mainly to a restructuring of the agri-food chain, characterized by a great economic concentration of the commercial and, above all, distribution stages and by a growing worldwide interconnection between numerous different areas, producers and consumers.

In both countries most of the produce is sold to the big distribution brands, prepared and packed for display on supermarket shelves; the remaining part is sent to central markets and wholesalers. However, both commercial chains require large quantities of supplies and are heavily dependent on the end demand for containing prices as well as ensuring efficiency in delivery schedules. In any case, the agri-food chain requires low-cost pickers, who are highly flexible and can be recruited quickly at peak harvest times.

Given the general fall in prices paid at the lower levels of production, farmers and traders prefer to employ immigrant labour, which allows for a considerable reduction in production costs. In sum, formal and informal systems of brokering seasonal agricultural workforce are similar in their social effects and economic aims. The traditional flexibility of seasonal work is emphasized by the citrus market and 'just in time' migrants are recruited, employed and organized in the two areas through systems and with work conditions that are apparently different but are ultimately very similar.

## Notes

1 The citrus-growing area in the Gioia Tauro Plain is commonly known as 'Rosarno' by migrants, as well as both among national and international public opinion.

2 Both censuses cited here are part of a inquiry by the European Union into the structure of farms, carried out in all EU member countries during 2009 and 2010. Despite the different publication dates of the two countries' data, they both refer to methodology and quality criteria established by the Community Regulation (CE) No. 1166/2008 of the Parliament of the European Council.

3 The agreement on agriculture of Uruguay Round within GATT, which entered into force in 1995, has caused a reduction in direct subsidies, contributions for exports and the protection of internal prices (as stipulated by the CAP) and has led to the progressive abolition of certain tariffs applied to the importation of fresh and transformed citrus fruit. A further series of bilateral agreements were stipulated over the following years with various third countries, which have facilitated the access of fruit and vegetable products onto the European market. For example, concessions have been made to Morocco, Tunisia and Israel (Wallach and Sforza, 2000).

4 ISMEA, in Italy, and the price observatory of the Ministry of Food and Environment in Spain regularly publish analyses of costs and prices among the different segments of the citrus fruit chain.

5 It is possible to consult the text of the *Convenio colectivo para la recolecciòn de cítricos de la Comunidad Valenciana,* valid for the campaign 2010–2014, at the following website: http://noticias.juridicas.com/base_datos/Laboral/475493-convenio-colectivo-de-recoleccion-ca-valenciana-2010–2014-r-html#a12

6 Article 12 of Legislative Decree No.138/2011, converted into Law No.144/2011, included the illicit mediation and exploitation of labour in the penal code.

## References

Abad, V. (1984). *Historia de la Naranja (1940–1962)*. Valencia: Comité de Gestiòn de la Exportaciòn de Frutos Cìtricos.

Ajuntament de Valencia (2013). Estadística. https://www.valencia.es/ayuntamiento/estadistica.nsf (last access on 20/2/2016).

Arlacchi, P. (1980). *Mafia, contadini e latifondo nella Calabria tradizionale: le strutture elementari del sottosviluppo*. Bologna: Il mulino.Arlacchi, P. (1983). *La mafia imprenditrice. L'etica mafiosa e lo spirito del capitalismo.* Bologna: Il Mulino.

Barndt, D. (2002). *Tangled Routes: Women, Work, and Globalization on the Tomato Trail.* New York: Rowman and Littlefield Publishers.

Bonanno, A. and Cavalcanti, J. S. B. (2014). *Labor Relations in Globalized Food.* Bingley: Emerald.

Burch, D., Dixon J., Lawrence G. (2013). 'Introduction to symposium on the changing role of supermarkets in global supply chains: from seedling to supermarket: agri-food supply chains in transition'. *Agriculture and Human Values*, 30, pp. 215–224.

Callegari, F. and Valentini, M. (2014). *Filiere d'Italia. Produzioni e reti dell'agroalimentare*. Roma: Donzelli.

Castro, E. M. and Arévalo, A. R. (2008). *El sistema de comercialización en origen de las frutas y hortalizas en fresco*. http://www.infoagro.com/frutas/sistemas_comercializacion_frutas_hortalizas.htm (last access on 20/2/2016).

Cavazzani, A. and Sivini, G. (1997a). *Dolci clementine: innovazioni e problemi di una agrumicultura sviluppata: la Piana di Sibari*. Soveria Mannelli (Catanzaro): Rubbettino.

Cavazzani, A. and Sivini, G. (1997b). *Arance amare: la crisi dell'agrumicoltura italiana e lo sviluppo competitivo di quella spagnola*. Soveria Mannelli (Catanzaro): Rubbettino.

Cesaretti, G.P and Green, R. (2006) *L'organizzazione della filiera ortofrutticola. esperienze internazionali a confronto*. Milano: FrancoAngeli.

Chirico, D. and Magro, A. (2010). *Il caso Valarioti: Rosarno 1980: così la 'ndrangheta uccise un politico (onesto) e diventò padrona della Calabria: un processo a metà*. Roma: Round Robin.

Colloca, C. and Corrado, A., a cura di (2013), *La globalizzazione nelle campagne. Migrazioni e società rurali nel Sud italia*. Milano: FrancoAngeli.

Corrado, A. (2011). 'Clandestini in the orange towns: Migrations and racisms in Calabria's agriculture'. *Race/Ethnicity: Multidisciplinary Global Contexts*, 4(2), pp. 191–201.

Facoltà di Agraria dell'Università degli Studi Mediterranea di Reggio Calabria. (2012). *Studio Preliminare Sullo Stato Dell'agricoltura Nel Comprensorio Della 'Piana Di Gioia Tauro'*. Reggio Calabria: Facoltà di Agraria dell'Università degli Studi Mediterranea di Reggio Calabria.

FAO. (2012). *Citrus Fruits – Annual Statistics 2012*. From http://www.fao.org/economic/est/est-commodities/citrus-fruit/it/

Friedland, W. H. (2001). 'Reprise on commodity systems methodology'. *International Journal of Sociology of Agriculture and Food*, 9(1), pp. 82–103.

Generalitat Valenciana. (2012). *Informe Del Sector Agrario Valenciano*. From http://www.agricultura.gva.es/la-conselleria/publicaciones/informes-del-sector-agrario

Gereffi, G. and Korzeniewicz, M. (1994). *Commodity Chains and Global Capitalism*. Westport: Greenwood Press.

Gereffi, G., Humphrey, J. and Sturgeon, T. (2005). 'The governance of global value chains'. *Review of International Political Economy*, 12(1), pp. 78–104.

Gertel, J. and Sippel, S.R. (2014). *Seasonal Workers in Mediterranean Agriculture. The Social Costs of Eating Fresh*, London: Routledge.

Henderson, J., Dicken, P., Hess, M., Coe, N. and Wai-Chung Yeung, H. (2002). 'Global production networks and the analysis of economic development'. *Review of International Political Economy*, 9(3): pp. 436–464.

Hermet, G. (1999). *Storia della Spagna nel Novecento*. Bologna: Il Mulino.

Hopkins, K. and Wallerstein, I. (1994). 'Conclusions about commodity chains' in Gereffi and Korzeniewicz (1994), pp. 17–20.

Illescas, J.L., Bacho, O. and Ferrer, S. (2008). 'Mercasa y la Red de Mercas. Al servicio de la cadena alimentaria'. *Distribución y Consumo*, No. 100, pp. 147–166.

INE. (2009). *Censo Agrario*. http://www.ine.es/CA/Inicio.do

ISMEA. (2008). *Report Economico Finanziario*. Roma: ISMEA.

ISMEA. (2011). *Report Economico Finanziario*. Roma: ISMEA.

Istat. (2012). *6° Censimento Generale dell'Agricoltura*. http://censimentoagricoltura.istat.it/

Lee, J., Gereffi, G. and Beauvais, J. (2012). 'Global value chains and agrifood standards: Challenges and possibilities for smallholders in developing countries'. *PNAS*, 109(31), pp. 12326–31.

Marx, K. (2015 [1867]). *Capital: A Critique of Political Economy, Volume 1*. Arsalan Ahmed.

McMichael, P. (2005). 'Global Development and the Corporate Food Regime' in Buttel F.H. and McMichael, P. (eds) *New Directions in the Sociology of Global Development*. Oxford: Elsevier, pp. 229–67.

Morice, A. and Michalon, B. (eds.) (2008). *Travailleurs saisonners dans l'agriculture européenne*, special issue of *Études rurales*, 182.

Mostaccio, F. (2012). *La Guerra Delle Arance*. Soveria Mannelli (Catanzaro): Rubettino.

Ohno, T. (1988). *Toyota Production System. Beyond Large-Scale Production* (1978). Portland, OR: Productivity Press.

Pedreño Cánovas, A. (ed.) (2014a). *De cadenas, migrantes y jornaleros: los territorios rurales en las cadenas globales agroalimentarias*. Madrid: Talasa.

Pedreño Cánovas, A. (2014b). 'Encadenados a fetiches. Del enfoque de las cadenas de mercancías a la sostenibilidad social de los enclaves de producción de la'uva global'', in Pedreño Cánovas (2014a), pp. 13–37.

Piselli, F. (1990). 'Sensali e caporali dell'Italia meridionale'. in Bevilacqua, P. (ed) *Storia dell'agricoltura italiana in età contemporanea*. Vol. II, Venezia: Marsilio, pp. 823–825.

Piselli, F. and Arrighi, G. (1987). 'Capitalist development in hostile environmnents: Feuds, class, struggles and migrations in a peripheral region of southern Italy', in *Review*, X, 4, pp. 649–751.

Ploeg, J. D. Van der (2008). *The New Peasantries: Struggles for Autonomy and Sustainability in an Era of Empire and Globalization*. London: Routledge.

Pugliese, E. (2012). 'Il lavoro agricolo immigrato nel Mezzogiorno e il caso di Rosarno'. *Mondi migranti*, 3/2012, pp. 7–28.

# 8 Migrant labour and intensive agricultural production in Greece

## The case of the Manolada strawberry industry

*Apostolos G. Papadopoulos and Loukia-Maria Fratsea*

### 8.1 Introduction

Agriculture remains a significant production and employment sector in southern European countries. Mediterranean crops show significant seasonality and are highly dependent on migrant workers. Southern European agriculture is not a homogeneous sector: on the contrary, it is highly diversified and unevenly developed within each country. Despite the stereotypical view of Mediterranean agriculture as a mosaic of small- to medium-scale family farms producing globally recognized quality food products, there exists a range of agricultural systems that vary from highly intensive vegetable production to extensive cereal farms (Moragues-Faus *et al.*, 2013). More important, the modernization of agriculture and the rise of 'agricultural productivism' have been major trends in many southern European countries. According to available EU data, the number of farm holdings is declining with a subsequent rise in the average size of holdings, the size of family labour is shrinking while the share of non-family wage labour is increasing, and commercial crops and stockbreeding are expanding at the expense of extensive cultivations (Eurostat, 2014). These trends comply with the wider aims of the Common Agricultural Policy, which is regularly reformed in an attempt to modernize agriculture and make it more market-oriented (Giannakis and Bruggeman, 2015; Papadopoulos, 2015).

The Agricultural Census 2010 indicates that non-family members provide 25 per cent of farm labour in the southern EU countries. This group is mainly composed of a non-regular labour force with a minority being made up of regular workers (Eurostat, 2014). For nearly all of EU agriculture, migrant workers provide the bulk of non-family labour. The indigenous population is increasingly less prepared to accept the working conditions and wages offered in intensive fruit and vegetable production and is therefore substituted by migrants who either work irregularly or under various forms of legal status.

In southern EU countries, in particular, irregular and/or regular migrant workers meet the need for seasonal and permanent labour. In many cases, informal brokers play a major role in the recruitment of migrant labourers, most of whom work irregularly. This system of labour recruitment has proved useful to employers in agriculture because it is both sufficiently flexible and it creates the preconditions for low wages, poor working conditions and inadequate housing or accommodation (De Zulueta, 2003: 4). The common practice of utilizing irregular migrants creates economic advantages for employers but it also distorts competition and denies migrant workers their social rights. In many cases, there are incidents of labour trafficking that raise questions about the respect of human rights in intensive agriculture areas (Dupraz, 2006).

This chapter focuses on the role of migrant wage labour in strawberry cultivation in the area of Manolada, in the Peloponnese region of south-western Greece. This locality has recently been in the public eye as a result of the frequent mobilizations of migrant labourers who have demanded higher wages and defended themselves against the severe labour controls exercised by local strawberry farmers.

Studies have already considered a number of features and processes pertaining to migrant labour in this agricultural area. For example, scholars have described the mobility trajectories of different migrant groups: for example, while Albanian migrants tend towards upward social mobility, Bangladeshi migrants appear to live in a sort of 'ethnic enclave' (Papadopoulos, 2009). Other studies have analysed the secondary labour market in which migrant labour is immersed (Papadopoulos and Fratsea, 2013). Most recently, during the post-crisis period, discussions have focused on the increasing labour precarity of migrants (Kasimis *et al.*, 2015), while the social clashes that took place in Manolada in 2013 have been interpreted as induced by the economic crisis (Carastathis, 2014; Gialis and Herod, 2014).

In this chapter, we focus on the fact that the expansion of strawberry industry in Greece, and in particular in Manolada (the nation's main strawberry production site), is primarily based on the availability of numerous migrant wage labourers. Thus, it is important to analyse the various ways in which migrant labour has been controlled and been made available for strawberry growers.

We base our analysis on fieldwork data collected over almost a decade of research. The first set of data was collected between 2006 and 2007, during which 103 questionnaires with migrants were collected in the area, while 15 qualitative interviews were conducted. Since this first period, there have been several site visits and occasional discussions and correspondence with locals and migrant workers. Between June and September 2015, we carried out eight additional qualitative interviews with migrants and local stakeholders. Finally, we gathered and analysed media reports for the entire period between 2007 and 2015; some parts of the media analysis have informed the empirical section of the chapter along with the qualitative material derived from the questionnaires and interviews.

The next section discusses the forms of migrant labour control in intensive strawberry production in the US and Spain, the world's two principal producers. This is followed by an account of the evolution of the strawberry industry in Greece. In Section 8.4, we describe how migrants of different nationalities arrived in this agricultural area and how this migration created a segmented labour market, but also a number of social and labour conflicts. Through this historical account, we aim to demonstrate the distinct forms of migrant labour control in Manolada, which have been essential for the rapid expansion and modernization of the strawberry production system; the precarious legal status of migrant labourers; the 'ethnic' segmentation of the labour market; and, in some cases, the physical violence of supervisors and growers.

## 8.2 Migrants in the strawberry fields: US and Spain

The most well-known piece of research on migrant labour in the 'strawberry fields' was carried out by Myriam Wells between 1976 and 1989 in California (Wells, 1996). Californian agriculture – and in particular its strawberry production – have been important for studying the transformations of intensive agricultural production systems (Walker, 1997). Over history, California has experienced a succession of reserve armies of seasonal agricultural labour that have met the labour needs of growers. The Chinese were the first national group to work as seasonal farm labourers in the nineteenth century, followed by the Japanese, who were then replaced by Mexicans at the turn of the twentieth century. In the postwar period, the Bracero Program was the first agreement that introduced a seasonal migrant labour system in US agriculture, which was accompanied with the entry of 'irregular' migrants, who crossed the US–Mexico border in search of employment (Burawoy, 1976, pp. 1064–1065).

In this context, Wells' major aim was to 'explore the bases of class mobilization and labour process change in California's central coast strawberry industry' and she was 'particularly concerned with the conditions underlying workers' tendencies to challenge the terms set down by employers and owners' tendencies to reconfigure employment relationships to increase their control over labour' (Wells, 1996, p. 11).

Strawberries are one of the most labour-intensive crops, with labour constituting about half of total production costs. New cultivation methods and plant strains as well as the development of transportation, handling and quick-freezing methods had an enormous effect on strawberry production in California, which became the nation's (and world's) leading producer. The timing and steady availability of labour is crucial because any deviation from a carefully organized timetable causes impediments to production. The specificity of the strawberry, given its high value, yields and perishability, makes harvest interruptions extremely costly. Furthermore, the labourers' capacity to correctly handle the fruit and plants is crucial to maintaining top-quality and high-value produce. The importance of harvest labour is in part due to the fact it cannot be eliminated by the growers, but also because it is possibly the only cost that they are able to control (Wells, 1997).

The employment of migrant labour has been important for achieving labour control, which, in turn, has been key to safeguarding profitability. Labourers have developed their own social networks of job acquisition and security with a specific focus on the crop and the region (Wells, 1996, p. 17). Despite experts' predictions that technology will render migrant labour obsolete, the recruitment of migrants has been a structural factor for the profitability of the strawberry industry (Schlosser, 1995). The strawberry, which is known by Mexican migrants as *'la fruta del diablo'* (the fruit of the devil), demands a great deal of toil and effort on the part of labourers in terms of handling, treating, harvesting and packing the crop. The harvests are unpredictable, the labour process is difficult to organize, the working and living conditions are harsh, and the wages of labourers are severely affected by downward pressures due to an oversupply of people hoping to pick strawberries. For all these reasons, the Californian model of labour control eventually switched to sharecropping. In fact, sharecropping has been a strategy of farmers at different periods in history, starting in the post-Civil War era, then in the first half of the twentieth century with Japanese Americans and, more recently, in the postwar period with Mexicans (Wells, 1984; Manion, 2001). Lately, the typical arrangement is that the grower assigns a portion of a strawberry field to a farm worker – the sharecropper – and his family, and they share the production costs. The sharecropper undertakes the task to hire the strawberry pickers and arrange for their payment and other labour costs, while the grower is responsible for all other production costs and the overall management of the strawberry farm. In this arrangement the sharecropper assumes a large part of the risk associated with migrant labour and its regular or irregular status. Through this system of labour control, some sharecroppers became growers while others maintained their original status (Schlosser, 1995; Wells, 1996).[1]

Another model for migrant labour control was introduced in strawberry production in Spain and is known as the 'Huelva model' (Marquez Dominguez *et al.*, 2009; see Reigada; Hellio, this volume). The coastal province of Huelva became prominent in Spain from the 1960s onwards for the production of strawberries, locally dubbed 'red gold'. By 2008, Spain was producing some 300,000 tonnes of strawberries per year, most of which was exported to Germany, the United Kingdom and France. Currently, Spain is one of the leading exporters of strawberries, producing almost 10 per cent of world production of this crop. Huelva is the main site of strawberry production in Spain, and, given the recent expansion of the industry, it has also become a place where the demand for migrant labour increased greatly. The 'Huelva model' involves recruiting migrant labourers from their countries of origin (*contratacion en origen*). The workers are compelled to work hard under the threat of being replaced by other migrant labourers the following year; and they are encouraged to return home with the promise that they will have another opportunity to earn money for their family (Mannon *et al.*, 2012, p. 98). It is important to note that the labourers recruited through this programme are female migrants from Morocco who are considered more prone to succumb to the demands of the strawberry growers (Plewa and Miller, 2005; Zeneidi, 2011; Hellio, 2014; Hellio this volume).

This model of migrant labour control has been criticized by the labour unions for two reasons: first, employers fail to comply with existing regulations and agreements regarding seasonal work; second, by increasing barriers to migration and offering only rare windows of opportunity for non-EU labourers to work legally in Spain (and in the EU more generally), the vulnerability of migrants has increased alongside their growing dependence on their employers and other intermediaries in charge of their recruitment (FIDH, 2012, p. 29).

The suggested seasonal migration projects, which seem to be a 'resurrection' of the guest-worker system initiated in the post-war period, promoting circular migration patterns for labourers, are certainly implementing policies that overstress the economic functions of migrants and underplay their incorporation opportunities within the local societies in which they are invited to work (Castles, 2006). In Spain it seems that some lessons have been learned from previous struggles of migrant labour (Martinez Veiga, 2014) and, thus, promotion of seasonal migration patterns are initiated in an organized manner (Plewa and Miller, 2005).

To sum up, two of the most important strawberry production sites in the world have developed different models of migrant labour recruitment and control. As we will see, the Manolada case shares at least one important feature with both these cases: the substitution and competition of migrants of different nationalities in the labour market. Nonetheless, it presents a number of peculiarities that deserve to be studied.

## 8.3 The evolution of the strawberry industry in Greece

During recent years strawberry cultivation in Europe has changed considerably in terms of cultivated areas, growing techniques, varieties and produce. The strawberry is a short-statured, perennial plant, but it is now increasingly cropped for no more than four years, in part because young plants tend to have higher-quality fruit and also because it allows for better disease and pest control (Chandler *et al.*, 2012, p. 307). Different cultivation systems are used including: open field culture; use of single or multiple light plastic tunnels, with limited influence on the plant growing cycle; and plastic and glass houses in order to advance or delay the harvest period. Moreover, different varieties are cultivated depending on climatic conditions: in central and northern Europe new everbearing varieties are grown, while in Southern European countries low-chilling June-bearing varieties are cultivated (Neri *et al.*, 2012). Currently, a principal goal in strawberry cultivation is to extend the fruiting season and thus increase production efficiency and marketing options (Chandler *et al.*, 2012). This is being achieved by a combination of factors such as the use of different varieties according to the climatic conditions, specialized growing techniques and crop protection and forcing systems (Neri *et al.*, 2012, p. 1021).

The Greek strawberry industry has followed the evolution of strawberry cultivation in Europe. Production is located presently in three regions: the Prefecture of Pieria in northern Greece; the prefecture of Aitoloakarnania in Western Greece; and, since the 1970s, the prefecture of Elia (Manolada) in Southern Greece.

The transformation of the industry has been strongly associated with four basic structural developments of the industry at a global level. First, a number of Greek strawberry growers have shifted to fresh bare-rooted plants, which with proper management can produce large, well-shaped and high-quality fruit during an extended harvest season (January–June) (Neri *et al.*, 2012, p. 1027). Second, more intensive cultural practices were incorporated into Greek strawberry culture such as the use of greenhouses. This intensification of the culture is observed also in other parts of Europe such as Spain (Mannon *et al.*, 2012) and the UK

(Evans, 2013). Third, in some areas there was a gradual shift from a perennial to a biennial or annual crop in order to maximize production. Finally, a number of modern cultivating practices (i.e. pest control, fertility practices) were adopted. All these changes contributed to the intensification of production, a sharp increase in yield and to a gradual shift from an extensive open field system to a more intensive production system (i.e. protective tunnels or greenhouses). Modern cultures use high-yielding hybrids with a planting density of 7,000 plants per stremma (which is one-tenth of a hectare), with a yield of up to 2–5 tonnes of produce per stremma (Agronews, 2012).

As shown in Figure 8.1, the cultivation of strawberries in Greece has increased significantly both in terms of production and cultivated area. During the 40 years up to 2007, the average annual cultivated area was 5,500 stremmas, while the average annual production was 7,873 tonnes. These numbers increased considerably after 2007. More particularly, after 2007, the average cultivated area surpassed 11,000 stremmas and reached 18,000 stremmas in 2013. While in 2007 the average production was 9,400 tonnes, by 2013 it reached 79,700 tonnes (FAO, 2015). Currently, over 90 per cent of strawberry production is cultivated in a rural area around the small town of Manolada in the former Vouprassia[2] municipality in the north-western part of the Peloponnese peninsula. In addition to strawberries, this area is characterized by intensive agriculture of dynamic fruit and vegetable crops (tomatoes, potatoes, watermelons, melons and citrus fruit), as well as vines and olives. The agricultural production of Vouprassia extends over 86,400 stremmas, with an average of 43 stremmas per family holding. Agriculture is the main economic sector of the area and accounts for 46 per cent of total employment.

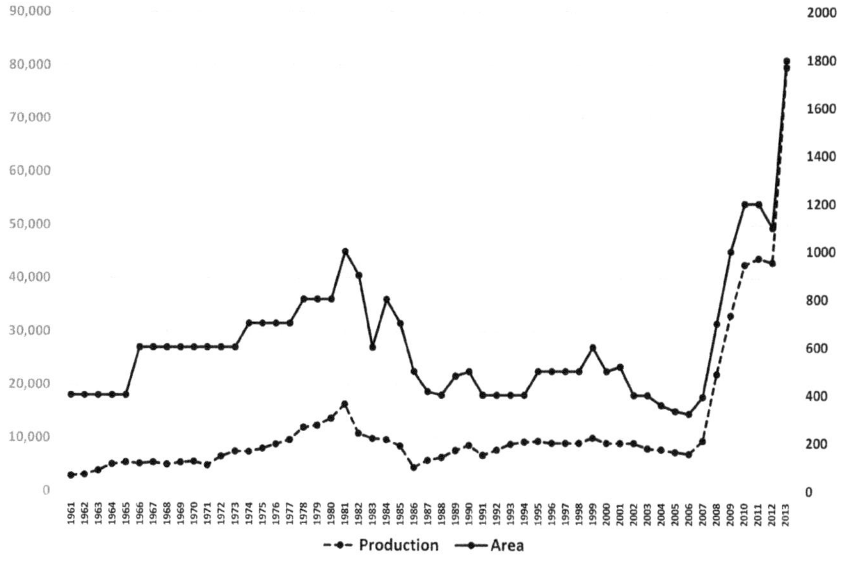


*Figure 8.1* Evolution of strawberry cultivation in Greece, 1961–2013.

As mentioned above, strawberry cultivation in the Manolada area dates back to the 1970s. In 1974 a pioneer producer from northern Greece initiated cultivation of approximately 300 stremmas in the area. Following the success of the culture, a number of potato growers gradually switched to the cultivation of strawberries. During this period, strawberry cultivation in Manolada represented a negligible proportion of the whole country's production. Nevertheless, from the 1980s onwards the culture expanded and this trend was offset for just one year following the nuclear accident at Chernobyl when production remained unsold for a year (*Fanis, strawberry grower, interview in Manolada, March 2007*).

On the basis of our field research, we consider that four major factors contributed to the expansion of strawberry culture in the wider region of Manolada. First, the frozen strawberry plants were replaced by fresh plants, which exhibit better organoleptic characteristics and allow for a longer harvesting period. In 1993, the strawberry culture in the area did not exceed 700 stremmas of frozen-planted strawberry plants with a harvesting period of 15 days earlier than other Greek regions and a commercial period of 40–45 days. Over the following three years, fresh strawberry plants imported by a local company were planted, which extended the harvesting season to between January and early June. This shift contributed to the Manolada area obtaining a dominant share in the national strawberry market.

Second, a wider intensification and modernization of the crop production took place in terms of cultivating practices: new methods of protecting the culture were applied, which provided for higher potential yields. While about 5,000 strawberry plants could be planted in one stremma using traditional cultivation methods, with more intensive farming practices and the conversion to annual plants, one stremma could accommodate up to 25,000 plants. Additionally, new innovative crop protection methods, such as polyethylene-covered protective tunnels and greenhouses, were used. The installation cost for greenhouse cultivation is €8,500 per stremma during the first year and thereafter the annual cost is estimated at €5,500–6,000 per stremma (Agronews, 2012). All these methods have contributed to an increase in both yield and marketable yield. Furthermore, the latter can be increased by eliminating or reducing losses due to disease, arthropod damage, fruit malformation, and cracking (Chandler *et al.*, 2012).

The third significant factor for strawberry expansion in Manolada was the setting up of a group of strawberry producers named 'IRMINI' by fifty producers in 2003. With the establishment of this cooperative, producers were able to promote their product on the market and to give the culture an export-oriented character. In 2004 the cultivated area increased to 1,600 stremmas (Agronews, 2012). The strawberry was first exported to Western European countries (such as Switzerland) and in more recent years it has been exported also to Eastern Europe (including Russia, Bulgaria and Romania), mainly through supermarket chains. This transition of the Greek strawberry industry to an export-oriented culture is mirrored by recent trade figures. In 2012 Greece ranked as the world's sixth largest exporter of strawberries, accounting for 3 per cent of total exports, which represented an increase of 240 per cent compared to 2008. Since 2005, strawberry exports to Russia have continued to rise, and in recent years Greece has consistently commanded the largest share of this market. With the development of the Russian market, the cultivated area increased by 7,500 stremmas and related investments in greenhouses amounted to €37.5 million, while the annual production costs reached €33 million. Growers claim that these investments are solely due to the opening and development of the Russian market and, moreover, that the quality requirements for strawberries have been determined solely according to the preferences of Russian consumers. This investment trend occurred in all other related economic sectors supporting strawberry production (packaging, transport companies, etc.) (Agronews, 2014).

In 2013 the major export countries were Russia (48 per cent), Italy (7.6 per cent), Moldova (6.2 per cent), Bulgaria (6 per cent) and Germany (4.8 per cent). This positive trend was offset to a certain extent by the embargo imposed by Russia on agricultural products in 2015 (*Takis, farmer, interview in Manolada, September 2015*). In fact, the share of strawberry exports to Russia decreased to 39 per cent in 2014, while during the same period exports to Bulgaria, Moldova and Romania increased (Figure 8.2). We estimate that a proportion of strawberries exported to those three Balkan countries have possibly ended up on the Russian market.

The fourth factor that allowed the sharp increase in strawberry culture in the area was the availability of a migrant labour force, as acknowledged by the local stakeholders we interviewed. In some cases it was argued that growers planned their culture according to the availability of the migrant labour force. In fact, strawberry culture is both capital and labour-intensive. It is worth noting that the production cost is around €1.10 per kilo of strawberries, with labour costs dominating since the crop is labour demanding, especially during the harvesting season. It is estimated that the culture requires 70–75 daily wages per stremma per year, which accounts for as much as 40 per cent of the production costs.

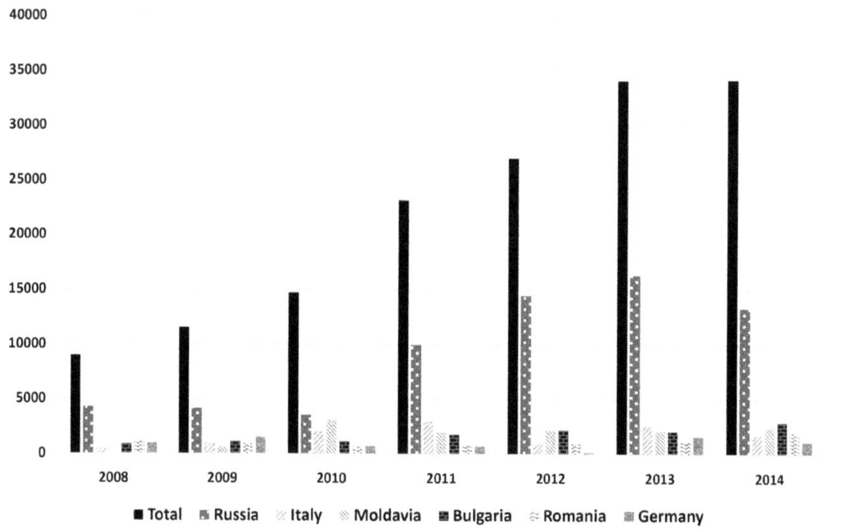


*Figure 8.2* Evolution of exports and main exports countries, 2008–2014 (tonnes).

From the late 1970s until the mid-1980s, local workers mainly met farm labour needs. It was usual practice for both local men and women to work in the fields. As the cultivated area and the labour needs increased, internal migrants from other rural regions of the country, and particularly Central Greece, arrived especially during harvest time. This situation changed in the late 1980s and early 1990s, when the employment of migrant labourers – mostly Albanians – started to increase.

## 8.4 Migrant labour in Manolada fields

International migration in the Manolada area dates back to the early 1990s when the collapse of communist regimes in Central and Eastern Europe, coupled with the strategic geopolitical position of Greece as a gateway to the European Union, saw Greece shift from an emigration to an immigration country. During this period a small number of Albanians, Egyptians, Pakistanis and Bangladeshis arrived in Manolada looking for employment in the emerging intensive agricultural sector. Soon they were followed by groups of Bulgarians and Romanians. By the mid-1990s migration to the Manolada area was on the rise. On the one hand, Albanian men who had been living and working in different, mainly rural regions of Greece arrived in Manolada looking for employment opportunities either in agriculture or in construction. In Greek studies on the geographical mobility of migrants (see Labrianidis and Sykas, 2009; Papadopoulos, 2011; Papadopoulos and Fratsea, 2013), Albanian migrants were seen to be very mobile, as they tended to 'chase the wages' in different parts of the country. On the other hand, Bulgarians, Romanians and Bangladeshis were more likely to arrive directly from Athens by using information drawn from their social networks. As one Bangladeshi migrant noted:

'When I arrived in Athens, I asked my compatriots where I could find work. They told me to go in Manolada. I came here and I stayed' (*Abdul, Bangladeshi Farmworker, Interview in Manolada, September 2015*).

The evolution of migration in Manolada must be seen within the wider context of two developments at local and national level. First, the agricultural restructuring of the area with the expansion of intensive strawberry production created additional labour demand. Second, a series of regularization laws (1997, 1998, 2001 and 2005) resulted in the legalization of a significant number of migrants in Greece, although a considerable part of the migrant population remained undocumented.

In the early 1990s the majority of the migrant population in the area was of Albanian origin, numerically followed by Bulgarians, Romanians and a few Bangladeshis. The increase in migration coincided with the steady withdrawal of the indigenous population from '3-D jobs' (dirty, degrading and dangerous) in intensive agriculture of the area, as occurred in other rural regions of Greece (Kasimis and Papadopoulos, 2005; Kasimis *et al.,* 2010). The subsequent deficiencies or 'gaps' in farm labour were filled by a migrant labour force. Their undocumented and precarious status was paralleled by low wages, which, in turn, kept down farm labour costs for the local growers. During this period the cultivation of strawberries was limited to around 700 stremmas. However, migrants worked on other crops such as potatoes, tomatoes, watermelons and olives.

The first legalization programme between 1997 and 1998 set the stage for the employment mobility of the immigrant population. As an Albanian migrant Aristos explains, recalling his early years of residence in Greece:

'The issue with the papers [legalization] changed things both for us [the migrants] and for the locals. They [the growers] were no longer afraid, so they took us on without problems' (*Aristos, Albanian agricultural supervisor, interview in Manolada, October 2007*).

During this period, the number of Bulgarian and Bangladeshi migrants increased. They found employment mainly in the strawberry fields. The entry of these migrant groups in the local labour market had a significant impact as it increased the available labour force, but also prevented wages from further increasing.

During the five years after this first legalization programme the migratory profile of the area changed considerably. The local migrant population steadily increased reaching almost 12 per cent of the local population, and represented more than one-fifth of the local labour force, while nearly 60 per cent were employed in the agricultural sector. Half of the migrant residents were of Albanian origin, 27 per cent were Bulgarians, 8 per cent were Romanians, and 7 per cent were Bangladeshi (ELSTAT, Population Census, 2001). Differences also existed in terms of gender and family situation. Even though Albanian men were among the first to arrive in the area, they were shortly followed by Albanian women who found work in agriculture or the local service sector. Both Bulgarians and Romanians were also living in the area. Many Bulgarian men work in the fields together with members of their family, while Romanians are either single men or couples working in strawberry processing units. In contrast, the vast majority of Bangladeshis were married young men whose families remained in their country of origin.

The majority of migrants in Manolada fuel the so-called 'secondary labour market', which consists of seasonal, menial, low-wage and unstable jobs. In fact, Albanians followed a different employment trajectory from other migrants in the area. In the 1990s, Albanians were employed in various agricultural jobs aiming at increasing their income but also moving from the unskilled to skilled agricultural tasks. Again Aristos' description is eloquent:

'I have worked in various jobs. After [picking] strawberries I moved on to pruning in the fields. I have pruned every field in the area' (*Aristos, Albanian agricultural supervisor, interview in Manolada, October 2007*).

According to the census data for the area, in the 1990s Albanians were mostly employed in agriculture (56 per cent), but a significant proportion was also employed in the construction sector (29 per cent). Almost two-thirds of Bulgarians and Romanians were working in the primary sector, while one-fourth of Romanians and one-fifth of Bulgarians were employed in construction. More than half of Bangladeshi migrants (55 per cent) were working in agriculture (ELSTAT, Population Census, 2001).

More so than other migrant groups, Albanians aimed to 'move up' the occupational ladder, and thus searched for new employment opportunities in the construction sector or better-paid and permanent employment in agriculture (Papadopoulos, 2009).

Indeed, soon after the first legalization programmes and more particularly by 1999, Albanian migrants working in strawberry fields went on strike to demand an increase in their wages. According to interviews with Albanian migrants, Bulgarians and Bangladeshis broke the strikes. Nevertheless, the daily wage increased from €12 to €15 and two years later it increased further to €18.

As time went by, Albanians acquired more skills and also increased their chances to improve their income and position in the local labour market. It should be noted that by 2003 the average daily wage in agriculture was €22.50, while in the construction sector this could reach €45. Over the years, the gap left by Albanian migrants, as they moved towards other employment sectors, was filled mainly by Bulgarian, Bangladeshi and newly arrived Albanian migrants.

Before the economic recession, it became apparent that the local labour market in Manolada was characterized by an 'ethnic' and gender hierarchy. First, the *regular skilled agricultural workers* largely consisted of Albanians: they had better, higher placed jobs with more demanding and specialized responsibilities such as supervising the planting and harvesting tasks. In some cases, they worked as strawberry pickers, but mostly as a complementary income to their employment in construction. Second, the *regular unskilled agricultural workers* were mainly Bangladeshi migrants who worked in planting and harvesting strawberries, both in the greenhouses and in the open fields. They usually worked in groups in which a single person – usually the one who spoke the Greek language – was responsible for negotiating the wages with the farmer. Bangladeshis are frequently described by the locals as 'quiet people' who are prepared to work under difficult conditions in the greenhouses, are more obedient and stay 'out of sight' from local society. Usually, they were paid less, but they still aimed to put aside money in order to send remittances to their families.

'[T]hey are very quiet people. They wouldn't hurt a fly. And this plays its part [. . .]. They are more . . . kind to each other. So far at least . . .' (*Nabil, Syrian Doctor, interview in Manolada September 2007*).

'[Banglandeshis] are good and quiet; they are mostly in strawberry cultivation' (*Antonis, Mayor of Varda, interview in Manolada July 2007*).

Third, *non-regular and seasonal migrant workers,* in the majority Bulgarians, tended to move with their family members, following a circular migration pattern. They were typically employed in unskilled, precarious, seasonal jobs without social security benefits. A significant proportion of Bulgarians arrived in the area to work temporarily for between 4 and 9 months and accepted lower wages (even €10–15 per day). In the interviews it emerged that their apparent readiness to accept lower wages than other workers was related to the fact that Bulgarian citizens do not have to pay for their social security to ensure their legal stay in Greece.

Finally, as in the case of Huelva, there are *female regular and non-regular workers* from Albania, Bulgaria and Romania who come with their families to work on strawberry culture. They are often undocumented despite the fact that their husbands may have legal working permits. They are employed in agriculture as assistants of their spouses and they are the lowest paid migrant group.

The wage level was often a point of contention among unskilled migrants and sometimes there were clashes between them in terms of who got the jobs. In the process, they often accepted to work for longer hours and/or for lower payment. Moreover, in many cases Bulgarians and Bangladeshis live in unfit conditions, in old shacks or huts built from plastic.

This situation led in 2008 to nearly 1,500 migrants – mostly from Bangladesh and the Balkan countries – refusing to work. The main demand of this collective mobilization was the payment of withheld wages, but they also claimed better daily rates and improved working and living conditions. Their demands were met with brutal violence from around 60 people, mostly strawberry producers, who in collaboration with their henchmen began beating the migrants. Two journalists from the daily newspaper *Eleftherotypia* exposed the story, revealing at the same time the dreadful housing and employment conditions. This drew the attention of the public authorities (Ministries of Employment, Public Order and Health) who conducted extensive inquiries in greenhouses in Manolada, confirming the reports. This 'heroic' event saw the daily wage for migrants increase to between 25 and 28 euros.

The availability of a cheap labour force contributed significantly to the expansion of the crop. Given that the possible reduction in capital investments (in greenhouses, fertilizers, etc.) was rather limited, cutting down the labour cost was a way to minimize the primary production cost. Thus, the availability of cheap labour has been crucial for the viability of the farm. It should be noted nevertheless that from the point of view of growers, migrant labour costs have risen considerably, although they admit that:

'You can't find a Greek who would want to do these jobs. This is something that we have had to accept as a fact' (*Fanis, strawberry grower, interview in Manolada, March 2007*).

As noted above, farmers plan their crop size based on the availability of migrant labour:

'[The grower] asked us. How many of you are looking for work? I tell him that there are about 18 or 19 of us. And based on this figure, the farmer decided on the number of hectares to plant' (*Aristos, Albanian agricultural supervisor, interview in Manolada, October 2007*). In other words, the principal agricultural production of the area was based upon an instantly available flexible workforce. For local farmers, this development was both a positive and negative consequence of migrant labour in the area. Before the arrival of migrant labour force, farmers were more prudent as to how much land they would cultivate:

> [In the past] there was a confinement of intensive cultures. Now there isn't [such limitation]. Just one grower may plant up to 500 stremmas [. . .] Today one may cultivate as much land as he wants. This is because he can find labour force.
>
> (*Petros, Agricultural Association representative, Elia, March 2007*)

Some growers argued that they would have abandoned their farm if it had not been for the availability of migrant labour, which allowed them to expand their cultivated land. By 2008 there were 4,000 stremmas of strawberry culture in Manolada.

It is important to note that after 2010 migrant wages in Manolada fell back to €22 per day, which was considered reasonable by strawberry growers who wanted to maintain labour costs at a low level.

By 2013, Manolada's strawberry fields had returned to the centre of public attention. On 17 April, 33 Bangladeshi migrant strawberry pickers were shot by their supervisors. The shootings occurred after around 200 migrant workers demanded to receive six months of unpaid work amounting to €150,000. Eight of them were seriously injured. This resulted in four suspects being arrested: the farm's owner and three supervisors. Although the campaign was unsuccessful in raising wages, it resulted in the prosecution of 80 employers for illegally hiring undocumented workers. The news was picked up by the international media which described the inhuman exploitation suffered by migrants working in the strawberry fields of the area. A significant campaign was launched, which called for a boycott of 'blood strawberries'.[3]

The practice by some farmers of withholding migrants' pay acts as a kind of 'labour control'. On the one hand it is a means of retaining the workforce at work and guaranteeing the constant availability of labour. On the other hand, it serves as a disciplinary mechanism that keeps the workforce in 'their place'. Of course, undocumented migrants are more likely to be disciplined and, are therefore to be more vulnerable to exploitation than their documented colleagues.

Currently, about 4,500 Bangladeshis are employed in strawberry culture in Manolada, and a further 900 Bangladeshis who arrive in the area during peak seasons, as well as a significant number of Bulgarians and Albanian migrants. Most Bangladeshi migrants are undocumented, although those who have been living in Greece for many years have been able to acquire legal status. Their working and living conditions are often harsh and even inhuman.

The construction sector during the economic crisis has shrunk. Some Albanian migrants have returned to their country of origin, while a good number of them have looked for employment in the local primary sector. A hierarchy is still evident in the local labour market, although it could be argued that this is now more closely related with the legal status of migrants. The agricultural jobs offered are not only distinguished by the different wages, but also by different working conditions and relations with farmers.

Over the last six years it seems that the economic recession has had very little impact on strawberry growers compared with the rest of the country. In other words, the economic crisis 'has not affected the local strawberry sector'. The crop has continued to expand and has reached 12,000 stremmas. As one local farmer notes: 'the whole area has become one big greenhouse' (*Takis, farmer, interview in Manolada, September 2015*). The wider coastal area around Manolada, Nea Manolada and Varda has seen a rapid expansion of strawberry fields. On the basis of recent observations, the crop has spread so much that it has virtually entered the environmentally protected zone of Strofylia.

The economic measures related to the economic recession could have a serious impact upon the production costs of strawberry production: the suggested increase of Value Added Tax on agricultural supplies will probably lead to the increase of the prices of the main agricultural inputs. Thus, the only available way for growers to curb production costs and lower investment risks is to lower labour costs. At a time when farm labour wages range from €20 to €22 per day, it appears that if strawberry cultivation is to continue to expand, the only way to manage the cultivation risks is to further increase the precarious conditions of migrant labour.

## 8.5 Conclusions

Highlighting the conditions under which intensive agriculture operates opens up a discussion about the social sustainability of rural areas. The movement of migrants towards rural areas has been a major basis for securing the ongoing development of agriculture. This population in Manolada consists of both permanent and temporary migrants. In the latter case, it is possible to distinguish different sub-types such as seasonal, casual or circular migrants.

A key issue is whether rural migrants are able to sustain the economic activity and, consequently, the social conditions that are necessary for the general well-being of rural areas. For employers, migrant populations represent a 'godsend gift' that minimizes costs in agricultural production and maintains greater flexibility (Rivoal, 2012, p. 203). Wages are kept at a low level, working time is extended or shortened according to production needs, there is a constant availability of low-cost labour through various channels, employment is informalized and workers' output is maximized.

Migrant labour has been of immense importance for increasing productivity in labour-intensive agricultural systems, while it is evident that in Greece and other countries its impact on local societies and economies is highly disputed by a segment of the indigenous population. The hierarchy of migrants, the 'ethnic' and gender divisions of labour, and the often dramatic employment and living conditions of migrants represent ways of controlling labour and lowering production costs in agriculture.

The availability, vulnerability and insecurity of migrant labour have been significant preconditions for the success of the labour process in the strawberry industry, which combines high technological and labour inputs. In each case, the place-based production systems have developed their own forms of migrant labour control. The labour input is possibly the single most important factor that allows for the increasing profitability of strawberry growers who are increasingly less able to manage the other production costs.

The antagonisms and social struggles between migrant labour and farmer are strongly influenced by the changing conditions of production in strawberry cultivation, which is highly competitive and greatly dependent on the capacity of export markets. The specific places in which strawberry production develops should be considered 'hotspots' of intensive agricultural systems, but also as locales where social struggles of migrant labour are particularly prominent.

The sharecropping system in the US (Wells, 1996) and the circular migration of female labourers recruited through the *contratacion en origen* in Spain (Hellio, 2014 and this volume) both represent major attempts to curb labour costs and to control and discipline migrant labour in the strawberry fields. In Manolada, the goal of maintaining cheap wages and keeping migrants in their insecure places at the bottom of the social pyramid of local society have been obtained through a number of factors including: the precarious legal status of migrant labourers; the 'ethnic' segmentation in the labour market; the informal system of recruitment; the practice of delaying the payment of wages; and, in some cases, the use of physical violence by supervisors and growers against their labourers. Thus, the Manolada case has become an example of how the claims of migrant labour have been contained and their participation in the local economy and society has been kept at a minimum level without leading to social unrest in the area.

## Notes

1 There is an extended discussion over the role and functionality of sharecropping in strawberry production and more generally in Californian agriculture, but it is not our aim to expand further on this issue here.

2 The former municipality of Vouprassia and its administrative centre of Varda is located in the Prefecture of Elia, in the Region of Western Greece. Following administrative reform initiated by the 'Kallikratis programme' (Greek Law 3852/2010), the Municipality of Vouprassia became part of the wider Municipality of Andravida-Kyllini. By 2011, Varda had a population of 3,072, followed by Nea Manolada with 2,006 and Manolada with 1,184 people (ELSTAT, 2011).

3 http://bloodstrawberries.tumblr.com/

## References

Agronews (2012). 'Agricultural lessons delivered by the strawberry'. *Agronews*, 28 February. Available from http://www.agronews.gr/?pid=162&la=1&aid=77450 (last accessed 24/9/2015). [in Greek]

Agronews (2014). 'We made a product exclusively for Russia'. *Agronews*, 11 August. Available from http://www.agronews.gr/agora/organoseis/arthro/117190/ftiaxame-proion-apokleistika-gia-ti-rosia-lene-oi-fraouloparagogoi/ (last accessed 8/9/2015). [in Greek]

Burawoy, M. (1976). 'The functions and reproduction of migrant labour: Comparative material from Southern Africa and the United States'. *American Journal of Sociology*, Vol. 81, No 5, pp. 1050–1087.

Carastathis, A. (2014). 'Blood, strawberries: Accumulation by dispossession and austere violence against migrant workers in Greece'. Paper presented in the *World Economics Association Conference 2014.*

Castles, S. (2006). 'Guestworkers in Europe: A resurrection?'. *International Migration Review*, Vol. 40, No 4, pp. 741–766.

Chandler, C. K., Folta, K., Dale, A., Whitaker, V. M. and Herrington, M. (2012). 'Strawberry' in Badenes, M.L. and Byrne, D.H. (eds.). *Fruit Breeding. Handbook of Plant Breeding 8*, Berlin: Springer, pp. 305–325.

De Zulueta, T. (2003) 'Migrants in irregular employment in the agricultural sector of southern European countries'. Report to the Committee on Migration, Refugees and Demography, Doc. 9883, Parliamentary Assembly, Council of Europe.

Dupraz, J. (2006). 'Agriculture and illegal employment in Europe, Report to the Committee on the Environment, Agriculture and Local and Regional Affairs'. Doc. 11114, Parliamentary Assembly, Council of Europe.

ELSTAT (2001). *Population Census 2001.* Athens: ELSTAT.

ELSTAT (2011). *Population Census 2011*. Athens: ELSTAT. Available from http://www.statistics.gr/en/statistics/-/publication/SAM03/- (last access on 20/2/2016).

Eurostat (2014). *Farm Structure Statistics*. Brussels: Eurostat. Available from http://ec.europa.eu/ eurostat/statistics-explained/extensions/EurostatPDFGenerator/getfile.php?file=195.251. 31.245_1443022349_25.pdf (last access on 20/2/2016).

Evans, N. (2013). 'Strawberry fields forever? Conflict over neo-productivist Spanish polytunnel technology in British agriculture'. *Land Use Policy*, Vol. 35, pp. 61–72.

FAO (2015). *FAO Statistical Yearbook*. Rome: FAO.

FIDH (2012). 'Importing workers, exporting strawberries: Working conditions on strawberry farms in the Huelva Province (Spain)'. Report of International Federation for Human Rights. Available from http://www.fidh.org (last access on 20/2/2016)

Gialis, S. and Herod, A. (2014). 'Of steel and strawberries: Greek workers struggle against informal and flexible working arrangements during the crisis'. *Geoforum*, Vol. 57, pp. 138–149.

Giannakis, E. and Bruggeman, A. (2015). 'The highly variable economic performance of European agriculture'. *Land Use Policy*, Vol. 45, pp. 26–35.

Hellio, E. (2014). ''We don't have women in boxes': Channeling seasonal mobility of female farmworkers between Morocco and Andalusia', in Gertel, J. and Sippel, S.R. (eds) *Seasonal Workers in Mediterranean Agriculture: The Social Costs of Easting Fresh*. London and New York: Routledge, pp. 141–157.

Kasimis, C. and Papadopoulos, A.G. (2005). 'The multifunctional role of migrants in the Greek countryside: implications for the rural economy and society'. *Journal of Ethnic and Migration Studies*, Vol. 31, pp. 99–127.

Kasimis, C., Papadopoulos, A.G. and Pappas, C. (2010). 'Gaining from rural migrants: Migrant employment strategies and socioeconomic implications for rural labour markets'. *Sociologia Ruralis*, Vol. 50, pp. 258–276.

Kasimis, C., Papadopoulos, A.G. and Zografakis, S. (2015). 'The precarious status of migrant labour in Greece: Evidence from rural areas' in D. Della Porta, S. Hänninen, M. Siisiäinen and T. Silvasti (eds) *The New Social Division: The Making and Unmaking of Precariousness*, London, Palgrave Macmillan, pp. 101–119.

Labrianidis, L. and Sykas, T. (2009). 'Geographical proximity and immigrant labour in agriculture: Albanian immigrants in the Greek countryside'. *Sociologia Ruralis*, Vol. 49, pp. 394–414.

Manion, J.T. (2001). 'Cultivating farmworker injustice: The resurgence of sharecropping'. *Ohio State Law Journal*, Vol. 62, pp. 1–19.

Mannon, S.E., Petrzelka, P., Glass, C.M. and Radel, C. (2012). 'Keeping them in their place: Migrant women workers in Spain's strawberry industry'. *International Journal of Sociology of Agriculture and Food*, Vol. 19, No 1, pp. 83–101.

Márquez Domínguez, J.A., Gordo Márquez, M. and García Delgado, F.J. (2009). 'Temporary 'contracts in origin' as policy to control immigration in Spain: The 'Huelva model''. *Cahiers de l'Urmis*, 12 June, published online. Available from http://urmis.revues.org/index878.html (last access on 20/2/2016).

Martinez Veiga, U. (2014). 'The political economy of El Ejido: Genealogy of the 2000 conflict', in Gertel, J. and Sippel, S.R. (eds) *Seasonal Workers in Mediterranean Agriculture: The Social Costs of Easting Fresh*. London and New York: Routledge, pp. 103–111.

Moragues-Faus, A., Ortiz-Miranda, D. and Marsden, T. (2013). 'Bringing Mediterranean agriculture into the theoretical debates', in Ortiz-Miranda, D., Moragues-Faus, A. and Arnalte-Alegre, E. (eds) *Agriculture in Mediterranean Europe: Between Old and New Paradigms*. Bingley: Emerald, pp. 9–35.

Neri, D., Baruzzi, G., Massetani, F. and Faedi, W. (2012). 'Strawberry production in forced and protected culture in Europe as a response to climate change'. *Canadian Journal of Plant Science*, Vol. 92, No. 6, pp. 1021–1036.

Papadopoulos, A.G. (2009). 'Begin from the bottom and move up': Social mobility of immigrant labour in rural Greece'. *Méditerranée*, No. 113, pp. 25–39.

Papadopoulos, A.G. (2011). 'Transnational immigration in rural Greece: Analysing the different mobilities of Albanian immigrants', in Hedberg, C and do Carmo, R.M. (eds) *Translocal Ruralism: Mobility and Connectivity in European Rural Spaces*. Dordrecht: Springer, pp. 163–183.

Papadopoulos, A.G. (2015). 'The impact of the CAP on agriculture and rural areas of EU Member States'. *Agrarian South: Journal of Political Economy*, Vol. 4, No. 1, pp. 22–53.

Papadopoulos, A.G. and Fratsea, L.M. (2013). 'The social and occupational mobility of migrants as a form of labour market integration'. *Geographies*, No. 22, pp. 73–90. [in Greek]

Plewa, P. and Miller, M.J. (2005). 'Postwar and post-Cold War generations of European temporary foreign worker policies: Implications from Spain'. *Migraciones Internacionales*, Vol. 3, No. 2, pp. 58–83.

Rivoal, C. (2012). 'Social responsibility in agriculture' in *CIHEAM, MediTERRA 2012*, Presses de Sciences Po (PFNSP), pp. 197–210. Available from http://www.cairn.info/mediterra-2012-english–9782724612486-page-197.htm (last access on 20/2/2016).

Schlosser, E. (1995). 'In the strawberry fields'. *The Atlantic Monthly*, November. Available from http://www.theatlantic.com/doc/199511/guest-workers (last access on 20/2/2016).

Walker, R.A. (1997). 'Commentary: Fields of dreams, or the best game in town', in Goodman, D. and Watts, M. (eds) *Globalising Food: Agrarian Questions and Global Restructuring*. London and New York: Routledge, pp. 273–284.

Wells, M.J. (1984). 'The resurgence of sharecropping: Historical anomaly or political strategy?'. *American Journal of Sociology*, Vol. 90, No. 1, pp. 1–29.

Wells, M.J. (1996). *Strawberry Fields: Politics, Class and Work in California Agriculture*. Ithaca, NY and London: Cornell University Press.

Wells, M.J. (1997). 'Legal discourse and the restructuring of Californian agriculture: Class relations at the local level', in Goodman, D. and Watts, M. (eds) *Globalising Food: Agrarian Questions and Global Restructuring*. London and New York: Routledge, pp. 173–187.

Zeneidi, D. (2011). 'Circular migration and misrecognition: the experience of spatial injustice of Moroccan women doing seasonal agricultural work in Huelva (Spain)', *Justice spatiale* [*Spatial Justice*], No. 3, pp. 1–10. Available from http://www.jssj.org (last access on 20/2/2016).

# Part III

# Restructuring of agri-food systems in Maghreb and the Middle-East

# 9 Contested red gold

## The tomato in the context of European–Moroccan relations

*Sarah Ruth Sippel*

Good day, my name is Masoussi.[1] A pretty name, isn't it? I was born in Morocco. A wonderful place. Yes indeed, I insist. An extraordinary sun-dappled country. In short, an ideal place. I mean, for a modest tomato like myself. Modest? Not really! I'm a Massoussi tomato! So I'm a star! [...]. Imagine me surrounded by more than five thousand people who jealously supervise my career as a star tomato from my birth to your shop. You don't believe me? Then take three minutes to listen to the story of my life. I'm a tomato born under the Moroccan sun [...]. The most beautiful sun in the world. And this is my tale ...

(Booklet of the Masoussi company, obtained in the Souss region in 2008, author's translation from French)

### 9.1 Introduction

With these words, the 'Masoussi tomato' invites us to learn more about its life from 'seed to plate' in the advertising campaign of the Moroccan–French company Masoussi. In this campaign, the company presents itself from the perspective of a 'cute' tomato that recounts its biography from greenhouse production and packaging in Morocco to the international distribution platform in Perpignan, France, and on to its arrival in the shopping basket of the consumer. Narrated in a naïve language and illustrated with appealing, simple pictures in a storybook style, the campaign creates a character that represents the company in a childlike way while appealing for sympathy. The tomato's life story connects with the central messages of the company: in terms of the compliance with quality standards, we learn that 'education is rather strict', and as for the requirement of traceability, we discover that 'it only takes a wink to learn all about my life'. Additionally, the principles of phytosanitary measures are referred to as 'the ladybirds protecting me against the nasty vine louses' and the company's social responsibility is advertised as follows: 'if they are doing that many things for me and my country of origin Morocco at Masoussi, then it is because they appreciate that the future of everyone of us is made today'.

It is not a coincidence that a tomato has been chosen as the congenial character of this advertising campaign: while tomatoes are among the most important Moroccan agricultural export products – for which the European Union (EU) is the main market – their entrance into the EU market is highly restricted and contested. The Moroccan–French company Masoussi is one example of the export-oriented tomato producers[2] in Morocco that aim at benefiting from an advantageous climate, access to natural resources, and low labour costs. While the export production is characterised by multifaceted interlinkages and forms of cooperation between European and Moroccan actors, it is simultaneously marked by economic and political ambiguities, conflicts and unequal power relations. The cute and harmless advertising character of the 'star tomato' has been created to present Morocco as a 'sun-dappled' production site fulfilling high-quality standards. However, the tomato has in fact been everything but a 'harmless' export product in Moroccan–European trade relations. On the contrary, it has been the subject of fierce negotiations over export quotas for several decades. These negotiations have not only been influenced by the respective interests of European and Moroccan producers but also by the foreign policy goals of EU and Moroccan politics. The tomato commodity chain from Morocco to the EU thus demonstrates how trade-related interests are coupled with security and geostrategic considerations regarding territorial conflicts, resource exploitation and migration.

This chapter uses the commodity chain of tomatoes from Morocco to the EU as a lens to address the multifaceted aspects that are influencing the trade of agricultural produce across the Mediterranean. Despite prevailing free trade rhetoric, agricultural commodities are still largely governed by political institutions (Raynolds, 2004; Talbot, 2009). This is particularly evident in the case of certain fruit and vegetables such as tomatoes, which are considered to be politically and economically sensitive by the EU and therefore are subject to the EU entry price system (Goetz and Grethe, 2009). At the same time, political institutions – in this case the EU – and the rules they set are embedded within constantly changing political constellations. Their governance can be seen as a result of multilayered and often conflicting political goals, interests of member states, or the influence of powerful lobby groups. By drawing on geographies of marketisation, Berndt and Boeckler (2012) have argued that the global movements of agricultural goods always involve both debordering and bordering processes, which constantly (re) draw spatial and territorial borders. Ambivalent border regimes, they contend, are a necessary condition for the construction of global markets and trade systems. Taking up this idea, this chapter demonstrates that the drawing and fixing of borders along agricultural commodity chains also draws on certain concepts of space that are equally ambivalent. The various actors and institutions involved in the tomato trade between Morocco and the EU employ, both explicitly and implicitly, spatial and territorial concepts to achieve their respective goals. The chapter will analyse these underlying concepts of spatiality and territoriality (Massey, 2005) to reveal the various interests that are involved in, and are actively shaping, the trans-Mediterranean tomato trade.

I argue that these interests become notably visible at three particular levels, which here I label as 'apple of discord', 'red gold' and 'occupation tomato'. The remainder of this chapter will address these three symbolic roles of the Moroccan tomato in the context of European–Moroccan relations. Section 9.2 focuses on the trade regulations set by the EU for the importation of tomatoes from Morocco. It explains why the tomato has become a constant 'apple of discord' in trade relations between Morocco and the EU and how the tomato export is currently governed. Section 9.3 then turns to Morocco and asks who in this country is actually producing tomatoes for export. It describes how tomatoes represent a 'red gold' from which not only Moroccan but also European producers are eager to benefit, often in the form of binational joint ventures. Section 9.4 addresses the recent relocation of tomato production to the territorially contested Western Sahara. It demonstrates how the 'Moroccan tomato' has been presented as an 'occupation tomato' by the Sahrawi resistance movement to protest against the exploitation of natural resources in Western Sahara. Empirically, the chapter draws on qualitative and quantitative data on the agricultural export industry in the Moroccan Souss region that was collected during nearly 12 months of field research between 2006 and 2009 (Sippel, 2014a).[3] In particular, I will refer to a selection of 37 qualitative interviews that I conducted with mid- and large-scale Moroccan export producers.

## 9.2 Apple of discord: negotiating export quotas

> About 100 Spanish farmers threw 200 kilogrammes of tomatoes at the European Parliament offices in Madrid Tuesday to fight against an EU-Morocco agricultural trade deal. [...] 'EU, don't betray our agriculture,' read a banner held by demonstrators who came from the southern province of Andalusia, heavily dependant [sic] on agricultural exports. 'The European Commission's agriculture policy deserves tomato-throwing, like an artist that performs badly,' said Andres Gongora of the Spanish farming body Coordinator of Farmers' and Stockbreeders' Organisations (COAG).
>
> (EU business, 2012, n.p.)

The stance of European agricultural policy towards Morocco has frequently raised objections among Spanish producers. As with the 2012 demonstration cited above, which was targeted against the negotiations of the EU–Morocco Agreement on Agricultural, Processed Agricultural and Fisheries Products (from now on referred to as the 'supplementary agreement'; *Journal officiel de l'Union européenne,* 2012), the tomato is often symbolically and physically present at the very core of protests. The representatives of the Spanish farmers have argued that Moroccan tomatoes are threatening Spanish production and thereby also employment in Spain. They claim that production and labour costs in Morocco are cheaper and that lower environmental, social and quality standards are allowed. It is along similar lines that European–Moroccan agricultural trade negotiations have been opposed since the 1990s by Spanish producers and their interest group the *Coordinadora de Agricultores y Ganaderos* (COAG). Already in 2000, the protest movement had gained such prominence that it had led to talk of a 'tomato war' (Martínez Veiga, 2014). How and why, therefore, is the tomato such a contested export good that it should represent an 'apple of discord' in European–Moroccan trade relations?

In 2013, Morocco exported 366,000 tonnes of tomatoes to Europe, which is the equivalent of 80 per cent of tomatoes imported to the EU from non-European countries (EU28 Extra-EU trade; EC, 2013). While the result of many years of trade negotiations, this amount also indicates Morocco's privileged position in the tomato trade with the EU (Chemnitz and Grethe, 2005). Currently, Morocco is the only country worldwide that has the right to export a certain amount of tomatoes to the EU at a privileged entry price below the most favoured nation entry price.[4] Due to the structure of the preferential agreement, Moroccan tomatoes are mainly exported within the indicated time period (October–May) and according to the quantity limits established by the entry price quota. Furthermore, an 'economic rent' is generated because the fixed entry prices function de facto as a minimum price for tomato imports. This price might be higher than the price for which Moroccan producers would have sold their produce had the entry price not existed.

The preferential treatment for Moroccan tomatoes is the result of historical roots as well as reasons related to the country's current political position. Historically, the preferential treatment has to be seen against the backdrop of the introduction of tomato production in Morocco. French settlers first established tomato production for the French market in the 1930s (Swearingen, 1987, p. 34 f.). Following Morocco's independence from France in 1956, tomato production was adopted by Moroccan producers and ever since – albeit under new political circumstances – this has been fostered within the context of an export-oriented agricultural development policy. Hence, in the recent *Plan Maroc Vert* – which was launched in 2008 and delineates Morocco's agricultural strategy until 2020 – the tomato remains a key agricultural commodity (Akesbi, 2011). In the decades after Morocco's independence, the export of tomatoes to Europe became increasingly constrained. A first limitation occurred at the end of the 1960s within the framework of the Common Agricultural Policy (CAP)[5] and was intensified when Greece, Spain and Portugal joined the European Community (EC) during the course of the 1980s. Morocco's agricultural exports to Europe were first limited by the association agreement of 1969; in the following cooperation agreement of 1976, export quotas and import calendars were introduced to shift exports to the counter season, i.e., the European winter months (M'barek, 2002). At the same time as the EU reached 99 per cent self-sufficiency for tomatoes after the accession of the southern European Mediterranean countries (White, 2001, p. 76), Moroccan tomato exports declined, averaging around 100,000 tonnes annually between the 1970s and 1990s (Redani, 2003, p. 24).

This development has to be understood against the backdrop of the expansion of intensive tomato production in the Spanish province of Almería (see Map 9.1). Initiated in the 1950s under the Francoist Dictatorship, the once socioeconomically marginalised province of Almería would later develop into the 'vegetable garden of Europe'. Since the 1980s, vegetable production in the area has accelerated. Key factors supporting this boom were the favourable natural and climatic conditions, state funding, EU subsidies for rural development, the opening up of European export markets after Spain's entry into the EC, as well as cheap migrant labour which, in the beginning, mainly originated from Morocco (Gertel and Sippel, 2014). Currently, there are about 30,000 hectares of vegetable production in greenhouses in Almería and about 70 per cent is directed at export markets (2,100,000 tonnes in 2012) (Aznar-Sánchez *et al.*, 2014, p. 112 f.). The farm structure is still relatively small: around 14,000 farmers cultivate on average 2.4 hectares, while an estimated number of between 70,000 and 80,000 people are directly employed in the vegetable production industry, most of them (irregular) migrants (Pumares and Jolivet, 2014, p. 130; Aznar-Sánchez *et al.*, 2014, pp. 115–118). Vegetable production contributes 24 per cent to the gross domestic product of the province and is thus of crucial social and economic importance. Moreover, agriculture is the only sector of the province that has not been affected by the recent economic crisis, mainly due to its strong export orientation (Aznar-Sánchez *et al.*, 2014, pp. 113–119). In 2013, the countries of the EU imported 2,656,000 tonnes of tomatoes from EU member states, with 36 per cent (or 947,000 tonnes) originating from Spain (EU28 Intra-EU; EC, 2013).

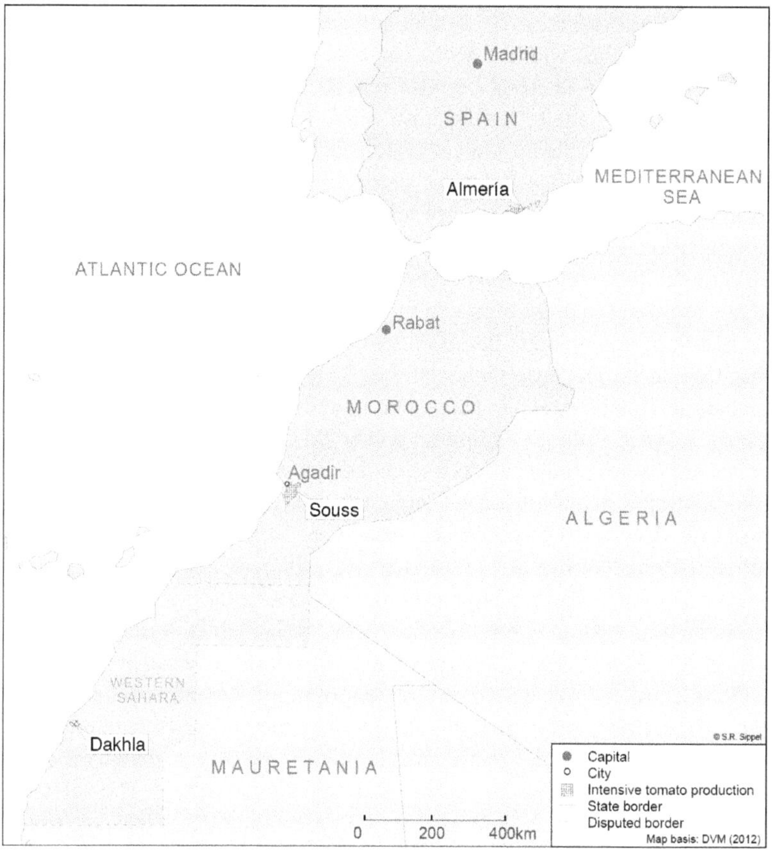


*Map 9.1* Intensive tomato production sites.

The economic and social importance of Spanish tomato production and its overlapping harvesting season with Morocco clearly explain why the Spanish growers strongly oppose the extension of the tomato trade with Morocco. Their position, however, is partly in conflict with the European Mediterranean policy that aims at 'democratisation and stability' within the framework of the Euro-Mediterranean Partnership in existence since the mid-1990s.[6] This policy has fostered the extension and successive liberalisation of economic relations with countries in the southern Mediterranean region.[7] While the EU aims at opening up markets for the export of industrial products, the import of sensitive agricultural products such as tomatoes is still restricted. One important instrument is the EU entry price system (Goetz and Grethe, 2009). At the same time, preferential trade agreements with certain countries for certain products do exist, as in the case of Moroccan tomatoes. The Moroccan entry price quotas have been increased regularly since the association agreement of 2000, and most recently in the supplementary agreement mentioned above, which, despite the protests of the Spanish farmers, entered into force on 1 October 2012 (EC, n.d.).

At $379 million, tomatoes have the highest export value of agricultural exports from Morocco (FAOSTAT for 2011) and, moreover, as I explain below, production is closely interlinked with the Moroccan elite. The supplementary agreement is a concession to these interests but also reflects aspects of EU foreign policy that go beyond purely trade-related interests. First, it is related to the upheavals in North Africa and the Middle East in late 2010 and 2011. As a strategy paper of the European Council on Foreign Relations states: 'if Morocco becomes less stable, this will impact directly on EU member states – whether in the form of increased illegal immigration, energy supply disruptions or political pressure from Moroccan diaspora communities within Europe' (Dennison *et al.,* 2011, p. 9). The paper continues that it was time to grant Morocco further trade privileges, namely for those products that until this moment had been less covered, which particularly meant agricultural products. The agreement can thus be interpreted as a means to foster political and social stability and to prevent undesired migration via economic trade concessions. As part of the EU's foreign policy, this goal has been placed above the interests of Spanish producers. As a second dimension, Morocco's cooperation in the 'war on terror' needs to be considered, which is of specific interest to Spain due to its close vicinity to Morocco (Dennison *et al.*, 2011).

It becomes clear that the EU still adheres to certain principles of protecting sensitive agricultural products within its borders: the EU entry price system serves as an instrument to separate the European trading space, which is defined by EU membership, and thereby seals this space against unwanted external produce such as potentially cheaper tomatoes from non-member third countries. The Spanish producers are referring to this spatial concept when they claim to maintain their protected 'trading space'. Preferential treatment as in the case of tomatoes, however, selectively opens this space whenever politically opportune. The selective opening and closure of trading possibilities becomes a political measure, which is also used to obtain foreign policy goals such as political stability and migration control. While the preferential treatment puts Morocco in a privileged position in comparison with other non-member competitors such as Turkey, from a

Moroccan perspective tomato exports to the EU nevertheless remain restricted. But who produces export tomatoes in Morocco?

## 9.3 Red gold: producing export tomatoes in Morocco

The Moroccan production of export tomatoes is mainly concentrated in one region in the southwest of the country: the Souss plain located between the High Atlas Mountains in the north, the Anti-Atlas mountains in the south and the Atlantic Ocean in the west (see Map 9.1). Ninety-seven per cent of tomatoes are exported from this region (EACCE, 2009a). Similar to the Almería region, export production takes place in greenhouses and relies on the labour of both male and female seasonal workers. Currently, the total number of people working in fruit and vegetable production of the Souss is estimated at more than 100,000 (Sippel, 2014a, p. 106). The boom in intensive agriculture has generated a large labour market that has triggered a high influx of internal labour migrants with many former and especially smaller farmers now securing their livelihoods as agricultural labourers (Bouchelkha, 2003; Sippel, 2014b). The greenhouses cover almost 4,400 hectares and about half of this area is dedicated to tomatoes (ORMVA/SM, 2008).[8] Annually, about 650,000 tonnes of tomatoes are produced and half of them are exported (ORMVA/SM, 2007), of which more than three-quarters as privately, mainly GlobalGAP-certified produce (Chemnitz, 2007, p. 10).[9] The export production of tomatoes is highly concentrated and internationalised.[10] A small number of people control large parts of production and exportation and are closely connected with the Moroccan elite, including the Moroccan King and significant economic and political figures, such as the Mayor of Agadir. One-tenth of farms accumulate almost half of the tomato growing area, while the four largest packing stations together process more than 40 per cent of exported tomatoes (see Tables 9.1 and 9.2). Three of these belong to a Moroccan–French group in which the Moroccan partner owns 75 per cent of the shares.

*Table 9.1* Greenhouse production of tomatoes in the Moroccan Souss

<table>
<tr><th colspan="2" rowspan="2"></th><th colspan="3">Farms</th><th colspan="3">Production</th></tr>
<tr><th colspan="2">Number</th><th>Share (%)</th><th colspan="2">Area (ha)</th><th>Share (%)</th></tr>
<tr><td rowspan="2">≤5 ha</td><td><2 ha</td><td>83</td><td rowspan="2">281</td><td rowspan="2">54.6</td><td>89</td><td rowspan="2">672</td><td rowspan="2">17.4</td></tr>
<tr><td>≥2 to 5 ha</td><td>198</td><td>583</td></tr>
<tr><td rowspan="2">>5 to 15 ha</td><td>>5 to 10 ha</td><td>103</td><td rowspan="2">166</td><td rowspan="2">32.2</td><td>694</td><td rowspan="2">1,435</td><td rowspan="2">37.3</td></tr>
<tr><td>>10 to 15 ha</td><td>63</td><td>741</td></tr>
<tr><td colspan="2">>15 ha</td><td colspan="2">68</td><td>13.2</td><td colspan="2">1,744</td><td>45.3</td></tr>
<tr><td colspan="2">Total</td><td colspan="2">515</td><td>100</td><td colspan="2">3,851</td><td>100</td></tr>
</table>

Source: Personal communication in 2008, Office Régional de Mise en Valeur/Souss Massa (ORMVA/SM); date of data not provided.

*Table 9.2* Tomato export by packing stations

| | *Packing stations* | | *Tomato export* | |
|---|---|---|---|---|
| | *Number* | *Share (%)* | *Total tonnage (t)* | *Share (%)* |
| ≤1,000 t | 14 | 29.2 | 3,393 | 1.0 |
| >1,000 to 5,000 t | 16 | 33.3 | 52,088 | 15.8 |
| >5,000 to 10,000 t | 8 | 16.7 | 52,587 | 16.0 |
| >10,000 to 15,000 t | 3 | 6.3 | 36,105 | 11.0 |
| >15,000 to 20,000 t | 3 | 6.3 | 47,541 | 14.4 |
| >20,000 t | 4 | 8.3 | 137,896 | 41.8 |
| Total | 48 | 100 | 329,610 | 100 |

Source: Personal communication in 2008, Etablissement Autonome de Contrôle et de Commercialisation des Exportations (EACCE); data provided for 2007/08.

Since the 1990s, French producers, in particular, have invested in tomato production, while since the 2000s, Spanish entrepreneurs have also become common in the Souss, focusing primarily on growing and exporting green beans (Sippel, 2014b). European investment in the region responds to the goal of European retailers to provide their customers with fresh fruit and vegetables all year round. This requires complementary production and delivery during the European winter months. The Souss region has become a favoured counter-seasonal production site due to its proximity to Europe, the advantageous climate, access to natural resources, low labour costs, as well as stable political conditions and an investment-friendly economic policy. The percentage of European actors and their total share are difficult to quantify as they are producing and exporting both individually and in cooperation with Moroccan partners, whose numbers and shares in businesses also fluctuate. According to my own empirical data, around one-third of the 85 packing stations for vegetables were (partly) founded[11] with European capital, which include those with a significant share in exported produce (own data 2009). European producers, who export a part of the contested quotas on their own or in cooperation with Moroccan partners, are thus among the main beneficiaries of the 'red gold'.

The most prominent example of European investment is a Moroccan–French company that was established as a partnership in 1988 and was one of the first vertically integrated export businesses in the Souss. Since its foundation, the company has expanded considerably and has also undergone several internal restructuring processes, including the creation of a spin-off company that follows the same business model. Currently, the two companies alone produce vegetables in about 1,000 hectares of greenhouses in the Souss and contribute around one-third of exported tomatoes (own calculation, based on data obtained in 2008). The group has also invested in greenhouse production in Dakhla (see below). While this cooperation is by far the most prominent case, there are several other examples of Moroccan–European partnerships, with some more institutionalised than others. The company Moraprim is an example of a much smaller business.

Set up as a joint venture between a Moroccan apple producer and a French food-processing company in 1992, this company owns 25 hectares of greenhouses, 20 of them dedicated to tomatoes, and additionally works with around 10 Moroccan contractors who cultivate between 2 and 30 hectares. The exported produce is mainly directed at the French parent company. The fierce competition surrounding the 'Moroccan tomato' – which, as demonstrated above, is strongly opposed by Spanish farmers and only selectively admitted to European space – is therefore, at least in part, a territorially relocated variant of 'European' competition. Given this situation, how are European agricultural policy and European investments perceived by the Moroccan export producers?

Three types of Moroccan export producers can be distinguished: 'family businesses', 'young entrepreneurs' and 'investors'. 'Family businesses' consist of large family holdings that often include several generations of family members. These families originate from the Souss region and have often been able to realise a remarkable degree of upward social mobility within the context of the export sector. The 'young entrepreneur' designates a group of producers who have been able to enter the (vegetable) export sector due to their high level of education and a special credit programme offered by the Moroccan state (*crédit jeunes promoteurs*). The category of 'investors', in turn, refers to Moroccan, often urban, actors who are not necessarily agricultural producers in the first instance but consider agriculture as an investment asset. All three types of producers can be integrated into the export market either as suppliers, or as members of cooperatives or export groups. Alternatively, they may export within the framework of individual partnerships or as vertically integrated businesses (Sippel, 2014a). Below I quote from interviews with Moroccan export producers who can be classified as family businesses and young entrepreneurs. They belong to the mid- and large-scale producers in the Souss region and are all very well integrated into export chains. These producers possess an ambivalent attitude towards the strong presence of investors from 'Europe', which itself is loaded with multifaceted connotations.

Three forms of identification with, or distanciation from, 'Europe' can be distinguished, depending on whether this refers to European trade policy, Europe as a competing producer, or Europeans as trade and investment partners. To begin with, Europe is considered without doubt the most important export market to which there are no real alternatives. At the same time, European trade policy is regarded as highly restrictive on Moroccan tomato exports. Spain, in particular, is perceived to be the pre-eminent opponent and of taking, due to its EU membership, an unfair position with regards to Morocco. Morocco as a non-European country is in turn characterised as disadvantaged on the basis of political interests rather than its level of competitiveness. At the same time, however, my interviewees expressed their awareness that there exist complex competing agricultural interests also within Europe, as the following quote demonstrates:

> Our only chance to stay in business is Europe, we don't have another market. [...] What we are asking is that Europe supports us more ... but not financially, not financially! [...] Just one thing: open your market! Opening your

> market means allowing me to produce. […] That's all, it's that simple – well, simple, that's easily said, for sure it's much more complicated. We know there are Spanish producers in Europe, … who defend their earnings, French producers, Dutch producers – it's an equation with several variables.
>
> (Aziz Rachik, export producer with 11 hectares of greenhouse production at the time of interview in 2006)

The European investments in the Souss add a further dimension to the sealing off of the European market through the competition it creates with European producers in the Souss. This implies competition for scarce natural resources as well as scarce export quotas, which are both exacerbating the situation. Here, the motives of the Moroccan state are called into question regarding the support of foreign investment and their implications for smaller producers while European policy appears even more paradoxical. From the perspective of the Moroccan producers, European investors do not only exploit scarce water and land resources at the expense of the local population but also siphon off the already scarce tomato quotas:

> We have to call a spade a spade. We took a political decision at the national level, and it is difficult to oppose political decisions. As you know, Morocco is an open country. […] But the development of foreign agriculture in Morocco, to put it bluntly, scares us a bit. […] Frankly speaking, these people are welcome but we would also like them to remember to defend the Moroccan quotas. […] My wish would be that if they come here and produce 1,000 tonnes, then these should not count as part of the [Moroccan] quota, because we are blocked, we are not allowed to exceed the quota, we have to respect the entry prices!
>
> (Nabil Bouguenouch, export producer with 20 hectares of greenhouse production at the time of interview in 2006)

Nonetheless, Europeans are not only viewed as the dominant producers favoured by market restrictions or as competing investors in Morocco. They are also indispensable trade partners in the export business and can take on the role of important financiers for joint ventures in the Souss. Here, a third dimension appears: Europeans as important business and investment partners. These partnerships can offer opportunities as well as risks, but if they are successful, they can enable projects to be realised that otherwise would very likely not have been possible. This has been the case for the producers Youssef Lkam and Fouad Achouri. In the following quote, Youssef Lkam explains why he has opted to participate in a joint venture with European investors:

> The advantage is … I cannot do this just by myself, it's a partnership with Europeans, a kind of joint venture – if this wasn't the case I would not have been able to do this [project]! […] They are large firms that are interested in establishing themselves in Morocco, through us if you like. They want guaranteed production, that's why they are searching for a partnership. […]

> A partnership means someone shares the risks with you, at 50 per cent […], it buffers the risks as well!
>
> (Youssef Lkam, export producer with 145 hectares of greenhouse production at the time of interview in 2006)

The opportunity to make investments on a larger scale was also a motive for Fouad Achouri to attempt to re-establish his business with European partners on several occasions. After a number of failed projects, he has now been working with a French company for more than ten years with which he is now a partner. The partnership does not only give him the financial means to invest in production and packaging in the Souss, but has also opened up for him new possibilities of action in Europe where he, as he himself puts it, is no longer a 'stranger': 'I'm almost like a European citizen, I have a visa for two, three years […], I can move freely in Europe, without any problems' (Fouad Achouri, export producer with 35 hectares of greenhouse production at the time of interview in 2006).

Lastly, the large European–Moroccan joint ventures are also regarded as 'advocators' for Moroccan produce in Europe. According to Anouar Layachi, as market leaders they have enabled and promoted the success of Moroccan produce on the European market. This situation, he stresses, should not be ignored when European production in the Souss and its share of export quotas are both criticised:

> They [the companies] add a lot to the value of Moroccan produce in Europe, that's normal …. […] I could not even imagine what the situation would be like without the large groups in Europe … I don't think Moroccan products would be able to achieve their present status in Europe if this were not the case, all of this would be finished. […] They have done much for the label 'Maroc', that's for sure.
>
> (Anouar Layachi, export producer with 11 hectares of greenhouse production at the time of interview in 2006)

The attitudes of Moroccan export producers towards 'Europe' are thus complex and multilayered. A clear position exists regarding the agricultural policy of the EU. EU policy is considered to discriminate against Moroccan tomatoes for political reasons because Morocco is not a part of the EU trading space. Here, Moroccan producers call for an opening of the European market. This call, however, does not take into account Morocco's privileged and therefore protected position against other non-European competitors. Competitors such as Turkey could be potentially cheaper if a 'total' liberalisation of the market were to occur. European investments in the Souss are, in turn, read in a much more ambivalent way. The European quota system is regarded as increasingly paradoxical as it establishes a highly selective import system based on criteria of national territoriality, which is, however, blind to the deterritorialised, border-crossing character of actors and financial flows. Following the territorial logic of the import system, the export quotas are considered as 'Moroccan' and, as such, reserved for 'Moroccans'. At the same time, the manifold interlinkages between Moroccan and European actors make it increasingly difficult for producers to draw and adhere to these national boundaries: Europeans are not only indispensable trading partners, they are also key actors whose cooperation is of crucial importance and can yield significant benefits.

## 9.4 Occupation tomato: dislocating to Western Sahara

In addition to the relocation of European production to Moroccan territory since the 1990s, there has been a second wave of relocation to the south. Currently, the region of Dakhla, situated about 1,200 kilometres south of Agadir, is being developed for intensive greenhouse production, primarily for high-value crops such as cherry tomatoes (see Map 9.1). Dakhla is both a strategic and territorially contested production site because it is located in a part of Western Sahara that has been occupied by Morocco since the end of the 1970s.[12] The interests of the Moroccan state lie especially in the exploitation of Western Sahara's (assumed) rich resources, mainly phosphate and fishing industries (Smith, 2013; Torres-Spelliscy, 2014). In a similar vein, the promotion of intensive agriculture aims at exploiting natural resources while at the same time serving to substantiate territorial claims. Recently, this production in Dakhla has drawn the attention of the Sahrawi resistance movement. Within this context, the Moroccan tomato acquires a third connotation. It is symbolically turned into an 'occupation tomato' and once again represents a conflict of interests, in this case between the Moroccan state and a number of large-scale producers, on the one hand, and the Sahrawi resistance movement, on the other.

In the early 2000s, producers from the Souss first started to acquire land in Western Sahara for vegetable export production. The group Les Domaines Agricoles, owned by the Moroccan King and the Moroccan–French company Masoussi, was one of the first investors. According to my own data collected in 2009, four of the largest companies of the Souss also produced in Dakhla while a fifth was about to acquire land. Currently, the production in Dakhla is estimated to take place in around 500 hectares of greenhouses (EP, 2012a). The 2012 report by Western Sahara Resource Watch stated that there were eleven farms exporting close to 60,000 tonnes of vegetables, the lion's share of which were tomatoes (WSRW and EMMAUS Stockholm, 2012, p. 4).

Agricultural production in Dakhla is mainly backed by a small group of export producers who belong to the largest producers in the Souss. They pursue a number of strategic goals as the interview with Charles Bertrand, one of the main investors, reveals. A first key issue is the favourable climate, which allows for earlier production and therefore a more lucrative placement of the produce on the European market. The availability of water resources, he explains, is a second important factor given the overexploitation and foreseeable depletion of groundwater resources in the Souss:

> I believe the region has substantial, even enormous potential because the problem we have here [in the Souss] is the availability of water … it's difficult to say but we maybe have ten, fifteen years at the most! […] This

> problem doesn't exist over there where water is abundant [...], there are fossil groundwater tables that have existed for thousands of years [...], there is a very large groundwater table.
>
> (Charles Bertrand, partner in a Moroccan–French joint venture, 2006)

Against the backdrop of the restricted access to the EU market, a third layer of interests is evident. As more and more investments have been made in the Souss, the tomato export quotas have become increasingly scarce. Accordingly, Charles Bertrand stresses the importance of opening up new markets, particularly the US market. In contrast to the Souss, where agricultural produce would not be approved for export to the US due to phytosanitary reasons, exports from Dakhla would be allowed.[13] This makes investment in the region all the more attractive:

> As you know, there are export quotas in place for Europe, which means we can't export as much as we would like to. [...] In the meantime, as you can imagine, if more people are coming and investing, we are hindered from exporting our produce. And that's why we are in Dakhla: it's our goal to export to the US and this is a region [...], which has been approved for export by the Americans.
>
> (Charles Bertrand, partner in a Moroccan–French joint venture, 2006)

While Charles Bertrand acknowledges that Western Sahara is a territorially contested region, he neither considers this as an obstacle to investment nor does he expect a fundamental change of the geopolitical situation:

> It's a region which is not yet ... politically it's a bit difficult, a bit unstable, as you know there are a few problems, but in the end Morocco is present over there and I don't think this will change – it has been 30 years now and that won't change.
>
> (Charles Bertrand, partner in a Moroccan–French joint venture, 2006)

Hence, Dakhla is a strategic production site due to its climatic conditions and natural resources, which further combine with considerations regarding the saturation of export markets in the context of export quotas as well as the goal of opening up new markets against the backdrop of phytosanitary regulations. It should be stressed, however, that agricultural production in Dakhla requires massive financial investment as well as political contacts on site and is therefore only an option for very powerful exporters.

In recent years, the situation has attracted the attention of the Sahrawi resistance movement, which has started to document production in Dakhla on its website under the headlines of 'occupation' and 'conflict' tomatoes (Hagen, 2009; WSRW, 2009). With the financial support of the Swedish NGO EMMAUS Stockholm, Western Sahara Resource Watch published a report in 2012 directed at three audiences: the EU, European retailers and European consumers (WSRW and EMMAUS Stockholm, 2012). With respect to the EU, the report criticised, in particular, the negotiation of the supplementary agreement of 2012, which continued to not define the national borders of Morocco. The 'vague territorial scope' of the agreement essentially allowed Morocco to determine the border of its national territory. As a result, vegetables produced in Western Sahara but labelled as '*Produit du Maroc*' by the export control agency, the *Etablissement Autonome de Contrôle et de Coordination des Exportations* (EACCE), could be exported to the EU. This would be against the EU Directive 2005/29 on Unfair Commercial Practices (Official Journal of the European Union, 2005) and contrary to the treatment of produce from the occupied territories in Palestine. The NGO thus claimed:

> The [European] Commission must clarify the territorial scope of the Agreement with Morocco. Any agreement between the EU and Morocco can only apply to the territory which is recognised under international law as 'Morocco'. As a result, any waiving of import duties can only be applied to Moroccan produce, not to Western Saharan produce. The Commission must inform importers that they cannot claim preference when importing goods from Western Sahara.
>
> (WSRW and EMMAUS Stockholm, 2012, p. 21)

Besides the EU – which would be in charge of guaranteeing that falsely labelled produce could not cross its borders – the campaign also addressed the responsibility of the private sector and the ethical awareness of consumers. The report requested European retailers to control the correct origin of their produce and to make sure they were not selling to their customers produce from Western Sahara falsely labelled as originating from Morocco. Finally, it aimed to reveal how 'unaware European consumers unwittingly contribute to perpetuating an illegitimate and brutal occupation with dire human rights consequences, by purchasing products that are being systematically mislabelled with the wrong country of origin' (WSRW and EMMAUS Stockholm, 2012, p. 2). To prevent this, the 'ethically minded' European consumer was called upon to boycott certain labels and supermarkets featured in the report, and was asked to support the organisation by identifying and detecting false labels of origin. Ultimately, the consumer is advised to question the retailer about the 'true origin' of all products that 'claim to be Moroccan' (WSRW and EMMAUS Stockholm, 2012, p. 21). Hence, not only were tomatoes of 'Moroccan origin' symbolically charged with being 'occupation tomatoes', but produce originating from Morocco in general has been placed under suspicion of false labelling and associated with occupation and the violation of human rights.

Although the supplementary agreement – which Western Sahara Resource Watch sought to block – was finally signed, the campaign received considerable attention. For example, it was raised during the European parliamentary debate on the supplementary agreement by the rapporteur to the Committee on International Trade, José Bové, who problematised the territorial question as follows:

> Several times over the past few months, the rapporteur has raised the question of the territorial range of the agreement between the European Union and Morocco. [...] As the Commission and Parliament's Legal Service hold diverging views on this issue, the rapporteur feels unable to guarantee that this free trade agreement will comply with the international treaties binding the European Union and all its Member States.
>
> (EP, 2012b, n.p.)

Moreover, the campaign urged representatives of the Greens to pose a parliamentary question to the European Commission to verify the data on agriculture in Western Sahara, which was one of the reasons why the Greens opposed the supplementary agreement (EP, 2012b; The Greens in the European Parliament, 2012). Lastly, the media also referred to the WSRW report in their coverage of the EU trade agreement and agriculture in Western Sahara (Govan, 2012; Quarante, 2014). Whether European retailers and consumers might effectively change their purchasing and consumption behaviour remains to be seen. Nevertheless, the campaign attracted considerable public attention and thus achieved one of its most important goals.

It is unlikely, however, that the issue of tomato exports from Western Sahara will lead to a political change at EU level. First, tomato production remains marginal in comparison to the exploitation of phosphate and fishery resources. Furthermore, Moroccan resource exploitation in Western Sahara is not necessarily against international law, which highlights the complex constellation of interests at play. Regardless of whether Morocco is considered either 'de facto administrator' or an 'occupying power', as Torres-Spelliscy points out (2014), international law does not apply an absolute bar to the development of natural resources in non-self-governing territories because economic development activities are considered potentially beneficial to the local population. Thus, the economic development of natural resources in Western Sahara is permitted if two conditions are met: 'first, any such activities must be, objectively speaking, in the interest of the local population; and second, they must be done in consultation and coordination with the local population' (Torres-Spelliscy, 2014, p. 250). Whether this also applies to the production of tomatoes would require clarification. Further to the legal situation, as Gillespie (2010, p. 89) notes, the resolution of the Saharan conflict never made it onto the EU policy agenda but has been delegated to the United Nations. Gillespie identifies the main reasons for this as being the intractability of the conflict and the different positions of EU member states, specifically France and Spain. Nevertheless, the complex situation has not prevented the EU from seeking to reinforce European–Moroccan relations, an observation supported by the case of the tomato trade.

To conclude, the 'occupation tomato' symbolically represents a further dimension within European–Moroccan trade relations, especially with regard to the national status of Western Sahara. While the Moroccan state uses the production of tomatoes to underpin its territorial power, those companies that are involved in the industry pursue mainly resource- and market-oriented interests, for which the unresolved territorial status is of no objection. The EU, in turn, leaves the territorial question deliberately undetermined to avoid a clear position in the face of conflicting interests among its member states. This subsequently leaves the Moroccan state to determine the demarcation of its territorial border. The NGO Western Sahara Resource Watch used this situation to denounce the false labelling of produce and, on behalf of European consumers, called for an 'unambiguous territoriality' in the definition of designations of origin.

## 9.5 Conclusion

Tomatoes are a very lucrative and thus contested commodity in European–Moroccan trade relations. This chapter has focused on the complex constellations of interests that have had an impact on the trade of this 'red gold' in the Mediterranean region and it has specifically addressed the underlying concepts of space and territoriality employed by various actors and institutions. The EU has set up a closed trading space to protect especially sensitive products against potentially cheaper competition. The EU entry price system works as a gatekeeper, protecting the space while simultaneously opening it for selected products, such as Moroccan tomatoes, during certain time periods and according to carefully determined quotas. These selective openings are not only influenced by trade-related considerations but also the EU's foreign policy goals in relation to stability and security. In addition, the chapter has presented the perspectives of Spanish and Moroccan producers, both of whom aim to defend and extend their interests within this system while at the same time trying to influence the system itself by maintaining as well as questioning existing borders. Some actors also exercise cross-border mobility and engage in transnational partnerships, thereby leading to a constant blurring of the opposition between 'European' and 'Moroccan' actors and produce. European production has been relocated to Moroccan territory, which has resulted in a paradoxical situation where some of the cheap Moroccan tomatoes contested by Spanish farmers in Europe are produced and exported by European producers themselves. At a further level, questions of sovereignty and self-determination in relation to Western Sahara are impacting upon the tomato export industry. In this case, more recently the Sahrawi resistance movement has instrumentalised the tomato export for its own purposes of mobilising against Moroccan occupation. Finally, in terms of symbols of product quality, various actors are trying to promote particular images of the Moroccan tomato, be it the falsely labelled 'occupation tomato' or the cute 'star tomato'. Conflicts of interests pertaining to agricultural products in the Mediterranean region are thus carried out at many levels, from the physical quality and price of the product to the power over spaces and discursive branding.

## Notes

1 All the names used for companies and interviewees in this chapter are pseudonyms.
2 In addition to tomatoes, the company also produces other fruit and vegetables for export markets.

3 My field research was financially supported by the German Research Foundation (DFG), for which I am very grateful.

4 For a detailed analysis of the preferential trade agreement for tomatoes from Morocco, see Chemnitz and Grethe (2005) and van Berkum (2013). Reduced entry price quotas during certain time periods are also in place for other fruit and vegetables from Morocco (*Journal officiel de l'Union européenne,* 2012, pp. 7–8/12). In all other cases, either the EU entry price system (Goetz and Grethe, 2009) or the usual tariffs (for those agricultural products that are not subject to the EU entry price system) are applied (Grethe and Tangermann, 1999; Grethe *et al.*, 2005).

5 The CAP, developed by the European Community (EC) in the 1950s and outlined and agreed upon in the Treaty of Rome (1957), set European agricultural policy over the following decades. One of its key objectives was a policy of import substitution of agricultural products. Among its major results, the EC overcame the food shortages of the 1950s, achieved self-sufficiency, and then generated considerable surpluses that were exported. Since the 1980s, financial constraints and a changing international agricultural context have set in motion a reform process of the CAP that is still ongoing (Tangermann and von Cramon-Taubadel, 2013).

6 Since 2008, these explicitly normative goals have been replaced by a commitment to democracy, pluralism, constitutional legality, and fundamental human rights within the context of the Union for the Mediterranean (Jünemann, 2009, p. 59).

7 See the portal of the European Commission on the Euro-Mediterranean Partnership (http://ec.europa.eu/trade/policy/countries-and-regions/regions/euro-mediterranean-partnership/); regarding Moroccan–European trade relations, see also Brunel (2009).

8 The Souss is also a major region for the production of other fruits and vegetables. More than 90 per cent of Moroccan vegetable exports originate from the Souss, among them bell peppers (98 per cent), courgettes (92 per cent), and green beans (80 per cent) (EACCE, 2009a). The production of vegetables other than tomatoes has intensified over recent years due to the restriction on exports. Furthermore, two-thirds of citrus fruit exports originate from the Souss region (EACCE, 2009b).

9 The Global GAP standard (originally EurepGAP) was developed in 1997 by the Euro-Retailer Produce Working Group in order to create a standard for certifying 'good agricultural practices'. The standard covers food safety and traceability, protection of the environment, working conditions as well as animal welfare, and adopts various crop, pest and quality management systems (see www.globalgap.org).

10 The intensive export production mainly relies on groundwater irrigation, which has led to a lowering of the groundwater tables. This has had a massive impact on rural livelihood securities, which I elaborate upon elsewhere (Sippel, 2014a, 2014b).

11 Ownership structures can have changed since the establishment of the packing station.

12 There are two opposing rights in the West Saharan conflict: the right to self-determination claimed by the Sahrawian population and the principle of national sovereignty claimed by the Moroccan state (Maghraoui, 2003; Joffé, 2010). The history of the conflict and its geopolitical context are highly complex (Pham, 2010; Gillespie, 2010; Saidy, 2011; Boukhars and Roussellier, 2014). In short, when the former colonial power Spain withdrew from Western Sahara in 1976 both Morocco and Mauritania laid claim to the territory, which led to a military conflict with the liberation movement *Frente Polisario* (Frente Popular para la Liberación de Saguia el-Hamra y Río de Oro). After Mauritania withdrew from Western Sahara in 1979, Morocco has controlled 85 per cent of the territory. Following the ceasefire in 1988, Polisario and Morocco agreed to a UN peace plan in 1991 that foresaw a referendum to resolve the conflict. To date, however, no such referendum has taken place. The UN considers Western Sahara as a 'non-self-governing territory'.

13 However, Western Sahara is not included in the free trade agreement between Morocco and the US, which entered into force in 2006 (Brunel, 2009, p. 223).

## References

Akesbi, N. (2011). 'Le Plan Maroc Vert: une analyse critique'. *Questions d'économie marocaine 2011*. Association Marocaine de Sciences Economiques, Presse Universitaire du Maroc, Rabat, pp. 9–48.

Aznar-Sánchez, J., Belmonte-Urena, L. and Tapia-León, J.T. (2014). 'The industrial agriculture: A model for modernization from Almería?' in Gertel, J. and Sippel, S.R. (eds) *Seasonal Workers in Mediterranean Agriculture: The Social Costs of Eating Fresh*. London: Routledge, pp. 112–120.

Berndt, C. and Boeckler, M. (2012). 'Mobile Grenzen, entgrenzte Orte und verortete Waren: Das Beispiel des Agrarhandels zwischen Marokko und der EU' in Gertel, J. and Breuer, I. (eds) *Alltagsmobilitäten: Aufbruch marokkanischer Lebenswelten*. Bielefeld: Transcript, pp. 219–239.

Bouchelkha, M. (2003). 'La serriculture: Evolution et dynamisme d'un nouvel âge agricole au Maroc. Le cas de Souss-Massa'in Bouchelkha, M. (ed.) *L'espace rural dans le Souss. Héritage et changements*. Université Ibn Zohr, Faculté des lettres et des sciences humaines Agadir/Groupe d'études et de recherches sur le sud marocain, Actes du Colloque organisé le 15 et 16 Mars 1996, Agadir: Sud Contact, pp. 149–178.

Boukhars, A. and Roussellier, J. (eds) (2014). *Perspectives on Western Sahara: Myths, Nationalisms, and Geopolitics*. Lanham: Rowman and Littlefield.

Brunel, C. (2009). 'Morocco-EU Trade Relations' in Hufbauer, G.C. and Brunel, C. (eds) *Capitalizing on the Morocco-US Free Trade Agreement: A Road Map for Success*. Washington, DC: Peterson Institute for International Economics, pp. 221–236.

Chemnitz, C. (2007). 'The compliance process of food quality standards on primary producer level: A case study of the EUREPGAP Standard in the Moroccan tomato sector'. Working Paper No. 81, Wirtschafts- und Sozialwissenschaftlichen Fachgebiete der Landwirtschaftlich-Gärtnerischen Fakultät der Humboldt-Universität zu Berlin, Berlin.

Chemnitz, C. and Grethe, H. (2005). 'EU trade preferences for Moroccan tomato exports – who benefits?'. Paper prepared for presentation at the 99th seminar of the EAAE (European Association of Agricultural Economists) *The Future of Rural Europe in the Global Agri-food System*, Copenhagen.

Dennison, S., Popescu, N. and Torreblanca, J.I. (2011). 'A chance to reform: How the EU can support democratic evolution in Morocco'. *Policy Brief*, European Council on Foreign Relations.

DVM (Digital Vector Maps) (2012). Digital-vector-maps.com/WORLD/WM-1979-Free-Vector-World-Maps.htm (last access on 21 June 2013).

EACCE (Etablissement Autonome de Contrôle et de Coordination des Exportations) (2009a). 'Bilan des statistiques d'exportation des produits maraîchères 2008–2009'. Casablanca, http://web2.eacce.org.ma/Publications/Bilans Statistiques/tabid/162/Default.aspx (last access on 12 July 2010).

EACCE (Etablissement Autonome de Contrôle et de Coordination des Exportations) (2009b). 'Bilan des statistiques d'exportation des agrumes 2008–2009'. Casablanca, http://web2.eacce.org.ma/Portals/0/BILAN%20AGRUM ES%20ET%20SYNTHESES %202009.pdf (last access on 12 July 2010).

EC (European Commission) (n.d.). 'Countries and regions: Morocco'. http://ec.europa.eu/trade/policy/countries-and-regions/countries/morocco/, access on 12 August 2014.

EC (European Commission) (2013). 'Export helpdesk: Statistics'. http://exporthelp.europa.eu/thdapp/display.htm?page=st%2fst_Statistics.html&docType=main&languageId=en, access on 6 November 2014.

EP (European Parliament) (2012a). 'Subject: Agricultural activity in western Sahara', Parliamentary question, 2 March 2012. http://www.europarl.europa.eu/sides/getDoc.do?pubRef=-%2f%2fEP%2f%2fTEXT%2bWQ%2bE-2012–002451%2b0%2bDOC%2bXML%2bV0%2f%2fEN&language=EN (last access on 10 November 2014).

EP (European Parliament) (2012b). 'Recommendation on the draft Council decision on the conclusion of an Agreement in the form of an Exchange of Letters between the European Union and the Kingdom of Morocco concerning reciprocal liberalisation measures on agricultural products, processed agricultural products, fish and fishery products, the replacement of Protocols 1, 2 and 3 and their Annexes and amendments to the Euro-Mediterranean Agreement establishing an association between the European Communities and their Member States, of the one part, and the Kingdom of Morocco, of the other part'. http://www.europarl.europa.eu/sides/getDoc.do?pubRef=-//EP//TEXT+REPORT+A7-2012–0023+0+DOC+XML+V0//EN (last access on 10 November 2014).

EU business (2012). 'Spanish farmers chuck tomatoes to fight EU-Morocco deal'. http://www.eubusiness.com/news-eu/spain-morocco-farm.f6z (last access on 25 June 2014).

FAOSTAT (2011). Food and Agriculture Organization of the United Nations Statistics. faostat.fao.org, Data for 2011 (last access on 12 February 2014).

Gertel, J. and Sippel, S.R. (2014). 'Seasonality and temporality in intensive agriculture' in Gertel, J. and Sippel, S.R. (eds) *Seasonal Workers in Mediterranean Agriculture: The Social Costs of Eating Fresh*. London: Routledge, pp. 3–22.

Gillespie, R. (2010). 'European Union responses to conflict in the western Mediterranean'. *The Journal of North African Studies* 15, 1, pp. 85–103.

Goetz, L. and Grethe, H. (2009). 'The EU entry price system for fresh fruits and vegetables - paper tiger or powerful market barrier?'. *Food Policy* 34, 1, pp. 81–93.

Govan, F. (2012). 'King of Morocco to be biggest benefactor of EU trade agreement'. *The Telegraph*, 29 January, http://www.telegraph.co.uk/news/worldnews/africaandindianocean/morocco/9047659/King-of-Morocco-to-be-biggest-benefactor-of-EU-trade-agreement.html (last access on 12 August 2014).

Grethe, H. and Tangermann, S. (1999). 'The EU import regime for fresh fruit and vegetables after implementation of the results of the Uruguay round'. Diskussionsbeitrag 9901. Paper prepared for the Commodities and Trade Division FAO Economic and Social Department, Göttingen.

Grethe, H., Nolte, S. and Tangermann, S. (2005). 'Entwicklung und Zukunft der EU-Agrarhandelspräferenzen für die südlichen und östlichen Mittelmeeranrainerstaaten'. *Agrarwirtschaft* 54, 7, pp. 300–313.

Hagen, E. (2009). 'Coop stops import of occupation tomatoes'. http://www.wsrw.org/a141x1085 (last access on 11 August 2014).

Joffé, G. (2010). 'Sovereignty and the western Sahara'. *The Journal of North African Studies* 15, 3, pp. 375–384.

Journal officiel de l'Union européenne (2012). 'Décision du conseil du 8 mars 2012 concernant la conclusion de l'accord sous forme d'échange de lettres entre l'Union européenne et le Royaume du Maroc relatif aux mesures de libéralisation réciproques en matière de produits agricoles, de produits agricoles transformés, de poissons et de produits de la pêche, au remplacement des protocoles nos 1, 2 et 3 et de leurs annexes et aux modifications de l'accord euro-méditerranéen établissant une association entre les Communautés européennes et leurs États membres, d'une part, et le Royaume du Maroc, d'autre part'. L 241, 7 September. eur-lex.europa.eu/LexUriServ/LexUriServ.do?uri=OJ:L:2012:241:FULL:FR:PDF (last access on 6 November 2014).

Jünemann, A. (2009). 'Zwei Schritte vor, einer zurück: Die Entwicklung der europäischen Mittelmeerpolitik von den ersten Assoziierungsabkommen bis zur Gründung einer Union für das Mittelmeer' in Hrbek, R. and Marhold, H. (eds) *Der Mittelmeerraum als Region*. EZFF Occasional Papers No. 35, Tübingen: Europäisches Zentrum für Föderalismus-Forschung, pp. 26–59.

Maghraoui, A. (2003). 'Ambiguities of sovereignty: Morocco, The Hague and the western Sahara dispute'. *Mediterranean Politics* 8, 1, pp. 113–126.

Martínez Veiga, U. (2014). 'The political economy of El Ejido: Genealogy of the 2000 conflict' in Gertel, J. and Sippel, S.R. (eds) *Seasonal Workers in Mediterranean Agriculture: The Social Costs of Eating Fresh*. London: Routledge, pp. 103–111.

Massey, D. (2005). *For Space*. London/Thousand Oaks, CA/New Delhi: Sage.

M'barek, R. (2002). *Der nordafrikanische Agrarsektor im Spannungsfeld einer euro-mediterranen Freihandelszone: Wohlfahrtsökonomische Auswirkungen einer Liberalisierung des Agrarhandels zwischen der Europäischen Union und den Maghrebstaaten Marokko und Tunesien*. Berlin: Logos Verlag.

Official Journal of the European Union (2005). 'Directive 2005/29/EC of the European Parliament and of the Council of 11 May 2005 concerning unfair business-to-consumer commercial practices in the internal market and amending Council Directive 84/450/EEC, Directives 97/7/EC, 98/27/EC and 2002/65/EC of the European Parliament and of the Council and Regulation (EC) No 2006/2004 of the European Parliament and of the Council ('Unfair Commercial Practices Directive')'. eur-lex.europa.eu/legal-content/EN/TXT/PDF/?uri=CELEX:32005L0029&from=EN, (last access on 10 November 2014).

ORMVA/SM (Office Régional de Mise en Valeur Agricole du Souss-Massa) (2007). 'Evolution des superficies et productions moyenne des cinq dernières campagnes: Total zone d'action'. Agadir.

ORMVA/SM (Office Régional de Mise en Valeur Agricole du Souss-Massa) (2008). 'Situation des superficies maraîchères de primeurs, campagne 2007/08'. Agadir.

Pham, J.P. (2010). 'Not another failed state: Toward a realistic solution in the western Sahara'. *Journal of the Middle East and Africa* 1, 1, pp. 1–24.

Pumares, P. and Jolivet, D. (2014). 'Origin matters: Working conditions of Moroccans and Romanians in the greenhouses of Almería' in Gertel, J. and Sippel, S.R. (eds) *Seasonal Workers in Mediterranean Agriculture: The Social Costs of Eating Fresh*. London: Routledge, pp. 130–140.

Quarante, O. (2014). 'Fish, phosphates and tomatoes: Morocco exploits western Sahara's natural resources'. *Le Monde diplomatique*, 7 March 2014, http://mondediplo.com/2014/03/07sahara (last access on 12 August 2014).

Raynolds, L.T. (2004). 'The globalization of organic agro-food networks'. *World Development* 32, 5, pp. 725–743.

Redani, L. (2003). *Analyse du potentiel agro-exportateur marocain et des advantages comparatifs avec l'Espagne: Etude de cas de la tomate primeur*. Série Master of Science No. 58, Institut Agronomique Méditerranéen de Montpellier, CIHEAM-IAMM, Montpellier.

Saidy, B. (2011). 'American interests in the western Sahara conflict'. *American Foreign Policy Interests* 33, 2, pp. 86–92.

Sippel, S.R. (2014a). *Export(t)räume. Bruchzonen marokkanischer Landwirtschaft*. Bielefeld: Transcript.

Sippel, S.R. (2014b). 'Disrupted livelihoods? Intensive agriculture and labour markets in the Moroccan Souss' in Gertel, J. and Sippel, S.R. (eds) *Seasonal Workers in*

*Mediterranean Agriculture: The Social Costs of Eating Fresh*. London: Routledge, pp. 186–198.

Smith, J.J. (2013). 'Fishing for self-determination: European fisheries and western Sahara – the case of ocean resources in Africa's last colony' in Chircop, A., Coffen-Smout, S. and McConnell, M. (eds) *Ocean Yearbook 27*. Leiden/Boston: Koninklijke Brill, pp. 267–290.

Swearingen, W.D. (1987). *Moroccan Mirages: Agrarian Dreams and Deceptions 1912–1986*. Princeton, NJ: Princeton University Press.

Talbot, J.M. (2009). 'The comparative advantages of tropical commodity chain analysis', in Bair, J. (ed.) *Frontiers of Commodity Chain Research*. Stanford, CA: Stanford University Press, pp. 93–109.

Tangermann, S. and von Cramon-Taubadel, S. (2013). 'Agricultural policy in the European Union: An overview'. Diskussionspapiere, Department für Agrarökonomie und Rurale Entwicklung, no. 1302.

The Greens in the European Parliament (2012). 'EU-Morocco Trade Agreement/Western Sahara', 26.01.2012. http://www.greens-efa.eu/de/eu-morocco-trade-agreementwestern-sahara-5202.html (last access on 10 November 2014).

Torres-Spelliscy, G. (2014). 'The use and development of natural resources in non-self-governing territories' in Boukhars, A. and Roussellier, J. (eds) *Perspectives on Western Sahara: Myths, Nationalisms, and Geopolitics*. Lanham, MD: Rowman and Littlefield, pp. 235–259.

van Berkum, S. (2013). 'Trade effects of the EU-Morocco Association agreement: Impacts on horticultural markets of the 2012 amendments'. *LEI Report* 2013–070, Wageningen.

White, G.W. (2001). *A Comparative Political Economy of Tunisia and Morocco: On the Outside of Europe Looking In*. New York: State University of New York Press.

WSRW (Western Sahara Resource Watch) (2009). 'Occupation tomatoes reached the US'. http://www.wsrw.org/a141x1147 (last access on 11 August 2014).

WSRW (Western Sahara Resource Watch) and EMMAUS Stockholm (2012). 'Label and liability: How the EU turns a blind eye to falsely stamped agricultural products made by Morocco in occupied western Sahara' http://www.emmausstockholm.se/wp-content/uploads/Label-and-Liability-tomater-fran-Vastsahara.pdf (access on 25 June 2014).

# 10 Refugees in the agricultural sector

## Some notes on Syrians in Hatay province, Turkey

*Selma Akay Erturk*

### 10.1 Introduction

International labour migration is usually supposed to move from 'underdeveloped' or 'developing' countries in the global South to 'developed' countries in the global North. However, this orthodox notion of labour migration, however inaccurate in the past, has been increasingly challenged during the last three decades (Massey and Taylor, 2004; Bartram, 2005; Castles and Miller, 2009). Turkey used to be regarded as an emigration country, but since the 1990s it has become a country that receives migrants of different national origins (Mutluer, 2003). The reasons for this shift include: Turkey's geographical position (as a crossroads between East and West and between North and South); its recent economic development; the economic transition period of the old Eastern Bloc countries following the collapse of the Soviet Union; and the conflicts and wars in the Middle East and African countries. Moreover, during the same period, thanks to increasing Turkish investments in Russia, Central Asia and the Caucasus as well as the Middle East and North African (MENA) countries, white-collar and blue-collar workers have begun to move from Turkey to these countries to work. As such, since the 1990s, South–South migration has risen in importance for Turkey, as it has for migration networks in other parts of the globe.

Labour migrants have found (mainly irregular) employment in the care, domestic, construction and textile sectors, particularly in Istanbul and other large Turkish cities. There exist a significant number of academic studies on migrant workers in the non-agricultural sectors in Turkey (Toksoz, 2006; Erder, 2007; Kaska, 2007; Akalin, 2010; Lordoglu, 2010). Foreign migrant labour in the agricultural sector in Turkey is a quite recent phenomenon, even if internal migration of temporary agricultural workers has existed for some time. For example, according to the report of Kalkinma Atolyesi (2014), seasonal internal migrant workers employed in the hazelnut harvest in the Western Black Sea Region experience a number of problems, which include difficult working and living conditions, low salaries and recruitment activities of informal brokers.

Undoubtedly, international mobility in Turkish agriculture needs to be analysed in the context of mobility processes and agricultural restructuring across the whole of the Mediterranean basin. In effect, over the last three decades agricultural migrant labour has been generally on the increase in southern European countries. Since the early 2000s, migrant workers' involvement in the agricultural sector has been a recurrent issue of analysis in European Union (EU) member countries such as France (Sippel and Gertel, 2014), Italy (Corrado, 2013), Spain (Arango, 2000; Bayona-i-Carrasco and Gil-Alonso, 2013), Portugal (Fonseca, 2008) and Greece (King *et al.*, 2000; Hugo and Morén-Alegret, 2008; Kasimis, 2008; Kasimis *et al.*, 2010).

Migrant labour in the agricultural sector in Turkey dates back to the early 1990s. However, as labour migrants working in rural areas are less visible than those in urban areas, they have received less attention. Turkish scholarly interest in migrant agricultural workers is only very recent and only a few studies have been produced from a social science perspective (Ulukan and Cigerci Ulukan, 2009a, 2009b). Media reports and the limited academic research indicate that foreign labour migrants are employed usually without formal work permits in agricultural areas in many different geographical regions of Turkey. For instance, Georgians work in hazelnut and tea plantations in the eastern Black Sea region of Turkey (Ulukan and Cigerci Ulukan, 2009a; 2009b), while labourers from Central Asian countries (Uzbekistan, Turkmenistan, Kazakhstan and Kyrgyzstan), with whom Turkey has mutual cultural ties, and ethnic Turks from Bulgaria, are involved in stockbreeding and fruit and vegetable cultivations in the Marmara region, in western Turkey. Since 2011, a substantial number of refugees escaping from the Syrian civil war work irregularly in the agricultural areas of Hatay province (in the cultivation of olives, cotton, citrus fruit and carrots), Sanliurfa province (cotton), Denizli province (in greenhouse horticulture) and Antalya province (greenhouses and citrus and flower cultivation) (ORSAM, 2014, p. 16). Due to the irregular nature of this work, the presence of migrants and refugees in Turkish agriculture is not recorded in official statistics but is only mentioned in the media.

This chapter deals with Syrian refugees in the agricultural areas, especially in olive cultivation in Hatay province which is located in the eastern Mediterranean region of Turkey. Forced migration from Syria to Turkey has had significant social, economic and spatial effects not only in Hatay province but also in the other border regions of southern Turkey and in large cities, particularly Istanbul. A total of 2,291,900 Syrian refugees were living in Turkey at the end of December 2015 (UNHCR, Government of Turkey).[1] Syrian refugees now live alongside local inhabitants in cities, districts and villages throughout the country. The Turkish State has allocated a significant amount of financial resources to these refugees. Camps of tents and containers have been established and a number of schools and government buildings in the cities near to the Turkey–Syria border have been transformed into emergency accommodation.[2]

Refugees have also had a serious impact on the labour market in the regions where they have settled. As 'irregular' workers, they earn below the minimum wage, reportedly around $250–300 a month, which is just enough to cover their living expenses. Those who are able to save a bit extra send remittances back to their families in Syria (Cagaptay and Menekse, 2014; ORSAM, 2015).

This chapter is based mainly on the examination of the relevant academic literature and the data and reports prepared by the Food and Agricultural Organization of the United Nations (FAO), the Turkish Statistical Institute, the Hatay Provincial Directorate of Agriculture and the Eastern Mediterranean Development Agency (EMDA). In addition, I conducted a field study in Hatay province in April 2014 in order to better understand the effects of the mobility of Syrian refugees upon agricultural production and the labour market in the area. I interviewed the public institutions (officials from Hatay Provincial Directorate of Agriculture and Altinozu District Directorate of Agriculture) and non-governmental organizations, private sector representatives, olive growers and a small number of Syrian refugees who were working in local agriculture at the time.

This chapter first provides some general information about the study area and details about the effects of post-2010 conflicts in the Middle East on Turkey and in particular on Hatay Province. It then describes olive cultivation in Hatay Province before finally considering the presence of Syrian refugees and asylum seekers in the olive sector in Altinozu, one of the Province's 15 districts. I argue that the forced mobility of Syrians in Turkey, and their informal employment in the agricultural sector in border regions, represents a case of proletarianization, which is peculiar in the context of Mediterranean agriculture, although there are some similarities with the 'refugeeization of the workforce' in southern Italian rural areas (Dines and Rigo, 2015), that is the growing participation of asylum seekers and refugees in the agricultural labour market. From a broader perspective, my case study shows how geopolitical conflicts and civil wars – such as the war in Syria – can have unexpected effects on the restructuring of agriculture in the Mediterranean basin.

## 10.2 Study area

Hatay is located on the eastern Mediterranean coast of Turkey and is the country's most southerly province. Agriculture, commerce and tourism (Akova, 2009; Serbetci Savran, 2011) are the principal economic sectors in the coastal and flatter districts of Hatay province, while stockbreeding is more common in mountainous areas (Caliskan, 2002).

According to the Turkish Statistical Institute, the total population of Hatay province in 2013 was 1,503,066 and the population of Antakya, the capital of the province, was 347,947. At the end of 2014 the number of Syrian refugees in the province was estimated to be around 75,000 (DEMP, 2013). Altinozu district is located in the south-east of the province on the border with Syria. Its population is 61,882 people; it has a strong rural character and agriculture is the most significant economic activity.

Just over 50 per cent of Hatay Province's agricultural land is irrigated. The majority of agriculture in the province is given over to crop production. The crops cultivated mostly consist of fruit and vegetables (lettuce, persimmons, turnips, chard, plums, parsley, onions, olives, citrus fruit and pomegranates). Laurel trees and cotton are the other important crops in the province. The Mediterranean region of Turkey, in which our study area is located, is second after the Aegean region in terms of the country's olive production (Yaman Kocadagli, 2009).

Some of the agricultural products grown in Hatay Province, especially fruit and vegetables, are sold on the domestic market in Turkey, especially in the country's principal cities. However, a significant portion of the production is exported. In 2012 agricultural exports accounted for 33 per cent of total exports of Hatay Province. The main external markets are MENA countries and Russia.

Since the 1960s, a huge number of unemployed young people living in rural Turkey have moved to the country's major cities. As most of the middle-aged and elderly population have remained in the villages, the labour for agricultural activities has substantially decreased. The circumstances in Altinozu's villages are not dissimilar to the general situation across the rest of Turkey. Given the lack of local labour, seasonal internal migrant workers, particularly from eastern and south-eastern Turkey, have traditionally worked in the agricultural sector in Hatay Province. Since the start of the Syrian civil war, Syrian refugees have become another key source of agricultural labour in the province, which has led to a process of 'refugeeization' of the local workforce and labour market.

## 10.3 The conflicts in the Middle East after 2011 and the Turkey–Syria border

In order to understand the process of 'refugeeization' of agricultural labour, this section addresses the question of the Turkey–Syria border and, in particular, the border posts in Hatay. The land border between Turkey and Syria is 877 kilometres long, the longest of Turkey's borders with its neighbours. There are 10 border posts on the Turkey–Syria border located in the provinces of Hatay, Sirnak, Mardin, Sanliurfa, Gaziantep and Kilis. Of all these provinces, Hatay has the longest land border with Syria (276.9 km), which represents almost a third of the total land border between the two countries.

In 2011, popular demonstrations in a number of MENA countries, collectively known as the Arab Spring, pressed for a series of socio-economic and political changes. A major uprising in Syria gradually turned into a full-scale civil war, which continues today. These events have led to significant developments in the politics of the MENA countries (see also Gana, this volume). There is no doubt that Turkey has been affected by these events due to its proximity to Syria and other Middle Eastern countries. Prior to the civil war in Syria, there was intensive interaction along the border between Turkey and Syria, particularly in terms of commercial activities. The relative ease of applying for a daily visa also stimulated tourism in the local area. In addition, people on both sides freely crossed the international border on religious days to pay visits to their relatives.

The civil war in neighbouring Syria has affected Hatay Province socially, economically, culturally and spatially. Trade and tourism between the two countries ceased, while the border economy, one of the prominent sources of revenue of Hatay Province, collapsed. Hatay's economy depends mainly on international transport, tourism and agriculture. Since 2007, Turkey had seen an expansion of trade with Syria (with which it had signed a free trade agreement) as well as the wider region. The number of loaded Turkish trucks crossing from Hatay into Syria nearly doubled every year after 2007, increasing from 15,634 trucks in 2007 to a peak of 108,591 trucks in 2010, underlining Hatay's role as Turkey's principal trade route to the south (Collinsworth, 2015, p. 120). Trade with Syria dropped after March 2011 when Syria's civil conflict began to spread: the number of loaded trucks crossing into Syria from Turkey fell to just over 6,000 between January and July 2012, one-ninth of the level during the peak year of 2010, although roughly the same number as in 2007 (Collinsworth, 2015, p. 120; see also ORSAM, 2015). Atasoy *et al.* (2012) note that most of the commercial activities performed legally before the war in the Turkey–Syria border region are now carried out illegally.

During this same period, a great number of refugees escaped from Syria to seek sanctuary in Hatay province as well as other provinces along the Turkey–Syria border, and many others have since moved on to other parts of Turkey. At the time of writing, Syrian refugees are continuing to flee to Turkey.

At the end of December 2015, the United Nations High Commissioner for Refugees (UNHCR) reported that there were 4,390,439 Syrian refugees, and, of these, 2,291,900 were located in Turkey, which means that this one country accounts for more than half the total number of refugees. Since the Syrian crisis began in 2011, according to UNHCR, Turkey's emergency response has been of a consistently high standard, declaring a temporary protection regime and ensuring *non-refoulement* and assistance in a network of 24 camps that accommodate more than a quarter of a million refugees (UNHCR, 2015).

At the end of 2014, 15,404 Syrian refugees – the 7.7 per cent of the total number of Syrians hosted in refugee camps in Turkey – were located in five refugee camps in Hatay province (Altinozu 1, Altinozu 2, Altinozu Apaydin, Yayladagi 1 and Yayladagi 2), which are run by the Disaster and Emergency Management Presidency (DEMP) under the direction of the Turkish Government and UNHCR. In addition, around 60,000 refugees were estimated to live outside the camps, probably by renting in Antakya city and other districts and villages of Hatay Province. According to a survey conducted by DEMP in 2013, most of the refugees in Turkey were from Syrian regions close to the Turkish border where intense clashes have taken place. A large number of Syrian refugees have attributed geographical closeness and accessibility as the reason for fleeing to Turkey instead of another country. About 36 per cent of the Syrian refugees taking sanctuary in Turkey have been placed in 20 camps in 10 cities in Turkey. The remaining 64 per cent have settled outside the camps. The 10 cities with refugee camps are generally located in the south and south-eastern parts of country near the Syrian border. Approximately 45 per cent of the refugees living outside camps have been registered by DEMP and nearly 20 per cent have obtained a residence permit.

About 42 per cent of the refugees living in camps and 45 per cent of those living elsewhere are aged between 19 and 54 years. In Hatay Province, 52 per cent of male inhabitants of the refugee camps and 48 per cent of females are in this same age group, while 42 per cent of males and 45 per cent of females living outside camps are in this group (DEMP, 2014, p. 60). This means that a large percentage of Syrian refugees are probably willing to enter the labour market in Turkey.

A large number of the Syrian refugees living outside camps declared that they were seeking work after moving to Turkey. About 49 per cent of male respondents and nearly 64 per cent of female respondents living in the camps declared that they were seeking work. According to the same statistics, 77 per cent of male and female refugees living outside the camps have sought work at least once (DEMP, 2013, p. 52).

## 10.4 Olive cultivation in Hatay Province and Altinozu district

The olive tree is perhaps the most characteristic natural symbol of the Mediterranean Region. In 2012, Turkey ranked sixth behind Spain, Tunisia, Italy, Morocco and Greece in terms of the area of land dedicated to olive cultivation (805,500 hectares), while in terms of actual olive production, it ranked fourth behind Spain, Italy and Greece (FAO, 2012). According to data of the Turkish Statistical Institute, the total olive production in Turkey in 2013 was 1,676,000 tonnes. However, the Turkish olive industry has encountered a number of problems regarding quality, marketing and production technology. Moreover, the Common Agriculture Policy (CAP) of the EU has introduced tariffs on Turkish olives. Thus, Turkey has tried to export to different markets like Russia, USA, Japan, Saudi Arabia and China.

Olive production in Hatay dates back to ancient times and today there are more than 14 million olive trees in the province. According to the data of the Turkish Statistical Institute, in 2013, the total area dedicated to olive cultivation was 51,384 hectares, and production amounted to 158,419 tonnes of olives, over 87 per cent of which was destined for oil production and the rest for table olives. According to records of the Hatay Provincial Directorate of Agriculture (2013), there are 92 olive oil production facilities in the province; the highest number in the whole of the eastern Mediterranean region of Turkey. Most of these facilities use dated machinery: 83 of the 92 production units are able to process just over 1,000 tonnes of olives a year, while only three facilities with more modern equipment have an annual processing capacity that exceeds 2,250 tonnes. The olive growers in the study area receive state aid for diesel fuel and fertilizer, and may be granted additional aid if they prove that they produce olive oil.

The Turkish agricultural sector and farmers have been greatly affected by EU quotas, World Trade Organization decisions, the power held by the big global producers in determining the prices and their reduced competitiveness due to the increasing cost of agricultural inputs (Ozturk, 2012; López *et al.*, 2013). As already noted, as a result of these changes, the population in some rural areas, especially in the poorer southern border regions, has decreased due to internal migration. As a consequence, local farmers have started employing migrant workers and Syrian refugees who work for lower wages.

The Altinozu district of Hatay Province was selected in order to study the insertion of Syrian refugees in the Turkish agricultural labour market. According to records of the Altinozu District Directorate of Agriculture (2014), Altinozu has 4,223 registered farmers and is one of the leading olive-growing districts in the area, producing 24.6 per cent of the total olive production in Hatay Province. In 2013, 39,047 tonnes of olives were cultivated in the district on 15,791 hectares of land. These olives are processed either in the district itself or in Antakya, and a substantial percentage is turned into olive oil. Most of the processed olives and oil are consumed locally or on the domestic market in Turkey, although a number of companies export olive oil to foreign markets, including the United States, Germany, Saudi Arabia and Russia. In all cases, Turkish traders resident in the destination countries play a decisive role in exports.

For the most part, olive cultivation in Altinozu takes place on small family-owned farms, which employ family members and temporary seasonal workers (either internal migrants or Syrian refugees). The olive crop in the study area is rainfed rather than irrigated. Most of the farmers in the district are middle-aged or elderly, while younger people tend to work in commercial, industrial and service sectors in the city of Antakya. Some of them continue to maintain connections with their farming families, but usually only spend their weekends in the village. As a result, there is a lack of agricultural labour force in Altinozu, especially during harvest time and, for this reason, Syrian refugees play a very important role in sustaining olive production in the area.

## 10.5 Syrian refugees in the olive-growing industry in Altinozu district

As mentioned, foreign migrant workers in Turkish agriculture have come generally from neighbouring countries. Clearly, the experience of Syrian refugees in Turkey is different from that of migrant workers from Georgia and Central Asian countries, with the former mainly 'economic' migrants, while the latter have arrived in Turkey having suffered deprivation and trauma, and most have since depended upon special welfare.

Foreign nationals in Turkey who have a valid residence permit (for at least six months, except for educational purposes) can apply to the Ministry of Labour and Social Security for a work permit. Syrian refugees, who possess a six-month or one-year residence permit, but not those with temporary protection, are also entitled to apply for a work permit. This said, most migrants and Syrian refugees employed in the agricultural sector do not have a work permit. Moreover, in most cases there is no formal work agreement between the employer and the employee. As a result, there are no official statistical records of the number of migrants and Syrian refugees working in Turkish agriculture.

The Turkish State provides humanitarian assistance (shelter, nutrition, free health care and education) to Syrian refugees living either in or outside camps. There are three refugee camps in Altinozu hosting just over 9,000 people, as well as a sizeable number of Syrians who reside among the local population. The total number of refugees in the district therefore exceeds the native population of the town of Altinozu (7,399 inhabitants), the district's principal urban centre.

After meeting their needs for housing, the Syrian refugees in Altinozu district have started to work not only in agriculture, but also in construction, small- and medium-scale enterprises, domestic and care work, and nearly always irregularly. In the case of olive cultivation, refugees are employed in numerous stages of production, from planting and hoeing to pruning, spraying and harvesting.

Serious conflicts (including racist violence) between migrant workers, employers and local inhabitants that have taken place in recent years in EU countries (Corrado, 2011; Perrotta and Sacchetto, 2014) have not occurred in Turkey. However, tensions with the local population have been reported.[3]

During my fieldwork and interviews carried out in April 2014, I was able to observe how Syrian refugees arrived at the worker collection places, usually along the main roads in Altinozu, in the early morning and agreed on a daily or weekly wage with the employer. The employer then drove them to their places of work. An evident degree of trust existed between those refugees and employers who had already worked together. This trust also leads to the two parties contacting each other when there is new work to be done. As noted, on almost all occasions no official, written agreement is made between them.

Only the refugees in 'Altinozu 1' camp have permission to leave the camp during the day to go to work. Employers apply to the Camp Administration whenever they want to hire workers from the camp.

Informal brokers of both Turkish and Syrian nationalities played an important role in providing labour to the local farm. Most of the local inhabitants living in Hatay Province can speak Arabic and so they are no communication problems with the Syrian refugees. The informal brokers bring together refugees and organize them into teams for agricultural work. They also organize other services, such as the transportation of workers, although they do not provide legal assistance to Syrian refugee workers for applying to work permits. At the end of the work, farmers pay the workers' wages through informal brokers who deduct a fee for their services.

Border districts such as Altinozu have been able to benefit from the refugee crisis in other ways. For instance landlords have, in some cases, tripled rents, especially given the housing shortage. In addition, small supermarkets have opened since the Turkish Red Crescent and World Food Programme started distributing food vouchers to refugees in camps (Collinsworth 2015, p. 123; ORSAM, 2015).

In order to provide a more detailed picture of the situation of Syrian refugees in the local agricultural labour market, here I describe the experiences of two Syrian refugees among those who I was able to interview in the field study. The first interviewee is Anas, a man of 48 years old, married with five children, three of whom are married. He fled to Turkey from the Caludiye settlement in Syria, in 2011. He and his family live in Altinozu 1 camp. He used to make his living in agriculture: before the war, he used to cultivate wheat, olives, apples, plums and apricots on the 1.5 hectares of land that he owns and he would sell this produce on the local market. Shortly after he moved to Turkey, he began to work on someone else's land for the first time in his life. Since arriving in Turkey, he has only worked in agriculture and has not sought employment in any another sector. A day's work lasts from 8am to 5pm: during the ploughing and hoeing carried out in spring and summer, he earns 30 Turkish liras (or about 10 euros), although when the workload intensifies during harvest time in September and October he is able to earn 35 Turkish liras. He has been working with the same olive farmer for three years. His four siblings have also moved to Turkey and settled down in Altinozu camp, while his elderly parents have remained in Syria despite the war. Indeed when we met in April 2014, he had just been to Syria to pay them a short visit. His wish is to go back to Syria as soon as the war ends. He feels that he is lucky because he owns a bit of land, but he believes that those refugees who do not own land may not be willing to go back to Syria and are more likely to continue living in Turkey even after the war ends.

The second story is that of Sami, a man of 40 years old, married with seven children. He moved to Turkey in 2014 from the Cneydo settlement in Syria, while his elderly parents remained in Syria. Having found it very hard to live in the camp in Altinozu, he had decided to rent a house in the local area. Four of his children study in Altinozu School. Before the war, he had owned a supermarket, the revenue from which allowed him to provide a decent standard of living for his family. He claimed that he and his family would like to continue to live in Turkey, even if they were here out of obligation, and in any case, he would be willing to move back to Syria after the war. He said that he earned between 25 and 30 Turkish liras a day from hoeing weeds in the olive grove. Following a first stint of employment, he had returned to the same employer on several occasions.

These brief accounts indicate a faint process of proletarianization among Syrian refugees. Following the exodus of a huge number of Syrians and the lack of EU institutional and legal mechanisms to facilitate their reception, many have remained in Turkey with limited possibilities of participating formally in the local labour market. Moreover, the tightening of EU border controls has forced those refugees seeking to move onto Europe to risk their lives crossing the Aegean Sea to Greece. The lack of access to work permits coupled with the recruitment strategies in the agricultural labour market have forced a huge number of Syrian refugees to work in the informal economy. They often do dirty, difficult and dangerous jobs for extremely low wages. Finally, even if serious conflicts have yet to occur between refugees and the local population, this forced proletarianization risks eventually creating tensions with Turkish workers.

## 10.6 Conclusion

The agricultural sector remains important for Turkey's economy. In comparison with EU countries, Turkey still has a substantial rural population (22.7 per cent in 2012).[4] Moreover, 22.1 per cent of the population work in the agricultural sector, which is relatively high when compared with key EU member countries (for example, the equivalent rate is 2.9 per cent in France and 4.4 per cent in Spain) (Eurostat, 2013). Until recently, the domestic workforce has mainly satisfied the need for labour in the Turkish agricultural sector, although this has included seasonal internal migrant labourers. For this reason, the employment of foreign migrants in the agricultural sector in Turkey is a relatively new phenomenon in comparison with EU countries. Migrant workers, especially Syrian refugees, settle in areas where seasonal internal migrants are employed. However, in recent years a shortage of agricultural labour has arisen due to the progressive exit of locals thanks to alternative economic opportunities. Syrian refugees usually work on an informal basis and accept lower wages than Turkish agricultural workers. In the specific study area of Altinozu district, Syrian refugees have hence played a very important role in sustaining local olive production.

The geopolitical reordering of Syria and of the wider MENA region is an upshot of armed conflicts and the scramble for the control of land and natural resources (gas, minerals, water, oil) that intersect with neoliberal economic restructuring driven by 'accumulation by dispossession' (Harvey, 2004). Forced migrants (who are sometimes themselves displaced farmers) are turned into precarious and poor proletarians who enter agricultural labour markets that are squeezed by state and market regulations and supply chains. Whether Turkish agriculture permanently transforms under the current Syrian refugee crisis is something that will need to be considered in future research.

## Acknowledgements

My colleague, Geographer Ozlem Kirkici Carcar, and the olive farmers translated the answers and questions from Arabic to Turkish and vice versa during the interviews with the Syrian refugees. I am very grateful for their kind assistance and support in this study, as well as the cooperation of the Syrian agricultural labourers.

## Notes

1 For UNHCR data on Syrian refugees in Turkey see http://data.unhcr.org/syrianrefugees/country.php?id=224 (last access on 20/2/2016).
2 In 2014, Turkey also witnessed an unprecedented increase in asylum applications from Afghans, Iraqis and Iranians. See UNHCR country operations profile – Turkey: http://www.unhcr.org/pages/49e48e0fa7f.html.
3 According to the findings of a survey conducted by the Ankara-based Centre for Middle Eastern Strategic Studies (ORSAM) on the economic impact of Syrian refugees on Turkey (ORSAM, 2015), over 40 per cent of local people who lost their jobs in border cities believe that they lost their jobs due to the arrival of Syrians. See also 'Syrian refugees attacked, urged to leave in Antalya', *Hurriyet/Daily News*, 23 December 2015, http://www.hurriyetdailynews.com/syrian-refugees-attacked-urged-to-leave-in-antalya.aspx?pageID=238&nID=76056&NewsCatID=341.
4 Turkish Statistical Institute (2012).

## References

Akalin, A. (2010). 'Yukaridakiler–asagidakiler: Istanbul'daki guvenlikli sitelerde gocmen ev hizmetlisi istihdami' in Pusch, B. and Wilkoszews, T. (eds) *Turkiye'ye uluslararasi goc toplumsal kosullar – bireysel yasamlar*. Istanbul: Kitap Yayinevi, pp. 111–134.

Akova, B.S. (2009). *Dogu Akdeniz Kiyilarinda Nufus*, Istanbul: Cantay Kitabevi.

Altinozu District Directorate of Agriculture (2014). *Agricultural Statistics, Crop Production Statistics Database, Fruits, Beverage and Spice Crops* (CPA classification).

Turkish Statistical Institute. Ankara, http://rapory.tuik.gov.tr/18–01-2016–13:50:56–83252475764108546784775896 7.html (last access on 20/2/2016).

Arango, J. (2000). 'Becoming a country of immigration at the end of the twentieth century: the case study of Spain' in King, R., Lazaridis, G. and Tsardanidis C. (eds) *Eldorado or Fortress? Migration in Southern Europe*. London: Macmillan, pp. 253–176.

Atasoy, A., Gecen, R. and Korkmaz, H. (2012). 'Siyasi cografya acisindan Turkiye (Hatay) – Suriye siniri' in *TUCAUM VII. Geography Sympozium 2012 Proceeding Book*, Ankara. http://tucaum.ankara.edu.tr/yayin/sempozyum/semp7_13.pdf (last access on 20/2/2016).

Bartram, R. (2005). *International Labor Migration. Foreign Workers and Public Policy*, New York: Palgrave Macmillan.

Bayona-i-Carrasco, J. and Gil-Alonso, F. (2013). 'Is foreign immigration the solution to rural depopulation? The case of Catalonia (1996–2009)'. *Sociologia Ruralis*, 53 (1), 26–51.

Cagaptay, S. and Menekse, B. (2014). 'The impact of Syria's Refugees on Southern Turkey'. *Policy Focus*, 130. The Washington Institute for Near East Policy, pp. 1–32.

Caliskan, V. (2002). *Amik ovasinin beseri ve iktisadi cografyasi*, Istanbul: Istanbul University Social Sciences Institute, Unpublished PhD Thesis.

Castles, S. and Miller, M. J. (2009). *The Age of Migration*, 4th edition, Basingstoke: Palgrave Macmillan.

Collinsworth, D. (2015). 'fonseHatay: the Syrian crisis and a case of Turkish economic resilience'. *Turkish Policy Quarterly*, 12 (1), 119–124.

Corrado, A. (2011). '*Clandestini* in the orange towns: migrations and racisms in Calabria's agriculture'. *Race/Ethnicity*, 4 (2), 191–201.

Corrado, A. (2013). 'The global countryside: migrations in rural South of Italy: sustainable local food systems for rural resilience in time of crisis'. *XXV European Society for Rural Sociology*, Florence, Italy.

DEMP (2013). *Syrian Refugees in Turkey, 2013 Field Survey Results*. Ankara: Disaster and Emergency Management Presidency of Republic of Turkey Prime Ministry.

DEMP (2014). *Turkiye'deki Suriyeli kadinlar.* Ankara: Disaster and Emergency Management Presidency of Republic of Turkey Prime Ministry.

Dines, N. and Rigo, E. (2015). 'Postcolonial citizenships between representation, borders and the 'refugeeization' of the workforce: critical reflections on migrant agricultural labor in the Italian Mezzogiorno', in Ponzanesi, S. and Colpani, G. (eds) *Postcolonial Transitions in Europe: Contexts, Practices and Politics*, London: Rowman and Littlefield, pp. 153–174.

Erder, S. (2007). 'Yabancisiz kurgulanan ulkenin yabancilari, Turkiye'de yabanci isciler' in Ari, A. (ed.) *Turkiye'de yabanci isciler*, Istanbul: Derin Yayınları, 1–82.

Eurostat (2013). European Union Labour force survey – annual results 2012, http://ec.europa.eu/eurostat/statistics-explained/index.php/Archive:Labour_force_survey_overview_2012 (last access on 20/2/2016).

FAO (2012). FAOSTAT Production Statistics. FAO, http://faostat3.fao.org/browse/Q/*/E (last access on 20/2/2016).

Fonseca, M. L. (2008). 'New waves of immigration to small towns and rural areas in Portugal', *Population, Space and Place*, 14 (6), 525–535.

Harvey, D. (2004). 'The 'new imperialism: Accumulation by dispossession', *Socialist Register*, 40, 63–87.

Hatay Provincial Directorate of Agriculture. (2013). *Production statistics of olive, Crop Production Statistics Database, Fruits, Beverage and Spice Crops* (CPA classification),

Turkish Statistical Institute. Ankara and Hatay Provincial Directorate of Agriculture, Hatay, http://rapory.tuik.gov.tr/18–01-2016–14:20:51–21354255218567205247263790 88.pdf (last access on 20/2/2016).

Hugo, G. and Morén-Alegret, R. (eds) (2008). 'International migration to non-metropolitan areas of high income countries. Editorial Introduction'. *Population, Space and Place,* 14 (6), 473–477.

Kalkinma Atolyesi. (2014). *Findik Hasadinin Oyunculari (Actors of Hazelnut Harvesting)*, Ankara: Altin Matbaasi. http://www.kalkinmaatolyesi.org/v2/en/programs/social-development/seasonal-labour-immigrance/actors-of-hazelnut-harvesting/ (last access on 20/2/2016).

Kasimis, C. (2008). 'Survival and expansion: Migrants in Greek rural regions'. *Population, Space and Place,* 14, 511–524.

Kasimis C., Papadopoulos A. G. and Pappas C. (2010). 'Gaining from rural migrants: migrant employment strategies and socioeconomic implications for rural labour markets'. *Sociologia Ruralis*, 50 (3), 58–276.

Kaska, S. (2007). 'Ev ici hizmetlerin kuresellesmesi ve Turkiye'deki gocmen kadinlar' in Ari, A. (ed.) *Turkiye'de yabanci isciler.* Istanbul: Derin Yayınları, pp. 225–240.

King, R., G. Lazaridis, and Tsardanidis C. (eds) (2000). *Eldorado or Fortress? Migration in Southern Europe*, London: Macmillan.

López, R. C., García-Álvarez-Coque, J. M. and García zcárate, T. (2013). 'EU-Mediterranean relations in the field of agriculture: The example of Morocco and Turkey'. Policy Paper No. 91. Paris: Jacques Delors Institute.

Lordoglu, K. (2010). 'Turkiye'de calisma hayatinin bir parcasi olarak yabanci calisanlar' in Pusch, B. and Wilkoszews, T. (eds) *Turkiye'ye uluslararasi goc toplumsal kosullar – bireysel yasamlar.* Istanbul: Kitap Yayinevi.

Massey, D. S. and Taylor, J. E. (2004). *International Migration: Prospects and Policies in a Global Market (International Studies in Demography)*, New York: Oxford University Press.

Mutluer, M. (2003). *Uluslararası gocler ve Turkiye kuramsal ve ampirik bir alan arastirmasi Denizli/Tavas*. Istanbul: Cantay Kitabevi.

ORSAM (2014). 'The situation of Syrian refugees in neighboring countries: Findings, conclusions and recommendations'. ORSAM Report No. 189. Ankara: Tesev.

ORSAM (2015). 'Effects of the Syrian refugees on Turkey'. ORSAM Report No. 195. Ankara: Tesev.

Ozturk, M. (2012). *Agriculture, Peasantry and Poverty in Turkey in the Neo-liberal Age*, Wageningen: Wageningen Academic Publishers.

Perrotta D. and Sacchetto, D. (2014). 'Migrant farmworkers in Southern Italy: ghettoes, *caporalato* and collective action'. *International Journal on Strikes and Social Conflicts*, 1 (5), 75–98.

Serbetci Savran, Z. (2011). *Evaluation of Cultural Tourism Potential in Terms of Geography in Hatay*, Istanbul: Fatih University, Institute of Social Sciences, Geography Department, Master Thesis.

Sippel, S.R. and Gertel, J. (2014). 'Shared insecurities? Farmers and workers in Bouches-du-Rhone' in Gertel, J. and Sippel, S.R. (eds) *Seasonal Workers in Mediterranean Agriculture: The Social Costs of Eating Fresh.* London: Routledge, pp. 37–48.

Toksoz, G. (2006). *Uluslararasi emek gocu.* Istanbul: Istanbul Bilgi Universitesi.

Turkish Statistical Institute (2012). Population of Province / District Centers and Towns / Villages by Years, Census of Population – ABPRS, Results of Address Based Population Registration System, 2007–2012, Turkish Statistical Institute, Ankara,

Turkey Link: http://www.turkstat.gov.tr/PreIstatistikTablo.do?istab_id=1587 (last access on 20/2/2016).

Turkish Statistical Institute (2012–2013). Address based population censuses and crop production statistics, Turkish Statistical Institute. Ankara, http://www.turkstat.gov.tr/PreTablo.do?alt_id=1059 (last access on 20/2/2016).

Ulukan, U. and Cigerci Ulukan, N. (2009a). 'Findik uretiminde calisma iliskileri ve mevsimlik isciler: Persembe ornegi' in *Ulusal Sosyal Bilimler Kongresi*, Ankara: Bildiriler Kitabi, ODTU.

Ulukan, U. and Cigerci Ulukan, N. (2009b). 'Kriz ve goc: Turkiye Gurcistan arasi nufus hareketleri uzerinden bir tartisma' in *Turkiye Ekonomi Kurumu Ulusal Sempozyumu,* Zonguldak: ZKU.

United Nations High Commissioner for Refugees (UNHCR) (2015). http://data.unhcr.org/syrianrefugees/country.php?id=224 (last access on 18/1/2016).

Yaman Kocadagli, A. (2009). 'Turkiye'de zeytincilik faaliyetlerinde Edremit korfezi kiyilarinin onemi' *Cografya Dergisi*, 19, 28–58.

# Part IV

# Restructuring of agricultural labour markets in Southern Europe and Maghreb

# 11 Persistent unfree labour in French intensive agriculture

## An historical overview of the 'OFII' temporary farmworkers programme

*Frédéric Décosse*

> One day or another you should see them, arriving en masse on special trains for the grape harvests, dishevelled and exhausted from three days of travel, burdened with their wretched luggage: a few poor clothes, the dish for the Sunday paella and bags of salted fish. No one is waiting for them, except a few farmers still in need of workers, who move from group to group. Those who have contracts, those who can be counted on, wait – interminably – to be collected. The women's faces are tense with fatigue; the adolescents are amused and astonished by the new world around them. The names and addresses on the contracts are endlessly and carefully re-read.
>
> (Privat, 1966, p. 43)

While the massive migration of whole families of seasonal contract workers in France described half a century ago by Privat (1966) is now largely a thing of the past, foreign labour remains a key element in present-day systems of intensive agricultural production. The importance for the farmers of the recruitment and 'just in time' mobilization of these migrant workers and of their willingness to work overtime thus justifies the maintenance of a temporary worker migration scheme, under contracts arranged by the OFII (*Office français de l'immigration et de l'intégration*), referred to in 'emic'[1] (i.e. native) terms as 'OFII contracts'.[2] It is true that the workforce systems of contemporary industrial agriculture are no longer based solely on this category of workers, since during the peak harvest period their employment is now combined with that of an army of casual workers hired on the 'black' (or 'grey') labour market or through employment agencies, and with a growing number of temporary workers, increasingly despatched to France by foreign companies, and mostly from non-European countries (Latin America and the Maghreb). Nonetheless, the persistence over time of this atypical form of mobilization of a foreign labour force invites the researcher to examine the history of variable capital in the process of intensification of French agriculture.

This chapter therefore aims to understand the OFII seasonal migrant worker scheme in its diachronic and utilitarian dimensions by analysing how it has been managed (and thus constantly reinvented and transformed) by the state and the producer organizations to meet the labour 'needs' of an agriculture which has been intensified at varying rates over time and across the country. By focusing on the different types of agriculture that have historically resorted to seasonal foreign workers (sugar beet, rice, grapes and most recently horticulture), I aim to grasp a little known but central dimension of the process of 'modernization' of agriculture. The analysis covers the period from 1945 to the present, with the immediate post-war years marking the moment when the state created the *Office national d'immigration* (ONI) and the seasonal contracts to which, by metonymy, it gave its name, and when, with the Marshall Plan and the generalized use of tractors, France entered the age of industrialization of its agricultural production.

The present chapter draws on my doctoral research (Décosse, 2011). This was based on fieldwork in Morocco, Spain and Southern France between 2004 and 2010, during which I collected 160 qualitative interviews, conducted archival research and undertook several months of participant observation in the *Collectif de défense des travailleurs agricoles saisonniers* (CODETRAS, a network that coordinates the action of several trade unions and associations in the Bouches-du-Rhône). On the basis of this long-term research, my discussion is structured as follows: I start by outlining the OFII scheme, and then proceed to examine the pioneering role played by the sugar beet industry, and the subsequent importation of this employment system into the rice and wine sectors. I then turn to the question of seasonal contracts in the fruit tree and market gardening industries, before finally considering the mobilizations of migrants to free themselves from OFII status.

## 11.1 From migratory utilitarianism ... to unfree labour

Originally created by a ministerial decree on 2 November 1945 to regulate the entry and residence of foreigners, the OFII seasonal worker contract is a simplified employment contract through which a farmer requests from the state authorities the entry of a seasonal worker onto French territory for an employment period presently ranging from three to six months. However, for a long time this work permit also served as a residence permit (at least until the creation of a multi-year 'seasonal worker' residence card in 2007), thus reflecting the extent to which the presence of the foreigner was both legally bound and politically justified by his productive function. The scheme thus epitomises what Morice (2004) calls 'migratory utilitarianism,' in the sense that migration is understood and organized solely in terms of the economic advantage it offers to the 'host' country. Although this channel for the mobilization of foreign labour has historically concerned other sectors,[3] more than 90 per cent of the seasonal workers have been concentrated in the agricultural sector.

The term 'OFII contract' in fact refers to two distinct realities. First, it designates an atypical form of employment, which in legal terms signifies a short-term employment contract (*Contrat à durée déterminée*, CDD) without the benefit of certain rights, such as the payment of the 'precarity bonus'[4] or complementary payments by the employer in the event of illness or a workplace accident. In terms of employment, then, the OFII contract constitutes a wage form with reduced rights, in which seasonality produces precarity. Second, it refers to the status of a foreign worker brought into France on the basis of this system. While some farm labourers have worked for 10, 20 and even 30 years on the same farm, their entry and their right to work are conditional, on the one hand, on the employer's renewal of their contract and, on the other hand, on the outcome of the administrative procedure aimed at protecting the employment of local, national and EU workers, even if, in reality, this procedure is largely fictitious. Foreign nationality in turn removes a certain number of rights either directly guaranteed by the seasonal CDD (including the clause relating to the renewal of the contract from one year to another) or directly linked to the wage (such as family benefits and the allowance for the return to employment).

The OFII contract is thus the product of a combination of legal categories ('CDD', 'seasonal', 'foreigner') which legally create inferiorization and subjection in employment relations, and which are maintained and reinforced by mechanisms associated with this precarious status, such as individual recruitment by co-option dependent on family or village networks, paternalism, racism, and debt. Debt is both psychological – in the sense that it merges with a duty of loyalty towards the employer (Jounin, 2006) – and financial, in that the majority of contracts are bought, which generates a 'black market in rights to emigrate to and work in France' (Berlan *et al.*, 1991, p. 56). This in turn represents a windfall that is exploited both by the employers themselves and the supervisors who hail from the same villages as the labourers and double up as labour brokers. Such brokers have long been an important link in the system of recruitment and management of teams in the workplace, to the extent that over time this figure has assumed different names according to the waves of migration that the contracts have successively structured: for example the Belgian *ploegbaas* of the immediate post-war period were later followed by the Italian *caporali*, who in turn were replaced by the Spanish *enganchadores.*

The seasonal contract system for migrants, in fact, has always combined two major elements. First it incorporated the traditional mobility of the rural world through which peasant economies periodically derived supplementary income from outside the family production unit, and which was fostered by the asymmetries between territories, types of agriculture and modes of production. Second, it has functioned as a way of 'disciplining' the movement of worker populations, as areas of production became more concentrated and specialized, and as the productive systems became dependent on a migrant labour force, first external to the farm, then to the village and region and ultimately to the country and continent of production. Immediately after the Second World War, this dependence led the French state and the organized producers to set up stable recruitment channels aimed at providing a secure source of foreign labourers willing to accept the employment and working conditions of intensive agricultural production. For, as Berlan has noted,

> as soon as a region (or farm) starts to specialize in one or more intensive crops, it needs the corresponding labour resources and so there has to be a reliable social mechanism that can supply the employers with the necessary workers.
> (Berlan, 1986, p. 15)

The seasonal contract scheme allowed a shift from a migratory system based on self-organized mobility to a bureaucratic system of importation and controlled hiring of foreign labour. The state thus turned the temporary migrant farm worker into an inferiorized and bridled wage earner. As Moulier-Boutang observes,

> the control of the flight of dependent workers[5] is the major element determining the birth, supersession and replacement of various forms of unfree labour and the genesis of social welfare and the status of the free and protected wage-earner as established by the Employment Code (*Code du travail*).
> (1998, p. 16)

However, the unfree character of work under this scheme does not mean that the migrants are unwilling to participate and remain in such a programme. On the contrary, the seasonal OFII workers are, like their counterparts in the Canadian Seasonal Agricultural Worker Program studied by Basok (1999),[6] 'free to be unfree'. In this sense, their bridled wage condition (Moulier-Boutang, 1998) is the product of the perverse alliance between powerful mechanisms of migratory and employer discipline and a certain form of what could be called, for lack of a better expression, 'voluntary servitude' (La Boétie, 2014) or, to put it another way, an encounter of interests that are certainly asymmetrical but are, at the same time, irreducibly convergent.

## 11.2 The sugar battle and its mercenaries

In the immediate post-war years, seasonal contracts were almost exclusively issued for the beet crop in central northern France. The migrants were mainly concentrated in the three departments of Aisne, Marne and Oise and were assigned to work in the fields (hoeing and picking) and in processing activities (distilling and sugar making). At that time, the sugar beet labour force system was in a quandary: while Belgium had traditionally represented an accessible pool of labour, the devaluation of the French franc in 1945 significantly worsened the exchange rate between the two countries, justifying the application of an expensive system of wage 'bonuses' paid to Belgian seasonal workers to make up for the loss (Lenoble, 1984). Just as the setting-up of the *Société générale d'immigration* had made it possible to hire Polish and Czech workers between the wars, so the creation of ONI contracts allowed producers to recruit workers from further afield. Recruitment thus turned to Italy in 1947, then to Spain in 1953, to Portugal in 1959, and finally, but very marginally, to Morocco and Tunisia in 1964. Each time, the employers' organizations – first the *Confédération générale des planteurs de betteraves* (CGB), and then from 1953 the *Fédération professionnelle agricole pour la main-d'oeuvre saisonnière* (FMO) – played a key role in extending recruitment to other countries. In Spain, for example, the FMO recruited with the agreement of the Ministère du Travail, three years before the signing of the official bilateral workforce convention of 1956, which the Federation had a direct hand in negotiating (Lenoble, 1984, p. 49).

As a result, an average of 35,000 workers were recruited each year between 1953 and 1966 (Décosse, 2011). Recourse to seasonal workers from further South was, however, a false solution for the sugar beet sector. It raised the stakes: the greater distance between the farms and the areas of origin of the migrants increased the transport costs and led to an extension of the contracts. Whereas the Belgians returned to Flanders between the hoeing and harvesting periods, the Italians and Spaniards were too far from home[7] to go back to their respective countries, which meant producers had to resort to seasonal contracts to employ them across the entire growing and productive period and not simply for distinct seasonal tasks within this cycle. The proportion of seven-month contracts increased greatly during the 1950s, comprising between 45 and 60 per cent of all contracts issued by the end of the decade (Lenoble 1984: 34), while wage costs tripled between 1955 and 1967 (Guigou *et al.*, 1969, pp. 72–73).

This increase in labour costs was remarkable given that it occurred at a time of national and international overproduction, resulting in the rationing of production and a reduction of cultivated land between 1953 and 1967 (Guigou *et al.*, 1969, p. 71). In fact, this situation stimulated the development of chemical products, such as herbicides to replace the traditional hoeing in early summer, as well as greater mechanization. As with other crops, capital–labour substitution took place very rapidly from the mid-1950s on: ten years later, more than 80 per cent of the land was ploughed and harvested mechanically (Lenoble, 1984, p. 32). Hoeing was in turn revolutionized by the introduction in 1966 of single-seed sowing, marketed by a Swedish company, which removed the need to pick out the excess plantlets, and also by the improved precision of the seed drills. In the space of fifteen years, the figure of the seasonal migrant worker disappeared completely from the sugar beet industry. In the meantime, mainly Spanish and Portuguese migrant workers came on short three-month contracts to do the hoeing, and then returned south to harvest fruit and vegetables in the Loire, Garonne or Rhône valleys. Consequently cycles of seasonal work and migratory routes began to be established, such as the one taken by Mediterranean migrants during the month of July, which took them from the sugar beet plains of Caen to the tomato farms of the Comtat Venaissin (Hérin, 1971, p. 256). The pioneering work of the organized sugar beet producers to enlarge the scope of recruitment also opened up possibilities for producers of other crops, such as rice.

## 11.3 'As soon as I rise in the morning / Off to the ricefield I must go'

The rice producers' organizations persuaded the administration to adapt the scheme to meet their own 'needs'. Introduced in the nineteenth century, rice-growing had stagnated until it was successfully reintroduced in the Camargue (and to a lesser extent in the Périgord Noir) by the *Ouvriers Non-Spécialisés indochinois de la Main-d'Oeuvre Indigène* (ONS-MOI, Indochinese Semi-Skilled Workers of the Native Workforce) in 1942 (Drot *et al.*, 2007, p. 50; Daum, 2009). In the immediate post-war years, the producers recruited Italian *mondine*, female workers from Tuscany, Emilia-Romagna, Veneto and Lombardy, specialized in hoeing and replanting rice in the Po valley,[8] who 'illegally' extended their migration to the departments of Bouches-du-Rhône and Gard. At the time, this 'irregular' mobility was not subject to the verification of documents, and can thus be considered representative of an alternative and discreet form of migratory utilitarianism based on the founding principle of liberalism, '*laissez faire, laissez passer*'. Other sources of labour at the time included the '*gavots*', workers from the highlands of the neighbouring Massif Central, and to a lesser extent the 'native' ('Muslim French') workers from the colonial empire who had accompanied the Moroccan and Algerian *Pied-noir* back to France from the 1950s onwards. The rice workers were well organized and regularly forced the producers to raise piece rates in the course of the harvest (by 50 per cent in 1950, for example). As a contemporary commentator explained,

> this cosmopolitan group of workers unionized mainly through the CGT (*Confédération générale du travail*). Strikes were used when necessary. The rice industry seems to have only accentuated a class struggle that was still latent. The working class increasingly took a stand against the exploitative owners.
> (Varin d'Ainvelle, 1954, p. 99, quoted by Bethemont, 1962, p. 184)

Thanks to the initiative of the FMO, the employers' organization, the *Syndicat des Riziculteurs de France* was offered the chance to abandon this troublesome group of workers, when in 1954 it started to recruit *collas* (teams) of several dozen experienced workers, mostly from the rice-growing region of Sueca in the Province of Valencia. Spanish immigration provided the workforce required for the renewal of rice production in the Camargue in the 1950s and 1960s – financed mainly by the arrival of *pieds-noirs* and the investment of financial groups from North Africa – which was concentrated essentially in industrial-type farms (Bethemont 1962: pp. 179–184). The rice-growing area practically doubled in size between 1953 and 1960 only to decline again over the next decade (falling from 33,500 ha in 1963 to 19,000 in 1972). However, during this same period the productive units tripled in size, as four-fifths of farms became absorbed into larger plantations. At the peak of production in 1963, the Camargue rice industry employed 4,000 permanent and 7,600 seasonal workers, out of which 7,200 were Spanish (Beau, 1975, p. 59).

This new channel for temporary worker immigration brought several major changes to the labour system. First, the seasonal population became mainly male: at most the various *collas* brought with them two or three women to prepare meals (Moreno, 1994, p. 140). Next, even if some Italians continued to be hired as permanent workers, the seasonal workers in the rice fields were from this period onwards mainly Spanish and 'legal'. Finally, the system of seasonal recruitment was sufficiently flexible to meet the needs of the producers. Although the majority of the contracts were issued for transplanting work, which lasted around 90 days and enabled the Valencian workers to do a first season of replanting at home before leaving for France, a growing number of 'nursery workers' participated in the whole productive cycle over the course of five to seven months (i.e. from preparing the ground, terracing and maintaining irrigation channels through to sowing, weeding, replanting and finally harvesting the rice [Hérin, 1971, p. 248]). This situation resembled the pattern already identified in the context of sugar beet production. As well as meeting the employers' initial wish to break the workers' organization in the early 1950s, the success of the scheme was largely explained by the elasticity of the contracts, which could be extended to more than half the year or limited to a few weeks.

Here is an example of a farm with just under 500 ha near Arles in the early 1960s. As in many agricultural businesses in the region, rice had progressively replaced the grazing lands, where 2,000 sheep had once roamed, and the vineyards, that had been removed in 1957 in the wake of wine overproduction and the deregulation that came with the creation of the European Common Market. The labour system was mainly based on seasonal migrants from the eastern Spain and Catalonia and had benefited from the flexibility of the ONI scheme:

> From 15 March a first team of about fifteen Spaniards settled on the estate where it remained until 15 August. Since 1952, this team had always consisted of the same men or men from the same families and the same village who had always been overseen by the same supervisor who was responsible for the nursery, the planters and the watering of the crop. The team came with him to prepare the nursery, which was sown at the rate of 1,500 kilos per hectare. The transplanting phase took place from 19 to 25 May, with the aid of a second Spanish team, which brought the number of planters to 190 men. [...] Once the weeding was finished, the second Spanish team left, generally around July 15th. The 15 men in the first team did not leave until a month later.
>
> (Bethemont, 1962, p. 194)

By the mid-1960s, ten years after it was first considered a miracle solution, the dependence of rice cultivation on a Spanish workforce had become problematic. The experienced planters, whom the farm owners had come to depend upon, had been raising their demands, and between 1958 and 1966 the wage and piece rate for a hectare of replanted rice increased by 30 per cent (La Cognata, 1967, p. 244). This rise in the cost of labour, in a context where the workforce generated 47 per cent of the total costs of production, led the farmers to rapidly implement a capital–labour substitution. The introduction of chemical weeding and direct seeding sounded the death knell of the replanting activity from 1968 onwards and led to a 'progressive reduction of the permanent workforce and a complete halt to recruitment of seasonal labour' (Beau, 1975, p. 59).

## 11.4 A special regime for the grape harvests

The contract used by the rice planters inspired the ONI and the employers' organizations of the wine-growing sector to draw up the 'special regime for Spanish grape-pickers' in 1960 which made it possible to issue short-term contracts lasting from two to six weeks (Débarre, 1990, p. 43). The employers' need to systematize and guarantee the recruitment of foreign workers coincided with the government's desire to legalize and organize the employment of Spanish grape pickers, in order to regulate the labour market in the wine sector and collect the relevant social security contributions. Since 1956, regional labour offices had been in the habit of issuing work permits to migrants who had entered France as 'tourists' to take part in the grape harvests (Carrière and Ferras, 1968, p. 8). A decade later, 90 per cent of the 24,000 seasonal workers employed in the specific department of Hérault possessed ONI contracts (Hérin, 1971, p. 232); while by 1974, 'grape harvest' contracts accounted for 61 per cent of the 144,500 seasonal entries (in 1974), and this percentage remained more or less stable until the late 1980s, even if the number of employees dropped following the introduction of grape-harvesting machines.

The first mechanized grape harvest took place in France in 1971, but the first generation of machines was only adopted on the largest estates, due to their high price and size, and above all their inappropriateness for the vineyards of the time (which were small plots with narrow corridors between rows and lacking the necessary trellising). In 1976, a second generation of smaller and towable machines were better fitted to the needs of small and medium-sized vineyards (Débarre, 1990, pp. 73–76). After 1980, the reorganization of land, the steady fall in prices in line with market developments, and the arrival of a third generation of machines equipped with closed 'shaking' systems and bucket chains, as well as a new 'straddling' chassis suitable for difficult terrains, led to the adoption of these machines everywhere and the replacement of the foreign seasonal labour, which had, by then, become more expensive and restrictive.

The 'Spanish grape pickers' scheme is, in several respects, an exception to the standard seasonal work regime. First, it only applied to the winegrowers of Languedoc-Roussillon and imported migrant labourers from relatively nearby, since the pickers mostly came from down the coast in the Communities of Valencia and Murcia. Second, the cost of entry was relatively low, since the fee paid by the employer to the ONI was 20–50 per cent of the usual entry fee (Carrière and Ferras, 1968, p. 9). Finally, there was a greater degree of tolerance regarding the age of the workers, because, in order to allow for the traditional familial composition of the *collas,* no upper age limit was set and young people could legally be employed from the age of 16 (or 18 in the case of women), with special exemption for accompanied minors over 14 (or 16 in the case of females). In the Charente department in 1983, women made up 40 per cent of Spanish grape pickers and were divided into two main age groups: 16–28 and 47–58 (Débarre, 1990, pp. 163–165). This is similar to the findings of studies in other areas (De Prado, 1966; Carrière and Ferras, 1968; Hérin, 1971; Roudié, 1987) and confirms the familial form of this type of labour migration.

The example of the 'Spanish grape picker' contracts thus shows how the system could evolve according to the requirements of different actors. The seasonal scheme had to be accessible to all members of the same family so that they would agree to come (the short period of employment generated a 'small'[9] income for the family unit of production, which maximized its earning capacity by migrating and working as a group[10]). It also had to be sufficiently inexpensive for the employers to agree to replace 'illegals' with contracted pickers. Furthermore it had to enable the migrants to move on to another crop, not only to increase the attractiveness of migration for the workers, but also in order to give the labour administration the means of meeting other needs of local or national production.

On this last point, the case of Charente is illuminating, since in the 1970s and 1980s the labour administration of the department and the winegrowers' federation jointly organized the transfer of some of the foreign grape picking workforce from Languedoc-Roussillon or Gironde to the Cognac and Pineau production areas, where harvests took place later (Débarre, 1990). In this redeployment of the seasonal labour force, the mobility of the workers was strictly controlled: once their contracts were extended, the workers were transported by train or bus to new areas where they were distributed among the vineyards that needed them. While this transfer satisfied all parties – the pickers earned more money, the employers shared the registration fees and the administration provided the workforce without having to bring them from their country of origin – it reflects the Janus-faced aspect of the utilitarian migratory logic. On the one hand, this strictly limited the foreigner's residence to a specific seasonal activity; on the other, however, it extended the migrant's period of residence and work under a seasonal CDD according to the needs of the producers. This continual switching between these two positions is most apparent in the sector known as 'other agricultural activities,' a catch-all category which today essentially refers to fruit tree and market gardening industries.

## 11.5 The deft fingers of the greenhouses and orchards

'The Alpine regime', 'the Catalan regime', 'the Pyrenean procedure': the history of the seasonal worker scheme represents a series of exceptional procedures through which the administration has sought to legalize and channel migrant labour towards the market gardens and orchards of the regions adjoining Italy and Spain. But whereas these businesses mainly assigned migrants to genuinely seasonal tasks (lasting approximately one month), the permanent suspension of economic immigration in 1974 transformed the very nature of this employment system. This change was made possible by the spread of greenhouse farming in fruit and vegetable production in the 1970s and 1980s. The progressive artificialization of market gardening favoured the deseasonalization of tasks, which in turn led to an extension of the working and residence periods of imported migrant labourers. Whereas in the 1960s hundreds of Spaniards came on 'twenty-day contracts' to pick cherries in Languedoc-Roussillon and strawberries in the Rhône valley (Hérin, 1971, pp. 241–243), by the early 1980s around a third of the contracts in the 'other agricultural activities' sector were originally issued or extended for a period of six to eight months (Raynaud *et al.*, 1981).

This change did not occur uniformly across time and space, and did not eliminate the diversity that still prevails in the market gardening and fruit tree sector.

The type of workforce system is strongly correlated with the particular type of productive system that depended on a range of variables including the existence or absence of a diversity of crops on the farm, the nature and intensity of the use of mechanical and chemical techniques and the integration of additional tasks (such as washing, grading and packing) into the production process. The combination of these different variables influences the number of teams of seasonal workers that the producer recruits and the length of the contracts for each team. It is possible to outline a broad typology of the estates in this sector: first, productive units which, due to their retention of permanent staff and the monocultural nature of their activity, only require seasonal workers on short contracts for their harvests; second, businesses that have introduced mechanical and chemical methods into their production cycle and have replaced their former permanent employees with long seasonal contract workers who tend to the single crop and supervise the group of shorter-term seasonal workers during picking and packing phases; and third, those whose production is diversified and which therefore only use long-term seasonal migrants who move from one activity and one crop to another.

From a general perspective, it would appear that employers willingly adapt their productive system in order to maximize the (administratively sanctioned) opportunity to hire temporary workers who accept low wages, illegally long working hours and poor working conditions. The producer then spreads out his labour needs by developing an additional crop, which enables him to hire seasonal workers for the entirety of their authorized employment period. The possibilities of recruiting migrant labour and thus modifying the labour systems has enabled employers to alter existing crop systems. This productive logic is all the more significant if one considers that the cost of labour normally constitutes roughly 50 per cent of production costs and, according to the employers, is the only variable which they can act upon, when they find themselves caught between the demands of purchasers,[11] on the one hand, and those of banks and suppliers, on the other.

## 11.6 Contesting the OFII status to break free of it

As the seasonal scheme has become increasingly distorted and the employment of migrants has become near permanent within an increasingly deseasonalized fruit and vegetable sector, the struggles of agricultural workers to break free from their status as temporary contract workers and to secure full rights of residence and work have grown. Due to the lack of space,[12] only some key, salient features will be mentioned here. A first dispute took place in Avignon in 1974, when seasonal workers from North Africa, backed by the *Mouvement des travailleurs arabes*, occupied churches and went on hunger strike to demand their residence and work permit. Although the movement ultimately failed to obtain its demands, it nonetheless publicly highlighted what was at stake following the shift from temporary to permanent immigration. The question arose again in 1980 in Loiret, but this time in a trade-union context, when seasonal workers denounced their 'bogus contracts' and went on strike with the support of the CGT. Although the strike ended in negotiations leading to an increase in the rates of the collective agreement and verdicts from employment tribunal against a number of market garden employers, it was not until the 'Mitterrand regularization' of 1982, which issued 6,000 permanent residence permits, that seasonal workers were able to secure an improvement to their administrative situation. This exceptional measure, taken by a new Socialist government seeking to introduce a clear break into French society, had, in any case, been legitimated by the 1980 strike (Décosse, 2013).

Fifteen years later, the Socialists had adopted a neo-liberal ideology that aligned with the migration policies of conservative agenda. Backed by the CGT, the seasonal workers of Chateaurenard asked to be included in the Chevènement regularization of 1997, which excluded them on the grounds that they already possessed documents. Although the union obtained work contracts from the employers, these were never fulfilled because it failed to bring the migrants out on strike.

In July 2005, 240 seasonal workers went on strike on a farm in Crau which produced 10 per cent of French peaches and nectarines. The movement was initially spontaneous and self-managed but was later supported by the CGT. Although the union won a tribunal verdict against the employer and provoked unprecedented media coverage of the migrants' poor working and housing conditions, it failed again on the question of documents, and, moreover, the strikers were blacklisted so that they would receive no further contracts. Two years later, the CODETRAS, a network coordinating the action of several unions and associations in Bouches-du-Rhône which since 2001 had been trying to make political use of the law,[13] took legal action against the Prefecture of the Department on the basis of an observation that had been made during all the previous experiences of struggle: the use of these contracts was against the law and amounted *de facto* to permanent productive activities. Backed by employee career records, some of whom had been coming to France for 20 to 30 years for eight months of the year, as well as crop calendars of the companies hiring them, the argument was accepted by the court, which ordered the administrative authority to issue residence permits to a thousand seasonal workers.

## 11.7 Conclusion

Having come to the end of this historical reconstruction, it is important to note that we are now probably witnessing the demise of a scheme that, for 70 years, accompanied the industrialization of French agriculture. In the sugar beet and rice sectors, machines and chemicals very quickly replaced the migrant seasonal labour, as the latter became less cost effective and more challenging for the employers to mobilize.[14] On closer inspection it is evident that the ONI contracts enabled producers to delay a capital–labour substitution that the agricultural model had made inevitable (as a result of the expansion of the cultivated area, the pressure to increase yields per hectare and the decline in margins due to overproduction and the speculative turn taken by the market). In other words, producers were able to benefit as long as possible from a precarious, bridled and cheap labour force to which the scheme gave them access.

In the wine-growing sector, the disappearance of seasonal workers has been less dramatic, which should certainly be seen as the corollary of the benevolence on the part of the authorities towards a culturally and economically important industry that historically has wielded great influence in the political sphere. The maintenance of very small properties and the technical constraints linked to the varieties of vineyards for a long time prevented capital–labour substitution, and it was not until the 1980s that Spanish grape pickers rapidly disappeared from the French rural landscape. A similar development in the horticultural sector took place later. The mechanization of work was not readily compatible with quality requirements, which meant that fruit and vegetables had to be picked by hand, even if in fruit tree industry, for example, the workers increasingly moved around on overhead walkways to pick the fruit.

It is for this reason that this sector continues to employ the majority of the several thousand contracted seasonal labourers who still come to France each year to work on harvests. In contrast to sugar beet, rice and grapes, fruit and vegetable production continues to be partly based on migrant labour. However, the role of the OFII scheme in this sector has sharply declined since the campaign by CODETRAS for the permanent residence of foreign workers in Bouches-du-Rhône in 2007–2008. This decline in OFII numbers is matched by an increase in the hiring of temporary workers through European or extra-EU temporary staffing agencies (Mésini, 2014). This further renewal of migratory utilitarianism would appear to disprove the French historian Ronald Hubscher who declared that 'the historical role of migrants in [French] agriculture now seems to be over' (2005, p. 403).

## Notes

1 For a theoretical discussion of the use of *etic* vs *emic* categories in the social sciences, see Olivier de Sardan (1998).

2 The abbreviations ONI, OMI, ANAEM and OFII refer to the same public agency responsible for managing migration in France and therefore the organization responsible for the seasonal scheme studied here. Their use in the text depends on the period in question. The *Office national d'immigration* (ONI) was set up in 1945; it became the *Office des migrations internationales* (OMI) in 1988, the *Agence nationale d'accueil des étrangers et des migrations* (ANAEM) in 2005, and finally the *Office français de l'immigration et de l'intégration* (OFII) in 2009.

3 This was particularly true in the hotel and restaurant trades and the car industry after May 1968, when it enabled employers in the Paris region to put pressure on the unionized permanent workers. For example, in 1969 and 1970, some 3,500 Moroccans were hired on a seasonal basis in the car factories east of Paris (*Statistiques de l'immigration*, Office national d'immigration, Paris, 1970–1971). On the connections between the postcolonial management of 'North-African labour' in the car industry and industrial disputes, see Pitti (2002) and Linhart (1981).

4 The precarity bonus normally provides 10 per cent additional pay to all short-term contracted workers in France.

5 For Moulier-Boutang, bridled labour covers

> a very wide spectrum of different situations which, between slavery or serfdom and the canonical free wage earner, includes the true ancestors of international migrant labour, deported labour, apprenticeship and indenture, and the contracted

foreign worker, subject to the contract limiting his mobility and his freedom to break the relationship of dependent labour, because he was a foreigner, while the indentured servant or apprentice became exogenous labour, because they were subject to their contract for a fixed time.

(1998, pp. 677–678)

6 Based on the 'guest worker' (*Gastarbeiter*) model, various Temporary Foreign Worker Programs (TFWP) have historically supplied labour for intensive farming systems throughout the world, such as the Bracero Program (1942–1964) in the USA (Castles, 1986). Largely abandoned in the 1970s, such systems are now again expanding (Castles, 2006) and international organizations such as the International Organization for Migration, the World Trade Organization and the World Bank promote them and present them as win-win models for the management of human mobility on a world scale. For a detailed study of current TFWPs, see Sanchez and Lara (2015).

7 Moreover, the origins of emigrants in the source countries shifted over time: in Italy, Puglia in the South progressively took the place of Emilia-Romagna and the Po valley; while in Spain, Andalusia took over from Aragon (Lenoble, 1984, pp. 46–50).

8 On the *mondine* (from the Italian *mondare:* to clean, hoe), see the film *Bitter Rice* by Giuseppe De Santis (1948), which depicts the dualism of the system of work used to produce rice, since the documented female planters are opposed to the 'illegals' ('*clandestine*'), recruited by gang-leaders and who are made to compete against them in the same rice fields in order to drive up work rates. This confrontation is expressed in the popular work songs, as in an early version of the famous partisan tune *Bella Ciao*. This is a translation of the words evoking the working conditions of the *mondine*:

As soon as I rise in the morning
Off to the ricefield I must go
And among the bugs and mosquitoes
I must toil
And the foreman standing with his stick
And us bent down working
O Good Mother what a torment
I call on you every day
And all the hours we spend here
We lose our youth
But you'll see that one day, such as we are
We shall work in freedom.

9 Hérin estimates the earnings per person at between 500 and 700 francs, twice the average wage of a worker in Spain. This amount varied depending on whether the work was paid by piece-rate (which enabled experienced harvesters to double their earnings) or by the hour, on the nature of the task (cutting, carrying, carting, etc.). There was also payment in kind, such as accommodation and wine, while local expenditure was limited by virtue of the food being prepared by a woman of the group and provisions being brought from Spain (1971, pp. 263–265).

10 A quantitative study based on 1,700 questionnaires completed at the Franco-Spanish border provides some details on the profile of the grape pickers who came to Languedoc-Roussillon in the 1960s: a third of respondents was inactive in Spain (housewives, young people, retired workers); those who worked earned on average 100 to 150 pesetas for a day's work; the professional agricultural workers managed to find work for eight to nine months during the year (in orange, rice, grape and other fruit crops); and only 4.5 per cent said they wanted to settle permanently in France (De Prado, 1966). On this last point, although the figure should be taken cautiously in the light of how it was produced (small sample, survey in a local branch of the ONI in Figueras), it is

echoed by findings in Débarre (1990, p. 169) and confirms the fact that the migration of Spanish grape-pickers genuinely took the form of seasonal displacement for work, in the sense that, for those involved, it was not intended to be permanent. While this observation is not valid for all agricultural activities or all nationalities, it nonetheless requires the observer to reject the mechanistic and determinist vision of a shift from temporary migration to permanent migration and to analyse in fine detail the individual and collective/systemic reasons that lead seasonal workers to remain in a temporary pattern or, conversely, to try to move to a permanent employment and/or residence status.

11 In the case of this oligopsony market, the control of the purchasing groups over the producers is exerted both through the fixing of prices (surplus-value appropriation) and through the externalization of their logistical constraints.

12 See Décosse (2011) for further information.

13 On the notions of the political mobilization of law and 'cause lawyering,' see for example Israël (2001) and Noreau and Vallet (2004).

14 This was in part the result of trade union activity, but was also due to the forced extension of contracts and to the fact that the sources of recruitment were ever more distant from the places of work.

## References


Basok, T. (1999). 'Free to be unfree: Mexican guest workers in Canada'. *Labour, Capital and Society* 32(2): 192–221.

Beau, J. P. (1975). 'La culture du riz en Camargue, aspects techniques et commerciaux actuels'. *Méditerranée* 22(2): 53–68.

Berlan, J.P. (1986). 'Agriculture et migration'. *Revue européenne des migrations internationales* 2(3): 9–32.

Berlan, J.P. (dir.) (1991). *L'intégration des immigrés en milieu rural.* Marseille: INRA/CEDERS/Université Aix Marseille II.

Bethemont, J. (1962). 'Le riz et la mise en valeur de la Camargue'. *Revue de géographie de Lyon* 37(2): 153–206.

Carrière, P. and Ferras, R. (1968). 'Les vendangeurs espagnols en Languedoc et Roussillon'. *Études rurales* 32: 7–42.

Castles, S. (1986). 'The guest-worker in Europe: An obituary'. *International Migration Review* 20: 761–778.

Castles, S. (2006). 'Guestworkers in Europe: A resurrection?'. *International Migration Review* 40: 741–766.

Daum, P. (2009). *Immigrés de force, les travailleurs indochinois en France (1939–1952).* Arles: Solin/Actes Sud.

Débarre, M. (1990). *Les travailleurs saisonniers étrangers dans l'agriculture française.* Mémoire de maîtrise de géographie, Université de Poitiers.

Décosse, F. (2011). *Migrations sous contrôle: Agriculture intensive et saisonniers marocains sous contrat 'OMI'.* Thèse de sociologie, EHESS, Paris.

Décosse, F. (2013). 'Immigrés, solidarité! Histoire d'une lutte, envers d'un slogan'. *Hommes & Migrations* 1301: 109–117.

De Prado, E. (1966). 'La migration saisonnière espagnole des vendanges'. *Économie méridionale* 54: 37–40.

Drot, C. (dir.) (2007). *Histoire et mémoires des immigrations en Aquitaine.* Rapport d'étude final, ACSE/DRA.

Guigou, J. (dir.) (1969). *Les salariés étrangers dans l'agriculture française.* Montpellier: École Nationale Supérieure Agronomique.

Hérin, R. (1971). 'Les travailleurs saisonniers d'origine étrangère en France'. *Travaux et documents, Cahier de l'INED* 59: 221–286.

Hubscher, R. (2005). *L'immigration dans les campagnes françaises (XIX-XXe)*. Paris: O. Jacob.

Israël, L. (2001). 'Usages militants du droit dans l'arène judiciaire: le cause lawyering'. *Droit et société* 3(49): 793–824.

Jounin, N. (2006). *Loyautés incertaines. Les travailleurs du bâtiment entre discrimination et précarité*. Thèse de sociologie, Paris: Université Paris VII.

La Boétie, E. (de) (2014) [1574]. *Discours de la servitude volontaire*. Paris: Larousse.

La Cognata, G. (1967). 'Vers une suppression du repiquage en Camargue'. *Méditerranée* 8(3): 239–253.

Lenoble, R. (1984). *La main-d'œuvre saisonnière betteravière en France: Historique des migrations, des origines à 1984*. Paris: Fédération Professionnelle Agricole pour la Main-d'œuvre saisonnière.

Linhart, R. (1981). *L'Établi*. Paris: Minuit.

Mésini, B. (2014). 'The transnational recruitment of temporary Latino workers in European agriculture' in Gertel, J. and Sippel, S. (eds). *Seasonal Workers in Mediterranean Agriculture. The Social Costs of Eating Fresh: Earthscan Food and Agriculture*. New York: Routledge: 71–82.

Moreno, P. (1994). 'L'émigration maghrébine dans l'agriculture espagnole: un effet indirect des politiques d'ajustement structurel?'. *Options Méditerranéennes* 8 (série B, Études et Recherches): 136–140.

Morice, A. (2004). 'Le travail sans le travailleur'. *Plein droit* 61, juin: pp. 2–7.

Moulier-Boutang, Y. (1998). *De l'esclavage au salariat: Économie historique du salariat bridé*. Paris: PUF.

Noreau, P. and Vallet, E. (2004). 'Le droit comme ressource des minorités nationales. Un modèle de mobilisation politique du droit' in Noreau, P. and Woehrling, J. (eds). *Diversité des appartenances culturelles et réaménagement des institutions politiques et de la citoyenneté*. Montreal: Wilson Lafleur.

Olivier de Sardan, J. P. (1998). 'Émique'. *L'Homme* 38(147): 151–166.

Pitti, L. (2002). *Ouvriers algériens à Renault-Billancourt de la guerre d'Algérie aux grèves d'OS des années 1970. Contribution à l'histoire sociale et politique des ouvriers étrangers en France*. Thèse d'histoire, Saint-Denis: Université Paris 8.

Privat, L. (1966). 'Les saisonniers agricoles dans le Midi de la France'. *Économie rurale* 67: 37–48.

Raynaud, F. (dir.) (1981). *L'immigration saisonnière dans l'agriculture de 1967 à 1981*. Paris: Office national d'immigration.

Roudié, P. (1987). *Les saisonniers étrangers en Aquitaine septentrionale*. Bordeaux: Publications de la MSH d'Aquitaine (Maison des Pays Ibériques).

Sanchez, M. and Lara, S. (dir.) (2015). *Los programas de trabajadores temporales. ¿Una solución a los retos de las migraciones en el contexto de la globalización?* Mexico D.F.: IIS-UNAM.

# 12 'They know that you'll leave, like a dog moving onto the next bin'

## Undocumented male and seasonal contracted female workers in the agricultural labour market of Huelva, Spain

*Emmanuelle Hellio*

> So, what is an immigrant? An immigrant is essentially labour power, and labour power that is non-permanent, temporary, in transit. According to this principle, an immigrant worker (which is itself almost a pleonasm), [...] is always defined and treated as provisional, and therefore dismissible at any moment. [...] The right to stay is subject entirely to the immigrant's labour, and is granted first and foremost to exist as an immigrant, and thereafter briefly as a human being – in effect, as a human being subject to the condition of being an immigrant.
>
> (Sayad, 1991, p. 50)

### 12.1 Introduction

Andalusia is today the leading exporting region of agricultural products for the European market. In the western part of this region, along the Atlantic coast, strawberry farming has developed considerably since the 1980s. The favourable climate of the Huelva Province and plant varieties imported from California make it possible for producers to export strawberries during the out-of-season period, from January to April. The industrialization of local agriculture is inscribed in the landscape: 7,000 hectares of greenhouses immerse visitors in a sea of plastic. The drop in profits stemming from higher input prices, the increased international competition from new production areas in the global South, and the role of supermarket chains as price setters (see Reigada, this volume), have led to the seasonal recruitment of a female workforce from Eastern Europe and Morocco, who have largely replaced undocumented male migrants from sub-Saharan Africa and Morocco in the local farm labour market. In fact, in 2000, the Spanish government launched a recruiting programme known as the '*contratación en origen*',[1] a contractual scheme aimed at organizing and controlling the international mobility of seasonal agricultural workers. Such contracts have been widely used in the strawberry industry to formally recruit farmworkers, while other agricultural sectors continue to rely on undocumented workers.

The *contratación en origen* is a response to the productivity imperatives of the strawberry industry, characterized by a long season during which workers must remain on call, without assurance of permanent employment. In addition, the fragmentation of tasks facilitates the training of women workers and does not require any coordination between them.

This type of contract therefore meets the employers' need for control and flexibility, which results from their position of dependence in the supply chain, both with respect to the upstream (biotech and seed industry) and downstream ends (large retail distribution sector). In comparison, undocumented workers are often considered too mobile. Other crop growers (olives, apricots, peaches, grapes and citrus fruit) usually hire undocumented workers because of the short harvest season, and their unwillingness to undertake lengthy bureaucratic procedures for such a short period. Moreover, the tasks involved in such cases require a sort of 'gang spirit' that is to be found more commonly in the 'community' or family spirit typical of certain groups of migrant workers, rather than through the more anonymous recruitment of the *contratación en origen*. Today, these two groups of migrant workers coexist and complement each other on Huelva's labour market.

This chapter starts by providing an overview of the history of labour recruitment in Huelva, with the aim of understanding the impact of migration policies on the political construction of the labour market. I describe how the recruitment of new groups of (migrant) workers – mainly Moroccan men in the late 1980s and those employed through the *contratación en origen* in the 2000s – represented, on both occasions, a response to labourers' collective demands and autonomous mobility, and a strategy for segmenting, and thus controlling, the agricultural labour force. I proceed to show, through a comparison of living and working conditions, the different and yet complementary roles assumed by Moroccan women recruited through the *contratación en origen* and undocumented sub-Saharan men within the local employment system. I argue that the programme of recruitment of seasonal farm workers aims to control and channel – rather than to 'protect' – migrant labour. Following Michael Burawoy (1976), I maintain that such programmes guarantee farmers' profitability in essentially two ways: first, by compelling contracted workers to return to their countries of origin at the end of the harvest season; and, second, by establishing a hierarchy and competition within the local market along the lines of nationality, gender and legal status.

This chapter is based on my PhD research that examined the mobility of contracted female Moroccan workers in Spain. During this research I carried out 70 interviews with seasonal workers, farmers, trade union officials, and representatives of institutions involved in the management of the foreign workforce, as well as conducting observations of workers' daily lives both on farms in Huelva province, between 2008 and 2011, and in their villages of origin in the Moroccan region of Gharb, between 2010 and 2011.

## 12.2 Mobilizing labour supply in Huelva

In order to be profitable given the high cost of various intermediaries in the supply chain, the production of strawberries – the local 'red gold' – needs to employ cheap migrant labour. Considering foreign labour as just another production 'input', Huelva's strawberry growers seek a reliable labour force without guaranteeing year-round work. This labour force must be displaced (or, put another way, rejected) once the season ends. Over the years, farmers have found diverse solutions to face this double imperative.

### *12.2.1 The* subsidio agrario *and the early recruitment of migrant workers*

The early development of strawberry farming was inseparable from the availability of a flexible family workforce that was able to match the changing workload on the farms. This family workforce used to be backed up during the harvest season by Spanish day labourers from neighbouring provinces. In the 1980s, the day labourer was quite a common figure among the Andalusian rural population and in a context of structural unemployment. In 1984, the region experienced increasing social conflicts as a result of the high proportion of under-employed rural labour. To avoid further tensions, the State set up the *subsidio agrario*, a public allowance system created specifically for Andalusia and Extremadura, in recognition of the existence of massive rural unemployment. In order to benefit from the programme, workers had to only work for a limited number of days each year, and to be enrolled in the agricultural social insurance scheme. After working 60 days, they received a maximum annual salary equivalent to 75 per cent of the minimum annual wage of 180 days' work (García, 2004). Initially, the obligation to work for a minimum number of days a year reinforced the traditional practice of internal seasonal mobility. As the strawberry picking season was long, it was a particularly attractive sector. Thus, the *subsidio* generated a reserve of labour in rural Andalusia, which permitted the development of crops requiring a large seasonal workforce, such as strawberries and olives.[2]

During the 1990s, the situation changed. Farmers increasingly tended to hire foreign workers. The massive rural employment of foreigners who lived locally can partly be explained by the legal changes made to the *subsidio agrario* during this decade. In 1995, a reform reduced the period of work required to contribute to social security from 60 to 40 days (and then to 35 in 1997). Moreover, Spanish daily labourers had adopted a more detached attitude towards agricultural work, and farmers had less and less control over their mobility. While for years the State allowance had been considered a 'totally secure social mechanism' that supplied the required amount of workers while at the same time guaranteeing a 'structural excess of labour' (Berlan, 1986), the *subsidio* eventually stopped being fully functional in both aspects. During the 1990s, one could notice the widespread presence of migrants in intensive farming all along the Andalusian Mediterranean and Atlantic coast, either permanently (as in Almería and Murcia) or seasonally (as in Jaén and Huelva), even if these areas registered very high unemployment rates among the autochthonous agricultural population. Farming gradually became one of the few sectors where undocumented migrants could find employment. At the same time, irregular employment was fundamental to the competitiveness of Huelva's strawberry production, as well as the intensive fruit and vegetable industry all over the Mediterranean (Berlan, 1987). This new labour source gave rise to a new strategy for the survival and expansion of intensive family farms. In turn, the possibility of finding employment in agriculture fostered the permanent or seasonal settlement of numerous foreigners in many rural towns. Nonetheless, by the end of the 1990s, the situation had changed again. A number of migrants of this 'first wave' managed to obtain a permit to stay in Spain. In a short space of time, farmers came to consider these migrants as too mobile. An explicit migratory utilitarianism emerged: employers protested at the ease of mobility of undocumented and legalized foreigners and hence pressed for a programme of recruitment of seasonal migrant workers: the *contratación en origen.*

### *12.2.2 The independent mobility of undocumented migrants versus the restricted mobility of foreigners under temporary contracts*

The *contratación en origen* was inspired by an experiment led by a Catalan union which had started to organize seasonal foreign labour in the farming sector as early as the mid-1980s. At the end of the 1990s, this programme of temporary migration was presented by a number of political and economic actors as a means of developing forms of so-called 'legal' migration, and thus rejecting other forms of residence, such as undocumented migration, with the subsequent tightening of border controls. At the national level, several parliamentary groups called on the government to develop public policy that could channel and regulate migration flows according to the needs of the Spanish economy and to society's supposed capacity to 'absorb' migrant labourers. On their part, employers considered this new recruitment mechanism as an answer to what Michael Burawoy (1976) called the failed reproduction of a migrant labour system.

Burawoy argues that, as soon as mechanisms of migration control are loosened or abandoned, new groups of migrant workers appear. In Huelva, migration control in the early 1990s had become a subject of public debate. After 1997, reports from farmers' meetings highlighted complaints about the lack of employment continuity and the collective desire to control the mobility of what farmers called *volanderos* (i.e. tramps or hobos). Indeed, the agricultural sector offered migrants an employment refuge and an entry into the labour market, but – as employers complained – many of them left agriculture for better opportunities 'as soon as they got legalized' (García, 2004).

In the meantime, locally, Maghrebi and sub-Saharan workers organized a series of protests, demonstrations and occupations of public spaces to demand the regularization of their legal status (Martín and Castaño, 2004). It was in this situation that the *contratación en origen* was approved in 2000.

The struggles and mobility of day labourers during both the late 1980s and the late 1990s represent the main causes for the recruitment of new groups of workers in the strawberry sector (on this question, see Moulier Boutang, 1998). In the late 1980s, the mobilizations of Andalusian day labourers were countered by the employment of Moroccan workers. This was part of a strategy of segmenting the labour force, which led to the demise of union activism among farm labourers.

Ten years later, the *contratación en origen* constituted a leap forward in the segmentation process and aimed to prevent the success of Moroccan male workers' claims for legalization and the improvement of their working conditions. As in other cases, these processes contradict the dominant idea that recruiting programmes act as an impetus for new migrations. On the contrary, the *contratación en origen* was a response to existing forms of spontaneous mobility that public authorities and farmers tried to 'channel' and 'govern' (Karakayali and Rigo, 2010). An executive of Fresdeloc, one of the biggest companies in the area, which was among the first to relocate production to Morocco at the end of the 1980s, recalls how foreign labour was regulated in Huelva during the period:

> The choice was between mechanization or an appropriate way of legalizing these people; otherwise it was an open door to a subterranean economy that doesn't provide sufficient protection. In Huelva a migration commission was set up that sought commitment from the companies. The aim was to channel migratory flows in a civilized way. The contracts guaranteed set periods of work. By being documented, [workers] were entitled to Spanish labour regulations. The matter was managed politically. Legalizing these specific flows of labour implied at the same time rejecting previous migratory flows. The public authorities threatened a few companies […]. We'd had some previous experience with Moroccan workers who had settled here and worked well […] From small numbers of migrants entering at random … we moved to the idea that we can't import all workers who ask for work, but rather we need to start to select them in their countries of origin.
>
> (Interview in Spanish with an executive from Fresdeloc-Morocco, Moulay Bouslem, Morocco, 22 July 2010)

In the above quotation it is possible to identify two key aspects in claims about the benefits of the move from spontaneous and illegalized migration to controlled and legal mobility. The executive interviewed starts by emphasizing the main objective behind such a shift: to ensure the planning of the season by counting on a secure labour force that meets the needs of the producers, in short, what Tanya Basok (2002) calls 'captive labour'. The interviewee goes on to legitimate migration channelling by distinguishing between two opposites: on the one hand 'legal' migration, that provides protection for workers; on the other 'illegal' migration, which is presumed to be a synonym for poor working and housing conditions. However, such discourses that highlight the advantages of legal migration contra the risks of illegal migration never explain why the former should improve the housing and working conditions of foreign workers. Rather, it is taken for granted that legalization automatically protects migrants from exploitation.

Even though the substitution of an illegalized workforce by contract labour has been managed by all the sector actors, a decade later, neither farmers nor institutions feel responsible for the persistence of slums and poverty endured by undocumented migrants, as if such a reality were totally independent of the farm labour market.

Concerning the causes, the underlying idea behind this model was actually to reject independent migration in order to secure a new controlled mobility. The *contratación en origen* appeared to be a consensual solution that was able to harmonize the diverse interests at stake: first, those of the State, which sought to avoid taking care of foreign workers during the off-season and to ensure the apparent maintenance of public order, which was otherwise challenged by the uncontrolled mobility of undocumented workers and the visibility of their settlements; and, second, those of the employers, who needed well-trained and regular labour available at all times (Achón, 2010). The development of the *contratación en origen* stemmed from the desire to go back to 'a stricter definition of immigration and immigrants [that] maximizes the (mostly economic) "advantages" of immigration, while reducing to a minimum the "costs" (particularly those of a social and cultural nature) imposed by their mere presence' (Sayad, 1991, p. 50).

The new scheme was consistent with the positions of international organizations such as the International Organization for Migration and the International Labour Organization, which promoted temporary migration within the wider frame of the so-called 'global' approach to migration (Kalm, 2010; Karakayali and Rigo, 2010; Pellerin, 2011; Décosse, 2011). Far from being more protective, mobility under the *contratación en origen* actually grants less mobility and freedom to workers than informal migration. In an article in a cooperative newspaper based in Almería Province, a farmer pointed out that the major advantage of contract recruitment was the greater degree of constraint placed on workers:

> We used to waste a lot of time and money on the legalization of workers. We used to give them documents, and then, once they had a valid work permit, they would leave to find work in another city, another company, or in a different sector. Thanks to the recruitment 'in origin', workers now come for a specified length of time and they cannot go to work elsewhere. The contract binds them to the company [...] if they leave, they lose their work permit and cannot remain in Spain: this is probably the biggest advantage of this kind of recruitment.[3]

Nicolas Jounin (2010) has used Emmanuel Terray's (1999) expression 'delocalization on the spot' (*délocalisation sur place*) to describe transnational subcontracting, arguing that Terray's concept applies better to posted workers – and, I would add, to temporary contracts – than to illegal work. 'Indeed, in both cases one can find the idea of a "transfer" organized and controlled by the company [...]. Both undocumented and posted salaried workers cross the border, but the latter's mobility is directly controlled by their employer' (Jounin, 2010, p. 70). In her analysis of the labour market in the Californian strawberry industry, Wells (1996) explained that temporary workers under contracts were more easily disposable than undocumented workers because they were well known to the authorities.[4] In fact what really distinguishes legalized from illegalized workers is the higher degree of control that both the State and employers have on the former compared to the latter. Several studies conducted in North America have shown that seasonal migrants themselves see irregular migration in some cases to be less constraining than legal forms of temporary migration (McLaughlin, 2010; Lutz and Bordi, 2007).

### *12.2.3 The* contratación en origen*: three waves of labour force within ten years*

Since it started in 2000, the new recruitment system has enabled employers to recruit seasonal workers in foreign countries to harvest strawberries in Huelva. The selection and contract agreement both take place in the country of origin. Workers are then sent to Huelva for a limited period of time (from three to nine months) at the end of which they must return to their country, in accordance with a signed repatriation agreement. In the first year in 2000, 600 Polish, around 200 Moroccans and a small number of Colombians and Ecuadorians were recruited. In 2003, the number of contract workers rose to 12,000; the following year this figure nearly doubled, while in 2007, 35,000 female workers came to harvest strawberries in Huelva Province (Table 12.1).

During this period, the *contratación en origen* thus became the major recruitment channel in the strawberry sector. In less than ten years, it fostered the arrival of three major national groups of female workers (in the following descending order): Poles, Romanians and Moroccans.[5] This new recruitment mechanism offered Huelva farmers the opportunity to maintain working and housing conditions well below the legal standards of the Andalusian agricultural sector (which actually offer little protection). As Yann Moulier Boutang (1998) has underlined in his study of situations in other historical periods, the persistence of the exogeneity of foreign labour is allowed not by the succession of different legal statuses of each individual, but by the succession of migrant individuals. The current local employment system is characterized by a diversified labour force: seasonal female workers from Eastern Europe who were initially introduced through the *contratación en origen* but who are now EU citizens, and thus free to move and work; undocumented and regular migrants from Morocco or sub-Saharan Africa; and female contract workers from Morocco. In his analysis of the functions of temporary migration programmes, Burawoy (1976) argues that such programmes guarantee employers' profitability not only through the return of temporary workers to a non-capitalist economy at the end of the season, but also through the coexistence and competition of differentiated types of labour. For the past 15 years in Huelva, a continuous process of differentiation has led to a triple segmentation of the workforce – along the lines of nationality, gender and legal status – and to competition between different groups of workers as well as among workers of the same group. The ultimate aim is to lower production costs to a minimum.

## 12.3 Opposition and complementarity of two labour groups in the local employment system

I now turn my attention to analysing the differences in terms of recruitment, transportation, housing and employment among the two main groups of migrant

*Table 12.1* Evolution of the *contratacion en origen* between 2000 and 2010 (number of contracts)

| *Season* | *Colombia* | *Ecuador* | *Philippines* | *Poland* | *Romania* | *Bulgaria* | *Ukraine* | *Morocco* | *Senegal* | *Total* |
|---|---|---|---|---|---|---|---|---|---|---|
| 1999–2000 | | | | 600 | | | | | | 600 |
| 2000–2001 | | | | 540 | | | | 198 | | 738 |
| 2001–2002 | 149 | | | 4,954 | 970 | | | 336 | | 6,409 |
| 2002–2003 | 177 | 15 | | 7,535 | 4,178 | | | 95 | | 12,000 |
| 2003–2004 | 105 | 8 | | 8,506 | 10,589 | 508 | | 620 | | 20,336 |
| 2004–2005 | 82 | 64 | | 7,361 | 13,186 | 604 | | 1,094 | | 22,391 |
| 2005–2006 | 8 | 26 | | 9,796 | 19,153 | 941 | | 2,330 | | 32,254 |
| 2006–2007 | 22 | 12 | | | 20,710 | 3,021 | | 5,277 | | 29,042 |
| 2007–2008 | 11 | 14 | 270 | | 20,364 | 4,656 | 557 | 13,600 | 749 | 40,491 |
| 2008–2009 | 0 | 11 | 0 | | 3,743 | 373 | 183 | 13,300 | 40 | 17,650 |
| 2009–2010 | | | | | | | | 6,153 | | 6,153 |

Sources: Statistics from the labour and migration service for the government of Huelva, communicated 29 July 2010; and INEM statistics, the Spanish employment agency.

agricultural workers during the period of my field research in Huelva province: Moroccan female seasonal workers recruited through the *contratación en origen*, and undocumented male workers, mostly from sub-Saharan Africa. The description of the latter group – especially the conditions of their accommodation, the hiring process, and the social networks that they develop during the season – can help highlight the specificities of the *contratación en origen*, particularly with regards to the control of workers' mobility.

### *12.3.1 Transportation and accommodation*

Let us recall the characteristics of the *contratación en origen.* Through this procedure, seasonal workers sign a temporary work contract at the end of which they promise to return to their country of origin, and then have to wait for an invitation from their employers for the following season. Workers who fail to return to their country of origin are declared illegal. This contract entitles migrants to a temporary job and residence permit, specifying the geographical area and activity sector in which they can work, and the duration of the contract. The worker is bound to her employing company, and is restricted from working for another employer unless a 'renunciation certificate' is provided by her initial employer, as explained by the local representative of the Ministry of Employment: 'We connect a person to a farm. If she doesn't like it and wants to quit, we need the employer to tell us that he agrees to let her leave and that another farm intends to employ her' (Interview, Huelva, 31 March 2010).

In addition, recruiting criteria play an important part in channelling contracted female workers. They are selected according to their marital status, preferably mothers with young children – 'attachment criteria are favourable for return rates'[6] – and, of course, their experience in the fields. Most female seasonal workers come from a rural background (mainly from the Gharb region, where the Spanish strawberry industry has delocalized production since the 1990s; see Hellio, 2014b) and are unable to locate the country where they are sent to work. From his interviews with migrant workers about their arrangements for the journey from Morocco to Spain, Ahlame Rahmi (2011) noted that some did not even consider they were travelling abroad (*alkharij*), but explained that they were simply being transferred from one place to another: from Tangier harbour to the farm that employed them.

> How do we get there? They escort us holding their hands over our eyes and remove them once we get there. When we arrive at the cooperative, all I see is the female boss waiting for the women workers. There's no translator to tell us: "this is Huelva, this is Sevilla, this is Rabat or Casablanca". They take you to the countryside then, straight away, aaahh: "*voilà* the strawberries".
>
> (Interview with Meriem, Moroccan seasonal worker, 35, married, in her home in a *douar* near Souk Larbaa, Morocco, 26 July 2010).

The workers' poor geographical knowledge, alongside their lack of migration expertise, means that most of them are unable to return home by bus or train.

Therefore, they cannot leave the farms outside collective transportation periods. Moreover, a set of tight constraints channel their passage between Morocco and Andalusia: the signing of a repatriation agreement, the discouragement of *h'rague*[7] through Moroccan intercultural mediators, sometimes the withholding of passports, or the consignment of their last salary and pay slip only as they step onto the return bus. These women are therefore much more dependent on their employers than undocumented workers who arrive independently.

Another advantage of the *contratación en origen* for employers is that part of the recruitment process and costs are subcontracted to Anapec (see Note 6), which organizes departures, ensures the flexibility and fluidity of crossings, and thus relieves employers from complications linked to the management of such a significant flow.

> The Foundation for Foreign Workers in Huelva gives us the employers' schedule and sets a date to meet in Tangier, while here in Morocco we manage the difficulties and problems that may arise [...] Women are always helped out by advisors on departure. As early as 6am, migration advisors arrive with the necessary documents. Police files are prepared beforehand and we make them sign the migration documents. Two advisors hand them out, and at around 9 or 10 am, everything is over. [...] We want to make the women's passage as smooth as possible.
>
> (Interview with the director of international placement for Anapec, Casablanca, 17 July 2011)

The accommodation provided during the period of work is a further constraint placed upon these women. Farm-based accommodation has developed with the *contratación en origen*, allowing employers to keep a reserve workforce on-site, and thus ensuring flexibility and a sufficient labour supply. Unlike in the case of undocumented workers, this system also makes migrant women 'invisible'. More so than undocumented people living in slums, the confinement of women on farms prevents them from socializing with the native population because they are isolated from the local social space. Villages are merely places of transit for contract seasonal workers, during arrival – when they are immediately dispatched to the farms – and on their return. Gatherings take place inside the cooperatives that centralize recruitment for all farmers.[8] Although they do go to shop in the villages, they seldom congregate there; on the contrary, they only surface in public space for very short periods of time. As such, their presence is far less detectable than that of undocumented or even regular male migrants who come to Huelva seeking employment, and who might stay for days, weeks or months without work and without accommodation.

Accommodating seasonal workers on the farms therefore means imposing tighter controls on the lives of the employees, particularly on their social and sexual relations, because employers fear that women might otherwise use external relations to abandon the workplace. Competition is organized between and within the diverse groups, and the resulting forms of self-control thus reinforce the rules of employers and supervisors.

In order to highlight the specific ways in which the workers' accommodation channels flows and fixes the place of foreigners in host towns, I believe it is appropriate to draw a comparison with the *chabola* (slum) settlements established by migrant itinerant workers who have been replaced by the contract workers and who now encounter difficulties in finding employment in the area. Unlike the lodgings provided by employers, the *chabolas* are self-built. They accommodate foreign workers transiting across Spain and on the *rueda temporera*, the 'seasonal cycle', which leads them from one harvest to the next (orange, olive, apples, peaches, etc.). These workers aim to obtain the required three-year presence in the country and/or the one-year contract that will eventually make legalization[9] possible.

Despite insalubrious housing conditions and very limited access to vital resources such as water, these settlements are still sites for building (mainly all-male) social ties, and places of freedom outside the control of farmers, where workers gather and couples are sometimes formed. The typical self-built shelter of independent, non-recruited migrants, although itself very much constraining due to its dire standards and temporariness, remains entirely different from the accommodation provided by a system whose goal is the 'integral management of migratory flows'.

The collective accommodation of female seasonal workers is a constitutive element of a general mechanism of control. In contrast, the *chabola*, where undocumented men gather, is a shelter and social space invented and created by homeless people. This space eludes the rules of the employers: it functions on a community basis, even if it is also shaped by power relations, both internal to the *chabola* and across the wider social space in which the *chabola* is situated. As Mohammed points out: 'One of the only good things, and I've only seen it here, is that the foreigners all know each another. They all live and mix together in the *chabola*' (informal conversation; fieldnote, Palos de la Frontera, 1 June 2010). Even though there is no comfort, one can breathe an air of freedom that cannot be found when working in the *campos*.[10] Intimate relationships are impossible on farms because employers forbid the entrance of men who do not work there. Couples formed during the season therefore get together in the *chabola*:

> They are not allowed to work or sleep with us because they are men. There are only women on our farm. Well, they can come to visit at night, when the supervisor is not around, and is not doing his evening round, which is usually at about 6 or 7pm, although at the moment he comes around 10pm! [...] He wants to know who goes out, who stays at home. We're afraid because we don't want any trouble with the boss. It's better to come here, that's it.
>
> (Informal conversation with Rebecca, Polish seasonal worker, *chabola de la madre*, Palos de la Frontera, 25 May 2011)

However, as already noted, tolerance for unregulated mobility has decreased as a result of the new system of recruitment. The *chabolas* are periodically destroyed by the police and thus can not guarantee stable settlement for workers. When I interviewed Mohammed (cited above), he had been living for three years in a self-built shack made from greenhouse plastic and wood that was hidden in a ditch. 'Here they can't see us. This is our place. And if they see your "house", they are sure that you are not staying for a long time. They know that you'll leave, like a dog moving onto the next bin'. Even if it is durable, the presence of this group of workers is accepted only in that it appears to be temporary.

### *12.3.2 Work*

As explained above, undocumented workers have largely been replaced by female contract workers. However, they still play a role on the fringe of the local labour market. According to the Mediterranean agriculture model formulated by Jean-Pierre Berlan (1986), these workers occupy the third, most flexible circle of the employment system, which is used only during harvest peaks. Employers usually consider them excessively mobile. Pedro, whose farm is located very close to a large slum, employs mostly people from sub-Saharan Africa who live there, but he complains about their lack of commitment to stay until the end of the season:

> They do not realize that this will cause them problems. They won't find work with another boss [...] I only have four harvesting days left: they only need to work four more days, and when they finish that, they get paid and can then go. [...] But they're leaving me now and I won't find them again. They go off the tracks, like Moroccans who now tend to manage to earn their living by other means.
>
> (Interview with Pedro, owner of a 10-hectare farm, Mazagón, 7 June 2011)

Daouda, an undocumented citizen from Burkina-Faso, explains that the 'liberation' brought about by the general regularization of migrants in 2005 has delegitimated African workers in the eyes of their employers:

> In 2005, many men asked their boss to fill in their forms, then they left. And when the boss called them back to work, they threatened to call the *guardias* [the police]. In the end, those who've remained in the *campos* are not *encargardos* [crew leaders], but the boss listens to them. As for those who left and are now coming back looking for work [because of the crisis], the bosses don't want to know. They keep saying: "*Moreno no vale, Moreno no vale na*" ["a black is no good (at picking strawberries), a black is no good at all"] [...] I've been to see this guy every day for the past five days; today he was repairing his tractor. When the engine stopped, I said hello, but he didn't even answer. He left, and I just stayed there. When he came back, he asked me "what do you want? Do you want a job?" I answered "yes!" Then he started with his speech: he had it all ready in his head! He was only waiting for somebody to listen to him. [laughter, then he imitates a high-pitched voice of an old angry man]: "*¿Moreno? ¡Nunca! Moreno no valen nada. Antes tenía cinco. Arreglas papeles y se van*" ["A black man? Never! Blacks are no good. I used to have five. You give them their papers, then they leave"].

Since the diffusion of the recruitment of temporary contract workers, farmers only employ African and Maghrebi men for what they consider to be male tasks, during periods of peak activity, or when they need quick replacements. For instance, planting or dismantling greenhouses may offer a few days' work.

> I now do the picking on a farm where I only used to plant, because the boss would always repeat: "a black man is no good at picking [strawberries]. A black man is good for planting because blacks are strong." But now all the women from Romania have gone, because the work is too hard; so he hired us. We are five black men and he has two Moroccan women [...] At the end of the season we may have to take down the greenhouses. They don't control that because it takes many men. And if you are lucky, you may get ten days' work.
>
> (Interview with Daouda, *Chabola de la Madre*, 4 April 2011)

As they are considered an auxiliary labour force, they are seldom accommodated on the farms. Settlements are recruiting grounds where neighbouring farmers can find workers for the peak season: 'The boss gave me some work [...] he didn't give me accommodation – I'm still in my shed – as he told me it was a temporary job.' In addition, they substitute seasonal workers who might want to leave early, they represent a reserve army of labour in case of strikes, or a source of labour for those employers who do not respect regulations and are therefore not entitled to the *contratación en origen.*

### *12.3.3 Fertile greenhouses ... for stereotypes*

Working teams are hierarchically organized according to the legal status of the diverse groups of workers, ranging from undocumented workers to EU citizens, and including third-country nationals under contract or new members of the EU with residence authorizations but without work permits. At the bottom of the pyramid are undocumented workers and female contract workers. The diversity of legal statuses boosts the performance of farms (Thomas, 1992), insofar as employment precariousness tends to compel workers to draw attention to themselves, whether it is female contract workers who want to ensure their re-employment for the following season, or undocumented workers who wish to earn the one-year contract that is synonymous with legalization.

It is important to insist on the objective working conditions of the different groups of migrants residing in the province, because local racism, sexism and class representations combine to naturalize relations among farm workers. The employment of each type of worker is justified by the essentializing discourses propagated by both employers and the workers themselves. Indeed, as temporary migration programmes typically authorize the recruitment of different national groups of workers, this leads employers to differentiate between and physically separate groups depending on their origin, thus exacerbating national divisions. The naturalization of differences is often complex: it is not solely the product of social relations but constitutes specific categories. For instance, one often hears that men cannot harvest strawberries, and yet it is expected that black men are more productive than Romanian women. The following extract from an interview with the recruiting manager of a cooperative provides insight into the stereotypes that prevail in the organization of labour in the fields and shows how they are the result of entrenched power relations (in this, with respect to gender and race):

> One day, an employer calls me and tells me that there is a problem with the blacks on his farm. I tell him: "listen, I didn't bring these black people to your place. What can I do?" He answers: "ok, but you brought me the Romanian women, and there is a problem with them". So I go to the farm, and he tells me that the black men aren't harvesting well, because black people usually pick faster than Romanian women. We go to the field, and there they were, moving up the field all in a single line. Then I see that the Romanian women are wearing mini-shorts and shirts with a plunging neck-line and no bra [...] I turn to the boss and tell him "how do you expect these black men to move faster when they have women dressed like that by their side?".
>
> (Interview with Eduardo, human resources agent for the COAG, a Cooperative of small and medium farmers, Palos de la Frontera, 23 June 2010)

The targets of stereotypes themselves tend to endorse certain discourses, sometimes with a sense of ethnic or gender pride: 'No white man can pick faster than a black man, a woman can, but not a white man'. 'Men cannot pick as fast as women: it hurts their back'. Groups are differentiated according to their nationality, gender, legal status, which leads to the ranking of performance and the workers' competitive selection, as a farmer explains:

> I put together intercultural working teams. I place a different nationality on each row: a Moroccan here, a Romanian there, then someone from Mali, a Polish woman then another Romanian woman. I mix them – I realized that this is much better for the pace of work. I've had the worst problems with Romanians: if one of them works too fast, the others stop her. "Calm down! You're only earning the boss more money!" When they are all of the same nationality, they feel they are stronger. But if you mix them, things are easier. They don't understand one another, so they can't argue! Or if they get angry, it's to my benefit, because when a Moroccan is angry with a Romanian, he'll try to harvest faster than the other, he'll try to pick more than the other. Once I employed a lot of Romanian workers, but now I tend to mix nationalities.
>
> (Interview with a farmer with four-hectare greenhouses in Palos de la Frontera, May 2008)

The productive system and labour organization in Huelva together provide a fertile ground for the proliferation of positive and negative stereotypes, and for the development of hostility between groups. Nadia, a Moroccan seasonal female worker, describes the relationships between Moroccans and sub-Saharans in Huelva:

> Among the black workers, you have those who pray, those who are Muslims, and those who aren't, like the Senegalese. Muslims get along well with Moroccans, but the others are no good. [...] I know a few who are very nice, they work with us and we get along well. But it is impossible with some of them. When they come, we call each other names and we quarrel. Then we have the Moroccans versus the Blacks and it gets vulgar. Black people say that we are dirty, and we tell them "beat it Negro, you stink!".
>
> (Interview with Nadia, Moroccan seasonal worker, 30, divorced, at her parents' in Ouled Ziane, Morocco, 30 July 2011)

Discourses that essentialize and differentiate between groups of workers are revived each time a new group arrives. For instance, the different groups of female workers (Polish, Romanian, then Moroccans) were all first praised for their 'feminine virtues' but were then criticized for their casualness once another group arrived to substitute them. Each new wave of workers is welcomed at first, and is used to draw comparisons in order to criticize the previous group. Prejudices are used *a posteriori* to justify changes in labour force hiring, to reject one group and legitimate the next one. Just as with previous groups, the recruitment system in Morocco contributes to construct the essentialized representation of the Moroccan female worker, which builds on the image of the 'good worker', the good mother, and more generally the responsible woman. Those who leave the system are by contrast compared to other female figures such as the prostitute or the victim of human trafficking. The use of negative and positive images to define the limits of legitimate female behaviour are manipulated by employers and institutions in charge of migration control, and serve to ensure their return to the country of origin as well as encourage competition between the different female groups. These points confirm Burawoy's observation that different types of racial relationships appear according to the type of migrant labour system implemented (Burawoy, 1976). He noted that when both the production of goods and the reproduction of the labour force are organized by the employer, this gives rise to a system of paternalistic relations; conversely, when these two processes are separated, as in the case of temporary migration programmes (where production is organized by the employer and reproduction is managed by the communities of the different groups of workers or the country of origin), the outcome is a system of competitive racial relations.

## 12.4 Conclusion

Since 2000 the EU, guided by international organizations and their experts, has restored the figure of the old 'guest worker' or '*gastarbeiter*' as a means to better governing international migration. Temporary legal migration has been presented as the alternative to irregular migration. In contrast to former migratory models now presented as deleterious, promoters seek to create a new consensus by presenting a form of temporary migration that has exclusively positive benefits (Ruhs, 2002, 2006; Schiff, 2004; Abella, 2006; Martin, 2003; Amin and Mattoo, 2005; Winters *et al.*, 2003; and for Europe, Fargues, 2008). In this approach, legal and illegal migrants are presented as diametrically opposed and yet are always mentioned in relation to each other, with temporary migration presented as the means to solve the problem of illegal migration.

My case study shows that, in certain instances, the substitution of an undocumented labour force by a legal workforce seems to serve more the goal of controlling migrant workers' mobility rather than defending their rights. This observation leads one to question the common rhetoric among international organizations that legal migration is more of a safeguard than illegal migration which is instead seen to be the cause for some of the worst labour abuses. Over the last few years, migration policies have aimed to promote temporary labour migration, both in Europe and in North America. In Huelva, this form of migration has been, in fact, more profitable to the interests of the strawberry sector than to the migrant labourers. The system allows for the externalization of the costs of labour mobilization by providing efficient selection in the countries of origin, as has occurred in Morocco which had long provided a reservoir of migrant labour. Despite the growth of the recruitment programme, undocumented workers continue to come to Huelva in search of employment. The relationships between the different groups of workers during harvest time are often of a competitive nature, but, conversely, they also represent a seasonal multi-ethnic society, which can become sometimes the breeding ground for acts of resistance to the dehumanizing controls imposed by employers.

## Notes

1 *Contratación en origen* can be translated as 'contract in origin' or 'at source'. Employees are selected and contracts are signed in the countries of origin.
2 The use of public unemployment allowances to finance labour during the off-season has also been described by Burawoy (1976) in California, Laliberté and Satzewich (1999) in Canada and Piro (2015) in Italy.
3 Extract from 'Agriculture employs 92% of immigrants "in origin"', *Almería en verde* (journal of the farming group Coexphal-Faeca) no. 51, January 2008.
4 Miriam Wells (1996) reminds us that Mexicans practiced different patterns of mobility in California, depending on their legal status. While the mobility of *Braceros* was tightly organized by government and employers, the movement of undocumented workers was often independent or remained underground, and was therefore impossible to fully trace or control.
5 I do not discuss here the origin of successive waves of the workforce (see, instead, Hellio, 2014a).
6 Interview with the Anapec placement supervisor in charge of the programme, Casablanca, 16 March 2010. Anapec (*Agence Nationale de Promotion de l'Emploi e des Compétences*) is the Moroccan public employment agency, which is charged with the organization of the recruitment and departure of workers employed through the *contratación en origen*.
7 This verb means 'to burn' in the local Arabic dialect. It is used in Morocco to refer to irregular border crossings. Despite being legally bound to return to Morocco at the end

of the season, many female workers attempt to remain illegally. The idea of crossing the border between the seasonal authorized time–space of the farm, and the forbidden out-of-season time–space beyond the farm and Huelva province, is expressed through the women's use of the terms *h'rague* (in reference to the potential or actual itineraries), and *harragats* (in reference to those who embark on them).

8 In Huelva, most of the farms are members of cooperatives that take charge of recruitment, packaging and commercialization.

9 In Spain, undocumented workers can be legalized in four ways: by applying for *arraigo laboral* (after one year of work declared by an employer); by applying for *arraigo social* (after a three-year stay and the written promise for one year of employment) or, like in other European countries, as an asylum seeker or through family reunification. They may also use the *contingente* in order to legalize their stay; a procedure makes it possible to obtain a one-year contract as on-site labour, prior to the substitution of labour from outside Spain. For further information, see: http://extranjeros.empleo.gob.es/es/InformacionInteres/InformacionProcedimientos/Ciudadanosnocomunitarios/Autorizresiexcep.html

10 From research conducted in the 1970s, Abdelmalek Sayad compared the workers' residences built by Sonacotra (the French national society for the construction of workers accommodation) with hostels where migrant workers chose to stay, often in order to maintain community ties. He noted that the former were 'legitimately' stripped of the social functions normally provided by housing: 'reduced to its sheltering role, [the Sonacotra residence] can be considered accommodation for men reduced to their sole function as workers'. In contrast, in the hotels of the 'sleep merchants', usually located in city centres, migrant workers used to gather according to their personal affinities, and the relationship to work did not prevail over other considerations (Sayad, 1991, p. 92).

## References


Abella, M. (2006). 'Policies and best practices for management of temporary migration'. *International Symposium on International Migration and Development*, United Nations Secretariat, Turín.

Achón, O. (2010). *Contratación en origen e institución local: estudio sobre el sistema de alojamiento de trabajadores agrícolas extranjeros en el Segriá (Lleida)*, Doctoral Thesis, Universitat de Barcelona.

Amin, M. and Matoo, A. (2005). 'Does temporary migration have to be permanent?'. *World Bank Policy Research.* Working Paper 3582, Washington, DC: Word Bank.

Basok, T. (2002). *Tortillas and Tomatoes: Transmigrant Mexican Harvesters in Canada.* Montreal: McGill-Queen's University Press.

Berlan, J.-P. (1986). 'Agriculture et migrations'. *Revue européenne de migrations internationales*, vol. 2, no. 3, pp. 9–32.

Berlan, J.-P. (1987). 'La agricultura Mediterránea y el mercado de trabajo: ¿Una California para Europa?'. *Agricultura y Sociedad*, no. 42, pp. 233–245.

Burawoy, M. (1976). 'The Functions and Reproduction of Migrant Labor: Comparative Material from Southern Africa and the U.S'. *American Journal of Sociology*, no. 5, pp. 1050–1087.

Décosse, F. (2011). *Migrations sous contrôle. Agriculture intensive et saisonniers marocains sous contrat OMI.* Doctoral Thesis. Paris : EHESS.

Fargues, P. (2008). 'Circular migration: Is it relevant for the South and the East of the Mediterranean?'. *CARIM Analytic and Synthetic Notes 2008/40.* Avalilable at hdl.handle.net/1814/8391 (last access on 20/2/2016).

García, T. (2004). *Mercado de trabajo en sistemas hortícolas intensivos: el caso de la fresa en Huelva.* Doctoral Thesis, Universidad Politécnica de Madrid.

Hellio, E. (2014a). *Importing Women to Export Strawberries: Labour Flexibility, Migratory Flux Control and Loopholes in a Global Monoculture*. Doctoral Thesis, Université de Nice.

Hellio, E. (2014b). 'We do not have women in boxes: Channelling seasonal mobility of female farmworkers between Morocco and Andalusia' in Gertel, J. and Sippel, S.R, (eds). *Seasonal Workers in Mediterranean Agriculture. The Social Costs of Eating Fresh*. London: Routledge, pp. 141–157.

Jounin, N. (2010). 'Des sans papiers locaux à la sous-traitance internationale. Trajectoire d'un métier du bâtiment: le ferraillage' in Morice, A. and Potot, S. (eds). *De l'ouvrier immigré au travailleur sans papiers: les étrangers dans la modernisation du salariat*. Paris: Karthala, pp. 69–94.

Kalm, S. (2010). 'Liberalizing movements? The political rationality of global migration management' in Geiger, M. and Pécoud, A. (eds). *The politics of international migration management*. New York: Palgrave Macmillan, pp. 21–44.

Karakayali, S. and Rigo, E. (2010). 'Mapping the European space of circulation' in De Genova, N. and Peutz, N. (eds). *The deportation regime: sovereignty, space, and the freedom of movement*. Durham, NC: Duke University Press, pp. 123–144.

Laliberté, R. and Satzewich, V. (1999). 'Native migrant labour in the southern Alberta sugar-beet industry: Coercion and paternalism in the recruitment of labour'. *Canadian Review of Sociology/Revue canadienne de sociologie*, vol. 36, no. 1, pp. 65–85.

Lutz, B. and Bordi, I.V. (2007). 'Entre el metate y el sueño canadiense: representaciones femeninas mazahuas sobre la migración contractual transnacional'. *Amérique Latine Histoire et Mémoire. Les Cahiers ALHIM*, no. 14.

Martin, P. (2003). 'Managing labour migration: Temporary worker programs for the 21st century' Special lecture on migration, International Institute for Labour Studies, International Labour Organisation (ILO), Geneva.

Martín, E. and Castaño, A. (2004). 'El Encierro de Inmigrantes en la Universidad Pablo de Olavide Sevilla' in *Atlas de la Inmigración Marroquí en España: Atlas 2004*, Madrid, Ministerio de Trabajo y Asuntos Sociales.

McLaughlin, J. (2010). 'Classifying the ideal migrant worker: Mexican and Jamaican transnational farmworkers in Canada'. *Focaal*, no. 57, pp. 79- 94.

Moulier Boutang, Y. (1998). 'Femmes, greniers et capitaux réveille du sommeil dogmatique'. *Journal des anthropologues*, no. 118–119, pp. 23–29.

Pellerin, H. (2011). 'De la migration à la mobilité: changement de paradigme dans la gestion migratoire. Le cas du Canada'. *Revue européenne des migrations internationales*, vol. 27, no. 2, pp. 57–75.

Piro, V. (2015). 'What is deemed to be ′fake`? The case of "fake agricultural workers" in South Eastern Sicily'. *Mondi Migranti*, no. 1, pp. 65–83.

Rahmi, A. (2011). 'Le soupçon migratoire: organisation sociale et traitement politique du travail saisonnier des ouvrières marocaines en Espagne' in Palidda, S. (ed.). *Migrations critiques: repenser les migrations comme mobilités humaines en Méditerranée*. Paris: Karthala, pp. 131–142.

Ruhs, M. (2006). 'Potentiel des programmes de migration temporaire dans l'organisation des migrations internationals'. *Revue Internationale du Travail*, vol. 145, p. 741.

Sayad, A. (1991). *L"immigration ou les paradoxes de l"altérité. 1, L"illusion du proviso ire*. Bruxelles: De Boeck Université.

Schiff, M. (2004). 'When migrants overstay their legal welcome: A proposed solution to guest-worker program', *Iza Discussion Paper*, 1401, Bonn: Iza.

Terray, E. (1999). 'Le travail des étrangers en situation irrégulière ou la délocalisation sur place' in Balibar, E., Chemillier, M., Costa-Lascoux, J. and Terray, E. (eds). *Sans-papiers: l'archaïsme fatal*. Paris: La Découverte, pp. 9–34.

Thomas, R.J. (1992). *Citizenship, Gender, and Work: Social Organization of Industrial Agriculture*. Berkeley: University of California Press.

Wells, M.J. (1996). *Strawberry Fields: Politics, Class, and Work in California Agriculture*, Ithaca, NY: Cornell University Press.

Winters, A., Walmsley, T., Kun Wang, Z. and Grynberg, R. (2003). 'Liberalising the temporary movement of natural persons: An agenda for the development round'. *World Economy*, vol. 26, no. 8, pp. 1137–1161.

# 13 The land of informal intermediation

## The social regulation of migrant agricultural labour in the Piana del Sele, Italy

*Gennaro Avallone*

### 13.1 Introduction

The Piana del Sele is a rich agricultural area located in the province of Salerno, in the southern Italian region of Campania. Since the 1980s, local agriculture has been characterized by diversified and intensive crop production that has been based increasingly on greenhouse cultivation. The rearing of cows and buffalos is also widespread and the local area is, in fact, one of the leading centres of mozzarella cheese production.

Both the growth of diversified production and the spread of new technologies have affected the social organization of local agriculture and, consequently, its labour market. Agricultural production has expanded increasingly across the entire year, even if some activities have maintained a seasonal character. This deseasonalization has transformed the quality and structure of the labour demand, which is oriented towards, on the one hand, stable workers for permanent production and, on the other, flexible workers for seasonal production and unexpected daily activities. This diversification has opened doors to new farmworkers who have partially substituted the local population in the open fields and plastic greenhouses as well as in livestock management. Since the mid-1980s, migrant workers have increasingly become key actors in local agriculture (Calvanese and Pugliese, 1991). The initial arrivals were mainly from Morocco and other North African countries; these were later joined by migrants from Romania and India.

This chapter describes the 'social regulation' of farm labour in the Piana del Sele. According to critical labour geography (Jonas, 1996, 2009; Peck, 1996; Peck and Theodore, 2012; Rogaly, 2008), the idea of the 'social regulation of labour' does not mean that relations between entrepreneurs and labourers are the result of simple and peaceful negotiations. This concept implies that these labour–capital relations are built by mixing formal and informal rules and arrangements. The relations of production are socially structured in the sense that social, political and cultural variables (especially nationality, race and gender) are important in constructing real labour regulations outside the realm of formal state law (Harriss-White, 2009).

In this framework, I aim to show how, in the Piana del Sele, over the last three decades, inexpensive farm labour has been reproduced in hostile social, spatial and institutional contexts. In particular, I argue that, in this area, the social regulation of labour is organized around a system of informal intermediation, which encompasses virtually all aspects of a migrant labourer's life: from recruitment, and the organization and supervision of labour, to the practices employed to obtain a regular permit of stay and to access housing, the public health service, and credit. This intermediation system reproduces practices which have been widespread in the area for decades, well before the arrival of foreign workers, in particular the informal method of recruiting farm labour known as *caporalato*[1] (Pugliese, 1984; Gribaudi, 1990; Perrotta, 2014). In other countries, as France and Spain, the recruitment of migrant farm workers has been – at least partially – guaranteed by state-led programmes (the *contrats OFII* in France and the *contratación en origen* in Spain, see Décosse, Hellio, this volume). Differently, in the Piana del Sele – as well as in other agricultural regions of Southern Italy (Perrotta and Sacchetto, 2014; Perrotta, 2015; Garrapa, this volume) – farm labour intermediation is mainly realized on informal and illegal basis. As I show in Section 13.4, in this area the '*decreto flussi*' – the Italian government-led programme for the recruitment of foreign workers in their countries of origin – has never functioned as intended by the law; on the contrary, it has often been used by informal intermediaries to cheat both the state and migrants.

The analysis is based on research that was conducted between 2011 and 2015, combining different sources and methods: statistical data analysis; in-depth interviews with trade union and employer association representatives, third sector managers, local politicians and migrant farmworkers; and fieldnotes that were produced during ethnographic research with groups of migrants.

The chapter is divided into four sections. The first section focuses on the principal transformations in local agriculture over the last three decades, which include changes in production technologies, types of crop and labour demand. The second section addresses agricultural labour market regulation and describes the informal intermediation of labour, and the social regulation of employment conditions. The third part shows how labour intermediaries usually act as brokers in other areas of migrants' lives, thus contributing to reproducing their subaltern condition. Finally, the fourth section discusses a number of aspects regarding the agency of migrant labourers.

## 13.2 The 'new' agriculture and labour demand

Since the 1980s, the introduction of new crops and technologies, and especially the spread of protected cultures have together transformed the Piana del Sele into one of Italy's most important and dynamic agricultural areas. This transformation has accelerated over the last 20 years due to the diffusion of 'fourth range' products – i.e., ready-to-eat vegetables, particularly baby leaf and rocket lettuce – as well as mozzarella cheese production. The restructuring of agriculture is increasingly oriented towards more programmable crop production based on greenhouse cultivation as well as livestock rearing, which are less affected by weather conditions and unpredictable factors. This change reflects a trend towards a 'new agriculture', which is characterized by increased industrial and technological organization, production with secure yields, guaranteed buyers and lower market risks than other kinds of farming activity.

As in other Mediterranean agricultural areas, particularly Spain (Jiménez, 2010; Moraes *et al.*, 2012), an increasing proportion of local agriculture has been able to produce vegetable crops year-round. These products are mostly sold in supermarket chains in Italy and other European countries, especially France, the UK, Switzerland, Germany and Scandinavian countries. Statistical data indicate a doubling of the greenhouse area (from 3,027 to 6,925 hectares in the province of Salerno) and greenhouse vegetable crops (from 1,378,380 to 2,566,540 quintals) between 2000 and 2010 (Istat, 2010). In 2009, about 30 per cent of the nation's cultivated land dedicated to fourth range production was located in the Piana del Sele (Baldi and Casati, 2009).

The development of this 'new agriculture' has opened the door to migrant workers who have partially replaced the local population in the fields and greenhouses, and almost completely in the case of livestock management. Census information for 2010 shows that about 3,700 agricultural workers in the area were non-Italian (42.6 per cent of the total farm workforce; Table 13.1), and if one adds informal labourers, migrants actually outnumber Italians. The National Institute of Agrarian Economy (INEA, 2013, p. 20) has estimated a presence of approximately 5,000 foreign-born farmworkers. The same source emphasizes that in both the Piana del Sele and the province of Caserta – another important agricultural area in the Campania Region (Filhol, 2013; Caruso, 2015) – there are almost as many irregular labourers as there are regular workers (Inea, 2013).[2]

The quality and the structure of the labour demand in the Piana del Sele's agricultural industry is more clearly defined than in the past. Two types of labour supply are required: first, a stable supply of workers for permanent production, especially fourth range products and other crops that are grown in greenhouses, as well as for livestock production; second, a flexible supply of workers for seasonal production (particularly open field crops such as tomatoes, fennel, cauliflower and artichokes) and for unexpected daily activities. Statistical data, as well as my own field observations, indicate that the first group mainly comprises Italian male and female workers, while migrants constitute the majority of the second labour pool. As we can observe in Table 13.2, there are more migrants on fixed-term contracts (88.0 per cent) than Italians (72.8 per cent) (Istat, 2010). Migrant farmworkers are exposed to higher levels of casual employment than Italians, although about 12 per cent of migrant workers are on permanent contracts. Moreover, as already noted, migrants are more likely than Italians to be employed without any kind of contract.

The migrant component of the labour force is further segmented by nationality and gender. In the 1980s and 1990s, most migrant farmworkers were from non-European countries, mainly Morocco and other North African countries. Male Moroccan farm labour was the key actor in the first phase of the 'new' local agriculture. Over the last fifteen years, however, competition has emerged between different national groups, especially between European and non-European migrants. Although the available data on gender and nationality

*Table 13.1* Total non-family farmworkers employed in the primary sector by citizenship (absolute and percentage values)

| *Territorial area* | *Labourers employed by citizenship* | | | | | | |
|---|---|---|---|---|---|---|---|
| | *EU27* | | *Extra-EU27* | | *Italy* | | *Total* |
| | *Absolute values* | *% values* | *Absolute values* | *% values* | *Absolute values* | *% values* | *Absolute values* |
| Italy | 134,474 | 14.3 | 98,581 | 10.5 | 705,048 | 75.2 | 938,103 |
| Province of Salerno | 2,753 | 8.5 | 2,735 | 8.4 | 27,040 | 83.1 | 32,528 |
| Piana del Sele | 1,960 | 22.4 | 1,759 | 20.2 | 5,017 | 57.4 | 8,736 |

Source: Italian Agricultural Census, 2010.

*Table 13.2* Other labour employed on a non-regular basis in the primary sector by citizenship (percentage values of the total non-family labour employed by citizenship; total non-family labour employed by citizenship = 100)

| *Territorial area* | *Labourers employed by citizenship* | | |
|---|---|---|---|
| | *EU27* | *Extra-EU27* | *Italy* |
| Italy | 89.6 | 79.5 | 81.7 |
| Province of Salerno | 87.0 | 87.8 | 87.2 |
| Piana del Sele | 90.0 | 85.8 | 72.8 |

Source: Italian Agricultural Census, 2010.

are insufficient, it is possible to draw a general picture of the migrant labour force. This mainly consists of three national groups: Moroccans, Romanians and Indians. Moroccan men and Romanian men and women are employed principally in agricultural activities, while Indian men are, for the most part, employed in livestock management.

The relationships between the labourers of the two main national groups (Moroccans and Romanians) are characterized by reciprocal mistrust, which has produced new divisions among farmworkers and increased the weakness of farm labour in the relations of production. As in other southern European areas (Hartman, 2008; Papadopoulos, 2009; Gualda, 2012; Torres and Gadea, 2012; Piro and Sanò, this volume), Romanian labourers usually accept to work for less money than Moroccans. This competition in the labour market has been further accentuated following the onset of the economic and financial crisis in 2008. A Moroccan farmworker summarized the situation in the following way:

> The problem now is that there is no work. [...] They [the farmers] don't want Moroccan workers. When I looked for a job, I met loads of Romanians, because they work for nothing, they do anything and accept the wage fixed by the employer.
>
> (Moroccan worker, interview, October 2014)

The arrival of Eastern European workers was both a cause and an indicator of a broader crisis of the social regulation of labour relations. This particular crisis has been shaped by two key developments. The first is the growing impoverishment of the farm workforce as real wages have declined or stagnated, despite an increase in farm investments and profits. Poor working conditions are widespread among both stable and temporary farmworkers. Interviews with Romanian and Moroccan workers reveal that wages for a day's work (7 hours) range from 27 to 33 euros, whereas monthly pay (based on 20–24 days) ranges from 500 to 800 euros, although in specific cases salaries may be higher because they are paid on a piece rate basis.

The second development has been the decline in political strength and compactness of migrant labour power. This is the result of a series of overlapping factors: (1) the national rivalries in the workforce, especially between Moroccans and Romanians; (2) the socio-spatial and socio-cultural separation between the main national groups of farmworkers; (3) the partial feminization of the migrant labour force, especially from Eastern European countries (Romania and Ukraine); (4) the increasing distance between migrant groups and the host society; and (5) changes in the system of informal labour intermediation, due to the arrival of new Romanian intermediaries who accept lower wages and worse working conditions than the more established Moroccan brokers.

Migrant farmworkers have become the 'structural' protagonists of the new agriculture in the Piana del Sele. They allow for an increase in the farms' competitiveness as well as the social and economic upward mobility of local farmers, as observed in other areas, for example Greece (Cavounidis, 2013; Kasimis and Papadopoulos, 2005). Nonetheless, their crucial role has been long overlooked by the key social, economic and institutional actors of the area. Local society and farmers consider migrants as a separate and subordinate population and as a useful and controllable source of labour power. As in other Mediterranean agricultural areas (Checa *et al.*, 2010; Colloca and Corrado, 2013; Moraes *et al.*, 2012; Pedreño *et al.*, 2014), migrant farmworkers enjoy few social or civil rights and endure poor economic conditions. The subaltern status of migrants, in turn, helps to preserve the availability of cheap labour for the local agricultural industry. In the next sections, I describe some of the processes that have contributed to this general situation: the informal organization of the labour market (Section 13.3); the development of forms of monetized intermediation in migrants' everyday lives (Section 13.4); and cultural attitudes towards migrants and migrants' agency (Section 13.5).

## 13.3 The informal intermediation of farm labour

Ever since migrants first arrived in the Piana del Sele in the 1980s, foreign farmworkers have intimately experienced the more disreputable aspects of local agricultural heritage, namely the informal system of labour intermediation and recruitment, and the particular employment relationships (Gribaudi, 1990).[3]

Access to employment in the Piana del Sele is a resource that is often controlled by private gatekeepers who act in collaboration with employers, outside of any institutional intermediation. These gatekeepers – known as '*caporali*' – are either 'professional' intermediaries or migrants employed to directly and indirectly link farms with labourers and to guarantee workers' skills and discipline. They match labour supply with demand and, as I explain in the next section, satisfy social needs. *Caporali* represent the ideal solution in a context where, on the one hand, workers look for jobs and are exposed to a reserve army, migration law (if they are non-EU workers) and the inadequacies of public employment services, and, on the other, employers search for inexpensive, disciplined and 'just-in-time' workers.

Informal intermediaries offer farmers teams of workers who are weakened by their incapacity to directly access farms and, thus, paid work, on their own. In other words, intermediaries sell a resource to workers that the workers do not have. Thus, the matching of workers with farms and money has been *de facto* privatized; and this kind of intermediation creates a feeling of forced gratitude on the part of migrant farmworkers towards *caporali*.

The picture is somewhat different in the livestock sector. The *caporalato* also exists in this sector; however, livestock production, more than protected cultivation, requires a permanent, stable and flexible workforce, due to the predominance of programmable activities and a more predictable market demand (see Azzeruoli, this volume).

Thus, migrants' access to farm labour can be described as sitting on a continuum. At one extreme, there exists a small number of workers who hold regular and stable employment at a farm or with livestock. At the other extreme, there are workers who ask for jobs on a daily basis outside the entrances to farms. In the middle, a larger portion of workers passes through the caporale and informal recruitment.[4]

There are many different forms of labour intermediation and recruitment. These include: (1) informal recruitment of a single labourer for a temporary job; (2) informal intermediation of a work squad for casual seasonal employment (for example during harvest), which allows for the just-in-time allocation of farm labourers who oversee agricultural production; (3) daily transport for farmworkers (otherwise not provided by local institutions); and (4) supervision in the workplace on the part of the *caporale*.

Informal labour intermediaries play a fundamental role in reproducing the socio-economic structure and power relations in local agriculture. *Caporali* simultaneously recruit and control part of the workforce and allow migrant men and women to obtain jobs that are usually informal and temporary. At the same time, they allow farms to employ labour that is not entirely 'free' in the labour market: for a number of reasons, which include their precarious legal status and housing segregation, the majority of migrant workers are not able to meet farmers without intermediaries; thus, they are 'bridled' by intermediaries and informal networks. Migrants often describe the key players in the informal intermediation services as particularly unpleasant people:

> The most annoying person in this whole affair is the *caporale*, who we call *'o sensale* [the broker], as the locals say in their dialect, because he earns money from our work, our wage and our transport. There are *caporali* who make a

> lot of money because they mediate for people who work hard for piece-rate wages, and who increase production in order to receive more pay.
>
> (Moroccan worker, interview, February 2015)

Local labour regulation is characterized by strongly asymmetrical power relations between growers and farmworkers. The informal recruitment through the *caporalato* system consolidates the informal and subordinate relationships that exist between a single worker and those who enable them to work. Farmworkers are not simply subordinated to the owner of a farm but to a greater 'enabling power' that manages their employment and employability and, thus, their social reproduction.

Two examples help to clarify this idea of 'enabling power'. The first example concerns non-EU migrants. *Caporali* (and growers) control not only the provision of employment, but also the allocation of regular work contracts. For non-EU migrants, the possibility to acquire a regular labour contract is essential for their legal status. In the absence of such a contract, a non-EU migrant becomes undocumented, and thus subject to 'deportability' (De Genova, 2013). It is worth underlining that, in this case, asymmetrical labour relations have been reinforced by the national immigration law, which, by linking labour – or more specifically employment contracts – to the permit to stay (*permesso di soggiorno*), has contributed to create a strong hierarchy in the local labour market. As a Moroccan farmworker affirmed:

> Documents are more important than the work. In fact, it is impossible to build union membership. Why would we want to organize a strike? In the name of whom? For yourself and your own rights. But the real problem is getting the documents and a permit to stay. The first permit to stay is often bought by paying for a labour contract, and so the main problem is solved. Then you can buy a new contract if you need to renew your permit.
>
> (Moroccan worker, interview, September 2014)

The *permesso di soggiorno* represents a major, ongoing concern for non-EU migrants. One of their main problems is to obtain and renew the permit, because its lack or loss automatically renders migrants irregular. Very often, non-EU migrants *buy* labour contracts from growers and *caporali*, who, in turn, control not only their employment, but also the possibility of regularizing their legal status. As such a civil right is commodified and becomes a marketable right.

The second example concerns the spread of piece-rate work in numerous farm operations, especially during planting and harvesting:

> They [growers] pay 40 cents for harvesting a kilo of rocket, which costs 4 or 5 euros in the supermarket, which means I'm able to earn up to 40 euros a day on the luckiest days, when the rocket is particularly good and has no yellow leaves. The length of the workday depends on [market] demand: the higher the demand, the higher the number of working hours.
>
> (Moroccan worker, interview, December 2014)

As this interview demonstrates, piece-rate wages are largely determined by demand and are dependent on market trends and the farms' pursuit of profit. As Karl Marx first recognized, the 'piece-wage is the form of wages most in harmony with the capitalist mode of production' (Marx, 2007, p. 608). Piece wages subordinate workers to the logic of maximum performance and sustain self-exploitation processes that are functional to much higher levels of production and productivity, as Marx remarks: 'given piece-wage, it is naturally in the personal interest of the labourer to strain his labour-power as intensely as possible; this enables the capitalist to raise more easily the normal degree of intensity of labour' (Marx, 2007, p. 606).

The two above examples highlight the hostile social and institutional environment that migrant farmworkers are forced to face. In a number of interviews, migrant farmworkers describe labour relations as a world in which they have to continually thank their employers, recruiters and supervisors. In the Piana del Sele there are no alternatives to the power wielded by farmers and *caporali.* In fact, the national law seems to contribute to this power imbalance.

For many years, local and national institutions addressed this issue with inadequate tools and resources. In January 2014, the local council of Eboli, one of the largest towns in the Piana del Sele, together with trade unions and an employers' organization, set up the 'Public Employment Service against Illegality' in agriculture (*Collocamento pubblico contro l'illegalità*). Farmworkers have been asked to register, and growers are encouraged to use the service to hire their employees, with the municipality acting as a guarantor for the intermediation. The service is free, but farms are not obliged to hire their workers through it. Of course, by recruiting workers through this channel, employers are compelled to offer regular contracts and wages to their employees. In fact, to date, no workers have been hired through this service.

## 13.4 The general domain of monetized informal intermediation

The informal intermediation of the *caporali* is not limited to labour recruitment and organization: it also affects various aspects of the everyday lives of migrants, from the practices geared at obtaining regular permits to stay, to access to housing, credit and health services.

The role of intermediation in procuring legal documents regards directly non-EU migrants, which in the case of the Piana del Sele, means especially Moroccans and Indians. As already noted, this service is fundamental for preventing situations of deportability and vulnerability in which undocumented migrants live. In many cases, migrants obtain a permit to stay (or, more precisely, the regular work contract that allows for the acquisition of this document) by paying a broker. Brokers – who are usually *caporali* who have 'extended' their business – provide this service for both potential migrants, who are in the country of origin and wish to travel to Italy with a regular visa, and migrants who are already in Italy. In the latter case, there are a number of situations in which migrants require the 'help' of a broker: (1) undocumented migrants, who have entered Italy as *clandestini* (illegals) or whose permit to stay has expired, and for whom there is no ordinary law that provides for their regularization; (2) migrants who work without a regular contract and who possess a permit to stay not related to work (for example, for health needs or for study) that cannot otherwise be converted to a labour permit; (3) migrants with a permit to stay but who are unemployed and wish to 'buy' a new labour contract in order to renew their permit.

Except for the very last case, brokers can offer their intermediation between (usually fake) employers and (real) migrants but only during favourable situations that are created by national legislation. One such situation is the amnesty law for undocumented migrants (known in Italy as a *sanatoria*), which since the early 1980s has constituted one of the main instruments for governing international mobility not only in Italy but across southern Europe (King *et al.*, 2000; Barbagli *et al.*, 2004). Most recently, two *sanatorie* were issued, in 2009 and 2012 (the former reserved exclusively for domestic and care workers). These amnesty laws require the employer to declare that she/he will hire the undocumented migrant, thus allowing them to obtain a permit to stay. The employer is supposed to pay a sum of money to the state, which, in reality, is usually paid by the migrant. Another favourable situation is created by the decree on annual immigration quotas for subordinate or seasonal work (known as *decreto flussi*). These decrees offer the brokers the opportunity to link employers with migrants, both those in their country of origin, and those who already live undocumented in Italy. Migrants are willing to pay high sums of money for this service of intermediation in the hope of obtaining regular documents (Botte, 2009; Colombo, 2012).

The *sanatorie* and the *decreti flussi* both signify that the permit of stay is subordinated to the employers' will to regularize labour relations. If, on the one hand, they represent an opportunity for irregular migrants to legalize their status, on the other these same procedures increase migrants' dependence on real or fictitious employers and intermediaries. Thus, such norms have worked to reproduce the subordinate position of migrants in relation to their Italian employers.

A second kind of auxiliary intermediation concerns housing, health and 'banking' services. In the Piana del Sele, migrants require informal intermediation in order to rent a house because they otherwise typically face economic, social and racial barriers in accessing accommodation. Migrants, especially Moroccans, often share houses with their compatriots to reduce costs. In addition, although migrants have access to the health service, some prefer to pay a compatriot to be present when they see a doctor. Finally, the *caporali* operate an informal banking service, often keeping back the workers' pay and giving them, when necessary, credit. Migrants trust them because:

> Everyone here knows who they are and where they live, and at the same time, the *caporali* guarantee that nobody steals their money. When a sum is made available, the broker sends money to the migrant's family via a money transfer service.
>
> (Moroccan farmworker, interview, March 2015)

A labour broker is only one of the many actors to sustain (and profit from) the mechanism of intermediation of migrants' labour, legal and social needs. For their part, migrants are embedded as subaltern actors in different networks and do not only occupy peripheral positions in the local structures of socio-economic power but also suffer directly from the lack of local policies oriented at safeguarding minimum wages, housing and health rights.

In contrast to other agricultural areas in Southern Italy, migrant farmworkers, and especially Moroccans, reside permanently in the Piana del Sele (although some, particularly Romanians, have a more seasonal presence). Nonetheless, there is a conspicuous absence of social and housing policies for migrants. It is very difficult for them to access welfare services for farmworkers, such as agricultural unemployment benefit. These obstacles increase the private costs of the social reproduction of these labourers – including the costs of intermediation – and reduce their social and economic power. The high costs of social reproduction are only reduced by under consumption, informal self-help networks and access to substandard housing conditions. Migrant workers find themselves propelled into a weak social condition that, in a vicious circle, legitimizes the rhetoric of pauperism and related policies targeted against them (Avallone, 2012). For migrants, money is crucial to accessing civil and social rights, within a completely commodified public life (Harvey, 2005). The more powerful the social, institutional and economic barriers become, the easier intermediaries are able to sell their services.

## 13.5 Labour agency, paternalism and national divisions

In spite of the discussion above, migrants in the Piana del Sele cannot be considered just as simply passive labourers. They play an active role in negotiating labour conditions and organizing their daily lives. Social conflicts and negotiations occur virtually in every workplace at a micro-level; not in the 'classic' collective and organized forms but in a range of ways that often depend on localized and individual or small group negotiations and adaptations. Labour agency is expressed through forms of resilience, reworking or resistance (Katz, 2004): different strategies with which migrants deal with hostile labour conditions and wider social relations.

For example, several informal interviews with women farm workers raised the issue of bodily vulnerability that is linked to the experience of subjection to their superiors in the workplace. Through what can be described as an act of resilience, the female migrant farm workers call on employers and intermediaries to respect a code of understanding: 'We work hard, but you have to control your male behaviour and respect our bodies. We do not create problems [at work] for you, but you prevent any [non-work-related] problem for us' (Romanian farmworker, interview, June 2014). On the one hand, this arrangement *de facto* reproduces unequal labour relations. On the other, these women avoid sexual harassment, which, according to one in-depth study in the same area, characterized the treatment of female farm workers during the 1980s (Gribaudi, 1990). This paternalistic style of managing labour relations is, to a certain extent, a legacy of southern Italy's agricultural past and is a reflection of a deeper social regulation of labour, as indeed exemplified by the persistence of the *caporale* as a fundamental labour broker.

Over time, however, Moroccan labourers, the *caporali* and Italian employers were able to regulate the local relations of production in an informal but recognized manner, which has led to the fixing of the daily wage rate and the length of the working day. Through informal relations, Moroccans have developed more favourable power relations than Romanians, which enabled them to demand (and, in some cases, to obtain) an increase in pay.

During the 2000s, Moroccan migrants often silently demanded better wages and housing conditions. At least on two occasions, Moroccan migrants publicly demonstrated their economic relevance to local agriculture and their marginality in relation to local institutions and society. The first event was a two-day strike, organized in September 2006 by the CGIL, the largest trade union in Italy, to claim better living and working conditions for migrant labourers, and regular permits to stay (Botte, 2009). However, this strike was not strong enough to have a positive impact. The second event was the eviction in November 2009 of an abandoned fruit and vegetable market area in San Nicola Varco in the municipality of Eboli, which since the early 1990s had been occupied by hundreds of Moroccans. The partial failure of the 2006 strike and the 2009 eviction hastened the weakening of the capacity of the Moroccan migrants to organize themselves in a collective and public way during the very same period in which they were competing with Romanian workers in the agricultural labour market. Without homes, money or clothes (and, in some cases, permits to stay) – the evicted Moroccans came to be considered publicly as people who were in need of 'humanitarian' aid. However, after the initial emergency died down, the voices and political demands of these migrant workers slowly faded out of public and policy debates.

Labour regulation has a strong informal and taken-for-granted nature that sustains the increasing invisibility of migrants. Consequently, every public action of or for migrants disturbs the usual labour relations between employers and farm workers. In the networks created by intermediaries, supervisors and employers have to reproduce the informal social regulation of labour and thus prefer silent relationships and modes of behaviour. The invisibility of migrants is a functional aspect of the current power arrangements.

Paradoxically, such invisibility is more easily guaranteed for migrants from new EU member states because these migrants are white, Christian and come from countries that are part of the Schengen area. Such features have favoured the integration of Romanian men and women into the local agricultural labour market.

## 13.6 Conclusions

Inexpensive labour and the reproduction of its material and symbolic conditions constitute a neoliberal strategy that includes wage repression (Harvey, 2010) and a regime of forced under consumption (Moore, 2014). The vulnerability of migrant farmworkers in the Piana del Sele is reproduced by a social regulation of the local labour market, in which informal intermediation plays a key role. Relationships between migrants and local society have been mainly structured through an 'enabling power' (comprising flexible networks of compatriots and formal and informal Italian intermediaries, supervisors and employers) that performs several gatekeeping functions. Migrants often do not have direct access to labour and other resources: their knowledge of local labour, social and institutional relations is mediated by a power structure that strengthens their subaltern position. As verified in other studies, 'mediated employment, recruitment and work practices mean [usually] increased precarity, vulnerability and insecurity' (Enrigh, 2013, p. 273).

The main recent change in the farm labour market and labour relations has been the reduction of the autonomy of migrant farmworkers and their ever-greater dependence on different forms of recruitment and employment intermediation. The more migrants are enclosed within their own national networks, the more dependent they become on the different services provided by their compatriots. The general effect has been the devaluation of migrant farmworkers who share similar material living conditions independent of their nationality. These similarities include: (1) low wages that create a generalized situation of working poverty; (2) irregular and illegal forms of employment; (3) a lack of access to agricultural welfare state provisions; and (4) a condition of social subjugation and reduced individual and collective autonomy.

Migrants are constrained by a comprehensive system of informal intermediation that impinges on their economic and daily lives. They are unable to access resources and rights in the Piana del Sele. In this situation, informal networks and intermediaries play an ambiguous role: on the one hand, they represent the only 'institution' that enables migrant workers to access employment and other resources; on the other, they reproduce the conditions that are favourable for local farms; first and foremost the presence of a subaltern, inexpensive and often fearful agricultural working class.

## Notes

1 The term used to define the informal intermediary of labour in Italy is *caporale*; this figure is similar to an unlicensed gangmaster in the UK (Brass, 2004; Rogaly, 2008; Strauss, 2013).

2 One could note that, within a deep transformation in production structure, migration processes, labour market, labour costs and conditions, one element has not changed in the 'new agriculture': the informality and irregularity in the regulation of labour relations.

3 At the same time, migrants have yet to encounter the more positive 'traditions' of local agriculture, namely the unemployment subsidies for agricultural labourers that Italian farmworkers were able to win after long struggles during the 1960s.

4 Even if informal intermediation holds a central role in local agricultural production, available information contradicts the common media discourse that sees the *caporalato* structured in a similar way to a mafia-type organization.

## References


Avallone, G. (2012). 'Presenti/assenti. I lavoratori migranti nell'agricoltura della Piana del Sele' in C. Colloca and A. Corrado (eds) *La globalizzazione delle campagne: Migranti e società rurali nel Sud Italia*. Milano: FrancoAngeli, 68–87.

Baldi, L. and Casati, D. (2009). 'Un distretto della IV gamma? Il comparto che 'vende tempo libero'. *Agriregionieuropa*, 16.

Barbagli, M., Colombo, A. and Sciortino, G. (eds) (2004). *I sommersi e i sanati. Le regolarizzazioni degli immigrati in Italia*. Bologna: Il Mulino.

Botte, A. (2009). *Mannaggia la miserìa: Storie di braccianti stranieri e caporali nella Piana del Sele*. Roma: Ediesse.

Brass, T. (2004). ''Medieval working practices'? British agriculture and the return of the gangmaster'. *The Journal of Peasant Studies*, 31(2), 313–340.

Calvanese, F. and Pugliese, E. (eds) (1991). *La presenza straniera in Italia. Il caso della Campania*. Milan: FrancoAngeli.

Caruso, F. (2015). *La politica dei subalterni: Organizzazione e lotte del bracciantato migrante nel Sud europa*. Rome: DeriveApprodi.

Cavounidis, J. (2013). 'Migration and the economic and social landscape of Greece'. *South-Eastern Europe Journal of Economics*, 1, 59–78.

Checa, J.C., Arjona, A. and Checa y Olmos, F. (2010). 'Actitudes recientes hacia los inmigrantes en El Ejido (España)'. *Convergencia*, 52, 125–154.

Colloca, C. and Corrado, A. (eds) (2013). *La globalizzazione delle campagne. Migranti e società rurali nel Sud Italia*. Milan: FrancoAngeli.

Colombo, A. (2012). *Fuori controllo? Miti e realtà dell'immigrazione in Italia*. Bologna: Il Mulino.

De Genova, N. (2013). 'Spectacles of migrant 'illegality': the scene of exclusion, the obscene of inclusion'. *Ethnic and Racial Studies*, 36(7), 1–19.

Enrigh, B. (2013). '(Re)considering new agents: A review of labour market intermediaries within labour geography'. *Geography Compass*, 7(4), 287–299.

Filhol, R. (2013). 'Les travailleurs agricoles migrants en Italie du Sud: Entre incompréhension, instrumentalisation et solidarités locales'. *Hommes et migrations*, 1301, 139–147.

Gribaudi, G. (1990). *A Eboli. Il mondo meridionale in cent'anni di trasformazione*. Venezia: Marsilio.

Gualda, E. (2012). 'Migración circular en tiempos de crisis. Mujeres de Europa del Este y africanas en la agricultura de Huelva'. *Papers, Revista de Sociologia*, 97(3), 613–640.

Harriss-White, B. (2009). 'Work and wellbeing in informal economies: the regulative roles of institutions of identity and state'. *World Development*, 38(2), 170–183.

Hartman, T. (2008). 'States, markets, and other unexceptional communities: informal Romanian labour in a Spanish agricultural zone'. *The Journal of the Royal Anthropological Institute*, 14(3), 496–514.

Harvey, D. (2005). *A Brief History of Neoliberalism*. Oxford: Oxford University Press.

Harvey, D. (2010). *The Enigma of Capital and the Crises of Capitalism*. London: Profile Books.

INEA (2013). *L'agricoltura nella Campania in cifre: 2012*. Guidonia: Imago editrice.

Istat (2010). *2010 Agricultural Census*, http://dati-censimentoagricoltura.istat.it/?lang=en (last access: 21/01/2016).

Jiménez, J.F. (2010). 'Migraciones en el Sur de Espana y desarrollo del Poniente Almeriense'. *Revista Internacional de Ciencias Sociales y Humanidades*, 20(2), 109–143.

Jonas, A. (1996). 'Local labour control regimes: Uneven development and the social regulation of production'. *Regional Studies*, 30, 323–338.

Jonas, A. (2009). 'Labor control regime' in R. Kitchin and N. Thrift (eds) *International Encyclopedia* of *Human Geography*. Amsterdam: Elsevier, 1–7.

Kasimis, C. and Papadopoulos, A. (2005). 'The multifunctional role of migrants in the Greek countryside'. *Journal of Ethnic and Migration Studies*, 31(1), 99–127.

Katz, C. (2004). *Growing up Global: Economic Restructuring and Children's Everyday Lives*. Minneapolis: University of Minnesota Press.

King, R., Lazaridis, G. and Tsardanidis, C. (eds) (2000). *Eldorado or Fortress? Migration in Southern Europe*, Basingstoke: McMillan.

Marx, K. (2007). *Capital: A Critique of Political Economy. Vol. III*. New York: Cosimo.

Moore, J.W. (2014). 'The end of cheap nature, or, how I learned to stop worrying about 'the' environment and love the crisis of capitalism' in C. Suter and C. Chase-Dunn (eds) *Structures of the World Political Economy and the Future of Global Conflict and Cooperation*. Berlin: LIT, 1–31.

Moraes, N., Gadea. E., Pedreño, A. and de Castro, C. (2012). 'Enclaves globales agrícolas y migraciones de trabajo: convergencias globales y regulaciones transnacionales'. *Política y sociedad*, 49(1), 13–34.

Papadopoulos, A. (2009). ''Begin from the bottom to move on`: Social Mobility of Immigrant Labour in Rural Greece'. *Méditerranée*, 113, 25–39.

Peck, J. (1996). *Work-place: the social regulation of labor markets*. New York: Guilford.

Peck, J. and Theodore, N. (2012). 'Politicizing contingent work: Countering neoliberal labor market regulation . . . from the bottom up?'. *South Atlantic Quarterly*, 111(4), 741–761.

Pedreño, A., Gadea, E. and de Castro, C. (2014). 'Labor, gender, and political conflicts in the global agri-food system: The case of the agri-export model in Murcia, Spain' in A. Bonanno and J. Cavalcanti (eds) *Labor Relations in Globalized Food*. Bingley: Emerald Group Publishing, 193–214.

Perrotta, D. (2014). 'Vecchi e nuovi mediatori. Storia, geografia ed etnografia del caporalato in agricoltura'. *Meridiana. Rivista di storia e scienze sociali*, 79, 193–220.

Perrotta, D. (2015). 'Agricultural day laborers in southern Italy: Forms of mobility and resistance'. *South Atlantic Quarterly*, 114(1), 195–203.

Perrotta, D. and Sacchetto D. (2014), 'Migrant farmworkers in Southern Italy: Ghettoes, caporalato and collective action'. *Workers of the World. International Journal on Strikes and Social Conflicts*, I(5), 75–98.

Pugliese, E. (1984). *I braccianti agricoli in Italia*. Milan: Franco Angeli.

Rogaly, B. (2008). 'Intensification of workplace regimes in British horticulture: the role of migrant workers'. *Population, Space and Place*, 14(6), 497–510.

Strauss, K. (2013). 'Unfree again: Social reproduction, flexible labour markets and the resurgence of gang labour in the UK'. *Antipode*, 45(1), 180–197.

Torres, F. and Gadea, E. (2012). 'Agricultura intensiva de exportación, inmigración y transformación rural. El caso del Campo de Cartagena 1990–2010 (Murcia)'. Paper presented at the meeting of *IX Colloquio Iberico de Estudios Rurales*, Lisbon.

# 14 From the *Al-Maghrib* to the *Al-Gharb*

## An anatomy of the recruitment and labour incorporation of Moroccan agricultural workers in the Algarve, Southern Portugal

*Dora Sampaio and Rui F. Carvalho*

### 14.1 Introduction

Over the last few decades, the process of economic modernisation in Southern European countries has resulted, inter alia, in an increasing demand for a young, low-skilled workforce to work in labour-intensive sectors such as tourism, civil construction and agriculture. Noteworthy among these changes has been the increasing incorporation of international migrants – a cheaper and less demanding workforce – as an active labour force in these sectors (King, 2000; Ribas-Mateos, 2004; Kasimis, 2009; Arnalte-Alegre and Ortiz-Miranda, 2013).

Even though international labour migration to rural areas does not constitute a recent phenomenon, research on migration and rural areas has focused mainly on outward movements (such as rural exodus) and their implications for the sending communities, rather than on rural areas as recipients of migrants (Kasimis, 2005). Moreover, it is fair to say that a significant proportion of the migrants moving into rural areas are (or will potentially be) employed in agricultural activities. Several factors from both the employee and the employer perspectives help explain the increasing incorporation of an international migrant labour force in these activities. On the one hand, the decline in the number of native workers available in rural areas as well as their lower willingness to accept poor working conditions; and, on the other hand, the employers' preference for migrant workers to whom they can more easily impose low salaries and long working journeys while avoiding paying social security contributions (Kasimis, 2005; Kasimis and Papadopoulos, 2005; Morice and Michalon, 2008; Mesini, 2009). In many Southern European countries such as France, Italy or Spain, the migrant labour force has thus become of structural importance to all labour markets, especially the low-skilled ones. The agricultural sector has not been an exception.

Even in the case of Portugal, where the admission of migrant workers to the agricultural sector was initially fairly restricted, recent evidence shows that the sector is now largely dependent on a migrant labour force (Kasimis *et al.*, 2003; Fonseca, 2008). The first waves of labour migrants arriving in Portugal (late 1970s), coming mostly from the Portuguese former colonies in Africa, had very little involvement in the agricultural sector. The high level of traditionalism, and the low-scale intensity and small size of the Portuguese agricultural businesses back then can potentially explain why these first migrants were not significantly absorbed into the sector (Corkill and Eaton, 1998).

Yet, similarly to what happened in other Southern European countries such as Spain or Greece, Portugal's accession to the European Union (EU) in 1986 induced important changes to both the country's agricultural sector and to its position in the European migration system(s). First, it brought a new, supra-national, legislative and regulatory framework, mainly in the ambit of the Common Agricultural Policy (CAP), which included new funding and investment for the modernisation and specialisation of the country's agriculture within the European common market. Second, and especially after the Schengen agreement, it established a new mobility regime, which entailed new regulations on the mobility of people (and workers) within the EU, sponsoring the rise of Portugal as a gateway for international migrants coming to Europe. This last shift was accompanied by internal changes to the legal framework regulating immigration in Portugal, implemented mainly through a set of extraordinary regularisation programmes that took place during the 1990s and early 2000s. These legal changes, especially that of 2001, came as a response to an exponential growth in the number of immigrants entering the country during the mid and late 1990s. This growth was accompanied by an ensuing diversification in the countries of origin of the immigrants residing in Portugal and also in their sectors of labour incorporation, with agriculture gradually increasing its relative importance as a receiving sector for a foreign labour force.

Thus, coming from remarkably stable and fairly residual numbers in the previous decades, a gradual increase in the percentage of migrants working in agriculture in Portugal has been witnessed since the 2000s. In 2005, a total of 2.6 per cent of all economically active immigrants living in Portugal were working in the sector (Fonseca, *et al.,* 2004; Fonseca, 2008). According to the latest official statistics available, the figure had risen to 5.3 per cent in 2011 (Portugal, Statistics Portugal, 2011a). At the regional level, these trends have been particularly visible in Portugal's most southerly regions, Alentejo and the Algarve.

Despite this noteworthy increase, and contrary to what is the case with other Southern European countries such as Spain (e.g. Corkill, 2005; Hellio, 2008, 2014; Mannon *et al.*, 2012) or Greece (e.g. Kasimis *et al.,* 2003; Kasimis, 2005, 2009; Kasimis and Papadopoulos, 2005), the incorporation of immigrant workers into Portuguese agriculture remains scarcely studied. Only two major studies were identified that specifically focused on the foreign agricultural labour force in Portugal: Fonseca *et al.* (2004) and Fonseca (2008). Their emphasis, however, is particularly on Eastern European migrants working in the Alentejo region. Concurrently, the only research on Moroccan immigrants in Portugal is that of Faria (2006, 2008) and Cabral (2007). These studies are nevertheless specific neither to Moroccan agricultural workers nor to those living in the Algarve.

Throughout this chapter, we aim at filling such a gap in the existent scholarship. We will do so by focusing on Moroccan workers (from *Al-Maghrib*) in the Algarve (*Al-Gharb*). Although the number of Moroccans in Portugal is negligible in terms of the total immigrant population, they are one of the most representative groups working in agriculture in the Algarve region. The choice to focus the analysis on a fairly small migrant group, although one of great importance for the Portuguese agricultural sector overall, has the potential to allow us to draw an in-depth diachronic anatomy of the recruitment processes and labour incorporation of these migrants into the regional agricultural sector in the Algarve. This may constitute a benchmark for what may have occurred with other migrant agricultural workers, not only in the Portuguese case, but also in other Southern European countries. Our goal is hence to show how the recruitment processes and the labour incorporation of the Moroccan agricultural workers in the Algarve has unfolded in recent years and how these elements help explain present dynamics and anticipate future trends, particularly those imposed by the current economic crisis.

Four main sections make up this chapter. It opens with a detailed contextualisation of both the agricultural sector and the immigrant agricultural labour force working in the Algarve, drawing particular attention to the Moroccan agricultural workers. This is particularly relevant given, as already mentioned, their almost complete absence in previous studies. This is followed by a section on methods and data. The third section assembles together the main debate, focusing mainly on the recruitment waves, migration process and labour incorporation of the Moroccan agricultural workers in the Algarve. Finally, the chapter rounds up by discussing and synthesising the main findings.

## 14.2 Moroccan agricultural workers in the Algarve: setting the scene

The arrival and settlement of Moroccans in Portugal and, more specifically, in the Algarve, is better understood by framing this migratory movement within the wider Iberian context. Previous research has shown that the first consistent arrivals of Moroccans to Spain occurred in the late 1980s (de Haas, 2007). Even though irregular entries were very significant in the first years, seasonal organised contracting schemes in Morocco have progressively gained relevance in explaining the arrival of Moroccan immigrants in Spain, and especially their entry into the Spanish agricultural sector (Corkill, 2005).

Notwithstanding the geographical proximity and historical relations between Portugal and Morocco, and contrary to the situation in neighbouring Spain, the consistent immigration of Moroccans to Portugal is more recent and numerically not as representative. The first Moroccan immigrants are believed to have settled in the north of Portugal in the early 1980s (Faria, 2006). These (very few) individuals were mostly nomadic street and market vendors who roamed from village to village trading in daily local and regional street markets (Cabral, 2007). More or less concurrently, the first arrivals of Moroccan fishermen were registered, particularly in port cities such as Lisbon and Setubal and small fishing villages in the Algarve. Initially these fishermen moved seasonally between Morocco and Portugal, and only later established themselves permanently in the country.

The first documented arrivals of Moroccan agricultural workers in Portugal occurred in the early 1990s (1992–1993). These pioneers, all men, came to the southerly regions of Alentejo and the Algarve (Faria, 2006). Apart from some episodic family reunification, the first women arriving in the country without their spouses or other male relatives came by means of collective work contracts to work in the agricultural sector. This occurred mostly towards the end of the 1990s and their final destination was the Algarve. As in Spain (Moreno, 2014), these women came mostly from the region of Kenitra, in northern Morocco. Initially bound by seasonal work contracts that obliged them to return to Morocco, many of these female workers ended up staying in the country, either by finding other jobs locally or simply by fleeing their employers and overstaying (Faria, 2008; Hellio, 2008).

According to Faria (2008), Moroccan migration to Portugal is generally characterised not only by its recent nature, but also by a noticeable socio-economic and educational heterogeneity. Migrants also originate from a range of regions in Morocco. The fieldwork carried out does not confirm these trends for the agricultural workers in the Algarve. In fact, our respondents are fairly homogeneous in their socio-economic and educational backgrounds and, contrary to the street vendors in the north of Portugal (Faria, 2008) they tend to present stable settlement patterns and come mostly from two or three agriculture-intensive regions in Morocco.

There does not seem to be a general consensus on the number of Moroccans living in Portugal, with different data sources suggesting different figures. In 2005, the Portuguese Foreign and Borders Service (SEF) reported a total of 1,539 Moroccan citizens residing in Portugal. In the same year, as noted by Faria (2006), a report from the European Commission, using data from the Moroccan Ministry of Foreign Affairs and Cooperation, presented a more generous figure of 2,866 Moroccans in Portugal. More recent data shows a steady growth of the Moroccan group between 2005 and 2008. According to SEF data, 2008 stands out as the peak year for the number of Moroccans in Portugal, with a total of 1,870 individuals. There has since been a slight decrease, with a total of 1,808 Moroccan residents reported in 2013 (Portugal, Service of Foreigners and Borders, 2008, 2013).

At the regional level, a total of 382 Moroccans were living in the Algarve in 2005 (Portugal, Service of Foreigners and Borders, 2005). Unlike the pattern registered in the country as a whole, the number of Moroccans in the Algarve has consistently risen in the last few years. From a total of 460 in 2008 this figure rose to 529 in 2011 to 567 in 2013 (Portugal, Service of Foreigners and Borders, 2008, 2011, 2013). The Algarve has hence seen an increase in its relative importance as a settling area for Moroccan migrants within the Portuguese context. In 2013, 31.4 per cent of the Moroccans settled in Portugal were living in the Algarve (up from 29.5 per cent in 2011), compared to 21.1 per cent in the Lisbon Metropolitan Area (LMA) and 11.6 per cent in the Oporto Metropolitan Area (OMA). These are particularly relevant figures considering that the vast majority of other immigrant groups in Portugal tend to heavily cluster around the LMA (Portugal, Service of Foreigners and Borders, 2011, 2013).

According to the former Portuguese Ministry of Solidarity and Social Security (MSSS) (currently the Ministry of Solidarity, Employment and Social Security), in 2009 the migrants working in agriculture in the Algarve amounted to 18.2 per cent of the total number of agricultural workers in the region. In 2012, the figure reached 27.7 per cent, a staggering growth of almost 10 per cent in just three years (Portugal, Ministry of Solidarity, Employment and Social Security, 2012). Also, a total of 46.7 per cent of foreign nationals labouring in the sector at the regional level were from non-EU European countries (especially Ukraine and Moldova). Romania and Bulgaria were the most important providers of agricultural workers from within the EU-27, the second most important statistical sub-region. African non-Portuguese-speaking countries – where Moroccans are included and contribute strongly to the overall figures – came third, representing 10.3 per cent of the foreign agricultural labour force available in the region (Portugal, Ministry of Solidarity, Employment and Social Security, 2009).

Focusing specifically on the most relevant nationalities, in 2009, Moroccans were the third most representative foreign nationality after Ukrainians and Romanians. By 2013, this had changed slightly, with Moroccans representing the fourth largest group of immigrants employed in agriculture-related activities in the region, now overtaken by Bulgarians. This is not related, however, to a decrease in the number of Moroccans working in the regional agricultural sector, but rather to a growth in the number of Bulgarians due to targeted recruitment campaigns. According to the MSSS regional cadres of staff for 2009 (Portugal, Ministry of Solidarity, Employment and Social Security, 2009), more than half (52.4 per cent) of Moroccans living in the Algarve were employed in primary sector-related activities, either as farmers and skilled agricultural and fisheries workers (41.3 per cent) or as non-skilled agricultural and fisheries workers (11.1 per cent). Overall, these figures show that Moroccans in the Algarve display a strong profile of work specialisation in the agricultural sector.

In terms of gender, recent data shows that 53 per cent of Moroccan immigrants in Portugal are male (Portugal, Service of Foreigners and Borders, 2013). This slight male predominance may be explained by the relatively recent nature of Moroccan migratory paths to Portugal, with men in many cases preceding the arrival of their families. Nevertheless, the latest trends seem to suggest a decrease in the relative importance of male Moroccans living in the country – in 2008 they represented 66 per cent of all Moroccans in Portugal. This can be linked to both an upsurge in the number of family reunions and to an increase in the numbers of Moroccan female workers coming to the country, a trend particularly visible in the Algarve's farm businesses (Portugal, Service of Foreigners and Borders, 2013). In fact, in 2009, about 60 per cent of Moroccan agricultural workers in the region were women (Portugal, Ministry of Solidarity, Employment and Social Security, 2009). This feminisation of the Moroccan agricultural labour force seems to be in line with previous trends registered in Spain and Italy (de Haas, 2007; Mannon *et al.*, 2012; Moreno, 2014).

The settlement patterns of Moroccan migrants at the regional level do not seem to occur in a uniform manner within the Algarve. Figure 14.1 illustrates the geographical distribution of the Moroccan migrants by municipalities in 2013. Three municipalities stand out as possessing the highest numbers of Moroccans – Silves, Faro and Olhão – the latter two henceforth being referred to as the Faro–Olhão axis. This does not come as a surprise as these municipalities are also those with a stronger presence of farming activities within the region, particularly fruit-related activities.

These settlement patterns are also intimately related to the types of crops produced and the type of labour force preferred in each area. Although the Algarve has been one of the regions to lose more farmland in the last few years, mostly to urban and tourist development, approximately one-third of the region's land is still used for farming. From an agricultural standpoint, the Algarve is traditionally best known for its fruit production. About 68 per cent of all orange trees and 80 per cent of mandarin trees in Portugal are found in the region. Together with three other regions, Trás-os-Montes, Ribatejo and Oeste, the Algarve accounts for

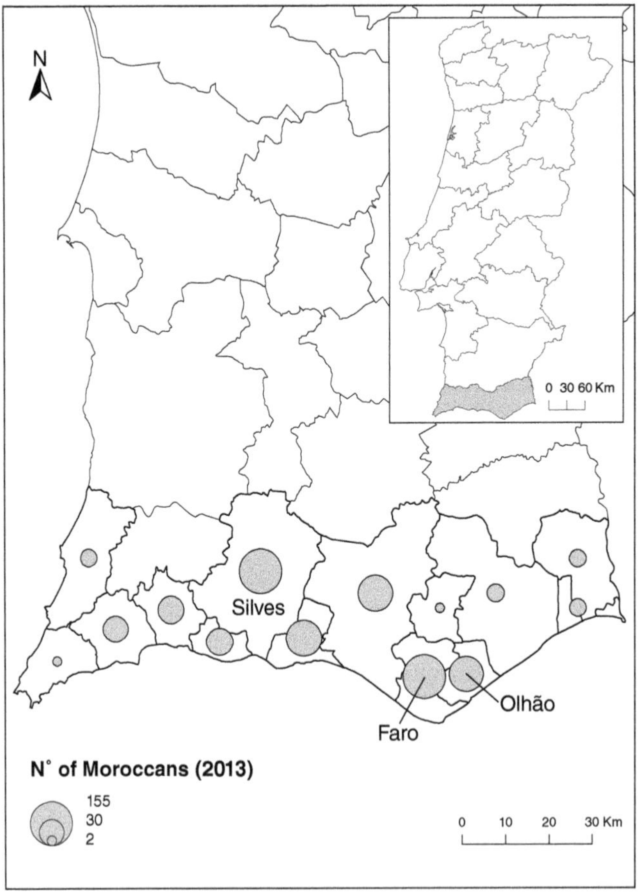


*Figure 14.1* Number of Moroccans per municipalities of the Algarve (2013).
Source: Portugal, Service of Foreigners and Borders, 2013.

the highest number of farms specialised in fruit production in the country. The region also possesses the biggest orchards in the country, three times larger than the national average. In 2009, 72 per cent of the farms in the Algarve were specialised in permanent cultures, with the citrus sub-sector dominant (17 per cent), followed by nut production (16 per cent), especially almonds and carobs, and the combined production of citrus, tropical fruits and nuts (24 per cent) (Portugal, Statistics Portugal, 2011b). The agricultural fabric in the Algarve is still strongly atomised, being mostly characterised by small family-oriented businesses with limited production capacity. It is estimated that only about 10 per cent of the farms in the region are larger than 20 ha and more than 60 per cent do not even reach 5 ha. For this reason, the citrus production in the region is mostly directed at national retailers, with only about 25 per cent aimed at export, with Spain ranking as the prime destination (Portugal, Ministry of Agriculture, Rural Development and Fisheries – Policy and Planning Council, 2007).

There is also significant local diversity in terms of the most important cultures. Silves, for instance, specialises in citrus production, with this sub-sector accounting for 61 per cent of its area of permanent crops (Portugal, Statistics Portugal, 2011b). Conversely, the Faro–Olhão axis shows a more diverse distribution. Relevant to this study is the production of fresh fruits which, despite representing no more than 13 per cent of the total area of permanent crops in these municipalities (Portugal, Statistics Portugal, 2011b), employs a large number of Moroccan workers. Women are generally preferred for these activities. Therefore, female Moroccans are strongly represented in these two municipalities (64 per cent of the Moroccan women included in our sample lived in these municipalities). On the other hand, men tend to cluster around Silves (60.7 per cent of the Moroccan men included in our sample), where the locally dominant citrus production requires more physical strength to harvest, carry and store the fruit. Men are also viewed as more skilled in working with the heavy machinery necessary for these tasks. It should be noted, however, that over the last few years family reunion mechanisms have added diversity to these patterns.

## 14.3 Data and methods

The analysis presented henceforth is based on an intensive period of fieldwork encompassing both qualitative and quantitative data collection in the ambit of a wider research project – THEMIS.[1] The fieldwork in the Algarve was carried out between April 2011 and May 2012. First, semi-structured interviews were conducted, followed by a larger survey. The information supporting this study is based on 15 interviews and 120 questionnaires to Moroccans working in agriculture-related activities in the Algarve.[2] The interviewees were selected following a set of initial contacts established with key local informants in the region. The sampling methodology used for the questionnaires was the so-called Respondent Driven Sampling (RDS).[3]

The respondents included in the study were deemed eligible according to five criteria: (i) they were born in Morocco; (ii) they were 18 years old or more at the time of the interview/survey; (iii) they were at least 16 years old when they arrived in Portugal; (iv) they had resided in Portugal for at least three full months at the time of the questionnaire; and (v) specifically for the purposes of this chapter, they were formally or informally employed in any type of paid work in the agricultural sector. Additional research techniques such as participant and non-participant observation and informal non-structured discussions with local agricultural employers were also used in the study.

The survey sample reflects a balanced gender distribution. The average age of the respondents is 35 years. This seems to be consistent with the relatively recent pattern of arrival of Moroccans in the Algarve. One of the most significant features of the Moroccans interviewed/surveyed is their low level of formal education: about 85 per cent of the respondents had attended school for four years or less. Furthermore, more than half of the respondents (55 per cent) had not completed primary education or had not attended school at all.

## 14.4 Moroccan agricultural workers in the Algarve: formation and establishment of a migrant labour force

The history of the arrival of Moroccan agricultural workers in the Algarve can be framed within three important periods or waves. The first-wave immigrants, henceforth referred to as *pioneers*, seem to have arrived during the early 1990s. Narratives of this first movement are consistent across the interviews: the pioneers came as part of a group of approximately 30 Moroccans who were brought by a Swiss employer with farming estates in Morocco and Spain, after he decided to expand his business to Portugal. These pioneers departed from Agadir (Southern Morocco). Some had previously migrated internally from a small agricultural town called El Kelaa des Sraghna, located on the outskirts of Marrakech. They settled in Odemira (Alentejo), a municipality bordering the Algarve, where they were hired to build greenhouses for strawberry growing. Later, when the employer died, the investment was discontinued and these migrants found themselves jobless. Some went back to Morocco, while others, taking advantage of their permanent residence in Portugal, moved to other countries in Europe. The remainder, between four and six – the number varying according to accounts – settled in the Algarve. The four we were able to contact during the fieldwork phase are still living in the region and continue to work in the agricultural sector. Over time, all of them have helped family members and other acquaintances come to Portugal, either through family reunion mechanisms, by arranging labour contracts, or by assisting them to settle in Portugal once they arrived in Europe, often after having crossed the Mediterranean irregularly.

The second wave can be identified as the *followers*, a group including both the pioneers' families and the first Moroccan immigrants to arrive in the region via consistent and organised recruitment campaigns. The first arrivals of this second wave took place in the late 1990s (1999) and lasted until the mid-2000s. This group comprised three main sub-groups: (i) the direct family members of the pioneers, especially their spouses and children; (ii) a group comprising about 15 to

20 women from Kenitra recruited to work in farming activities (mostly picking fruits and vegetables) by their employer in Morocco who was expanding his business to Portugal; and (iii) several undocumented migrants, mostly from El Kelaa des Sraghna and Agadir, who had entered Europe in makeshift boats or hidden in large cargo lorries. This second wave experienced its most consistent increases after 2001, mainly due to a rise in the number of entries following the 2001 extraordinary regularisation law, which granted residence status to all migrants holding a work contract in the country. Several of the Moroccans who had entered the country irregularly – from Morocco or other European countries such as Italy, Belgium or France and as a result of hearing about the opportunity for regularisation via word-of-mouth – were thus able to quickly regularise their situation in Portugal by arranging work contracts in agricultural businesses. They were often facilitated by compatriots who had arrived earlier in the region. Approximately one quarter of Moroccan immigrants included in our sample arrived during this period. As both the questionnaires and the interviews showed, it was also during this period that the first consistent and organised recruitment campaigns in Morocco took place. The particularity of this first stage of recruitment lies in the fact that it mainly involved the expansion of European agricultural companies (mostly French and Spanish) already established in northern Morocco, especially in the agricultural areas around Kenitra, to the Algarve. As Hayat[4] explains:

> Yes, it was a 'Portuguese' employer who helped them [Hayat's female cousins who later helped her to come to Portugal] come here to work. The employer isn´t Portuguese but he is living here and has greenhouses both here and in Morocco. He had people working for him in Morocco and then arranged for them to come here to work for him.
>
> (Female, 30, arrived in the Algarve in 2007)

The third wave of arrivals occurred after 2006 and consists mostly of family members of the followers and newly recruited agricultural workers, both hired and arriving in Portugal directly from Morocco or arriving irregularly from Spain before or after their seasonal contracts there had expired. According to the data collected, this period seems to account for the largest bulk of arrivals among the survey respondents (61.7 per cent). However, this is not a homogeneous trend. Again, a clear temporal distinction can be identified within this group. Looking in more detail at the migrants' arrivals per year, and considering 2008 as the beginning of the economic crisis in Portugal, it does not come as a surprise that 44.2 per cent of all the respondents arrived between 2006 and 2008, while a much more modest percentage (17.5 per cent) arrived between 2008 and 2012. As stressed by local employers, this de-growth cannot be detached from the crisis affecting the country, which not only impacted upon overall economic performance, but also led to a contraction in the international recruitment campaigns organised by Portuguese companies. Therefore, until 2007–2008 these migration patterns seemed to be maintained mostly by women recruited directly from Morocco to work in fruit growing and picking activities, especially oranges and red fruits.

Although some of these women went back to Morocco, many of them ended up leaving their employers before their contracts ended, while others were contracted by the same employers on a less seasonal (although still temporary) basis.

Some of those who left their employers moved to Spain, while others settled in other areas of the Algarve where they found employment with other companies. However, as stated above, after 2008 the recruitment campaigns, especially those directed at Moroccan immigrants, slowed down and the majority of arrivals from this year on occurred mostly due to: (i) family reunion mechanisms, mainly started by women already living in Portugal who brought their spouses and children; and (ii) irregular entries of recruited workers (mostly women) coming from Spain to the Algarve. Some of the individuals belonging to the first group claimed to have decided to come to the Algarve after hearing that, in spite of an overall lower availability of jobs and less generous payments, they would find less competition for job opportunities and better job stability (less constricted by seasonality), and it would be easier for them to regularise their visa situation. This is stressed, for example, in Skhatou's account:

> Here in Portugal there are no problems with papers. I know many Moroccans who work in Spain for three months and then come here. In Portugal you can get your papers with one year of social security contributions. In Spain and other countries it's not like that .... And I asked [a friend coming from Spain]: why don't you stay in Spain? Don't you make more money there? And she said: In Spain I couldn't get the papers. I stayed for 5 years, 6 years, and I still couldn't get the papers.
>
> (Female, 31, arrived in 2008)

Direct recruitment campaigns in Morocco have thus played an essential role in the establishment and maturation of the Moroccan workforce in the Algarve. Almost half (43.3 per cent) of the survey respondents arrived in the region already with a work permit. Of these, a total of 67.3 per cent were women, which seems to point to a strong gender bias in the recruitment campaigns. This is often related to an attempt to take advantage of women's vulnerability at family, cultural and symbolic levels (Hellio, 2014; Mannon *et al.*, 2012; Moreno, 2014). All in all, these campaigns seem to have evolved, since the second half of the 2000s, from intra-company recruitment, occurring in the context of a geographical expansion of businesses from northern Morocco (Kenitra) to the Algarve, to direct recruitment conducted by the largest Portuguese companies without any prior relations with Morocco. Emulating their Spanish counterparts, these companies started to expand their pool of potential workers to Morocco, where they could find a cheaper, more flexible and less demanding labour force, with the required know-how and previous experience in the sector. The recruitment campaigns took place mostly in northern Morocco, particularly in the area surrounding the city of Kenitra. Together, El Kelaa des Sraghna and Kenitra account for almost 75 per cent of all the Moroccans included in our sample of 120 questionnaires. Respondents from Kenitra generally came with a work permit or contract (during the first period) or through family reunion mechanisms (in the more recent period), while those hailing from El Kelaa des Sraghna (except for the pioneers) came either irregularly (mostly during the second wave) or as recipients of a family reunification permit (in the more recent period).

According to the manager of a large Portuguese agricultural company in the Algarve, the selection of new Moroccan workers is primarily driven by two main reasons: first, a recommendation provided by a current employee (usually seeking to bring family or friends to Portugal, or, less commonly, interested in 'selling' work contracts in Morocco) and, second, earlier working experience in the agricultural sector, particularly in the fruit and vegetable sectors. In the specific case of Kenitra, the agricultural specialisation here seems to be an important reason for explaining the recruitment campaigns conducted by Portuguese and Spanish companies in the region, especially those aimed at contracting women with prior experience in fruit picking and greenhouse work.

According to the data gathered during fieldwork, this process of recruitment in Morocco is conducted through an interesting mix of formal and semi-formal practices. Current employees advise their bosses on which persons to recruit, generally family members or close friends from the same region and often (although not always) with prior experience as agricultural workers. They also advise acquaintances to register with the local employment centres in Morocco. The employers then go to these job centres and seek to recruit workers tagged by their current employees. Even so, there seems to be a preference for hiring women. In spite of some references to an informal broker 'selling' contracts in the Kenitra region, this does not seem to be the dominant form of recruitment practised by Portuguese companies. Aicha's account sums up in a very clear way the process of recruitment that characterises this 'third wave':

> My boss wanted to get people from Morocco so he went to the Employment Centre over there. He wanted people from the countryside, not from the city, to work in fruit picking. So my sister-in-law [already working for this employer] said she knew my family. She also arranged [work contracts] for friends of mine but they always had to go to the Employment Centre in Morocco first.
>
> (Female, 41, arrived in 2008)

In all recruitment waves, the role of social and kinship networks with Moroccans already established in the Algarve stands out as an important vehicle for the labour incorporation of the new arrivals. In fact, more than 70 per cent of the 120 agricultural workers surveyed claimed to have received direct individual help to find their first job before or after arriving in the country. Men tend to be more active in providing help to find a work contract in Portugal (64 per cent of the total cases of help), with women being more prone to help only their spouses, children, sisters and other female cousins. In many cases, as already noted, this individual assistance comes in the form of friends and family already living and working in the Algarve requesting their employers to specifically prioritise their acquaintances during the recruitment and selection process. In the words of Kader, one of the pioneers:

> When I need to find a work contract for someone or I have family that wants to come over I talk to my boss. If he needs someone, I talk to my family and ask if anyone is interested in coming here to work. If they are, they send their passport, we arrange the work contract and the employer takes care of the rest.
> (Male, 50, arrived in 1990)

This propinquity to bring family and acquaintances was visible among both established workers and recent arrivals. In fact, more than 20 per cent of the survey respondents arrived through family reunion, with men representing approximately 60 per cent of the total number of Moroccan agricultural workers in our sample who came to Portugal with a permit based on family ties. This assistance mechanism seems to have become particularly important in the last few years, partly because of the maturation of the migration process from Morocco to the Algarve, and partly due to the decreasing importance of direct recruitment campaigns in Morocco in the current context of economic contraction.

## 14.5 Concluding remarks

This chapter has sought to add to the limited research on agricultural migrant workers in Portugal. Its focus has been on a relatively small and highly specialised group: the Moroccan agricultural workers in the Algarve. We have been able to build in great detail, and with a significant degree of representativeness – a relatively large sample for a small population – a genealogy of the migration and labour incorporation of the Moroccan agricultural workers in the Algarve. This would be naturally much harder to achieve with larger groups.

We have stressed the importance of an immigrant labour force for the agricultural sector in the Algarve. As in other southern European countries, immigrants have been recruited by agricultural businesses as a cheaper and more flexible work force, a practice that contributes to reduce production costs and increase or at least maintain margins of profit in a context of economic crisis. In Portugal, and specifically in the Algarve, this trend appears to be relatively recent, having occurred only during the last 10 to 15 years.

Our case study revealed that the recruitment campaigns targeting Moroccans increased significantly during the years between 2000 and 2008. The rural background of the majority of the Moroccan workers in the Algarve, combined with their prior acquaintance with the type of agriculture practised in the region and, in some cases, even with the employers themselves, seem, at least partially, to explain the preference for Moroccan workers among transnational and regional employers. Social and kinship networks are also instrumental in further feeding these processes of recruitment. Given its similarities with the agriculture practised in the Algarve – namely greenhouse work and fruit and vegetable picking – the Kenitra region in northern Morocco has become a key area of recruitment.

Regionally, the labour incorporation of Moroccans into the agricultural sector is intimately related to the type of crops produced and the skills required. Thus, while women tend to settle around the Faro–Olhão axis, where greenhouse work and fresh fruit production predominates, men tend to cluster in the municipality of Silves, specialised in citrus production.

However, changes to the regional economy of the agricultural sector have been visible in the last few years, especially since 2008. Although work opportunities in the sector still seem to be available at the regional level, Moroccan migrants have experienced an increase in informal employment and a generalised deterioration of their working conditions. The relative stability of the agricultural labour market – pointed out by many Moroccans as an advantage of the Portuguese context when compared, for example, with Spain – has been achieved at the expense of cumulative concessions in terms of working conditions. This includes the acceptance of lower wages and, in particular, an increase in non-contractual, informal work and underemployment schemes. Recruitment campaigns in Morocco have also practically disappeared since the inception of the economic crisis in 2008. More recent changes such as the enlargement of the EU to include new countries such as Romania and Bulgaria also influenced the recruitment dynamics of agricultural workers to the Algarve by allowing companies to recruit more easily workers within the EU or to simply take advantage of the inflows of unskilled Romanian and Bulgarian workers arriving in Portugal. This also enables companies to avoid onerous and more legally challenging recruitment campaigns such as those conducted in Morocco. In addition, the maturation of Moroccan migration to Portugal, with an increase in family reunification over the last few years, has also contributed to the growth of an available immigrant workforce at the regional level. This has led to increasing levels of unemployment (or at least underemployment) and to a stronger reliance upon family budgets, thus reinforcing these workers' willingness to accept even more precarious working conditions.

Unlike other immigrant groups working in agriculture in the Algarve such as Eastern Europeans, Moroccans tend to settle more permanently and experience less (upward and even lateral) professional, social and geographical mobility, therefore remaining longer in unskilled jobs in the agricultural sector. It is interesting to note that, despite being aware of the mounting economic uncertainty facing Portugal, the Moroccans surveyed do not generally seem to be considering a change to their migratory projects. Indeed, about 72 per cent of the respondents to our questionnaire expressed their intention to stay in Portugal. For most Moroccans then, certain features associated with Portugal and the Algarve are emphasised as counterbalancing the overall disadvantages encountered, thus justifying their permanence in the country and region. In particular, they perceive life in Portugal and the Algarve to be safe, easy going and to lack the levels of discrimination that exist in other European countries such as Italy or Spain. They also strongly value the idea that it is easier to have access to legal documents in Portugal. This helps to explain why, in a context of decreasing work opportunities and increasing competition for jobs, the Moroccans employed in agricultural activities in the Algarve seem to increasingly value work stability, even if this means accepting deteriorating labour conditions.

Finally, from a medium- to long-term local development perspective, Moroccan agricultural workers, like other immigrants, have made several positive contributions to the rural areas in the Algarve: first, their know-how and permanence in the agricultural sector have prevented fields remaining fallow for prolonged periods or abandoned altogether; second, their permanent settlement in rural areas has contributed to the revitalisation of small villages that would have otherwise lost most or all of their population. The future of the Moroccan presence in the Algarve is, however, fairly uncertain. This appears to depend on the interplay of various factors: the enduring economic crisis in Portugal (and its effects on the regional agricultural sector), the increasingly improving prospects for economic development in Morocco, and the growing awareness of better opportunities in other European countries, especially once the Moroccan migrants have acquired a legal status that allows them to freely circulate within the EU. This sense of an uncertain future resonates in other Portuguese (and southern European) rural and agricultural areas that have become increasingly dependent on a migrant labour force, both from a demographic and economic perspective.

## Notes

1 THEMIS (Theorizing the Evolution of European Migration Systems) was a four-year European research project coordinated by Oxford University (2010–2013). The Portuguese partner was the Centre for Geographical Studies/Institute of Geography and Spatial Planning of the University of Lisbon. For more information see: http://www.imi.ox.ac.uk/research-projects/themis.
2 These are part of a larger project sample of 25 interviews and 207 questionnaires.
3 For further insights on Respondent Driven Sampling see: http://www.respondentdrivensampling.org/
4 All the interviews have been anonymised and pseudonyms have been used. All quotations were translated into English by the authors.

## References

Arnalte-Alegre, E. and Ortiz-Miranda, D. (2013). 'The "southern model" of European agriculture revisited: Continuities and dynamics' in Ortiz-Miranda, D., Moragues-Faus, A. and Arnalte-Alegre, E. (eds) *Agriculture in Mediterranean Europe. Between Old and New Paradigms*. Bingley: Emerald, pp. 37–74.

Cabral, A. (2007). *Marroquinos na Venda Ambulante*. Oporto: Fernando Pessoa University.

Corkill, D. (2005). 'Immigrants and a regional economy in Spain: The Case of Murcia'. *International Journal of Iberian Studies* 18 (1), pp. 23–36.

Corkill, D. and Eaton, M. (1998). 'Multicultural insertion in a small economy: Portugal's immigrant communities'. *South European Society and Politics* 3 (3), pp. 149–168.

de Haas, H. (2007). 'Morocco's migration experience: A transitional perspective'. *International Migration* 45 (4), pp. 39–70.

Faria, R. (2006). 'Marroquinos em Portugal: Imigração, religião e comunidade'. *Lusotopie* XIV (1), pp. 205–221.

Faria, R. (2008). 'Identidades en tránsito: Portugal como nuevo país de inmigración marroquí'. *Revista de Estudios Internacionales Mediterráneos (REIM)* 6, pp. 145–150.

Fonseca, M. L. (2008). 'New waves of immigration to small towns and rural areas in Portugal'. *Population, Space and Place* 14 (6), pp. 525–535.

Fonseca, M. L., Alegria, J. and Nunes, A. (2004). 'Immigration to medium sized cities and rural areas: The case of the Eastern Europeans in the Évora Region (Southern Portugal)' in Baganha, M. I. and Fonseca, M. L. (eds) *New Waves: Migration from Eastern to Southern Europe*, pp. 91–118. Lisbon: Luso-American Foundation.

Hellio, E. (2008). 'Importer de femmes pour exporter des fraises (Huelva)'. *Etudes Rurales* 182 (2), pp. 185–200.

Hellio, E. (2014). '"We don't have women in boxes". Channelling seasonal mobility of female farmworkers between Morocco and Andalusia' in Gertel, J. and Sippel, S. R. (eds) *Seasonal Workers in Mediterranean Agriculture: The Social Costs of Eating Fresh*. London: Routledge. pp. 141–157.

Kasimis, C. (2005). *Migrants in Rural Economies of Greece and Southern Europe*. Migration Information Source. Online, available from: http://www.migrationinformation.org/Feature/display.cfm?ID=337 (last access on 20 February 2014).

Kasimis, C. (2009). 'From enthusiasm to perplexity and scepticism: International migrants in the rural regions of Greece and Southern Europe' in Jentsch, B. and Simard, M. (eds) *International Migration and Rural Areas*. London: Ashgate, pp. 75–98.

Kasimis, C. and Papadopoulos, A. G. (2005). 'The multifunctional role of migrants in the Greek countryside: Implications for the rural economy and society'. *Journal of Ethnic and Migration Studies* 31 (1), pp. 99–127.

Kasimis, C., Papadopoulos, A. G. and Zacopoulou, E. (2003). 'Migrants in rural Greece'. *Sociologia Ruralis* 43 (2), pp. 167–184.

King, R. (2000). 'Southern Europe in the changing global map of migration' in King, R., Lazaridis, G. and Tsardanidis, C. (eds) *Eldorado or Fortress? Migration in Southern Europe*. London: Macmillan, pp. 1–26.

Mannon, S.E., Petrzelka, P., Glass, C. M. and Radel, C. (2012). 'Keeping them in their place: Migrant women workers in Spain's strawberry industry'. *International Journal of Sociology of Agriculture & Food* 19 (1), pp. 83–101.

Mesini, B. (2009). 'Enjeux des mobilites circulaires de main d'oeuvre: L'exemple des saisonniers étrangers dans l'agriculture méditerranéenne'. *Méditerranée* 113, pp. 105–112.

Moreno, J. (2014). 'Labour and gender relations in Moroccan strawberry culture' in Gertel, J. and Sippel, S.R. (eds) *Seasonal Workers in Mediterranean Agriculture: The Social Costs of Eating Fresh*. London: Routledge, pp. 199–210.

Morice, A. and Michalon, B. (2008). 'Les migrants dans l'agriculture: Vers une crise de main-d'oeuvre?'. *Etudes Rurales* 182 (2), pp. 9–28.

Portugal, Ministry of Agriculture, Rural Development and Fisheries – Policy and Planning Council (2007). *Citrinos*. Lisbon: Ministério da Agricultura, Desenvolvimento Rural e Pescas – Gabinete de Prospetiva e Planeamento.

Portugal, Ministry of Solidarity and Social Security (2009, 2012). *Cadres of Staff* (unpublished data).

Portugal, Service of Foreigners and Borders (2005–2013). *Annual Report on Immigration, Borders and Asylum*. Oeiras: Serviço de Estrangeiros e Fronteiras.

Portugal, Statistics Portugal. (2011a). *Population Census*. Lisbon: Instituto Nacional de Estatística.

Portugal, Statistics Portugal. (2011b). *Agricultural Census 2009*. Lisbon: Instituto Nacional de Estatística.

Ribas-Mateos, N. (2004). 'How can we understand immigration in Southern Europe?'. *Journal of Ethnic and Migration Studies* 30 (6), pp. 1045–1063.

# 15 Agricultural modernization, internal migration and the formation of a wage labour market in the Souss region, Morocco

*Mohamed Bouchelkha*

## 15.1 Introduction[1]

Contemporary dynamics and developments in Moroccan agriculture have been studied from a range of perspectives, for instance through the modernity/tradition dichotomy or in terms of technological advances, exports or competitiveness. However, researchers and agriculture sector actors alike tend to disregard the social conditions of farmers and labourers. This is clearly confirmed in the case of the Souss region. Souss is the country's leader producer and exporter of numerous types of fruit and vegetable, including citrus fruit, tomatoes and bananas. It possesses the largest area of greenhouse cultivation in Morocco, and is the location for a substantial number of packaging factories and foreign investors (namely French and Spanish companies). However, issues related to agricultural labour and its economic and social implications are rarely taken into consideration.

Over recent years, the mainly temporary migration of workers from subsistence farming towards to the so-called capitalist agriculture has become a widespread phenomenon across Morocco. Souss is an exemplary case that deserves in-depth study. A number of poor regions of Morocco, including the neighbouring areas of the High Atlas and Anti-Atlas mountains, provide a reserve of labour for Souss, while at the same time, the modernization of agriculture in Souss has depended upon the social reproduction of cheap and vulnerable labour both inside and outside the region.

Agricultural migrant labour in the Souss region needs to be understood within a broader historical context. In fact, increased labour mobility reflects the particular development of Moroccan agriculture and accompanying changes to social relations in rural society (Sippel, 2014). This chapter is therefore organized in two sections. The first section outlines the evolution of agriculture in Morocco, and especially in Souss region, from the colonial era to the contemporary process of neoliberal globalization. The second section describes how the current agricultural labour market in Souss stems from internal migration and from the (forced) transformation of the marginalized rural population into agricultural wage labourers. It also considers the socio-demographic characteristics of this migrant labour force as well as their working and living conditions.

Data have been collected during a number of field surveys conducted between 2000 and 2013. These surveys mainly concerned agricultural workers employed in the tomato and green bean supply chains, which are among the most important crops exported to foreign markets (Bouchelkha, 2012b, 2013; van der Wal *et al.*, 2013; Fairfood, 2015).

## 15.2 The rise of capitalist agriculture

### *15.2.1 The sustained nature of agrarian capitalist accumulation in Souss*

Colonialism did not affect Souss as early as other Moroccan regions such as Doukkala and Haouz. The French Protectorate was imposed in 1912, but, due to the anti-colonial resistance, it was not until 1934 that the region was brought under the complete control of France and its countryside entered into a new social and economic era (Bouchelkha, 2007). The establishment of a market economy and the loss of the right of access to land gradually forced an increasing number of peasants to give up subsistence farming to look for wage labour in capitalist agriculture or in urban centres.

The colonial era triggered deep changes in the agrarian structure of the country. Vast irrigated plantations owned by French settlers produced citrus fruit and early fruits and vegetables for exportation to France or to Moroccan urban centres. This production was based on the partial mechanisation of farming operations as well as on motor pumps for underground water extraction for irrigation. The collapse of collective land tenure and the expropriation of a great number of small farmers from some or all of their property under different pretexts (for instance, the inability to prove property rights due to a lack of written records) led to the economic and social marginalization of smallholders and to an increase in the number of landless peasants. These new circumstances gave rise to two major developments: rural exodus and the development of agricultural wage labour.

If the modern/traditional dichotomy in Moroccan agriculture emerged during the colonial era and the arrival of French settlers, this would be further strengthened after the country's independence in 1956, which saw the transfer of the settlers' property to new Moroccan landowners. This also occurred in Souss, where settlers' plantations passed into the hands of high-ranking administrative figures and new local elites. The new stage in the development of capitalist agriculture that took shape after independence was concentrated in the downstream area of the Souss plain and focused on growing fruits and vegetables in open fields.

This type of agriculture remained dominant until the beginning of the 1980s when new production conditions and the international marketing of products ushered in a new era of Moroccan agriculture and particularly in Souss, with the rise of greenhouse cultivation. This was accompanied by a second wave of property takeovers during which land in Souss was increasingly coveted by both Moroccan and foreign capital. This period is also connected with the implementation of the Structural Adjustment Policy recommended by International Financial Institutions. The adjustment programme implemented in agriculture revolved around two major axes: the reduction of state involvement and trade liberalization (Akesbi, 1996, 2014; Kydd and Thoyer, 1992).

### *15.2.2 Souss agriculture between the national economy and global markets*

Colonial settlers first paved the way to export-oriented agriculture in Souss, particularly in the case of citrus fruits, early fruits and vegetables, and floriculture (Brien, 1952). The practice of an export-oriented agriculture was further developed following independence in a relatively conducive socio-economic environment. However, the expansion of the European Economic Community (EEC) raised barriers to the commercialization of Moroccan agricultural products on European markets, forcing producers to meet a rigid exportation schedules and standards (as set out in the 1976 and 1996 agreements) (Oulaalou, 1996; Berndt and Boeckler, 2011). Since 2008, Morocco enjoys an advanced status in its partnership with Europe that has contributed to alleviate these barriers (Akesbi, 2014).

Export-oriented and industrialized agriculture is considerably important for the Moroccan economy: it contributes between 15 and 20 per cent of its GDP and strengthens its balance of trade. As a major source of export income and employment creation, citrus fruits and vegetables have been accorded priority in agricultural development programmes since national independence.

In 2008, fruits and vegetables accounted for about 16 per cent of the national utilized agricultural area, out of a total of 1,320,000 hectares, 1,060,000 hectares consisted of fruit plantations, while 260,000 hectares were used for vegetable growing. The overall production for 2007 reached nearly 9 million tonnes: 3 million tonnes of fruit and more than 6 million tonnes of vegetables. Roughly 900,000 tonnes of early fruits and vegetables (400,000 of which for export) were produced by about 8,000 producers who created more than 12 million working days (Ministry of Agriculture, 2008). Souss is the national leader in terms of vegetable production and exports. In 2012, the utilized area for the cultivation of vegetables reached 24,476 hectares, a third of which (8,079 ha) were occupied by greenhouses. Tomato production alone uses 5,527 hectares (or 68.4 per cent) of all greenhouses, while field-grown tomatoes are far less significant and in decline (81 ha in 2012 compared with 205 ha in 2006) (ORMVA/SM, 2012). The cultivation of vegetables is concentrated in the province of Chtouka Ait Baha, which accounts for 58 per cent of the production of early fruits and vegetables and 82 per cent of all greenhouses (ORMVA/SM, 2010).

Souss has become the region with the largest area of greenhouses in the country. Greenhouses were initially used for growing indigenous fruit and vegetables for the domestic market, but they soon extended to include other varieties, which aimed at substituting costly imports, or at strengthening and diversifying exports, like bananas (Bouchelkha, 1997). Likewise, citrus fruit production, which on the eve of independence covered almost 5,000 hectares, had risen to 35,670 hectares in 2010 (ORMVA/SM, 2011). Furthermore, this system of production, which requires high capital investment and expertise, has reached an advanced level of technological development in Souss, with, for example, the introduction of state-of-the-art irrigation and fertigation systems and new growing methods. In short, this form of agriculture has almost reached the level of 'developed' countries. It is worth noting that in addition to the efforts made by local and national producers, foreign investors have also made a considerable contribution to the transfer of technology.

### *15.2.3 Outsourcing, or the new mobility of international capital*

Since decades, the capitalist agriculture in Souss has attracted national and foreign actors. According to my own research findings, 52 per cent out of 228 greenhouse producers in 2012 were Moroccan. Nevertheless, their activity is limited to only 24 per cent of the total cultivable greenhouse area. In fact, local producers are mainly small farmers who on average cultivate a surface area of less than 4.6 hectares. Meanwhile, foreign producers account for just under half of all producers but use 76 per cent of the total greenhouse surface area.

The number of European investors in the Souss region increased from 5 producers in 1988 to 39 in 2000 to 134 in 2012. Likewise, the area utilized by foreign investors increased from 1,124 hectares in 2000 to 2,948 hectares in 2012 (see Table 15.1). The larger plantations – mainly owned by foreigners but in a few cases also by Moroccans – have an area of 300 hectares or more, and are to be found principally in the area of Chtouka.

European investors are usually companies that produce fruit and vegetables for one or more European countries, and have found it convenient to outsource part of their production to Morocco. This process has been encouraged by two main factors: first, the higher production costs in European Union (EU) countries, particularly as a result of higher property taxes and labour costs; and, second, the favourable climatic conditions, which make Souss a natural greenhouse and thus further reduce production costs (while in Europe greenhouses often need to be heated).

*Table 15.1* Investor's nationality and surface area of plantations

| *Country* | *Number of investors* | *Number of plantations* | *Surface area (ha)* |
|---|---|---|---|
| France | 24 | 60 | 1,260 |
| Spain | 31 | 39 | 994 |
| Slovakia | 1 | 3 | 77 |
| Germany | 3 | 3 | 10 |
| Netherlands | 4 | 18 | 426 |
| England | 3 | 3 | 74 |
| Italy | 2 | 2 | 32 |
| Soudan | 2 | 2 | 27 |
| Yemen | 2 | 2 | 9 |
| Belgium | 1 | 1 | 9 |
| Palestine | 1 | 1 | 30 |
| Total | 74 | 134 | 2,948 |

Source: ORMVA/SM (2012).

Outsourcing has appealed mainly to foreign investors of EU countries that possess historical ties with Morocco. In fact, French and Spanish investors accounted for 74 per cent of foreign entrepreneurs in 2012. Some of them have set up partnerships with Moroccan investors. All of them are involved in the same production: early fruit and vegetables and new crops (such as beans and courgettes). Spanish investors cultivated 994 hectares in 2012, which amounted to almost 34 per cent of the total surface area used by foreigners. A number of the companies are based in areas of Spain specialized in fruit and vegetable production (such as the province of Almería in Andalucía) and have outsourced part of their production to Souss in order to be present on European markets all year round (Moreno Nieto, 2012; Hellio, 2008, 2014). Duroc is one of the most active Spanish companies, which began producing in Souss in 1989. Duroc is the result of a partnership between the Moroccan conglomerate Maresprim (which owns 60 per cent of shares), and the large Spanish firm DuranGranada. Meanwhile, French investors had production interests in about 1,260 hectares in 2012, 43 per cent of the total surface area connected to foreigners. Their production units have an average surface area of about 21 hectares. However, the Spanish presence has increased in recent years and their investments have already exceeded those of the French.

## 15.3 The development of an agricultural wage labour market

### *15.3.1 The transformation of a marginalized rural population: from* **khammass** *to wage labourers*

The emergence of agricultural wage labourers coincided with the changes in the Souss countryside during the early stages of the French Protectorate in Morocco. Among the first wage labourers were the *khammassis*. This term designated a traditional practice in which tenants received one-fifth of the harvest from a landowner in exchange for their labour. '*Khammassat*' has been considered as a form of slavery (Gerraoui, 1985; El Khayari, 1987), especially because by the end of the harvest the *khammass* had already used up their share and consequently recommitted themselves to their masters. According to Paul Pascon, although the French settlers certainly exploited the former *khammassis* as farm workers, the latter now received better wages and enjoyed better working conditions than they had under the pre-capitalist mode of production that once reigned in Moroccan society (Pascon, 1980). One of the causes of the emergence of agricultural wage labour was that a great number of small peasants had no means of survival other than agricultural work. For many, this entailed a break from subsistence agriculture.

The number of agricultural workers employed in Souss by settlers is estimated to have been around 3,500 workers immediately prior to independence (Pascon and Ennaji, 1986). In 1952, the daily wage was around 120 francs (Brien, 1952).[2] In contrast, the start of the colonial era certain activities had been characterized by forced labour, especially in road works between Taroudant and Agadir, but also in land reclamation for agriculture use, the preparation of citrus plantations, the fight against locust invasions and the clearance of indigenous Argan trees.

The colonial authorities contributed to create 'the social conditions necessary for the reproduction of the colonial model by encouraging the emergence of social groups that facilitated the preservation of the regime' (Ben Mlih, 1990, p. 39). Consequently, the penetration of settlers into the Souss countryside and the subsequent modernization of agriculture from the 1940s onwards, far from bringing benefits to local peasants, led to a new social stratification; agricultural workers were one of its key components.

Although agricultural wage labour began to emerge in Moroccan agriculture from the 1940s onwards, family labour, that was often unpaid, continued to dominate on family-owned plantations after independence and through until the 1970s. Young people were able to break free from this situation only by migrating to cities or to agricultural areas where they could find paid jobs on large plantations. The agricultural policies adopted by the Moroccan governments after independence in 1956 favoured the modernization of agriculture, which generated inter- and intra-regional imbalances, and consequently exacerbated the economic and social exclusion of peasants and increased their mobility towards other Moroccan regions and European countries.

### *15.3.2 Large-scale labour migration*

The recent changes to Souss agriculture have impacted upon the demographic structure of the region. The new type of agriculture requires a very large labour force, which has arrived from outside the region, such as the Middle Atlas mountains or coastal plains like Abda. Souss has experienced higher growth rates than other parts of Morocco and increased population densities. Internal migrants from the Middle Atlas refer to Souss as 'Morocco's Italy' because as Italy has represented one of the main foreign destinations for migrants, Souss has become an alternative destination for those who are unable or unwilling to move abroad.

In 2007, the two main cash crops (citrus fruit and vegetables) produced in the Souss region accounted for around 20 million working days. Vegetables were the most important labour recruiting sector, accounting for 67 per cent of this figure, while the citrus fruit industry provided the remaining employment (ORMVA/SM, 2007).

The Chtouka plain, the new pole of attraction for agricultural activities in the region, has witnessed the greatest population growth in the Souss region. For instance, the population of the municipality of Ait Amira increased from 13,820 in 1980 to 25,256 people in 1994 with an annual growth of 4.66 per cent, which was the highest growth rate in all the rural areas of Souss-Massa.[3] The municipality's population continued to increase, reaching 47,458 inhabitants in 2004 with an annual growth rate of 6.5 per cent between 1994 and 2004 (RGPH, 2004).

If the citrus-growing area has always been, since independence, an attractive destination for migrants from the Atlantic plains and plateaus, new fruit and vegetable crops of Chtouka attracted a working population mainly from the Middle Atlas. The various surveys I have conducted since 2000 confirm that over 70 per cent of the working population originates from this part of Morocco, mainly from rural areas around the towns of Khenifra, BeniMellal and Khemisset, as well as from neighbouring plateaus like Khouribga. The second major source of immigrants is the province of Safi in the region of Abda.

One of the main demographic characteristics of the migrant working population is that they are young: 65 per cent of those surveyed are aged between 20 and 35 and of these, 48 per cent are under 30 years old.[4] Indeed, the physically demanding nature of the work (the high temperatures in greenhouses, soil preparation, manual harvesting and the risks linked to spraying agrochemicals) makes it largely unsuitable for older people. For this reason, only about 13 per cent of workers are aged over 45 years old.

A further key aspect of this labour force is the predominance of women both on farms and in packing plants. They represent 68 per cent of the labourers I was able to interview in my 2012–2013 survey. As recent studies show, the feminization of the labour market has become a common feature of numerous agro-exporting areas in peripheral countries (Moreno Nieto, 2012). According to union representatives interviewed during my research, in Souss this is the result of the producers' preference to employ women, who they believe to be more submissive and willing to work. A large proportion of women are single: this category represents 45 per cent of the sample in my survey. In addition to young unmarried women (and men), single mothers also have a significant presence. This is a widespread phenomenon in Chtouka: according to a national study[5] carried out between 2003 and 2009, there were 38,623 births by single women in the region of Souss Massa Darâa. A significant portion of those giving birth at Agadir hospital and who found 'shelter' at the Oum El Banine Association[6] were young women who were working on farms or in agro-industries in Biougra and Ait Amira, two major areas of production and concentration of farm workers in the Chtouka plain (Arrazi, 2012). In addition, it is worth pointing out the presence of a substantial number of couples with children, but who do not possess marriage or civil status documents. Representatives of civil associations and local authorities have stated that this irregular situation poses serious difficulties for children to attend school.

Illiteracy is a major problem in rural areas. According to a survey conducted in 2004, in the province of Chtouka for example, more than half (52.5 per cent) of the population were illiterate, of which women represent 69.7 per cent (RGPH, 2004); over 72 per cent of the rural women of the same province were illiterate (RGPH, 2004). Nevertheless, the working population, mainly those who come from other regions, tend to have general literacy skills. My inquiries have found that 53 per cent of workers have completed primary or secondary education, while the remainder have not attended school. Most of my interviewees declared that their children attended school. In fact, all interviewees viewed school as a priority for their children. The wishes expressed to us are usually of the following kind: 'we wouldn't like our children to do the same hard jobs as us and have no future . . .' (farm worker, woman, 45 years old).

In addition, my fieldwork has shown that many couples and single women with young children have to endure a lack of childcare. The lack of nursery facilities has given rise to a new figure known as the '*mourabbia*', which in Arabic means 'educator'. The '*mourabbia*' is usually an old woman, no longer able to do agricultural work, who offers to take care of the young children of working mothers in her home. Her monthly wage ranges between 150 and 200 dirhams, which works out at about 9 to 13 per cent of the Guaranteed Minimum Agricultural Wage (GMAW).

Labour migration has also been accompanied by an increase in inadequate accommodation in the absence of decent housing facilities. With the intense demographical growth, uncontrolled and self-built housing has developed. Rural areas have seen the establishment of new *douars* (villages) with names that sometimes refer to the geographical or ethnic origins of workers, such as Laarab and Hmar, or simply to the construction material, for instance Douar Mika, which refers to the recycled plastic sheeting from old greenhouses.

A sizeable number of the labourers, who I have observed and interviewed in recent years, live in the workplace itself. This category is mainly made up of women coming from outside the region. This situation can be explained by the fact that these young migrants are unable to find housing in local towns and villages due to the population's reluctance to offer accommodation to female workers. These women generally live two or three to a room but, depending on labour needs, this can rise to five per room. This workplace accommodation usually provides water, electricity and other services like a shop or even a prayer room.

If the number of workers who pay a rent for their accommodation is still very high, a growing number of people in recent years have been able to buy property, for example in places such as the town of Ait Amira. This particular category of worker represents 38 per cent of the population according to the survey I conducted in 2012–2013. The growth of this category is partially encouraged by a favourable political environment[7].

### *15.3.3 Working conditions in fruit and vegetable production*

The changes to agriculture in Souss have led to a distinct division of labour within agricultural companies. Agricultural labour is classified according to a worker's specialization and permanence in the job. The importance of such a division of labour is not only due to the size of the farm but to the increased range of farming activities.

In Souss, unskilled labourers represent more than 80 per cent of the total farm workforce. On larger farms during harvest time, their numbers can exceed 200 workers. Generally, agricultural companies employ a small number of permanent workers to carry out specialized tasks and depend heavily on seasonal workers for large-scale farming operations. The total number of permanent farm workers at a national level does not exceed 140,000. This number includes mainly labourers working for big agricultural companies, such as SODEA and SOGETA.[8] Permanent agricultural labourers thus represent a privileged minority because the vast majority of workers are casual (Pascon and Ennaji, 1986).

The vast majority of those surveyed in Souss do not work with a formal contract.[9] Workers usually sign a fixed-term contract, which subsequently turns into an oral contract; 91 per cent of the surveyed workers find themselves in this situation. Some companies and tomato producers recruit farm workers in public places called *mouquef*,[10] and pay them at the end of each day without any written or oral obligation. This recruitment practice increases the job insecurity of workers. It should be underlined that the Moroccan Labour Code is based on the notion of flexibility at the expense of the right to work, which includes both the right to hold a job and the right to keep it.

The government has not yet delivered on its commitments to standardize the salaries of different sectors. Agricultural workers in Morocco are still discriminated in terms of wages, working hours and union rights compared to workers in the industrial sector. In principle, these workers should be paid according to the Guaranteed Minimum Agricultural Wage (GMAW). The GMAW currently stands at 63.36 dirhams per day or 7.92 dh per hour, while the Guaranteed Minimum Industrial Wage (GMIW) is currently 12.24 dh/hour. This meagre minimum daily wage (just under 6 euros) hardly guarantees farm workers a minimum living standard.

Wage differentiation may depend on a worker's seniority. If seniority is applied, it increases the wage by 5 per cent or more, depending on the years of service. Agricultural wages appear to be insufficient for the majority of workers who have to often provide resources for large families. Most households are below the poverty line as defined by the High Commissioner for Planning in 2004 (which was set at 1,700 dh per month). Moreover, the surveys that I conducted between 2012 and 2013 in tomato production chains showed that the 65 per cent of respondents had an unstable income due to the seasonal nature of the jobs. Consequently, there are some periods when workers are without any source of income.

For agriculture, the normal annual working time is fixed at 2,496 hours a year, which works out at 48 hours per week and is divided into periods depending on crop requirements. However, my inquiries have shown that the majority (69 per cent) of those interviewed work 8 hours a day, while a further 21 per cent work more than 8 hours a day. The latter group consists usually of those who work in packing plants and who have the opportunity to work overtime. There are slight differences in the number of hours because it depends on the season and on the labour needs of the company. In addition, piecework is a common practice on a huge number of farms, in which case a worker might work for just 5 instead of 8 hours a day and still receive the same wage on completing a given task.

Workers receive, in the best cases, 15 days of paid annual leave, but this all ultimately depends on the 'generosity' of agricultural companies. It should be noted that the value of annual leave depends on the seniority of the worker and the number of days worked in the year. In contrast, workers hired from the *mouquef* are deprived of this allowance because they are not officially recorded. During this 'leave', 61 per cent of those surveyed admit that they do nothing but wait for the beginning of the next agricultural year, 20 per cent are engaged in other activities, such as construction work and general housework, while 11 per cent look for work on other farms as day labourers.

My fieldwork found that the majority of workers contributed to their parents' budgets: 70 per cent of those surveyed, most of whom were women, sent money to their parents in their villages of origin. Meanwhile, the number of individuals that each worker supported varied from one to eight persons, which rendered the wages even more insufficient.

Due to the high proportion of casual and seasonal workers among the agricultural labour force, workers' social security benefits remain insignificant.[11] Considerable differences nevertheless exist between companies. Recent data show notable improvements to working conditions since 2009. Larger companies, in particular, have adhered to the pension and insurance fund of the CNSS (*Caisse Nationale de la Sécurité Sociale*).[12] Similarly, there are many more workers who are union members, particularly after years of labour struggles. Nevertheless, some companies are far from granting workers the right to benefit from the CNSS because they mainly hire them through the *mouquef*.

Labourers working in the fields and greenhouses in Chtouka Ait Baha live in neighbouring *douars* and villages and have long had to depend on inadequate means of transportation, although some companies have made substantial improvements in recent years. Nevertheless some of the workers use the trucks and pick-ups that are laid on by farms complain about overcrowdedness and the gender mix. In addition, road accidents, some of which fatal, are not uncommon.

Gender inequality is evident when it comes to granting privileges or promotions, and numerous managers and supervisors are known to practise favouritism. Moreover, the harassment of female workers in the workplace has often been denounced by trade unions, while the Moroccan Association for Human Rights and other organizations have even reported cases of rape on farms. Similar situations exist in other agricultural areas, such as the strawberry plantations in the north of the country, where sexual violence is a common occurrence (Moreno Nieto, 2012).

## 15.4 Conclusion

This chapter has aimed to show that the modernization of Moroccan agriculture – especially in the Souss region – has gone hand in hand with the formation of a wage labour market that has depended on the proletarianization of former small peasants and internal mobility. The importance of wage labour has steadily risen during the different stages of agricultural development in Morocco: from the birth of agrarian capitalism in the years following independence to the development of relations between Morocco and the EEC and later the EU, the impact of Structural Adjustment Programme and the globalization of supply chains and markets. The development of capitalist agriculture in Souss during the second half of the twentieth century gave rise to a process of land concentration that expelled peasants from their smallholdings and forced them to become wage workers. The formation of a wage labour market in the Souss region would be nurtured by former peasants from Souss itself and by internal migrants from other regions of Morocco.

Originating in particular from the Middle Atlas area of the country, and driven by poverty and unemployment, migrant workers constitute an uprooted and relatively docile labour force exploited by export-oriented agricultural companies, as local people have increasingly abandoned farm work.

Intensive agriculture as it is currently practised is undoubtedly a source of job creation. However, as I have shown, it also generates social marginalization and exclusion by consigning masses of workers to live under the poverty line. These social problems have led to a rise in union organization and an emergent class consciousness among workers. The most influential union is the *Fédération Nationale du Secteur Agricole* (FNSA, National Federation of Agricultural Sector), affiliate of the *Union Marocaine de Travail (*UMT, Workers' Moroccan Union). Holding meetings and staging strikes has become a common practice, although some militants and union officers have been arrested. This fact exposes the fragility of the workers' rights and the permanent risk of being unfairly dismissed or tried before the courts. In fact, the precarious condition and informal status of most migrant workers makes it difficult for them to engage in union activities. Their situation consequently contributes to keep wages low and to perpetuate the current poor working conditions for the majority of agricultural labourers.

## Notes

1 Some parts of the present chapter present ideas and findings published elsewhere (Bouchelkha, 2012a). It includes updated data from more recent investigations (see also Bouchelkha, 2012b, 2013).

2 Farm labour was sometimes paid in kind, particularly through the provision of sugar (500 grams per day per person).

3 According to the results of a survey conducted by the High Commissioner for Planning in 2007, two-thirds of the population of six villages of Ait Amira were internal migrants. Moreover, 48 per cent of the population had migrated to the area with the last ten years (HCP, 2007).

4 This is based on data from my survey conducted between 2012 and 2013. The investigation involved 153 workers, 104 of whom were women.

5 This study is entitled: "Morocco of single mothers: Diagnostic study of the situation, scale and reality of the situation. Actions itinerary representations and life experiences", April-December 2010. INSAF Association. Reference quoted by Arrazi (2012).

6 The Oum El Banin Association, based in Agadir, aims to help to women and children in difficult situations. The association provides accommodation and its main goal is to fully support mothers with newborn children.

7 It is worth noting that access to property was made easier by the events of the 'Arab Spring'. In fact, in response authorities displayed a lax attitude towards unauthorised building of new houses, which led to hundreds of families to build their homes in record time.

8 SODEA (Société de Développement Agricole) and SOGETA (Société de Gestion des Terres Agricoles) are government farm companies which assumed the management of the land of former settlers. Significantly, as of 2005, the government transferred the first part of these lands to private investors in the form of long-term leases.

9 Work contacts and rights of workers are regulated by the provisions of the Labour Code no. 65–99 of September 2003, which came into force in 6 May 2004.

10 In some *Moquef*, such as in Ouled Teima and Biougra, only women are recruited.

11 In 2000 at national level, only 30,000 out of 130,000 permanent workers were registered with the *Caisse Nationale de Sécurité Sociale* (CNSS), the national social security fund. Only 19 per cent of all workers in the farming sector, in other words 160,981 out of 840,000 workers, were registered with the CNSS in 2012, according to CNSS estimates.

12 Registering with the social security has become a means of improving the family income as workers with children are entitled to family allowances (200 dirhams per child per month for the first three children). Non-registration is therefore often a cause for workers' anger.

## References

Akesbi, N. (1996). 'La politique d'ajustement structurel dans l'agriculture au Maroc. Risquesetpérils du désengagement de l'Etat' in Mohamed Elloumi (ed.) *Politiques agricoles et stratégies paysannes au Maghreb et en méditerranée occidentale*. Tunis: ALIF-Les Éditions de la Méditerraneé, pp. 71–93.

Akesbi, N. (2014). 'Which agricultural policy for which food security in Morocco?' in Gertel, J. and Sippel, S. (eds) *Seasonal Workers in Mediterranean Agriculture. The Social Costs of Eating Fresh*. London: Routledge, pp. 167–174.

Arrazi, N. (2012). 'Workers in veil' under the guidance of the *Association des Femmes du Sud*.

Ben Mlih, A. (1990). *Structures politiques du Maroc colonial*. Paris: L'Harmattan.

Berndt, C. and Boeckler, M. (2011). 'Performative regional (dis)integration: transnational markets, mobile commodities, and bordered North-South differences'. *Environment and Planning A*, vol. 43, pp. 1057–1078.

Bouchelkha, M. (1997). 'Evolution récente et dynamique spatiale des cultures sous serres au Maroc, le cas du bananier de Massa'. *RGM*, vol. 17 (1–2), pp. 91–105.

Bouchelkha, M. (2007). *Les campagnes du Souss Massa. Mutations récentes et dynamiques socio-spatiales*. Marrakech: Imprimerie Al watanya.

Bouchelkha, M. (2012a). 'Agriculture capitaliste et développement du salariat agricole au Maroc à l'heure de la mondialisation: le cas du Maroc' in Bouchelkha M. (ed.) *Maroc du Sud et du Sahara. Défis et structurels et mondialisation*. Agadir: Imprimerie Chourouq.

Bouchelkha, M (2012b). 'Etude sur les conditions de travail et relations commerciales dans la production des haricots verts au Maroc: cas de la région du Souss Massa'. Funded by SOMO (*The Centre for Research on Multinational Corporations*) http://somo.nl/ (last access on 20/2/2016).

Bouchelkha, M. (2013). 'Etude sur les conditions sociales de production de la tomate dans la région de Souss Massa Draa'. Funded by *Fair food International*. http://www.fairfood.org/ (last access on 20/2/2016).

Brien, P. (1952). *La colonisation agricole européenne et l'évolution de la plaine du Souss*, mémoire de stage, ENA.

El Khayari, T. (1987). *Agriculture au Maroc*. Rabat: Okad Afrique.

Fairfood (2015). *The Fruits of Their Labour. The Low Wages Behind Moroccan Tomatoes Sold in European Supermarkets*. Amsterdam: Fairfood.

Guerraoui, D. (1985). *Agriculture et développement au Maroc*. Casablanca: Ed. Maghrébine.

Haut Commissariat au Plan (HCP) (2007). *Etude sur les conditions sociales au niveau de la commune d'Ait Amira*. Agadir: HCP.

Hellio, E. (2008). 'Importer des femmes pour exporter des fraises' in *Etudes rurales*, no. 182, pp. 185–200.

Hellio, E. (2014). '"We don't have women in boxes": Channelling seasonal mobility of female farmworkers between Morocco and Andalusia' in Gertel, J. and Sippel, S. (eds)

*Seasonal Workers in Mediterranean Agriculture. The Social Costs of Eating Fresh.* London: Routledge, pp. 141–157.

INSAF Association. (2010). 'Morocco of single mothers: Diagnostic study of the situation, the scale and the reality of the situation. Actions, itinerary representations and life experiences.' April-December 2010. http://www.insaf.ma/ (last access on 20/2/2016).

Kydd, J. and Thoyer, S. (1992). *Structural Adjustment and Moroccan Agriculture: An Assessment of the Reforms in the Sugar and Cereal Sectors*, Working Paper No. 70, OECD, Development Centre.

Ministry of Agriculture (2008). Annual Report.

Moreno Nieto, J. (2012). 'Faut-il des mains de femmes pour cueillir les fraises? Dynamiques de la gestion de la main d'œuvre et du travail dans le secteur du pérmétre irrigué du Loukkos (Maroc)' *Les Etudes et Essais du Centre Jacques Berque*, no. 11.

ORMVA/SM (Office Régional de La Mise en Valeur Agricole /Souss-Massa). (2007). Rapport d'activité de la campagne 2007/2008. Agadir.

ORMVA/SM (Office Régional de La Mise en Valeur Agricole /Souss-Massa). (2011). Rapport d'activité de la campagne 2010/2011. Agadir.

ORMVA/SM (Office Régional de La Mise en Valeur Agricole /Souss-Massa). (2010). Rapport d'activité de la campagne 2009/2010. Agadir.

ORMVA/SM (Office Régional de La Mise en Valeur Agricole /Souss-Massa). (2012). Rapport d'activité de la campagne 2011/2012. Agadir.

Oulaalou, F. (1996). *Après Barcelone ... le Maghreb est nécessaire*. Rabat: Les éditions Toubkal et l'Harmattan.

Pascon, P. (1980). *Etudes Rurales, idées et enquêtes sur la campagne marocaine*. Tanger: Ed. Marocaines et Internationales.

Pascon, P. and Ennaji, M. (1986). *Les paysans sans terres au Maroc*. Casablanca: Toubkal.

RGPH- Haut-Commissariat au Plan du Maroc (2004). Province of Chtouka Ait Baha CAB: Chtouka Ait Baha.

Sippel S. R. (2014). 'Disrupted livelihoods? Intensive agriculture and labour markets in the Moroccan Souss' in Gertel, J and Sippel, S. (eds) *Seasonal Workers in Mediterranean Agriculture. The Social Costs of Eating Fresh.* London: Routledge, pp. 186–198.

van der Wal, S., Scheele, F., and Theuws, M. (2013). *Spilling the Beans. Precarious work in Morocco's green beans production for Dutch supermarkets.* SOMO (The Centre for Research on Multinational Corporations). http://somo.nl/publications-en/Publication_3928/?searchterm= (last access on 20/2/2016).

# Part V

# Conflicts and resistances

# 16 Rural and farmers' protest movements in Tunisia and Egypt in the era of Arab revolts

*Alia Gana*

## 16.1 Introduction

Most analyses of the 2010–2012 'Arab revolts' have paid little attention to rural protest movements in the region. Yet both in Tunisia and in Egypt, the popular revolts that led to the fall of the Ben Ali and Mubarak regimes were preceded by numerous conflicts and social mobilizations, which had significant effects on rural and farming areas.

The 2010–2011 popular uprising in Tunisia originated in rural and inland areas and later spread to the major cities of the country. After the fall of President Ben Ali, protest movements in rural and agricultural areas grew and were characterized mainly by demands for better access to land and economic resources. Meanwhile, the violent conflicts that had shaken rural Egypt since the effective implementation of the 1992 land law were rekindled with the insurrectional movement of January 2011. While the uprising of 25 January 2011 in Egypt has often been characterized as an urban movement (Pagès El-Karoui and Vignal, 2011), several testimonies attest to a wide participation of peasants and young people from the countryside in the mass demonstrations in cities both before and after the ousting of Hosni Mubarak. In addition, until the military took over power, farmers and peasants continued to take an active part in different actions and in the renewal of the trade union movement.

This chapter is based on a review of press articles and on interviews conducted between 2012 and 2014 in Tunisia and Egypt with a range of different actors: farmers, peasants, members of farmers' unions, activists of civil rights organizations, representatives of the agricultural institutions and experts on rural issues. It has three main objectives: (a) to assess the role of farmers and peasants in triggering the popular revolts in Tunisia and Egypt; (b) to explore the processes behind rural protest movements and their links with the development strategies that were taking place in the two countries; and (c) to evaluate the capacity of rural and farmers' organizations to influence public policy and the orientation of agricultural development.

## 16.2 The underlying sources of the popular revolts in rural and farming areas

Far from being sporadic and localized events, the popular uprisings in Tunisia and Egypt had deep roots. They were both closely tied to the profound transformations that the two countries had experienced as a result of their engagement in a process of economic liberalization and their opening to the world market. Structural adjustment policies, which were initiated in Tunisia during the late 1980s and in Egypt in the early 1990s, would lead, in fact, to large-scale privatization, to the liberalization of prices and trade, and to significant cuts in public expenditure (such as lower consumption subsidies and a reduction of public employment). While reinforcing the orientation of their national economies towards the exports of goods and services (manufacturing industry, tourism, agricultural production), these policy reforms would expose both countries to the fierce competition of world markets (particularly in the case of the textile industry) and would have very negative impacts on employment. The structural adjustment policies also had major consequences on the agricultural sector and rural communities. By encouraging new forms of integration into the global economy, these policies implied a new role for the farming sector: that of reinforcing the contribution of agriculture to the balance of trade through the promotion of export-oriented farming and the expansion of irrigated areas for the production of fruits and vegetables (Ayeb, 2010; Blanc, 2012; Gana, 2012, 2013).

Structural adjustment in Tunisia resulted in a major shift in agricultural policy, with the privatization of state farms, cuts in farm subsidies, the liberalization of agricultural prices, the reorganization of the farm credit system and the gradual privatization of food marketing networks. These policy changes fostered the reallocation of economic resources towards large-scale and corporate agricultural enterprises to the detriment of the family-farming sector and rain-fed agriculture. The profound transformation to the economic environment of farming activities, the changing conditions of access to land, water and credit, and rising production costs, increased farmers' indebtedness but also land degradation, favoured the marginalization or even the exclusion of small farmers, especially in the rain-fed agriculture areas (Gana, 1998). These dynamics have been manifested in the major changes in patterns of rural livelihoods, and indicate a major break in the conditions that define households' access to land, i.e. a weakening of land rights based on family survival and a reconstitution of these rights in favour of those who can use farm land as a means of production (Gana, 1998). As a result of the changing farm production conditions and patterns of social reproduction, processes of differentiation began to increase, including within family farms themselves. With decreasing farm subsidies and growing competition for land resources, the capacity for reproduction of a large proportion of family farms became increasingly dependent on the diversification of income sources. The share of pluriactive farm households has been steadily growing and in recent years has represented almost 60 per cent of small farmers (MINAGRI, 2006). Among this group of landholders, survival strategies have depended increasingly on the off-farm wage labour of household members, indicating a progressive exodus from agriculture.[1] While calling into question the utilization of land as a means of livelihood and a mechanism of social redistribution, these processes have challenged the role of the state as a mediator in processes of liberalization and commoditization. Furthermore, as rural out-migration and non-farm employment opportunities have declined, small farms have become survival spaces for jobless household members (Elloumi, 2011), which has increased the pressure on family resources and exacerbated social frustrations in the same rural areas[2] where the movement of social protest first emerged.

The roots of the revolt in the rural areas of Egypt are also profound. They originate in the implementation of economic liberalization policies initiated in the mid-1970s by the regime of Anwar Sadat and which were expanded during the 1990s. Between the mid-1970s and the mid-1990s, liberalization policies in the agricultural sector consisted in the privatization of a large number of state-owned farms, the removal of crop area allotments, the elimination of fixed procurement prices (with the exception of cotton and sugar cane) and in the reduction of non-tariff barriers to imports and exports (Bush, 2007; Ayeb, 2010). The liberalization of Egypt's agricultural sector deepened in the late 1990s, with the elimination of the protection of property rights for small-scale and tenant farmers and the gradual implementation of the counter land reform law of 1992. Rent ceilings on land were lifted, allowing landowners to increase the number of agricultural leases. The 1992 land law also put an end to the heritability of agricultural leases. By subscribing to a liberal orientation of agricultural development that favoured export production (Blanc, 2012), the effective implementation of the counter land-reform law from 1997 resulted in a serious deterioration in the living conditions of the Egyptian peasantry (Saad, 2002; Ireton, 2006; Ayeb, 2010; Bush, 2007). In particular, the liberalization of agricultural leases and the end of their heritability aggravated the precarious status of tenants, placing them under the permanent threat of eviction by landowners. Saad (2002) reports that tenants' households, especially female-headed households, were often refused renewal of even temporary contracts. These dynamics were the root causes of the conflicts and protest movements that rose in rural Egypt from the late 1990s onwards.

## 16.3 The rise of rural conflicts and protest movements in Egypt and Tunisia

The conflicts in Egypt were initially caused by the expulsion of small farmers who had refused to pay rent increases demanded by owners, and very often took a violent form. Disputes over the access to land and of the expulsion of farmers between 1996 and 2006 led to nearly 300 deaths and 2,000 injured and resulted in the arrest of more than 3,000 people, according to a study conducted by the Land Centre for Human Rights (Ireton, 2006). Peasant mobilizations against rising land rents and their expulsion from the land they had owned for over forty years were often brutally repressed by the police in league with the big landowners. This repression, the absence of independent trade unions representing the interests of small farmers, but also the clientelist relations between farmers and land owners, as well as the pressure the latter exercised to impose their conditions, were all factors behind the limited extension of peasant mobilizations and their difficulty to transform into a mass movement. The implementation of the 1992 Act eventually resulted in the eviction of around one million tenant farming families or nearly six million rural people (Ireton, 2006). Burdened with debt, unable to pay exorbitant rents, and having in most cases no land of their own, these former tenants swelled the ranks of agricultural workers, the rural unemployed and the poorest categories of the population. In several areas of the Delta region, a severe deterioration in the living conditions of rural families occurred. This was manifest in the increase of malnutrition, in the drop in school attendance and in the growing number of children having to work in the fields as daily labourers (Saad, 2002). According to Saker El Nour, illegal migration also increased to Arab countries or Europe (El Nour, 2015).

Many conflicts also saw peasants opposed to former landowners who had been expropriated under the agrarian reform law of 1952. Taking advantage of the implementation of the 1992 law, a number of families of former landowners attempted to recover plots of lands, which had been redistributed to small farmers during the agrarian reform era. Exploiting the confusion between 'expropriated lands', which became property of the beneficiaries of the agrarian reform and 'sequestered lands',[3] these former landlords, or even farmers seeking to expand their production units, attempted to take control of land over which they had no legal entitlement. Often through the help of corrupt officials, they used various means to force beneficiaries of the agrarian reform off the land that had been in their possession for decades. These included procuring false ownership certificates, the theft of legal titles, intimidation and physical attacks, sabotage of irrigation equipment and the destruction of crops (LCHR, 2004; Ireton, 2006).

In several villages, these operations gave way to violent clashes between farmers, landowners' militias and police forces and often resulted in peasants being arrested and sentenced to long terms of imprisonment. Some of these conflicts, such as those between the peasants of the village of Sarando and the Nawar family in 2005, and the villagers of Izbet Mershaq and a large landowner in 2006, which in both cases led to the savage repression of the local population, received a great deal of attention from the national and international press (Sakr and Tarcir, 2007). To date these conflicts have not been entirely resolved, despite the support that farmers have received from Egyptian and international NGOs.

Farmers also mobilized against the rising costs of agricultural inputs, following the privatization of supply chains, and against the Agricultural Development and Credit Bank,[4] which was accused of practising usury and aggravating the indebtedness of farmers and the risk of having their means of production seized (Lesch, 2011).

The years before Mubarak's fall were also marked by conflicts over access to irrigation water, working conditions and the remuneration of seasonal farm workers (Ireton, 2006; Blanc, 2007). Access to water, one of the most acute problems in Egypt, gave rise to numerous mobilizations both in the cities and in the countryside. In 2007, 'the revolt of the thirsty' alerted the public about the serious problems of access to drinking water, which was accentuated by the gradual privatization of distribution services. One of the first major demonstrations mobilized ten thousand people in Burg al-Burullus in the governorate of Kafr al-Shaykh (Nile Delta) to protest against shortages and poor water quality that had forced local people to resort to the expensive services of water merchants (Dessouki, 2007). This demonstration was followed by other events in several regions of Egypt, leading to violence and multiple clashes between police and demonstrators, which were widely reported by the Egyptian press (Blanc, 2007).

Numerous mobilizations were organized by peasants to protest against the shortages of agricultural water. In July 2010, peasants from the south of Egypt held sit-ins in front of the offices of the central government in Cairo after the loss of their crops due to drought. Small farmers in the Fayum area, 130 kilometres southwest of Cairo, also protested against the clientelist practices that obliged them to pay bribes or join political networks to access water (McGrath, 2010). Mobilizations for access to drinking and agricultural water took place in all the country's governorates and led the government to adopt a contingency plan to supply water to areas experiencing acute shortages (Blanc, 2007).

This overview of the mobilizations in Egypt over access to land, water and agricultural inputs, which intensified during the 2000s, clearly shows how they were a direct result of the country's liberalization and privatization policies. The violent repression on the part of the police highlights the weak capacity of the rural population in asserting its right to land and water. The spontaneous and largely isolated character of these protest movements reflected the absence of trade unions capable of organizing and coordinating peasant struggles. In this regard, it is important to remember that independent trade unions were banned before the Egyptian revolution and that the agricultural branch of the one official trade union brought together only a small minority of farmers (Longuenesse and Monciaud, 2011).

As noted earlier, the processes of liberalization and state disengagement in Tunisia during the last two decades have profoundly transformed the conditions of farmers' access to agricultural resources. As in Egypt, these dynamics have favoured the rise of social tensions and conflicts in rural areas, particularly around demands over land and water. Since the late 1980s, the transfer of farm cooperatives to private companies has often faced strong opposition from former cooperative workers, many of whom have lost their jobs and livelihoods (Gana, 1998).

Similarly, the decentralization and transfer of water management from state agencies to local user associations, rather than reinforcing farmers' control has instead enabled the country's most influential economic actors to monopolize this key resource and has also enhanced the capacity of local authorities to interfere in the allocation of water to the detriment of small farmers (Gana and Amrani, 2006; Gana, 2012).

The rising discontent in rural areas also originated from farmers' growing indebtedness. Many of them, particularly small farmers were subject to lawsuits for failing to repay bank loans and were under the threat of land expropriation. In June and July 2010, farmers in Regueb and Sidi Bouzid demonstrated outside the headquarters of the Governorate against expropriation procedures they were facing and the lawsuits brought against them by the National Agricultural Bank (BNA). Twenty indebted families whose assets were liquidated staged a sit-in on their land to oppose expropriation. A protest outside the headquarters of the Governorate was subsequently organized and brutally dispersed by police (Rouissi, 2010). However, these protests received little media coverage.

The transfer of state-owned agricultural land to private investors, including members of families allied to the regime, continued to be a source of tensions between farm workers and employers, but also between the managers of large farm holdings and the agricultural administration. Although they were rarely successful in achieving their aims, protests by peasants and farm workers over state-owned farms would continue in many areas. As we will see below, the revolutionary dynamics since 2010 would contribute to the revival of land claims.

## 16.4 Peasants and farmers: actors of the political transition?

The protest movements in farming and rural areas in Tunisia and Egypt gained renewed intensity after the 2011uprisings, which reflected the growing aspirations for social justice and structural reforms. The period opened up by the fall of Mubarak in Egypt generated huge optimism among farmers, particularly among peasants who had been victims of spoliation, and was marked by an intensification of protests in rural and agricultural areas. Assisted in their struggles by independent trade union federations, they mobilized to voice their multiple demands: recognition of trade union rights of farmers; an end to the corruption that governed the organization of supply and marketing channels; the re-establishment of subsidies for fertilizers and agricultural prices; the improvement to irrigation networks and better access to land and other means of production; the cancellation of debts contracted with the Egyptian bank for credit and agricultural development; the release of imprisoned peasants. In Tunisia, multiple forms of collective action also took place and pursued various objectives, including access to land, water and financial resources, contestation of marketing conditions and pricing mechanisms, contestation of farmers' unions and users' associations, and better work conditions and remuneration.

### *16.4.1 Access to land, water and economic resources*

Land issues have represented a large part of peasants and farmers' demands in the post-uprising era in both countries. Claims on state-owned farmland in Tunisia have intensified, leading some political parties to lend their support to a project of agrarian reform that would improve access to land for small holders and farm workers. Immediately after 14 January 2011, a large number of state farms (more than 100 farm units representing 10,000 hectares of land), which had been previously transferred to private investors, found themselves the target of attacks by organized groups of landless farmers (Gana, 2012). Several of these farms were occupied by farm workers and landless peasants, who denounced the privatization of state farms and called on the transition government to redistribute state land in their favour (African Manager, 2011). These protests went so far as to call into question state ownership of agricultural land. Indeed, in many areas, farmers demanded the return of the land 'of their ancestors', first confiscated by French colonists (after 1881) and nationalized by the Tunisian state after independence (in 1956). A number of families undertook steps to obtain recognition of their rights on state land, based on the presentation of old titles. There were also sporadic occupations of large farms by smallholders and agricultural workers, which sought to block the ploughing at the start of the cropping season. These various forms of action were part of a more general desire on the part of the poor for the recognition of their right to access land and were thus highly political. The farmers' protests over land drew attention to the long-ignored social consequences of the privatization of state-owned farmland, which had deprived numerous rural families of a decent livelihood.

In Egypt, protests and demonstrations against the eviction of small farmers from their lands, continued throughout the transitional period and up to the military's ousting of President Morsi (who had been in charge from 30 June 2012 to 3 July 2013). As in Tunisia, land occupations were an important element of peasants' mobilizations (Kempf, 2011; Charbel, 2011). According to the Egyptian Ministry of Land and Irrigation, peasants occupied some 12,309 feddan,[5] 'without respect for property rights principally in the Nile Delta and Upper Egypt'. Attempts by the Ministry of Agriculture to recover these lands have had limited success (Charbel, 2011).

A number of associations, such as the Land Centre for Human Rights (*Markaz al Ard li Houqouq al Insan*), which had already been actively supporting the struggle of farmers affected by the implementation of the 1992 counter land reform law, now became involved in actions, such as providing legal support for farmers in their fight to recuperate land from landlords and the Agricultural Development and Credit Bank.

As in Tunisia, peasants' organizations called for the redistribution of reclaimed lands to small farmers – or *fellahs* – and the unemployed youth. However, these demands were largely unsuccessful. Only a handful of tenants were able to recover lands from which they had been expelled (Glain, 2012).[6] In contrast, the interests of private investors in obtaining reclaimed desert land were endorsed by the interim government and Morsi's presidency on the premise that they would create jobs that, in turn, would benefit small *fellahs*. As a small farmers' union representative told us:

> Nothing has changed since Hosni Mubarak. Our demands for the redistribution of the new land reclaimed in the desert in favour of small *fellahs* have fallen on deaf ears. The new land is for the businessmen. In the eyes of the government, small *fellahs* should work for large farmers.

Protest movements calling for better access to drinking and irrigation water intensified in both Egypt and Tunisia during the transition period that followed immediately the ousting of Ben Ali and Moubarak.

Farmers in several regions of Egypt organized sit-ins and road blockades to demand better access to irrigation water. According to one news report from the end of July 2012,

> on the same day that Egypt President Mohammed Morsi appointed former Minister of Water Resources and Irrigation Hisham Kandil as the country's new Prime Minister, [...] residents of seven Egyptian governorates [took] to the streets [...] to protest severe shortages of drinking and irrigation water.
>
> (Ooskanews, 2012)

Protests over water shortages and water pollution very often took a violent turn, as occurred in Beni Sueif governorate, Menoufiya, Minya and Fayyum. Other important water protests were also reported in 2013 in the Nile Delta where 'hundreds of farmers [...] blocked a highway to demand the administration release water for their crops' (Davies, 2013). As no efficient measures to improve access to water were taken, water protests continued to take place regularly in several regions of Egypt, both in rural and urban areas. The extent of discontent over the deficiencies of public services also led people in some rural villages to declare administrative autonomy, as occurred in the village of Al-Tahsin in the governorate of Daqhaliya, on 22 September 2012 (Charbel, 2012).

Water protests in Tunisia also intensified during the transition period that followed the uprising and conveyed a profound rejection of existing water management systems, especially at local level. A strong movement against the water users' associations (WUAs) – the bodies that had assumed management of water resources after liberalization – resulted in many WUA executive boards being broken up. In denouncing the mismanagement of WUAs and calling for their dismantlement, farmers and rural households stopped paying their water bills, demanded free access to water and that the state reassume the management of water resources. Protest movements have also targeted the question of drinking water, calling for the extension of water supply networks to deprived areas. Water conflicts and mobilizations extended to several rural areas and frequently took violent forms, such as sit-ins, road blockades and threats to destroy water pumping stations. These actions and demands, which often received positive responses from public authorities, reflected a widespread desire for more equal access and a greater sharing of water resources between social groups and regions. Protests also targeted the water transfer programmes in Tunisia given that these primarily benefited coastal regions and large cities to the detriment of the inhabitants of water providing areas.

### *16.4.2 Debt relief and the reform of supply and marketing networks*

Mobilizations in Egypt and Tunisia also focused on the problem of indebtedness that had led a number of smallholders to bankruptcy, and pressured governments to lift debts contracted by this category of farmers. In addition, peasants and farmers also contested the malfunctioning of supply and marketing networks. In Egypt, the distribution and scarcity of agricultural fertilizers continued to represent a major source of discontent among small farms and agricultural unions, who denounced the monopoly on fertilizer production held by four private companies and the subsequent upward pressure on fertilizer prices.[7] One of their demands was to allow cooperatives to take over the local distribution of fertilizers, a demand that, to date, has remained unfulfilled. In Tunisia, farmers' protests also targeted price increases following the privatization of grain collection. The contestation of new pricing mechanisms based on the evaluation of grain quality, led numerous farmers to refuse to sell their grain to private collectors and resulted in some farmers' groups calling for the re-establishment of state monopoly over the commercialization of grains. Horticulture and milk producers also organized several demonstrations and sit-ins to protest against the conditions of sale imposed on them by the agro-industry (Gana, 2012).

### *16.4.3 Contestation of farmers' unions and the renewal of the trade union movement*

Rural and agricultural mobilizations in Egypt and Tunisia also sought to create and reinforce autonomous organizations that would be in the position to represent the interests of various groups of farmers and peasants. Farmers played an active role in the renewal of the trade union movement in Egypt that followed the announcement of the 'Declaration on Freedom of Association' on 12 March 2011. Until the Egyptian revolution, the trade union landscape was dominated by the powerful General Federation of Trade Unions of Egypt (FGSTE), created in 1957, which had about four million members equal to roughly a quarter of the occupied workforce (Gamal Abdel Nasser Ibrahim, 1998). This organization, which was controlled by political authorities and had close ties with the business community, was an essential pillar of support of Mubarak's regime and its liberal reforms. Its action was mainly focused on containing or channelling social protests (Longuenesse and Monciaud, 2011). Farmers and veterinarians in the organization were represented by their own union branch, which was placed under the auspices of the Ministry of Agriculture. The union brought together 253,000 agricultural workers and farmers (out of a national total of three million farmers) (Gamal Abdel Nasser Ibrahim, 1998).

After the fall of Mubarak and the announcement of the Law on Freedom of Association, several independent unions were created to support demands for higher salaries and better working conditions, as well as the reinstatement of dismissed workers who had participated in strikes and demonstrations. Many of these new unions were affiliated to the Egyptian Federation of Independent Trade Unions. During the transition period, independent agricultural syndicates provided important support to peasant mobilizations for the recognition of their union rights, for better access to fertilizers, water and land. However, as explained below, the unions were not successful in organizing peasants and farmers as a political force, mainly because of their lack of coordination and their subservience to various political parties.

Mobilizations in Tunisia also contested the official farmers' union (UTAP, Tunisian Union for Agriculture and Fisheries) for being subordinate to the authoritarian regime and unrepresentative of their interests. Farmers organized numerous demonstrations, particularly in front of the government house in the capital Tunis, in order to demand the resignation of union leaders and a reform of UTAP's legal status (Mestiri, 2011). This wave of protests intensified in the first months that followed the fall of Ben Ali. Despite a strong mobilization, as attested by the occupation of a number of regional union offices, the organization of a large demonstration of farmers in front of government headquarters in Tunis in April 2011 and the replacement of national and regional representatives of UTAP, the 'reformist' movement met strong resistance. With the transitional government unresponsive to their demands, the 'reformists' set up an independent union, the Union of Tunisian Farmers (Synagri), on 10 December 2011. Bringing together farmers from different regions and different sectors, Synagri has since set itself the objective of defending the material and moral interests of farmers. By asserting its political independence, it has sought to become a credible interlocutor of public authorities and of the various economic and social partners. The new union recruits its members mainly among agricultural entrepreneurs. While Synagri represents without doubt a new counterbalance to State power, it has not, however, succeeded in expanding its social base and the large majority of farmers still has to resort to the services of main farmers' union, UTAP, which remains under the control of political power.

Farm workers have also been involved in the trade union movement in Tunisia, most of whom are employed on a seasonal basis. Sometimes with the support of UGTT (General Union of Tunisian Workers), these workers have organized numerous strikes and sit-ins calling for improved wages and work conditions. Farm workers have also sought to consolidate their presence within the framework of the union organization, although, to date, this project has been largely unsuccessful.

## 16.5 The continuing neglect of the voices of peasants and small farmers

This overview of farmers' protests and mobilizations in Tunisia and Egypt clearly reveals the rise of social struggles in the countryside and a profound contestation of former state policies. It also highlights the difficulty of farmers' unions to transform social discontent into efficient action that is able to influence policy decisions. In fact, the social demands of peasants and rural communities have continued to have little resonance in political debates and have not been translated into clear guidelines for agricultural development.

Although the opposition forces generally supported the demands of farmers and peasants, these same demands were largely disregarded by the post-uprising authorities in Egypt. First, the Supreme Council of the Armed Forces and the Military Council blocked the law passed on 12 March 2011 that would have legalized independent trade unions and it then proceeded to ban strikes. The election of Mohamed Morsi as President of the Egyptian Republic did not greatly improve the situation: farmers' demands remained marginal to the political agenda, while trade union pluralism continued to be denied. The Islamist Freedom and Justice Party's electoral promises to cancel small farmers' debts,[8] as well as President

Morsi's announcement about establishing a minimum price for rice remained largely dead letters. Campaigns for the redistribution of land to small farmers and unemployed youth have also had little success. Only a few tenants have been able to recuperate dispossessed land. The issue of the distribution of agricultural fertilizers continued to cause discontent among small *fellahs* and agricultural unions. Calls from agricultural unions to allow cooperatives to take over the distribution of fertilizers were rejected by the Ministry of Agriculture. Small farmers have therefore continued to purchase farm inputs from private traders and on the black market at increasingly higher prices. Several interviewees also pointed out that during the Morsi presidency, the price of diesel and seeds (including corn) rose significantly. In contrast, the price of livestock decreased significantly and farmers were heavily affected by the upsurge in the theft of animals. No action was taken to improve the supply of farm inputs and the marketing of agricultural products. On the contrary, illegal seed producers flourished, with negative repercussions for farmers whose crops deteriorated due to poor seed quality. Numerous representatives of independent agricultural trade unions report that members of the agricultural union 'Niqabat fellahin MESR', affiliated to the Freedom and Justice Party, took advantage of their position to develop profitable activities in the trade of agricultural products, buying farmers' products cheaply and selling them on the market at much higher prices. A number of interviewees felt that the Muslim Brotherhood party was especially eager to establish its control over agricultural services and that those close to the Islamist party were primarily concerned with the developing their own commercial activities. Representatives of small farmers' unions also pointed out that the Muslim Brotherhood had always supported the landowners and that they had never opposed the Land Law of 1992.

Consequently, while rural people and farmers overwhelmingly voted for Mohamed Morsi in the presidential elections, many of them also signed the petition calling for the removal of his government and participated in events that led to his overthrow. Indeed, large groups of peasants, supported by independent trade unions, participated in the demonstration on 30 June 2013 in Cairo that called for the toppling of the Muslim Brotherhood.

In Tunisia, the social mobilizations in rural areas, which were particularly important during the first phase of political transition, have continued to be largely disregarded by post-revolutionary authorities, especially the calls for structural reforms in land distribution and access to economic resources. The measures taken by both the transition and post-election governments indicated a lack of will to seriously tackle the issue of land. In addition, their response to calls for the removal of debts of small landholders (and, hence, the threat of expropriation) were deemed by farmers to be unsatisfactory.[9]

The collective demands for the reinstatement of public management of water resources were overlooked in favour of a reconfirmation of transferring this administration to users associations. Immediately after the 2011 elections, a campaign was launched to renew the water user associations, although, from my own observations in the field, it appeared that this was influenced by the desires on the part of the victorious Islamist party to ensure its control over these same structures. In a similar way, the National Constituent Assembly elected in 2011 was not particularly sympathetic to the emergence of independent agricultural trade unions. While the new farmers' union Synagri sought to become an autonomous organization, the UTAP, an organization subsidized by the state and subservient to the old regime, remained under the control of the post-revolutionary political authorities.

The tendency of increasing control over the administration of farmers' organizations reflects the lack of attention on the part of the post-revolutionary authorities to the demands for reform by different groups of farmers. Indeed, the policy priority has seemed to be oriented to other actors, such as foreign investors especially from the Gulf countries, with which agreements have been signed to develop agricultural projects on state lands (Dixon 2014). In a recent interview, the vice-president of the new farmers' union Synagri declared that the Tunisian revolution had not benefited the farming sector and lamented the subsequent lack of vision on the part of government with regard to agricultural development. The two farmers' unions have also expressed their concerns about the negative consequences on Tunisian agriculture of the Deep and Comprehensive Free Trade Area (DCFTA), the proposed agreement with the European Union that foresees the full liberalization of agricultural tariffs. As well as opening negotiations with the Tunisian government on the DCFTA on 19 October 2015, the European Union is also currently pressuring the Egyptian government to restart talks over a wider free trade deal that would include agricultural products.

## 16.6 Conclusion

This chapter has highlighted the often-neglected role played by peasants and rural actors in triggering popular revolts in Egypt and Tunisia. Exploring the processes behind the rise of farmers and peasants' protest movements, it has underlined the links between liberalization policies and the deterioration of the economic and social conditions of the farming population. The Egyptian and Tunisian revolutions both opened spaces of political expression for groups of farmers and peasants calling for better access to land and economic resources. Social protests and mobilizations also revealed the strong aspirations of rural inhabitants for social justice and for a better quality of life. Despite limited media coverage, these protests and mobilizations gave voice to poor farm workers and smallholders and contributed to transforming the questions of resource allocation and the organization of supply and marketing networks into topics of public debate. They also drew attention to questions of agricultural development, food security and the social role of farming activities. The post-uprisings transition period enabled the rise of independent farmers' trade unions seeking to assert their autonomy vis-à-vis political power and their capacity to influence the direction of policy. These dynamics, however, were not enough to instigate structural reforms or a real change in agricultural policy.

As we have seen, rural protests during the revolutions continued to be spontaneous and often violent and were largely unable to integrate themselves in legal and organized structures. In Egypt, the difficulty of the independent trade union movement to mobilize farmers and enlarge its social base was linked to a lack of coordination between a multiplicity of separate organizations. Furthermore, the proximity of trade unions with political parties in both countries, often led farmers to perceive these organizations as instruments in the service of partisan struggles, which deterred them from getting involved in union action.

Both in Tunisia and Egypt, the difficulty of farmers' movements to translate their demands into policy change and structural reforms was closely related to the configuration of political forces that emerged from the post-uprising elections. Some analysts have argued that the results of the first post-revolution elections, which in both cases brought to power Islamist parties, did not really reflect the main 'objective' roots of the popular uprisings (Van Hamme, Gana and Ben Rebah, 2014).[10] Rather than focusing on development issues, the action of the new authorities concentrated on political and constitutional reforms and sought to consolidate their position in state institutions. Following the retreat of Islamist forces from power, the new governments in both countries have continued to advocate land privatization and agricultural liberalization. This would appear to confirm the more general marginalization of revolutionary forces and progressive political parties. Nevertheless, despite the limited governmental interest towards the demands of peasants and farmers, the inspiration of previous struggles and a greater sense of collective courage would suggest that it would take little to reignite a rural protest movement, and that such a movement is likely to weigh heavily on the outcome of future elections.

## Notes

1 The share of agriculture in total employment in Tunisia declined sharply from 55 per cent in 1965 to 15 per cent in 2012 (ONAGRI, 2012).

2 Despite the lack of job opportunities, young people from rural areas have continued to migrate to cities. According to a recent report prepared by the World Bank in partnership with the Youth National Observatory of Tunisia, 90.2 per cent of rural households possessed family members who had migrated to urban areas. Rural out-migration continues to be an important form of escape for rural youth, especially men. Almost a quarter (24.6 per cent) of male rural migrants headed to the area of Grand Tunis, 31.7 per cent went to other cities, 15.3 per cent migrated abroad, while more than a quarter (28.4 per cent) moved to other rural areas (World Bank, 2014). As far as migrating abroad is concerned, and especially irregular migration, Hassen Boubakri (2013) reports an unprecedented outflow of young Tunisian migrants shortly after the collapse of Ben Ali's regime, with many departing towards Lampedusa. Departure areas, which were initially limited to the southwest of the country rapidly extended to the costal zones of Sfax, the Sahel and the CapBon.

3 This refers to lands that were seized by the government for a period but which were eventually given back to their owners.

4 The interest rates of the Agricultural Bank rose from 3 per cent in the 1970s to between 18 per cent and 20 per cent in 2015.

5 One *feddan* is the equivalent of 0.42 hectares or 42,000 square metres.

6 This is the case in Dakahlya and in Mansoura. However, precise data on these land reclamations are not available.

7 The production of agricultural fertilizers in Egypt is directed almost entirely for export, to the detriment of the local market. This exerts upward pressure on prices and encourages the development of a fertilizer black market.

8 In a presidential speech, Mohamed Morsi promised to cancel the debts that 44,000 small farmers owed to the Bank of Credit and Agricultural Development. However, only insolvent farmers (for non-payment) were ultimately affected by this measure, which meant that it was limited to only one in four farmers (El Nour, 2015).

9 In May 2014, the newly elected parliament ratified the government's decision to cancel debts under 2,000 Tunisians Dinars (approximately 1,500 US dollars), but this decision was considered inadequate by the farmers' unions.

10 In Tunisia, the Islamist party Ennadha (Renaissance) won 39 per cent of the seats for the National Constituent Assembly in the elections on 23 October 2011. While this vote no doubt expressed a deep rejection of the former regime, it also reflected the successful strategy of a political campaign built around a moral and religious discourse. Ennadha performed strongest in the south of the country, in the city of Kairouan (the religious capital of the country), and in the poor neighborhoods of the big cities. In contrast, it received the lowest share of votes in the Northwest and Midwest regions, which were the cradle of the Tunisian uprising.

## References

African Manager (2011). 'Tunisie: Terres agricoles et investisseurs, cherchent protection désespérément!' 26 June. http://farmlandgrab.org/post/print/1885408 (last access on 20/2/2016).

Ayeb, H. (2010). *La crise de la société rurale en Egypte. La fin du fellah*? Paris: Karthala.

Blanc, P. (2007). 'Le pain, la terre et l'eau: sujets de révolte en Méditerranée'. *Actualités du Moyen-Orient et du Maghreb*, IRIS, 3 December.

Blanc, P. (2012). *Proche-Orient. Le pouvoir, la terre et l'eau.* Paris: Les Presses de Sciences-Po.

Boubakri, H. (2013). *Revolution and International Migration in Tunisia*. Migration Policy Center Research Report, 2013/04, Florence: European University Institute. http://www.migrationpolicycentre.eu/docs/MPC-RR-2013–04.pdf (last access on 20/2/2016).

Bush, R. (2007). 'Politics, power and poverty: Twenty years of agricultural reform and market liberalisation in Egypt'. *Third World Quarterly*, 28 (8), Market-Led Agrarian Reform: Trajectories and Contestations, pp. 1599–1615.

Charbel, J. (2011). 'Co-opting Egypt's farmers no longer feasible after 25 January'. *Al-Masry Al-Youm*, 10 September.

Charbel, J. (2012). 'In opposition to Morsy, Mahalla declares autonomy'. *Egypt Independent*, 12 December. http://www.egyptindependent.com/news/opposition-morsy-mahalla-declares-autonomy/ (last access on 20/2/2016).

Davies, P. (2013). 'Farmers in Egypt press fights for land, debt relief'. *The Militant*, 77 (31), 26 August. http://www.themilitant.com/2013/7731/773154.html (last access on 20/2/2016).

Dessouki, N.H. (2007). 'Water crisis in Egypt: 2007 year of thirst revolution'. *Chroniques égyptiennes*, CEDEJ, pp. 180–191.

Dixon, M. (2014). 'The land grab, finance capital and food regime restructuring: The case of Egypt'. *Review of African Political Economy,* 41, pp. 232–248.

Elloumi, M. (2011). 'Tunisie: Pourquoi c'est à Sidi Bouzid que tout a commence'. *Mission Agrobiosciences*, 17 January.

El Nour, S. (2015). 'Small farmers and the revolution in Egypt: the forgotten actors'. *Contemporary Arab Affairs*, 8 (2), pp. 198–211.

Gamal Abdel Nasser Ibrahim (1998). 'Représentation syndicale et transition libérale en Égypte'. *Égypte/Monde arabe*, Première série, 33. http://ema.revues.org/1586 (last access on 20/2/2016).

Gana, A. (1998). *Agricultural Restructuring, Household Practices and Family Farm Differentiation: A Case Study of the Region of Zaghouan, Tunisia*. Ph.D. thesis, Cornell University.

Gana, A. (2012). 'Agriculteurs et paysans: nouveaux acteurs de la société civile et de la transition démocratique en Tunisie?' in Redissi, H., Nouira, A. and Zghal, A. (eds). *La transition démocratique en Tunisie. Etat des lieux*. Tunis: éditions Diwen, pp. 273–293.

Gana, A. (2013). 'Aux origines rurales et agricoles de la Révolution tunisienne'. *Maghreb/ Machrekh*, no. 215, pp. 57–80.

Gana, A. and Amrani, M. (2006). 'Crise hydraulique au Maghreb: raréfaction de la ressource ou problèmes de la gestion'. *Géocarrefour*, 81 (1), pp. 37–50.

Glain, S. (2012). 'Egyptian farmers make themselves heard'. *New York Times*, 27 June.

Ireton, G. (2006). 'La petite paysannerie dans la tourmente néolibérale' in Hassabo C. and Laus E. (dir.) *Chroniques égyptiennes*. Le Caire: Cedej, pp. 29–58.

Kempf, R. (2011). 'Les paysans dans la révolution égyptienne'. *Le Monde diplomatique*, March.

Land Center for Human Rights (LCHR) (2004). 'The conditions of human rights in Egypt during the last ten years between the freedom of the market and the deterioration of the citizens' conditions'. *The Economic and Social Rights Series*, no. 33.

Lesch, A.M. (2011). 'Egypt's spring: Causes of the revolution'. *Middle East Policy Council Journal*, 18 (3), pp. 35–48.

Longuenesse, E. and Monciaud, D. (2011). 'Syndicalismes égyptiens' in Battesti V. and Ireton F. (eds). *L'Egypte au présent, Inventaire d'une société avant révolution*, Sindbad-Actes Sud.

McGrath, E. (2010). 'Poor thirst as Nile taps run dry'. *Inter Press Service* IPS/IFEJ, CAIRO, 6 September.

Mestiri, B. (2011). 'Union tunisienne de l'agriculture et de la pêche . . . le dernier bastion du RCD?' *La Presse de Tunisie*, Tunis, 3 June.

Ministère de l'agriculture (MINAGRI) (2006). *Enquête sur les structures des exploitations agricoles 2005*. Tunis: MINAGRI.

Observatoire National de l'Agriculture, Tunisie (ONAGRI), (2012). *Agrégats économiques*. Tunis: ONAGRI.

Ooskanews (2012) 'Egypt: Water shortage protests are widespread and violent'. https://www.ooskanews.com/story/2012/07/egypt-water-shortage-protests-are-widespread-and-violent_151910 (last access on 20/2/2016).

Pagès-El Karoui, D. and Vignal, L. (2011). 'Les racines de la 'révolution du 25 janvier' en Égypte: une réflexion géographique' *EchoGéo*, Sur le Vif, 27 October, http://echogeo.revues.org/12627 (access on 18/12/15).

Rouissi, S. (2010). 'Les agriculteurs tunisiens manifestent pour conserver leurs terres'. *Les Observers*. http://observers.france24.com/fr/20100716-agriculteurs-tunisiens-manifestent-conserver-leurs-terres (last access on 20/2/2016).

Saad, R. (2002). 'Egyptian politics and the tenancy law' in Bush, R. (ed.). *CounterRevolution in Egypt's Countryside*. London: Zed Books.

Sakr, B. and Tarcir, P. (2007). 'La lutte toujours recommencée des paysans égyptiens'. *Le Monde diplomatique*, October, pp. 10–11.

Van Hamme, G., Gana, A. and Ben Rebah, M. (2014). 'Social and socio territorial electoral base of political parties in post-revolutionary Tunisia'. *The Journal of North African Studies*, 19 (5), pp. 51–769.

World Bank (2014). *Tunisia. Breaking the Barriers to Youth Inclusion*. Washington, DC: World Bank. http://www.worldbank.org/content/dam/Worldbank/document/MNA/tunisia/breaking_the_barriers_to_youth_inclusion_eng.pdf (last access on 20/2/2016).

# 17 Unionism of migrant farm workers

## The Sindicato Obreros del Campo (SOC) in Andalusia, Spain

*Francesco Saverio Caruso*

### 17.1 Introduction[1]

Over the last thirty years, in southern European countries, traditional trade unions have increasingly encountered difficulties in organizing new subjects of labour. Processes such as globalization, outsourcing, subcontracting, labour market deregulation and segmentation, as well as the fragmentation of production processes, constitute a context that is hostile to the collective safeguarding of workers' rights (Crouch, 2004; Gallino, 2012). Since 2008, the economic crisis has further exacerbated the situation. The crisis has affected mainly labour-intensive sectors and low-qualified workers, who work intermittently and on a temporary basis; in other words, those most in need of protection and for whom unionization and organization are more complicated.

Migrant day labourers in Mediterranean agriculture represent perhaps one of the clearest examples of these processes. In this sector, the general ethnic segmentation of labour markets (Portes and Sassen-Koob, 1987; Castles and Miller, 1993) is compounded by the greater social and economic vulnerability of workers. Among the key reasons for labourers' weak position in relation to their employers are the predominant seasonal and informal nature of labour relations, the lack of direct links between workers and employers, and, consequently, the difficulties in organizing collective bargaining mechanisms (Moraes *et al.*, 2012, p. 24).

In this chapter I describe the results of fieldwork conducted in Almería province in Andalusia, southern Spain. Here, thousands of migrants are employed in intensive agriculture. They can be considered the last link in agri-food supply chains that are dominated by the European large-scale retail corporations, which through their logistical platforms, are able to control the production and sale of fruit and vegetables. The restructuring of agriculture over the last 40 years can be considered to be situated at the intersection between the 'Californian model' of intensive agriculture (Berlan, 1987) and the informalization typical of southern European economies (Baldwin-Edwards and Arango, 1999) and of the 'Mediterranean model' of migration (King *et al.*, 2000). The exploitation of a temporary and vulnerable migrant labour force has represented one of the fundamental features of agricultural restructuring in this region.

In particular, this chapter aims to analyse the action and negotiation strategies of the *Sindicato Obreros del Campo* (Farm Workers Union; SOC from now on) in Almería. The SOC has a wholly unusual history within the context of European trade unions; it seeks to challenge the supposed 'unorganizability' and 'unrepresentability' of precarious workers, and to rethink the traditional union structure and activism in relation to neoliberal capitalism (Murgia and Selmi, 2011). I propose to read its characteristics by using the concept of Social Movement Unionism (Waterman, 1993; Moody, 1997). This concept has been developed over the past two decades to describe a number of self-organized unions in the southern hemisphere – such as the Central Unica dos Trabalhadores (Unified Workers Central) in Brazil, the Kilusang Mayo Uno (May First Movement) in the Philippines, and the Congress of South African Trade Unions. It has been used subsequently to analyse a number of labour unions in the United States (Turner and Hurd, 2001; Voss and Sherman, 2003). Social Movement Unionism is characterized by horizontal organization, the building of broad social coalitions, the recruitment of vulnerable subjects, non-professionalized grassroots activism, direct action and anti-bureaucratism. These features, as we will see, can be observed in the SOC, and contribute to distinguish it from traditional union organizations.

The chapter is based on fieldwork conducted in 2013 and 2014, which included interviews with trade unionists, workers and a variety of related actors, as well as participant observation in union activities at the SOC headquarters in the municipalities of Almería and El Ejido.

The chapter is structured in four sections. First, I provide a description of the agricultural sector in Almería province, and I show how this is embedded in global value chains controlled on the one side by biotech multinationals and on the other by Europe's principal retail companies. I then describe the relationship between the main Spanish unions and migrants; and drawing on the concept of 'cartel party' (Katz and Mair, 1995) I argue that these unions can be defined as 'cartel unions'. In the third section, I examine the case of SOC in the region of Andalusia and in particular in the province of Almería, paying attention to the unionization of Moroccan farm labourers. In the final section, I contend that the practices and strategies of this union can be analysed through the theoretical framework of Social Movement Unionism.

## 17.2 Almería's fruit and vegetable district within the global value chains

Many scholars have analysed how, over the last 40 years, a range of factors – technological development, the restructuring of forms of governance, liberalization policies and the progressive tearing down of trade barriers – have led to a redefinition of the organizational structure and boundaries of agri-food markets. One of the most prominent analytical approaches to studying these processes is the global value chains (GVC) perspective, which describes the structure of the connections of production at a global level. This approach pays attention to the management of flows and information that serve to reduce supply times and costs, satisfy consumer demand, and increase the added value of the entire production chain (Gereffi and Korzeniewicz, 1994; Gereffi, 1995). The agri-food sector (and especially the fresh produce industry) is probably one of the best examples of this: the quick deterioration of products requires a particularly efficient system of control of the production chain in order to cut supply times and costs through partnerships with suppliers and clients, to reduce uncertainty and guarantee better access to resources (Gereffi *et al.*, 2005).

Among the outcomes of these processes is the growing concentration of purchases in the hands of a few buyers/retailers, who possess an enormous negotiating power with their suppliers and wield control over the whole food supply chain. Retailers demand just-in-time production, the volumes of which are determined from the ground up following the flow of sales, which are monitored in real time. Retail-controlled supply chains have substituted producer-driven chains. Retailers have increasingly influenced production by not only determining the characteristics of the products, but also defining the ethical and social standards in labour relations (Reardon *et al.*, 2001; Gertel and Sippel, 2014).

From this point of view, Almería surely represents one of the most advanced cases of the integration between production, processing and retail of agricultural products (Ferraro and Aznar, 2008; see also Reigada, this volume). It was in this province that during the 1950s the National Institute of Rural Development and Colonization promoted policies aimed at subdividing uncultivated land into small farms. Three decades later, the province would become the largest European district for the production of counterseasonal fruits and vegetables. This cultivation takes place in greenhouses stretching over 30,000 hectares, through the so-called 'precision agriculture' (Watts and Goodman, 1997), where over 3 million tonnes of vegetables are extracted thanks to the most advanced agro-industrial technologies. The constant growth of the sector has been impressive, especially following Spain's entry into the European Union in 1986 and the removal of final trade tariffs for Spanish fruits and vegetables in 1996: from 100,000 tonnes of fruit and vegetables exported in 1980 (mainly winter tomatoes destined for the French market), production rose to 250,000 in 1985, 500,000 in 1990, 1.4 million in 1995, 2.3 million in 2000, and to 3 million tonnes of tomatoes, courgettes, cucumbers, aubergines, melons, watermelons, peppers and lettuce in 2013 (Cabrera and Uclés, 2013).

Over the last 35 years, the so-called 'Almería miracle' has been supported by mostly North American and European agrochemical corporations (Rijw Zwan, Bruinsma Seeds, Royal Sluis, Bayer's Nunhems, Swiss company Syngenta, AgrEvo, Probelte) which have supplied seeds and pesticides and, as such, have increasingly influenced producers' choices. Over 10,000 Almería farmers, each owning on average just under three hectares, have become progressively dependent on these corporations. In order to increase crop yield, farmers are obliged to buy back every year not only hybrid seeds but also a multiplicity of products and inputs necessary for the entire production cycle.

If biotech multinationals affect the production process, the same can be said of retail corporations. On a national level, the three biggest supermarket chains in Spain (Carrefour, Mercadona and Erosky) control approximately half of the food market; on a European level, 70 per cent of Almería agricultural production is absorbed by a handful of retailing companies – among which Tesco, Schwarz,

Rewe, Metro, Carrefour – through a system of 'lowest-bid auctions' at the *alhóndigas* (farm product exchanges).[2] These retailing giants impose on the farmers not only accelerated schedules and low prices, but also a rigid standardization of the product, which must be in line with specific quality control protocols and systems of certification.

Almería farmers therefore are caught in 'a technological and institutional system that resembles an agricultural 'factory' more than a farm, due to its high capital requirements, the high cost of productivity inputs, a large workforce, and manifold and active technological support' (Ferraro and Aznar, 2008, p. 354). Due to the loss of control over production, labour cost reduction is often the only strategy through which farmers are able to protect their profit margins. If the *convenio del campo*, the official union wage for this province, is 50 euros a day for a six-hour shift, actual daily wages are in the region of 30 euros for a daily shift of 8 to 9 hours. Migrant farmworkers – mainly Moroccans – usually accept informal, underpaid, intermittent, temporary jobs, which are also dangerous due to the constant risk of chemical poisoning in greenhouses.

In spite of the fact that numerous empirical studies have documented a widespread perception among migrants that Almería is the worst area of Spain for intolerance and racial discrimination (Izcara and Andrade, 2004; Checa, 2007), the province continues to be massively affected by labour mobility. Since the beginning of the economic crisis in 2008, the number and percentage of migrant farmworkers have been growing: in 2007, out of 39,400 labourers, 18,800 (47.7 per cent) were non-Spanish (Instituto de Estudios Socioeconómicos de la Fundación Cajamar, 2008); while these had risen to 33,800 (63 per cent) out of over 53,640 workers in 2014 (Cabrera *et al.*, 2015). These figures show, on the on hand, that the agricultural sector has an anti-cyclical function as a refuge for thousands of labourers when they are expelled from other sectors (chiefly construction and industry), and, on the other, that, despite the difficult situation of the Spanish economy, Almería's agribusiness sector appears not to be affected by the crisis, thanks to its integration with foreign markets.

## 17.3 Unions and migration in Spain

The trade union sector in Spain is dominated by the two largest labour organizations: the *Comisiones Obreras* (Workers' Commissions, CCOO) and the *Unión General de Trabajadores* (General Workers Union, UGT). In spite of the fact that these organizations have acquired greater importance in public life, Spain remains one of the countries with the lowest rate of unionization in Europe. The two largest unions – and especially the UGT – 'have invested more on negotiating with government and employers and less on grassroots political mobilization, and, as such, have favoured the development of depoliticized industrial relations modelled on the Scandinavian system' (Martínez Lucio, 1998, p. 430). After slowly emerging during the last years of the Franco dictatorship, the largest union organizations embarked on a strategy of top-down renewal based on institutional recognition, beginning with the Moncloa Pacts on wage moderation in 1977.

As for the relationship between unions and workers, both the UGT and the CCOO have concentrated on offering individualized services, such as assistance with benefits and tax returns, through a professional and bureaucratic infrastructure. In particular, union offices have progressively assumed the role of offering a meeting point and help for pensioners who encounter difficulties, for instance in dealing with bureaucratic issues. As such, and drawing on Katz and Mair's definition of 'cartel party' (Katz and Mair, 1995), I want to argue that these trade unions increasingly constitute a form of 'cartel unionism'. Indeed, many features of the cartel party can also be traced in Spain's main trade unions: the transition from competition to interparty collusion and mutual protection; professionalization and dependence on public funding; the non-mutual exclusion from public power; the interpenetration of party and the State; similar electoral programmes; and electoral democracy as a means to controlling the governed and not the governors.[3]

The tendency towards a 'service union' is even clearer when one considers migrant labour. Between 1995 and 2005, the number of foreigners in Spain grew from 650,000 to just over 6 million. During this period, unions played a key role at a political level and as a 'street-level bureaucracy' (Lipsky, 1980) in helping migrants navigate through red tape, laws, amnesties and legal voids. Each year, thousands of migrants continue to flock to the CCOO's Foreign Worker Information Centres (*Centros de Informacion para Trabajadores Extranjeros*) and the UGT's Guidance Centres (*Centros Guía*) in search of assistance in dealing with residency permits, family reunification, access to subsidies, and tax and pension benefits.

Notwithstanding its undeniable power of attraction for migrant labourers, the 'service union' model presents elements of ambivalence,[4] especially in terms of migrants' perception of union structures. The words of Nadir, a Moroccan day labourer in Almería, are eloquent in this regard: 'It was only after several years that I understood the difference between the help desk at the union and the help desk at the prefecture: I had always believed that in both cases I was dealing with civil servants' (interview with Nadir, Moroccan day labourer, November 2014).

The decision to join a trade union is a purely instrumental move. A union member is more a customer than a militant; migrants usually consider the union as a 'semi-public entity, if not as a state institution' (Miravet, 2005, p. 8). As a result, the rate of migrant union membership is lower than that of natives (1.9 per cent versus 7.4 per cent), and, not surprisingly, out of a total of 275,549 CCOO delegates, only 2,478 are foreigners (0.9 per cent).

Of course, in the context of neoliberal capitalism and economic crisis, and in a dual labour market, it is very difficult for trade unions to defend (migrant) workers' rights. A clear example of the difficulties facing unions is agricultural day labour. In a number of provinces in southern Spain, for instance during the 'orange strike' in Cordoba in 2009, certain unions, including the CCOO, launched campaigns against temporary employment agencies (*Empresas de Trabajo Temporal*) which they accused of distorting the agricultural labour market through quasi-slavery practices, back-breaking shifts, meagre wages and explicit forms of extortion with regards to food, lodging and transportation

(Gadea *et al.*, this volume). However, these mobilizations failed to produce union activism among the day labourers themselves.

One of the most important pieces of research on the relationship between unions and migrants in Spain, but which significantly omits agricultural labour from its analysis, spells out the key dilemmas:

> In spite of being one of the main immigrant job sectors, agriculture has been left out of this study due to the disappearance of native farm work in areas of intense agriculture where migrants work, and the inexistence or irrelevance of farm workers' unions in those areas. In fact, their equivalent is represented by small farmers' associations, whose position towards migrants is that of employer and not of fellow employee.
>
> (González, 2008, p. 92)

## 17.4 The SOC in Andalusia and in Almería Province

The SOC is a small but combative union made up solely of day labourers, which struggles to this day for 'workers' right to land'. Historically rooted in the provinces of northern Andalusia, where the land structure was characterized by the presence of huge estates, this union later managed to spread to coastal areas where smallholdings were more common. The freezing of social relations during the Franco dictatorship put the plight of day labourers on hold until the late 1970s and early 1980s, when thousands of day labourers – who were already networked through semi-clandestine *comisiones de jornaleros* – were finally able to overtly self-organize, which led to the setting up of the SOC. From its earliest years, the SOC clashed with the moderate policies of the main labour organizations and favoured direct action, especially the occupation of large estates that were still in the hands of the aristocracy. Over the past three decades, the SOC has occupied several thousand hectares of uncultivated land, in particular in the Lower Guadalquivir district and in southern Seville province. Among the various struggles is the famous case of the day labourers of the town of Marinaleda in the province of Seville, who managed to wrest 1,000 acres from the Duke of Infantado. They were led by the young mayor of Marinaleda, Juan Manuel Sánchez Gordillo, who has remained at the head of this small municipality uninterruptedly for 35 years. At the same time, the SOC fought xenophobic tendencies by encouraging mixed work gangs (*cuadrillas mixtas*) composed of natives and migrants in an effort to stave off infighting among the poor, the lowering of wages and the lack of respect for provincial contracts.

The extreme parcelling of land property in Almería left this area out of the great mobilizations and day-labour struggles that affected the great estates in the northern provinces of Andalusia from the mid-1970s onwards. Almería was historically the only Andalusian province where the SOC had never established a headquarters, a core group of activists, or even a symbolic presence. During the 1970s and 1980s, Almería's greenhouse farming and the Andalusian SOC grew in parallel, but never crossed paths. In the 1990s, intensive, counterseasonal greenhouse farming generated high profit margins for Almería's agricultural pioneers: the generational renewal was thus marked by an abandonment of labour and family self-exploitation, and by the availability of significant numbers of migrants willing to take on the most burdensome and strenuous jobs.

For many years the 'Almería miracle' took place apparently without the least hint of social and union opposition. In reality, the conflict had long been simmering underground. The well-known xenophobic violence and race riots in which Spaniards torched immigrant homes and shops in El Ejido between 6 and 9 February 2000, were not isolated events but rather the culmination of a long series of episodes of racial violence against Maghrebi workers (Forum Civique Européen, 2000; Checa, 2001; Veiga, 2014).

In reaction to the violence in El Ejido, migrants felt the need to organize and to build their own union. While the first reaction of labourers during the riots was to hide in isolated farms, they soon became aware that they could not return to work without taking a stand. As a result, Moroccan workers started to gather in spontaneous and self-organized assemblies and discuss about the prospect of going on strike. They organized sit-ins and pickets at the greenhouse access roads. These pickets turned into actual work stoppages, and were repeatedly attacked and dispersed by police. The strike took place in mid-February, an important period for Almería's agriculture, blocking the harvest and causing an estimated damage of 6 million euros. The action therefore scored a key victory, which was to highlight the productive power and the indispensable role of migrant day labour in sustaining the 'Almería miracle'. On 12 February, migrant representatives, local institutions, farmers' associations and official unions signed an agreement. It provided immediate assistance to migrants who were left homeless after the arson attacks, damages were paid to the victims of the violence, a programme was set up to build facilities for seasonal labourers, and the documents were issued to migrants without residency permits.

The self-organized action of the Moroccan labourers benefited from the support of organizers who had been sent by the Seville SOC to monitor the situation. Thanks to the participation of the more combative elements among the migrant workers, they decided to open the first SOC branch in Almería province. When it became clear that local institutions failed to comply with the February agreement, new mobilizations broke out: 100 migrants barricaded themselves in the Church of San Jose in the city of Almería for an entire month in September 2000. In January 2001, the SOC formally inaugurated its Almería offices; three among the leaders of the El Ejido mobilization become its local delegates. Two months later, they organized a sit-in at Almería University with several hundred migrants, to demand the legalization of undocumented workers. With this mobilization, they also managed to obtain their own so-called 'Barcelona Accords' (Barbero, 2013); in other words, their inclusion in an amnesty that had been won a few days earlier by over 1,000 migrants who had barricaded themselves for almost two months in Santa Maria del Pi cathedral and other churches in the Catalan capital.

In the early 2000s, the union Almería found itself operating in a contradictory situation in. On the one hand, Almería's greenhouses – and the whole national economy – experienced continuous growth, which brought a huge number of new migrants to the region; on the other, legislation in 2000 (Ley Orgánica 4) ushered in a crackdown on the rights and freedoms of migrants. In response, the SOC organized a large number of demonstrations for the legalization of migrants as well as protests against racist violence and attacks that continued throughout the province, and especially in El Ejido. During the same decade, this medium-sized town rapidly grew into a city of more than 100,000 inhabitants, over 30 per cent of whom were migrants. As the ultra-modern capital of Almería's greenhouse industry, high levels of wealth now stood cheek by jowl with poverty and social exclusion (Checa, 1998, p. 25). On 13 February 2005, the Moroccan day labourer and SOC member Azzouz Hosni was assassinated on his way out of a bar in El Ejido. The union called a demonstration in the city centre a few days after the murder but was banned by the mayor. The ongoing episodes of racist violence strengthened the bonds with a few small anti-racist organizations in NGOs in Almería province, which was structured through the State Network for Migrants' Rights (*Red Estatal por los Derechos de los Inmigrantes*). During this period, the SOC opened three branches in the province: one in the provincial capital, one in the eastern district of Nijar and one in the centre of El Ejido. The latter was established in a building that had been bought by the union with financial support from the European Civic Forum[5] (Getaz, 2015).

During the years of the horticultural boom in Almería, the SOC was the only union to denounce cases of racism and exploitation in the greenhouses. It was disparagingly referred to as the 'migrants' union', and faced ostracism from local inhabitants and farmers. The Almería local branch of SOC was composed almost exclusively of migrant members and militants, while in the other provincial SOC federations almost all the labourers were native Spaniards. Like the traditional unions, the SOC also set up help desks and provided assistance in tackling the bureaucratic procedures for obtaining Spanish residency. Nonetheless, a large number of migrant workers asked the SOC for union support and assistance in specific cases of labour exploitation, unpaid wages and overtime, and indiscriminate sackings.

Since 2008, the economic crisis along with the growing rigidity of Almería's 'unionized' employers, led to an intensification of these activities. It is no coincidence that the SOC – which in the meantime had merged with the Andalusian Workers' Union (*Sindacato Andaluz de los Trabajadores*, SAT) – was forced to use strategies of deception, which saw its activists disguise themselves as journalists, researchers and university students in order to gain access to the greenhouses, gather testimonies and organize individual and collective labour actions.

### *17.4.1 The response to the crisis: land occupations*

As noted above, the Andalusian SOC has, since its founding, used land occupation as its preferred instrument to defend and fulfil the day labourers' fundamental needs. 'Bread, land and work' has always been the slogan of its demonstrations and protest actions. As the economic crisis intensified and unemployment rose in

Andalusia – which in 2011 reached 38.4 per cent – the SOC decided to relaunch its traditional strategy in order to respond to the 'hunger for work' and to government measures to privatize over 20,000 hectares of public land, including land belonging to the Institute for Agrarian Reform in Andalusia, which was set up in 1984 and dissolved on 31 December 2010. On the eve of a public auction in March 2012 of the 540-hectare Somonte estate, owned by the Andalusian government in Córdoba province, hundreds of SOC day labourers marched to the estate and occupied it. The occupation continues to this day, where several dozen labourers are employed.

In the wake of the success at Somonte, on 1 May 2013, the SOC occupied three large estates in the northern Andalusian provinces. In all three cases, the occupiers were Andalusian labourers. First, 300 day labourers entered Las Turquillas, a military-owned 1,000-hectare estate in Osuna municipality, where only a few dozen hectares were used for a horse-breeding facility. According to the union, this estate could guarantee – as in the case of the 'El Humoso' farm in Marinaleda, which was of an equal size – about 50,000 working days a year. The demonstrators called for the Defence Department to cede the land to the municipality of Osuna, which is what already happened in 2008 with a 300-hectare lot where to this day, after a process of conversion to production, several dozen local day labourers organized into local cooperatives earn their living. Second, about 100 day labourers from SOC's Jaén provincial branch occupied La Rueda, a 600-hectare farm in the Sierra Magina district, for the seventh time. The estate numbered over 250,000 olive trees, whose fruit remained on the ground unharvested while Banco Bilbao bank, which had repossessed the property, raked in over 600,000 euros a year in EU subsidies just for owning the land. The Jaén SOC had been calling for years for a special permit – based on Law 34/79 on 'manifestly improvable agricultural land' – to hire 300 local unemployed day labourers to harvest La Rueda's thousands of tonnes of olives. Finally, a group of 200 day labourers marched on the Valdeojos-Hornillo estate in protest against municipal authorities, who ceded some 700 hectares to the Institute for Agrarian Reform. The Institute in turn sold the land to a local wealthy land-owning family. The union called on the Andalusian government to intervene against this agricultural 'counter-reform' and to reclaim the land that was being neglected by its new owners.

Following the success of day labourers' struggles in northern Andalusia, the migrant members of SOC in Almería decided to engage in the same form of struggle for the first time. In La Majonera municipality, which was located halfway between El Ejido and the town of Roquetas de Mar, a local entrepreneur, Simón Sabio, had abandoned the El Viso greenhouse farm with a mountain of debts, including over 500,000 euros in unpaid wages. On 10 May 2013, an assembly of approximately 130 Moroccan labourers employed on this farm decided to remain in their workplace. They decided to finish the tomato production cycle in a bid to recover at least some of their back pay and to defend their jobs. In the meantime, the union tried to mediate with a court-appointed receiver to verify the possibility of a temporary loan. They aimed to use part of the 36 hectares, by setting up a cooperative of former employees. The local authorities responded by cutting off the water and electricity supply to the company farmsteads where labourers had taken shelter, which made their living conditions even more difficult and precarious.

The workers and the union took up the gauntlet once more. They formed the *Jornaler@s Sin Patron* (Day Labourers without a Boss) association, and in September they began cultivating courgettes in the occupied greenhouses. These products were sold through alternative food networks. However, in the following months the local water management board cut off their water supply, impeding the vital irrigation of the land. The workers were forced to stop farming and to leave the greenhouses in a state of abandon and decline.

### *17.4.2 Alliance strategies between migrant labourers in southern Europe and consumers in northern Europe: the Bio Sol dispute*

The acquisition of negotiating power on behalf of highly vulnerable subjects remains a central goal for any union intending to defend the interests of migrant day labourers. Through its decades-long experience, the SOC has been able to identify and leverage one of the weak points of Almería's farmers: damaging their image vis-à-vis consumers, especially in other nations. The alliance between producers and consumers is at the core of the fair trade movement that connects the global South and North and the so-called Alternative Agri-Food Networks that promote social justice in Western economies (Goodman *et al.*, 2012). Here, a new kind of fair trade is at stake that regards the conditions of agricultural workers in the EU. While Almería's farmers may be able to trample the rights of seasonal workers with impunity, they cannot afford to upset the sensibilities of an increasingly aware and demanding cohort of consumers in central and northern Europe who are concerned about environmentally and socially sustainable food production. Day labourers may be interchangeable, but final consumers are far less so.

Over the years, the SOC has nurtured and encouraged ever-closer relationships with antiracist movements, NGOs, foreign trade unions and journalists as strategic resources to circumvent its weakness at the negotiating table.[6] The dispute against Bio Sol Portocarrero is an example of this strategy of internationalization. Bio Sol sells some 7,000 tonnes of organic fruit and vegetables, exclusively to foreign markets. Bio Sol, with some 20 affiliated farmers, grows these products in greenhouses stretching over 100 hectares in Almería's Nijar district. A number of certification bodies guarantee that the products are grown organically, and that the labour and union rights of its almost 300 employees are respected. Bio Sol adheres to GlobalGAP, a self-certification protocol adopted by leading European retail chains in response to growing consumer demand for food safety and respect for the environment (Campbell, 2005). It also adheres to the Leading Organic Alliance (LOA), the top European organic certification network. In addition, Bio Sol signed up to GRASP, GlobalGAP.'s add-on module to assess social practices and workers' health, safety and welfare. In 2010 the company allowed 32 GRASP audits, which vouched for the company's respect for the social dignity and rights of the workers employed in the various stages of production. Several studies and research reports have already pointed to the limitations of this certification system, which is managed by a private company with no public oversight (Moraes *et al.*, 2012): on the one hand regulatory ambiguity provides entrepreneurs with wide margins for manoeuvre – albeit subject to the payment of a rather steep membership fee – while on the other, its contents and findings are frequently publicized among northern consumers rather than among local workers (Korovkin and Sanmiguel, 2007, p. 18).

The Bio Sol case confirmed this critical reading of the privatization of regulations and controls, whereby new players such as multinational companies and private certification and inspection agents play a key role (Sassen, 2006). In fact, in Bio Sol's greenhouses, work relations are mainly based on fixed-term contracts and union rights are not fully recognized, in order to enforce constant wage cuts and ever longer working hours with no health and safety guarantees. SOC organizers allege that the firm's strategy of avoiding issuing permanent contracts consists in firing and then rehiring the same workers in the same workplace, through its different brands (Bio Sol, Econijar, Manipulados Parque Natural, etc.). After about two years, workers are finally laid off permanently. New hires are constantly blackmailed, and are forced to sign for false wage slips, to work unpaid overtime, to give up their holidays, to maintain elevated production rhythms even in cases of pregnancy or illness, and to avoid any contact with labour unions.

In October 2010, 13 Moroccan women workers on the packaging assembly line were fired when they were on the verge of completing two consecutive years of employment – after which, by law, employers must switch from fixed-term to permanent contracts – and were replaced with new Eastern European labourers. The SOC put the sacked workers in contact with a German journalist, who published their story in the Swiss national newspaper *Tages-Anzeiger*. Over the following days, several anti-racist groups distributed flyers outside Swiss supermarkets, denouncing what they called Bio Sol's 'bio-exploitation'. The campaign was effective. Bio Suisse, an organic farming organization that certifies products imported by the Swiss Coop supermarket chain, intervened in the labour dispute and asked the supplier for clarifications. It proposed itself as mediator, and ordered Swiss Coop to suspend all purchases from Bio Sol. On 14 March 2011, representatives from Bio Suisse, Swiss Coop and Campinia Verde Ecosol (a Spanish fruit and vegetable wholesaler, of which the major German supermarket chain Rewe is a significant shareholder) arrived in Nijar to talk to SOC union organizers and the sacked workers. Within a few days, the firm agreed to reinstate the workers and pay them their outstanding wages, to permanently stabilize seasonal workers and to open an SOC branch within the company. Hafida Mounjid, one of the 13 fired workers, was elected as union delegate.

The company also committed itself to ongoing dialogue with workers and to correct bad practices identified during a Bio Suisse public audit carried out in Almería with the participation of the SOC and other local social organizations. In 2012, a further agreement was signed putting in place a permanent and 'innovative system of dialogue and negotiation through a mediation agreement that includes the intervention of European consumers' (SOC/SAT, 2014).

## 17.5 Conclusions: Social Movement Unionism?

As the above description of labour disputes and SOC union practices demonstrates, this organization displays some of the characteristic elements of Social Movement Unionism: horizontal organization, the building of broad social coalitions, the recruitment of vulnerable subjects, non-professional grassroots activism, direct action and an anti-bureaucratic approach. This stands in sharp contrast with what I define as the 'cartel unionism' of the two main Spanish trade unions, the CCOO and UGT.

In recent years, the territorial and community-based 'worker centres' in the United States (Janice, 2006; Milkman and Ott, 2014), which recall the Industrial Workers of the World structures from the beginning of the twentieth century (Dubofsky and McCartin, 1969), have played a decisive role in the increased unionization of day labourers in metropolitan areas and agro-industrial districts. Similarly, the SOC branches in Almería have become important reference points for migrant day labourers. They can be considered a model of 'community unionism', blending the four ideal types of action employed by migrant rights organizations: the promotion of networks, political protest, legal protection and the provision of services (Ambrosini and Van Der Leun, 2015).

> I'm lucky because I work just a few kilometres away from here and with my bike I can come to this place [the El Ejido SOC union office] and visit my brothers, talk about my problems but also celebrate my birthday, play cards until late or watch football when my favourite team plays.
>
> (interview with Mohamed, Moroccan day laborer, November 2014)

This strong community-oriented model echoes many aspects of the most established experience of unionizing migrant day labour in the United States: the United Farm Workers of America (UFW) founded by Cesar Chavez, leader of the Mexican-American farm workers from the 1960s to 1980s (Araiza, 2014; Ganz, 2009). The SOC day labourers are mostly Moroccan, just as the majority of the UFW members were, and still are, Mexican. Moreover, there are strong analogies between the Bio Sol dispute in Almería and the renowned campaign by Justice for Janitors (Waldinger *et al.*, 1998), the social movement organization that has been fighting for the rights of cleaners across the USA and Canada since 1985. In both cases, the construction of broad social coalitions and the involvement of powerful subjects (tenants and homeowners in the US campaign and foreign consumers in the Spanish case) were the winning moves that bypassed the contractual weakness of migrant workers.

A further question concerns the particular nature of SOC's success in unionizing migrant farm labourers in Almería. It is difficult to envisage this model being automatically adopted and replicated in other agribusiness districts, due to both subjective elements and structural conditions. One needs only to recall the failure of the SOC to take root among the 30,000 day labourers employed in the strawberry industry in Huelva province. Here, the seasonal character of agricultural labour makes union intervention difficult. In fact, the SOC has only been able to win one labour dispute when, in 2008, Italian businesswoman Mirella Giorgi was expelled from the Freshuelva consortium after inspections revealed the inhumane living conditions of the workers segregated on her farm. It was no coincidence that this dispute had been brought about by approximately 70 Moroccan day labourers who had previously worked in Almería province. The permanent or semi-permanent presence of a consistent number of migrant day labourers, as well as the historic roots of migrant settlements in the area, are indispensable preconditions for the unionization of these workers.[7]

In addition, Andalusia has a number of particular characteristics that distinguishes it from the rest of Europe, which are the corollary of the persistence of the *cultura jornalera* in agricultural labour relations (Moreno, 1993). First and foremost, the longevity of the Franco dictatorship meant that old (native) and new (migrant) day labourers would cross paths through their involvement in union organization. This is consistent with the idea that the presence of home-grown activism does not undermine but, on the contrary, supports the emergence of new forms of social and union activism on the part of migrants (Ambrosini, 2014). In other Mediterranean contexts, such as Italy, the significant gap in terms of time between the cycle of native day-labour struggles and the arrival of migrants has created a gulf between autochthonous (sometimes 'fake') farm labourers – who enjoy health coverage and pension benefits and are mostly members of traditional unions (even when they do not work) – and the migrant day labourers who do most of the work in the fields, and in most cases do not carry a union card (Piro, 2015).

This said, the SOC experience, in sum, offers some useful lessons for future effective union organization of agricultural day labourers in other parts of the Mediterranean.

## Notes

1 This work is based on data collected within the 'Agri-Food Development, Markets and Policies' research project coordinated by the University of Calabria (Italy) in collaboration with the University of Almería (Centro de Estudio de las Migraciones y las Relaciones Interculturales – CEMYRI) and funded by Calabria Region (Regional Operational Programme, board IV 'Human Resource', European Social Fund 2007/2013).

2 *Alhóndigas* used to be the local agricultural markets. Today, they are institutions which connect local small farmers with big retailing companies.

3 It is worth noting that, in contrast to 'cartel unions', 'cartel parties' are in crisis in Spain, and across Europe, where they are challenged by new 'populist' parties (such as *Podemos* in Spain and the *Movimento 5 Stelle* in Italy).

4 In Catalonia, for example, the Government outsourced the management of the *contrataciòn en origen*, the Spanish seasonal agricultural workers scheme, to the Catalonian Farmers' Union (*Unió de Pagesos*) (Achón, 2011).

5 The European Civic Forum is a mutual aid organization set up by the leaders of the Longo Mai cooperatives, a network of self-managed farm cooperatives in France.

6 SOC is a member of the European Coordination Via Campesina (ECVC). This transnational movement brings together millions of peasants, small and medium-size farmers, landless people, women farmers, indigenous peoples, migrants and agricultural workers from around the world, in order to promote sustainable small-scale farming,

social justice and food sovereignty, and to organize against transnational corporations and neoliberal policies.

7 The case of the 2010 Rosarno riots in Calabria, Italy is emblematic. More than 1,000 undocumented migrant workers were granted extraordinary visas for 'humanitarian protection'. It is worth noting that the political management of the dispute was played out not in the orange-farming area of Piana di Gioia Tauro in Calabria but rather in Rome and the Castel Volturno area in Campania, where many of the seasonal day labourers move at the end of the citrus harvest, and where they have settled and been involved in union organizing for over a decade (Caruso, 2011).

## References

Achón, O. (2011). *Importando miseria: la alternativa a la provision de mano de obra agrícola*. Madrid: Los Libros de la Catarata.

Ambrosini, M. (2014). 'Networking, protest, advocacy, aid. Italian civil society and immigrants. migrant worlds'. *Mondi Migranti*, 3: 201–222.

Ambrosini, M. and Van Der Leun, J. (2015). 'Introduction to the Special Issue: Implementing human rights: civil society and migration policies'. *Journal of Immigrant & Refugee Studies*, 13: 103–115.

Araiza, L. (2014). *To March for Others: The Black Freedom Struggle and the United Farm Workers*. Philadelphia: University of Pennsylvania Press.

Baldwin-Edwards, M. and Arango, J. (1999). *Immigrants and the Informal Economy in Southern Europe*. London: Cass & Co.

Barbero, I. (2013). 'El movimiento de los sin-papeles como sujeto de juridicidad'. *Revista internacional de sociología*, 71: 37:64.

Berlan, J.-P. (1987). 'La agricultura Mediterránea y el mercado de trabajo: ¿Una California para Europa?'. *Agricultura y Sociedad*, no. 42: 233–245.

Cabrera, A. and Uclés, D. (2013). *Análisis de la campaña hortofrutícola de Almería. Campaña 2012/2013.* Almería: Fundación Cajamar.

Cabrera, A., Uclés, D. and Agüera, T. (2015). *Análisis de la campaña hortofrutícola de Almería. Campaña 2014/2015.* Almería: Fundación Cajamar.

Campbell, H. (2005). 'The rise and rise of EurepGAP: European (Re) invention of colonial food relations'. *International Journal of Sociology of Agriculture and Food*, 13 (2): 6–19.

Caruso, F. (2011). 'Il bracciantato migrante meridionale nel distretto della clandestinità: il movimento dei migranti di Caserta'. *Mondi Migranti*, 3: 229–243.

Castles, S. and Miller, M. J. (1993). *The Age of Migration: International Population Movements in the Modern World.* London: Macmillan.

Checa, F. (1998). *Africanos en la otra orilla. Trabajo, cultura e integración en la España Mediterránea.* Barcelona: Icaria.

Checa, F. (2001). *El Ejido: la ciudad cortijo. Claves socioeconomicas del conflicto etnico.* Barcelona: Icaria.

Checa, J. C. (2007). *Viviendo juntos aparte: La segregación espacial de los Africanos en Almería.* Barcelona: Icaria.

Crouch, C. (2004). *Post-democracy*. London: Polity Press.

Dubofsky, M. and McCartin, J. A. (1969). *We Shall Be All: A History of the Industrial Workers of the World.* Urbana: University of Illinois Press.

Ferraro, F. and Aznar, J. A. (2008). 'El distrito agroindustrial de Almería: un caso atípico' in Soler, M. V. (ed.) *Los Distritos Industriales.* Almería: Instituto de Estudios de Cajamar.

Forum Civique Européen (2000). *El Ejido, tierra sin ley*. Guipuzcoa: Hiru.
Ganz, M. (2009). *Why David Sometimes Wins: Leadership, Organization, and Strategy in the California Farm Worker Movement*. New York: Oxford University Press.
Gallino, L. (2012). *La lotta di classe dopo la lotta di classe*. Roma-Bari: Laterza.
Gerrefi, G. (1995). 'Global production systems and third-world development' in Stallins, B. (ed.), *Global Change, Regional Response. The New International Context of Development*. Cambridge: Cambridge University Press.
Gereffi, G. and Korzeniewicz, M. (1994). *Commodity Chains and Global Capitalism*. Westport, CT: Praeger.
Gereffi, G., Sturgeon, J. and Sturgeon, T. (2005). 'The governance of global value chains'. *Review of International Political Economy*, 12 (1): 78–104.
Gertel, J. and Sippel, S. R. (2014). *Seasonal Workers in Mediterranean Agriculture. The Social Costs of Eating Fresh*. London: Routledge.
Getaz, R. (2015). 'Spanien: Bitteres Obst und Gemüse'. *Archipelausgabe*, 233, http://www.civic-forum.org/de/artikel/spanien-bitteres-obst-und-gem%C3%BCse (accessed 17 June 2016).
González, C. (2008). *Los sindicatos ante la inmigración*. Madrid: OPI, Ministerio de Trabajo e Inmigración.
Goodman, D., DuPuis, E. M. and Goodman, M. K. (2012). *Alternative Food Networks: Knowledge, Practice, and Politics*. London: Routledge.
Forum Civique Européen (2000). *El Ejido, tierra sin ley*. Guipuzcoa: Hiru.
Instituto de Estudios Socioeconómicos de la Fundación Cajamar (2008). *Análisis de la campaña hortofrutícola de Almería. Campaña 2007/2008*. Almería: Fundación Cajamar.
Izcara, S. P. and Andrade, K. L. (2004). 'Inmigración y trabajo irregular en la agricultura: trabajadores tamaulipecos en Estados Unidos y jornaleros magrebíes en Andalucía'. *Mundo agrario. Revista de Estudios Rurales*, 4 (8).
Janice, F. (2006). *Worker Centers: Organizing Communities at the Edge of the Dream*. Ithaca, NY: Cornell University Press.
Katz, R. and Mair, P. (1995). 'Changing models of party organization and party democracy. The emergence of the cartel party'. *Party Politics*, 1: 5–28.
King, R., Lazaridis, G. and Tsardanidis, C. (eds) (2000). *Eldorado or Fortress? Migration in Southern Europe*. Basingstoke: McMillan.
Korovkin, T. and Sanmiguel, O. (2007). 'Estándares de trabajo e iniciativas no estatales en las industrias loricolas de Colombia y Ecuador'. *Iconos. Revista de Ciencias Sociales*, 29: 15–30.
Lipsky, M. (1980). *Street-level Bureaucracy. Dilemmas of the Individual in Public Services*. New York: Russell Sage Foundation.
Martinez Lucio, M. (1998). 'Spain: Regulating employment and social fragmentation' in Ferner, A. and Hyman, R. (eds) *Changing Industrial Relations in Europe*. Oxford: Basil Blackwell.
Milkman, R. and Ott, E. (2014). *New Labor in New York – Precarious Workers and the Future of the Labor Movement*. New York: ILR Press.
Miravet, P. (2005). *Trabajadores inmigrantes, sindicatos y participación*, Universidad de Valencia, Working paper.
Moody, K. (1997). *Workers in a Lean World: Unions in the International Economy*. London: Verso.
Moraes, N., Gadea, E., Pedreño, A. and de Castro, C. (2012). 'Enclaves globales agrícolas y migraciones de trabajo: convergencias globales y regulaciones transnacionales'. *Política y Sociedad*, 49 (1): 13–34.

Moreno, I. (1993). 'Cultura del trabajo e ideología: el movimiento campesino anarquista andaluz' in Moreno, I. (ed.) *Andalucia: identidad y cultura. Estudios de Antropología Andaluza.* Málaga: Editorial Librería Ágora.

Murgia, A. and Selmi, G. (2011). 'Inspira e cospira. Forme di autorganizzazione del precariato in Italia'. *Sociologia del lavoro,* 123: 163–176.

Piro, V. (2015). 'What is deemed to be 'fake'? The case of 'fake agricultural workers' in South Eastern Sicily'. *Mondi migranti,* 1: 65–84.

Portes, A. and Sassen-Koob, S. (1987). 'Making it underground: Comparative material on the informal sector in western market economies'. *American Journal of Sociology,* 93: 30–61.

Reardon, T., Codron, J.-M., Busch, L., Bingen, J. and Harris, C. (2001) 'Global change in agrifood grades and standards: Agribusiness strategic responses in developing countries'. *International Food and Agribusiness Management Review*, 2 (3): 421–435.

Sassen, S. (2006). *Territory, Authority, Rights. Assemblies from the Middle Ages to the Global Era.* Princeton, NJ: Princeton University Press.

SOC/SAT (2014). *Informe sobre la lucha de Biosol*, self-financed mimeograph, Almería.

Turner, L. and Hurd, R. (2001). 'Building social movement unionism: the transformation of the American labor movement' in Turner, L., Katz, H. C. and Hurd, R. W. (eds) *Rekindling the Movement: Labor's Quest for Relevance in the Twenty-First Century.* Ithaca, NY: Cornell University Press.

Veiga, U. (2014). 'The political economy of El Ejido: Genealogy of the 2000 conflict' in Gertel, J. and Sippel, S.R. (eds) *Seasonal Workers in Mediterranean Agriculture: The Social Costs of Eating Fresh.* London: Routledge.

Voss, K. and Sherman, R. (2003). 'You just can't do it automatically: The transition to social movement unionism in the United States' in Fairbrother, P. and Yates, C. (eds) *Trade Unions in Renewal: a Comparative Study.* London: Routledge.

Waldinger, R., Erickson, C. and Milkman, R. *et al.* (1998). 'Helots no more: A case study of the Justice for Janitors Campaign in Los Angeles' in Bronfenbrenner, K., Friedman, S., Hurd, R. W. *et al.* (eds) *Organizing to Win: New Research on Union Strategies.* Ithaca, NY: ILR Press.

Waterman, P., (1993). 'Social movement unionism: A new model for a new world'. *Fernand Braudel Center Review,* 16 (3): 245–278.

Watts, M. and Goodman, D. (1997). 'Global appetite, local metabolism: Nature, culture and industry in fin-de-siècle agro-food systems' in Goodman, D. and Watts, M. (eds) *Globalizing Food: Agrarian Questions and Global Restructuring.* London: Routledge

# 18 Entering the 'plastic factories'

## Conflicts and competition in Sicilian greenhouses and packinghouses

*Valeria Piro and Giuliana Sanò*

### 18.1 Introduction[1]

> It is still dark outside when the alarm of our phones tells us that it is time to get up. Outside, the streets are still lit by street lamps. We get in the car and we reach Hassan's house. When we get there, they are already in the car, ready to go, and we follow them. After a few metres, Hassan stops at the roadside. A young man gets in and the car sets off again. We cross Piazza Manin, better known as the "Square of Tunisians": from where the roads radiate out to the countryside. Someone is already there waiting for the employer. When the square and the city are some way behind us, we find ourselves in a completely new environment. Constructions of aluminium, wood and plastic devour up the land, consuming the scenery of carob trees and dry stone walls, to the point that the landscape disappears from view. At 7am we arrive at the district of Alcerito, our final destination. We get out of the car, as do Hassan, his wife, his son-in-law and Ahmed, the guy they had picked up from the roadside. Semi is there waiting for us. Semi is a Tunisian who lives in a little hut on the same land as Hassan's greenhouses. Valeria and I approach the rest of the team. They do not seem bothered by our presence. We get to the greenhouses and there are not that many of them. The land on which they stand is not very large. Hassan puts us to work immediately. Valeria, Sanah (Hassan's wife) and myself select the best tomatoes to be sent to market. Inside these very hot plastic factories, the three Tunisians relentlessly pick salad tomatoes and place them in boxes situated outside the greenhouses. On the back of a pickup van Valeria, Sanah and myself divide the tomatoes into first, second and third choice. "The best-looking tomatoes have to be placed on the top while the ugly ones go underneath". Sanah explains to us. No one speaks, except for us on the back of the van. From inside the greenhouses, all that can be heard is the sound of scissors as they remove the tomatoes as quickly as possible: tac, tac, tac.
>
> (Giuliana's fieldnotes, Vittoria, south-east Sicily, 5 March 2013)

In the south-east corner of Sicily, agriculture is 'protected' by a huge tract of plastic and polyethylene that stretches from Licata (in the province of Agrigento) along the coast to Pachino (in the province of Siracusa). This area, in fact, hosts the highest concentration of greenhouse farming in the whole of Italy. Like the rural areas of Almeria and Huelva in Spain and the Piana del Sele in Italy (see also Reigada, Hellio, Avallone and Caruso in this volume), this part of Sicily is characterized by the greenhouse cultivation of vegetables, especially tomatoes, aubergines, courgettes and peppers. The south-east province of Ragusa, where our ethnographic research was conducted, occupies the main, central section of this plastic landscape, which is commonly referred to as the 'Transformed Coastal Belt' (TCB), and where about 5,700 hectares are devoted to greenhouse crops (17 per cent of Italy's total greenhouse cultivation) (Istat, 2010). Protected crops in this area date back to the early 1960s, when local producers began to observe and experiment the advantages of early ripening of vegetables that could be attained thanks to placing plastic films over crops. Agronomic and technical transformations have led gradually to the deseasonalization of local agriculture, and have restored the fortunes of the primary sector as well as the general economy of the area. By greatly reducing the risks and problems associated with open field seasonal agriculture, greenhouse farming has enabled this particular province in Sicily to assume a prominent place in national and European production networks.

The high profits and the substantial turnover[2] connected with greenhouse farming are partly due to the strategic presence of one of Italy's largest wholesale fresh food markets, located in the nearby town of Vittoria. From here, tonnes of goods leave Sicily: local producers are able to deliver their produce daily to local fresh food markets as well as national and international supply chain platforms[3] – especially in northern European countries and, more recently, Eastern Europe.[4]

The improvement of economic conditions gave rise to an increase in workforce demand. Local people considered some agricultural tasks undignified, unprofitable and intrinsically *dirty, dangerous and demanding* (Cole and Booth, 2007). This led to a progressive shift from family labour to the employment of migrant workers and a process of labour market segmentation (Piore, 1979; Pugliese, 2009; Colloca and Corrado, 2013).

In the province of Ragusa, in 2013 there were 13,240 non-Italian agricultural workers, who roughly counted for half of the total workers working in the TCB. However, official statistics do not take into account the high presence of foreign workers hired 'off the books' in local agriculture or the significant number of Italian and non-Italian 'fake labourers' who are officially registered as employed but who either do not do the stipulated hours or do not work at all (Piro, 2015). The largest groups of foreign farmworkers are Romanians and Tunisians: out of the 13,240 workers, 4,349 are Romanian and 5,964 are Tunisian.[5] As in the case of Hassan, described in the fieldnote extract at the start of this chapter some of those Tunisians who arrived in the area during the early 1980s have recently started to rent greenhouses, and so have moved from the position of day workers to that of independent producers. This can be viewed as a social mobility strategy.[6]

Within the agriculture sector, gender divisions that have their bedrock in cultural constructions are particularly prominent and are functional to the division of labour in agri-food production. In packinghouses, women are hired more frequently than men, because they are considered to be quicker, more accurate and more attentive to the appearance of the produce. Conversely, men are more readily employed in greenhouses. Romanian female farmworkers represent an exception to this pattern. In this case, the traditional gender division has been exacerbated as the effect of a profound sexist and macho culture that tends to project onto these female workers the image of freely available women, and which has sometimes resulted in cases of sexual exploitation.

This chapter is based on ethnographic research conducted by the two authors during six months living in the town of Vittoria. Over this period we observed various workplaces, in particular greenhouses and packinghouses and, in some cases, we were able to participate directly in work. Workplace ethnography is necessary to acquire a more accurate understanding of the relationships between farmers and workers, and especially the strategies adopted by employers to capitalize on the efforts of their farmworkers. Indeed, the local dominant idea of agricultural productivity based upon a low-skilled, highly flexible and vulnerable migrant workforce is the premise for widespread precarious labour which sees thousands of men and women being randomly hired direct from the streets and squares, as in the case of Ahmed in the opening fieldnote (see also Theodore *et al.*, 2006). This organization of work also tends to generate deep conflicts – especially at a horizontal level – in the various workplaces.

In this chapter we analyse three conflicts that we were able to observe closely during our participation in operations in two greenhouses and a packinghouse. In the first case, a farmer justified the different wages paid to two national groups (Tunisians and Romanians) on the basis of differing work speeds which, in turn, led to a particular kind of competition within the greenhouse. In the second example, the high rate of precarious employment frequent in packinghouses was the cause for tension between us – as participant (and privileged) observers – and a team of female on-call workers who accused us of 'stealing their jobs'. In the final case, religious habits were the premise used to explain different levels of productivity in a dispute between Muslims of different nationalities.

The examples discussed here are not meant to be representative of the different kinds of conflicts that occurred in the workplaces we observed. Each case focuses on an analysis of horizontal conflicts, in other words disputes over wages and work conditions that take place between employees of different religious, national or social backgrounds, and not between farmworkers and their employer. We contend that these horizontal conflicts are the corollary of high levels of job insecurity but, at the same time, they represent ways through which workers also 'come to terms' with job precariousness. Through a mechanism similar to the 'games of making out' studied by Roy (1952, 1953) and Burawoy (1979), these negotiations resolve themselves in a division of labour, which is functional to the strategies of exploitation and value extraction inside agri-food system.

## 18.2 Theoretical inspirations and methodological strategies: a view from the field

In the study of the 'globalization of the countryside' (Colloca and Corrado, 2013), several authors have highlighted that salary reduction and the consequent degradation of agricultural work are the structural result of a gradual compression of a farm's profit margins due to the pressure of competition from international markets and retail corporations (see the Introduction to this volume; Holmes, 2013; Gertel and Sippel, 2014). Research has shown how the agri-food sector has been increasingly shaped by successive cycles of 'ethnic and gender substitution' in order to favour salary restraints through a continuous process of segmentation and competition (Berlan, 1986, 2008; De Bonis, 2005; Preibisch and Binford, 2007; Mannon *et al.*, 2011; Hellio, 2014). Moreover, it has been underlined that developments in agri-food production have been flanked by migration policies or mobility regimes often based on the temporality of migration, which are a root cause of the precarious condition of foreign workers (Morice, 2008; Morice and Michalon, 2008; Morice and Potot, 2010; Corrado and Perrotta, 2012; Décosse, 2013; Hellio, 2014; Lindner and Kathmann, 2014).

With this framework in mind, the aim of our research was to investigate these 'macro' dynamics through a 'micro' lens, looking in particular at how global processes influence and shape workers' everyday experiences in their workplaces. We thus posed ourselves some straightforward questions: what takes place on a daily basis in the work environments, namely, in our case, in the greenhouse and in the packinghouse? What mechanisms underpin the organization of production? What are the everyday conflicts? The main source of theoretical inspiration has been the sociology of labour, in particular the classic works of Donald Roy (1952, 1953), Alvin Gouldner (1954) and Michael Burawoy (1972, 1979) and other contributions that fall under the umbrella term of *workplace studies* (Heath *et al.*, 2000). From a methodological point of view, these scholars privilege the use of qualitative techniques and often draw on long-term observations in workplaces such as factories (Ngai *et al.*, 2015), building sites (Jounin, 2008; Perrotta, 2011) as well as the service industry (Ehrenreich, 2001; Alberti, 2014). In this direction, we provided a detailed description of agricultural work environments, more rarely considered by academic scholars, albeit with significant exceptions (Holmes, 2013; Castracani, 2014).

The possibility of conducting our field research together represented for us a great advantage. The fact of being together (instead of working separately) enabled us to access the field in an easier and safer way, and to take relatively higher risks and to feel more comfortable in a number of situations. Most important of all, it allowed us to deepen our reflexive approach, and to develop, between us, a greater degree of intersubjectivity that endowed our research with stronger 'validity' (Cardano, 2001). Too often, ethnographic research is limited through being constructed as an individual effort, with the ethnographer acting as a 'lone stranger in the hearth of darkness' (Salzman, 1994). Conversely, we are both persuaded of the importance of collective research methods (e.g. action research and workers inquiry) and have been inspired by several examples of joint ethnographic work (see, among others, Schneider and Schneider, 1976; Bourgois and Schonberg, 2009).

In any case, conducting participant observation in workplaces was not an easy task, primarily due to the difficulty for two young researchers to be hired in a labour market almost totally constituted by foreign workers, and mainly men in the case of the greenhouses. The structural differences – in terms of gender, social class and nationality – between the researchers and people normally employed in agriculture made access to the field particularly problematic. We opted for small periods of overt participant observation and mainly informal or unpaid work in a range of different workplaces: in the greenhouses of Hassan, a Tunisian farm owner in his fifties, over a total of 10 days; inside FreshCrops,[7] a medium-size farm managed by an Italian owner that 'hosted' us for 15 days (see Section 18.5); inside Just Tomatoes, a medium-size packinghouse where the Italian employer hired us for 15 days through an official seasonal contract. Also a period of covert participant observation was conducted on a small farm for about one week by just one of the two researchers (see Section 18.3).[8] In addition, in order to map the daily activities of the local fruit and vegetable market, we shadowed a broker as he went about his work at the wholesale market of Vittoria and in neighbouring towns. Finally, besides the life stories and informal conversations collected during the course of the research (with a total of 78 people), 43 semi-structured interviews were carried out with farmworkers and employers, members of local institutions, trade unionists and labour inspectors, priests, doctors and volunteers working with migrants in the province of Ragusa.

The accounts collected through the interviews and participant observation allowed us to analyse the daily processes of negotiation occurring in workplaces. Similar to the US shop floors studied by Roy and Burawoy, it was also possible to observe the deployment of several 'games of making out' and the emergence of micro-conflicts in the Sicilian 'plastic factories'. These different cases will be the focus of the following paragraphs.

## 18.3 SicilSerre: 'racing' during working hours

A first type of conflict, frequent in a labour market characterized by the presence of a foreign workforce, concerns the frictions that arise between workers of different nationalities. The example we discuss in this section is one of the most emblematic cases of how nationality explicitly becomes a significant issue during the definition of working conditions. Competitive pressures between Romanian and Tunisian workers emerged vividly during our short experience of covert participant observation in a small greenhouse farm, which we name SicilSerre. In this case, Ahmed, a Tunisian farmworker who we had met on a previous job, had managed to procure work for Valeria. Unlike Ahmed, who was informed of the purpose of our research, the employer did not know the reason behind the unusual presence of a young Italian woman in the greenhouse. During the same period inside SicilSerre, as well as the young researcher (employed on a temporary basis) and Ahmed, the farm owner had also hired off the books Nicola, a middle-aged Romanian man. This small group had just replaced the previous team, which had consisted of a young couple of Romanian workers. The arrival of the new workers had then prompted a delicate phase of negotiation to set the working conditions and, above all, to stipulate the 'fair' daily salary for each farmworker.

In order to determine the salaries, Giovanni, the employer, relied on a widespread convention in the TCB: that of paying a different salary according to the worker's nationality. At the time the research was conducted, the informal agreement in the area was €30 per day for Tunisians and €25 for Romanians.[9] As compensation for lower payment, the employer usually 'offered' Romanian workers the chance to live on the farm, generally in small houses (such as tool sheds or huts), which often cut them off from the services and places of sociability in urban areas. Moreover, hiring workers who lived 'in the countryside' gave employers other advantages besides paying lower salaries: it allowed them to demand more flexible (and often longer) working hours compared to workers living in urban areas. This overlap between places of production and reproduction largely limits the privacy of farmworkers: work and life tend to gradually coincide, lengthening the amount of time spent on the job and leading to a depersonalization and progressive loss of meaning of spaces and moments dedicated to personal life and intimacy (Ngai *et al.,* 2015; Andrijasevic and Sacchetto, 2015). Furthermore, the combination of work and home is a key deterrent against farmworkers abandoning their jobs, as loss of employment would mean also having to search for new accommodation.

The fact that there are farmworkers of different nationalities subject to diverse working conditions frequently encourages competition and conflict in the greenhouses. During our stay at SicilSerre, the competition turned into an actual 'race' where the prize was the chance to continue working with Giovanni. The 'competition' was deliberately fomented by the entrepreneur who suggested that the workers act 'as if they were in a boxing match', so that he could choose carefully and 'mathematically' the most productive worker to be hired (informally and irregularly) for long-term employment. The following long extract from fieldnotes recalls the declaration that Giovanni made once the competition was over. The result of the 'match' – the farmer's decision to employ both farmworkers, albeit with different working hours – suggests that the ultimate purpose of this recruitment procedure was the *competition itself,* which was deployed as a sort of device that induced employees to accelerate the pace of production (Burawoy, 1979).

*Giovanni:* I want to be clear once and for all. What you did [*referring to Nicola*], and what he did [*referring to Ahmed*] . . . was less compared with the work I do. Let's say, I do three *filagni* [*tomato rows*]: you [*N.*] do two and he [*A.*] does two and a half, just a little bit more. [*He pauses, as if to give greater solemnity to what he is about to say.*] Now, let's talk about money . . . [*Addressing A.*] How much do you think? €30? €30 is fine! [*Addressing Nicola*] What do you reckon? €25? So €25 it is! But, as for the work, you have to do at least as much I do. So,

I've done some calculations: 8 hours are not enough for you to do the work that I do. And the same goes for him. So to do the work I do, you're going to have to work 10 hours a day [*to N.*]. He's going to do 9 hours, because he's a little bit faster [*to A.*]. If that's fine by you, then we're sorted. If not [*he makes a sign with his hand to indicate that they can leave*] . . . *amici eramu e amici restammu* [friends as always]. This is the deal. It's fast work. If that's not all right for you there's nothing I can do about it.

*Nicola:* Let's try to do 10 hours . . . as this is my first day in the greenhouse for two years. Perhaps I can do 10 hours for a bit, then we'll see.
*G.:* What do you mean "then we'll see"? I don't get you!
*N.:* If you don't agree, I'll leave! You can't get mad because I can't be like you.
*G.:* You don't want to get mad?
*N.:* I don't want you to get mad. For now 10 hours is better.
*G.:* 10 hours is better?
*N.:* Because I'm not fast. It's right. Because I still have problems.
*G.:* Right? [*triumphantly*]
*N.:* Right!

(Valeria's fieldnotes, Vittoria, 13 June 2013)

From the outset, Giovanni takes for granted the principle according to which the two workers are hired on a different salary because of their different nationalities. He does not question the common practice of paying a Tunisian farmworker €30 and a Romanian farmworker €25 per day. In addition, Giovanni imposes different working hours for the two labourers, justifying this on the basis of their different pace inside the greenhouse. At a later point, Giovanni says:

> Watch out, because you're Italian, so you must understand me. It's not that I'm taking advantage of the situation. Do you understand? I do a calculation based on what I do. If I do two tomato rows, and you do one, then you're half of what I am. If I go to work, as Ahmed does, and someone says to me, 'how much do you want for a day?', and let's say I tell him: '€40', so I have to do a job for €40, which means going fast. *That's what it's all about: it's mathematical!*
>
> (Valeria's fieldnotes, Vittoria, 13 June 2013)

An arbitrary principle is built discursively as something objective ('it's mathematical'), which forecloses the possibility of any criticism. The farmer's 'recruitment procedure' could indeed be debatable; however, the rules set in that context are not negotiable. Ahmed, for instance, expressed strong disapproval, frustration and even rage at being treated like 'a racehorse', and understood clearly that the employer's purpose was to accelerate the rhythm of work and to extract workers' productive capabilities to his sole advantage. Nevertheless, both he and Nicola were not in the position to refuse to participate. So, when the competition took place, Ahmed maintained an air of detachment from the situation in which he was embedded, concentrating exclusively – and even agreeing – on the very purpose of the 'game'. Thus, competition in the greenhouse appeared to *become a value in itself.* As a 'game of making out', the fact of competing becomes a subjective frame to motivate the action: it provides (short-term) meaning to the work effort in the actual moment of its performance, and thus reduces the strain of the endless series of meaningless motions (Burawoy, 1979).

Moreover, the situation of conflict leads the two workers to use common national stereotypes to describe their experience of competitiveness at work. In commenting on the result of the competition, for instance, Ahmed says: 'The Romanian is less of a man than a Tunisian', to highlight his greater physical prowess, which he associates with a stronger 'virility' and, by implication, 'morality'. Thus, the competition instigated by the employer is, in turn, interpreted by the workers as a conflict that regards their nationality. The strength of the game of making out relies on modifying the sense of conflict that occurs in the workplace by partially obscuring the employers' intentions of maximizing labour productivity.

## 18.4 Just Tomatoes: precariousness and competition in a packinghouse

The competitive pressures that arise between female workers in the packinghouses partially reflect mechanisms akin to those described above. In the example that follows, nationality is not an issue because all the workers are Italian. However, two issues are even more evident than before: first, the agricultural workforce is segmented and this segmentation relates to the different types of employment and hiring options; and, second, competition among the workforce is exacerbated by employment precariousness.

An incident that directly concerned us (and which made us query the plausibility of continuing to do participant observation) occurred during our first work experience in a small packinghouse. Like most of the food packinghouses in the area, this had an almost exclusively female and largely Italian workforce. Although in this particular case the friction was mainly due to the presence of two researchers, who were external to the work environment, what happened was nonetheless emblematic of how high labour turnover and high levels of precariousness constitute a constant menace for workers, even if the workers here were all Italians and thus were more 'protected' by their legal status.

The company where we had just started to work, which we will name Just Tomatoes, employed 16 workers: 4 men and 12 women. Through the company's manager, we were able to organize a short period of unremunerated employment for the purpose of conducting our fieldwork.[10] As Carmela, the supervisor, explained to us, we were expected to work in lines, packing several types of vegetables (cherry tomatoes, aubergines and courgettes) into small plastic boxes, then inserting them in larger cardboard boxes. The packing process was organized so as to take into account both appearance and volume. Depending on the type of crop, we were expected to *do the cushion, use the hanky, do the pressed one, work the 20 and the 23 separately* and so on: expressions and tasks that were as nonsensical for the novice worker as they are for the reader. Obviously, no job is easy to perform at the beginning, and even those tasks that are deemed 'unskilled' require a degree of proficiency (Ehrenreich, 2001; Holmes, 2013). So, in the eyes of our workmates, we probably looked very clumsy and uncomfortable in our new roles. That was why Carmela, our team leader, and the other workers, laughed at us mockingly and started to become verbally aggressive.

During the course of the morning shift, Franca, a 31-year-old Italian employee, arrived at the packinghouse. She was one of the numerous female workers who were forced to balance the heavy burden of family life with more than one job. In fact, as employment in the packinghouse was so sporadic and poorly paid (on average €4 per hour[11]), it was not sufficient as a single source of income to cover everyday costs. Being employed in a packinghouse means being compelled to work on-call and for a number of hours that is usually not known in advance. In the majority of these small firms, in fact, shifts are usually not pre-planned: the amount of labour depends on the orders that the company receives on a daily basis and on the quantity of produce arriving from local growers. This just-in-time system of production transfers the social costs of eating fresh food onto workers (Gertel and Sippel, 2014). Workers live at the mercy of a phone call that asks them to be on the job in 20 minutes; a call that they might not receive for several days. In order to cope with her precarious working situation, Franca was doing night shifts for another local company in addition to her day shifts with Just Tomatoes. That morning, however, she had felt too tired to get up an early hour, and had phoned in sick so that she could stay at home and rest. However, her colleagues had warned her of our presence on the packing line and so she suddenly showed up. As she entered she started screaming:

*Franca:* I'm off work for just one day, and you lot immediately replace me with these two girls?
*Carmela:* No, calm down, they're only here to learn. They're from "school"!
*F.:* School?! *Io pure c'ho le scuol*e [I've been to school too!]

(Valeria's fieldnotes, Donnalucata, 19 March 2013)

Franca was highly concerned about the prospect of being called to work less frequently or being laid off altogether. High turnover is the principal fear for a packinghouse (and greenhouse) employee. The risk of being called up less than other workers employed on different contracts, as we were, often generated competitive tensions. In this case, the labourers' aggressive reaction to our presence epitomizes the high sense of insecurity faced by workers who are seriously concerned about losing their jobs. The conflict that is produced by a particularly precarious day-labour system, is also, in this case, dispersed; in other words the potential for *hierarchical* conflicts between workers and management is in effect replaced by *lateral* conflicts between workers. Precariousness does not only affect foreign farmworkers, but also the weakest fringes of the Italian workforce (in this case women). As shown, precariousness actually becomes an explicit reason for conflict inside workplaces.

## 18.5 'Who is a true Muslim?': a case of religious conflict in the Fresh Crops greenhouse

Horizontal conflicts were also a key element during our work with Mr Pippo, a tomato producer who we had met through a local young agronomist. The team of workers consisted of three Italians, one Tunisian, a couple of Albanians and a team leader, who was also Italian. The owner, who was aware of our intention to carry out research on the local agricultural system, was happy to give us work, especially as we were not going to be paid in return. We worked in Pippo's greenhouses for two weeks, during which period we were able to learn to harvest, prune and handle tomato seedlings.

As we were both inexperienced, we were put to work alongside other farmworkers. At the end of the first week, we were able to identify the characteristics of each worker regarding speed, accuracy and carefulness, and over the course of the day we decided who to stay with depending on our willingness to work more or less quickly. The Tunisian labourer and the couple of Albanians were the fastest workers. However, the Tunisian did not pay much attention to the quality of his work and attached little importance to the products themselves, whereas the two Albanians were unanimously considered the 'quickest and cleanest' of the team.

Apart from speed, the Tunisian worker and the two Albanians shared another thing in common: they were all Muslims, and this was a recurring theme in their conversations. There were some evident differences in the ways they expressed their faith. For example, the Albanian couple did not refrain from eating pork. During lunch, they would eat their ham sandwiches with us under a tree, while Gigi, the Tunisian farmworker, preferred to eat leftovers sitting on his own in the back of his car. During the lunch break, there was no sign of harsh feelings between the three Muslim farmworkers. On the contrary, during the working hours, the different eating habits of the three workers became a topic of banter. But while he worked at his tomato row, Gigi openly insulted the other members of the team and asked them: 'Who is the true Muslim here?' The Albanian couple took no offence at Gigi's provocations. The husband, Dimitri, who picked his tomatoes at high speed with a winning technique, replied: 'Who are we? We are number one'. We contend that, similar to the other examples above, here workers use religion as a means for managing competition in the context of a productive system that forces workers to side against each other.

As a number of studies have shown, religion can sometimes be a source of conflict in the workplace, with the workers using religious practices as forms of resistance against employers. A notable example is Aihwa Ong's study of spirit possession among female factory workers in Malaysia (Ong, 1987). Similarly, in one case observed during our fieldwork, fasting during the month of Ramadan turned out to be an act of defiance aimed at the employer. The abstinence from food and beverages on the part of Khaled, a Tunisian worker, greatly concerned his employer who, seeing him become weaker and weaker, encouraged him to drink and eat during working hours. However, the worker refused to give up fasting, and thus assured himself a lower volume of work and less physical fatigue. This ongoing 'arm wrestling match' between worker and employer, over the possibility of observing religious rites, offered us an opportunity to reflect on the potential role of religion as a source of resistance. However, the workers here do not use religion to exert pressure on the employer; rather, once again, its use reflects a horizontal conflict. In other words, the workers handle the competition that is encouraged by employers and compounded by the men's precarious situation by projecting it into a religious dimension.

Gigi appeared to maintain that his Islamic faith was more genuine and 'true' than that of his Albanian colleagues on the basis that he originated from an Arabic-speaking country and not an eastern European country. However, subsequent information obtained through other farmworkers led us to surmise that behind his claim to a more genuine and rooted faith, was a desire to compromise the relationship between the two Albanian farmworkers and the employer. Gigi played the role of a 'spy' within the team: in exchange for information he received favours and better treatment from the greenhouse's owner. Despite the fact that the three workers in question were the fastest members of the team, Gigi tried in every way to create discomfort for the other two. Each day he would offend his two colleagues in the hope they would get so fed up that they would end up abandoning the job. In reality, what usually happened was that the Albanians would accelerate their rate of work, rather than fall into the 'trap' set by Gigi.

We contend that the exacerbation of religious beliefs is, in this case, deceptive and is deployed instrumentally as a farce that aims to mask the 'real' source of the conflict between the three workers. Competition was accentuated by the fact that labourers wanted to work on this farm rather than others because it offered them the chance to obtain a semi-regular contract that allowed them, in turn, to access agricultural unemployment benefits. In addition, the greenhouse was run by a farmer who was generally considered to be honest and not that tough, who was helped by a reliable team leader. The chance of finding all these requisites in other companies was extremely remote. For this reason, the Albanian workers were careful to avoid any sort of conflict, frightened as they were by the idea of losing their job on Pippo's farm.

In the above case, religion can be viewed as a cause for conflict. Nonetheless, in order to fully understand the workplace conflicts that we observed, it is important to take into account the underlying mechanisms that engender a shift in the causes of conflict and the effects that this shift generates. The roots of the conflict, in fact, are to be found in the job precariousness of this sector, which compel workers to side against each other and find pretexts to increase competition in the workplace. The consequences of this are far from harmless; on the contrary, they contribute to the production of a social consensus (Burawoy, 1979, 1985). The competition between workers provokes an acceleration of the pace of work and provides the company with optimal productivity and better worker performance.

In other words, although he is never directly involved, the result ultimately satisfies the employer's production targets.

## 18.6 Conclusions

What was hidden behind these acts of competition staged by workers? What were the reasons that drove workers to line up against each other? Why did solidarity succumb to internecine rivalry and conflict?

We found answers to these questions during our ethnographic research in one of the largest and richest agricultural areas of Italy. In the province of Ragusa, the development of greenhouse farming has helped to reduce the critical threshold of seasonal work, allowing local farmers to extend the entire production process over the year, which, in turn, has had an overall positive impact on the local economy. Nevertheless, this intensive agriculture area continues to produce high levels of job insecurity and irregularity.

In this chapter we showed that if, at a first glance, workplace conflicts can be interpreted as dependent on nationality, religious habits or different hiring conditions, at a deeper level these conflicts reside in the structural nature of a production system that constantly threatens worker stability. Precariousness is, in ultimate analysis, the down side of the conflict: it permeates workplaces and erodes relationships between workers; the opposite to what one would expect in a context where greenhouse farming has achieved production stability.

Precariousness not only corrodes and corrupts work relations by encouraging competition, it accelerates the pace of work and increases the productivity of each worker. This occurs because speed and productivity are the yardsticks for assessing the farmworkers' performance, for determining labour costs, for negotiating 'fair' wages and, above all, for reconfirming the presence of day labourers in the workplace.

## Notes

1 Although the chapter overall is the result of collaborative research and analysis, Sections 18.1, 18.5 and 18.6 were written by Giuliana Sanò, while Sections 18.2–18.4 were written by Valeria Piro. The authors wish to thank Nicoletta Sciarrone, Pietro Saitta and the editors of the volume for their valuable comments and advice.

2 According to recent INEA data (INEA, 2013), the value of fresh and processed fruit and vegetables in Sicily stands at €309 million; 43 per cent of this figure is attributable to vegetables (70 per cent of which are tomatoes) whose production is concentrated above all in the province of Ragusa. In terms of the production of added value, the agricultural sector of Ragusa contributes 8.55 per cent of the provincial Gross Domestic Product (GDP), the highest rate in the whole of southern Italy, and surpassing the Italian average rate of 1.89 per cent by 7 percentage points. Data collected by Istituto Tagliacarne and processed by Toscano (2013).

3 Regarding the fruit and vegetable sector, the majority of market produce in 2012 was destined for the fresh market (94.1 per cent of approximately €291 million), of which, 40.7 per cent to retail chains and supermarkets without intermediaries, 46.1 per cent to the wholesale market and 7.3 per cent to other types of retail markets. These data refer

exclusively to produce marketed through producer organizations (POs) registered in eastern Sicily, 12 of which are in the Province of Syracuse, 11 in the province of Ragusa and 10 in the Province of Catania (INEA, 2013).

4 From an interview with L.F., working at *Vittoria Mercati*, a company in charge of the management of the local fruit and vegetable market, 70 per cent of the products from Vittoria are distributed to national markets, and 30 per cent to other European countries.

5 These data have been provided by Giuseppe Scifo, secretary of the Vittoria branch of FLAI-CGIL (Federation of the Agro-Industrial Workers within the General Confederation of Italian Workers; the FLAI is the main trade union of agricultural workers in Italy).

6 According to data from the last agricultural census, out of more than 12,500 farmers in the province of Ragusa, 51 are non-EU nationals and 13 are foreign EU nationals (Istat, 2010).

7 The names of the farms, as well as those of the individuals, have been changed to preserve anonymity.

8 Regarding the constraints, advantages and ethical concerns for conducting covert participant observation see, in particular, Bryman (2004), Christians (2005), Marzano (2012).

9 These figures refer to the year 2013, when the research was conducted. For the same period the Contract for agricultural workers and floral workers in the Province of Ragusa provided a daily salary of € 54.10 for 6.5 hours of work. During 2015, salaries continued to suffer a decline. During our research, however, we did not notice any salary differentiation based on gender, as frequently occurs in similar sorts of workplaces.

10 It should be underlined that access to these workplaces was not always straightforward. If the informal environment and lack of controls in the greenhouses often facilitated our access, the greater frequency of inspections in the packinghouses presented major limits.

11 This sum represents about half of the official union rate for this sector in the Province of Ragusa (€8.30 per hour).

## References


Alberti, G. (2014). 'Mobility strategies, 'mobility differentials' and 'transnational exit': the experiences of precarious migrants in London's hospitality jobs'. *Work, Employment and Society*, 28, 6, pp. 865–881.

Andrijasevic, R. and Sacchetto, D. (2015). 'Beyond China: Foxconn's assembly plants in Europe'. *The South Atlantic Quarterly*, 114, 1, pp. 215–224.

Berlan, J.P. (1986). 'Agriculture et migrations'. *Revue Européenne des Migrations Internationales*, 2, 3, pp. 9–31.

Berlan, J.P. (2008). 'L'immigré agricole comme modèle sociétal?'. *Etudes rurales*, 182, pp. 219–226.

Bourgois, P. and Schonberg, J. (2009). *Righteous Dopefiend*. Berkeley: University of California Press.

Bryman, A. (2004). *Social Research Methods*. Oxford: Oxford University Press.

Burawoy, M. (1972). *The Colour of Class on the Copper Mines: From African Advancement to Zambianization*. Manchester: Manchester University Press.

Burawoy, M. (1979). *Manufacturing Consent. Changes in the Labor Process Under Monopoly Capitalism*. Chicago: University of Chicago Press.

Burawoy, M. (1985). *The Politics of Production*. London: Verso.

Cardano, M. (2001). 'Etnografia e riflessività. Le pratiche riflessive costrette nei binari del discorso scientifico', *Rassegna Italiana di Sociologia*, XLII, 2, pp. 173–204.

Castracani, L. (2014). 'Lavoro non qualificato? La peculiarità dei lavoratori migranti temporanei per l'economia agroalimentare quebecchese'. Presentation in the international seminar *Migrant Labor and Social Sustainability of Global Agri-food Chains*, Murcia, 5–7 November.

Christians, C.G. (2005). 'Ethics and politics in qualitative research' in Denzin, N.K. and Lincoln Y.S. (eds). *The Sage Handbook of Qualitative Research,* 3rd edition. Thousand Oaks, CA: Sage, pp. 139–164.

Cole, J. and Booth, S. (2007). *Dirty Work. Immigrants in Domestic Service, Agriculture, and Prostitution in Sicily.* Plymouth: Lexington Book.

Colloca, C. and Corrado, A. (eds). (2013). *La globalizzazione delle campagne. Migranti e società rurali nel sud Italia.* Milano: Franco Angeli.

Corrado A., and Perrotta D. (2012). 'Migranti che contano. Percorsi di mobilità e confinamenti nell'agricoltura del Sud Italia'. *Mondi Migranti*, 3, pp. 103–128.

De Bonis, A. (2005). 'Processi di sostituzione degli immigrati di diversa origine nel mercato del lavoro agricolo' in Sivini, G. (ed.). *Le migrazioni tra ordine imperiale e soggettività.* Soveria Mannelli: Rubettino, pp. 157–178.

Décosse, F. (2013). 'Experimentando el utilitarismo migratorio: lo jornaleros marroquíes bajo contrato OMI en Francia' in Aquino, A., Varela, A. and Décosse, F. (eds). *Desafiando fronteras. Control de la movilidad y experiencias migratorias en el contexto capitalista.* Oaxaca, Mexico: Frontera Press, pp. 113–128.

Ehrenreich, B. (2001). *Nickel and Dimed. On (Not) Getting By in America*, New York: Holt.

Gertel, J. and Sippel, S.R. (eds). (2014). *Seasonal Workers in Mediterranean agriculture. The Social Costs of Eating Fresh*, New York: Routledge.

Gouldner, A.W. (1954). *Patterns of Industrial Bureaucracy*, Glencoe: Free Press.

Heath, C., Knoblauch H. and Luff P. (2000). 'Technology and social interaction: the emergence of 'workplace studies''. *The British Journal of Sociology*, 51, 2, pp. 299–320.

Hellio, E. (2014). 'We don't have women in boxes: Channeling seasonal mobility of female farmworkers between Morocco and Andalusia' in Gertel, J. and Sippel, S.R. (eds). *Seasonal Workers in Mediterranean Agriculture. The Social Costs of Eating Fresh*, New York: Routledge, pp. 141–157.

Holmes, S. (2013). *Fresh Fruit, Broken Bodies: Migrant Farmworkers in the United States,* Berkeley: University of California Press.

INEA (2013). *L'agricoltura nella Sicilia in cifre 2013,* available at: http://www.inea.it/pubbl/

Istat (2010). *6° Censimento Generale dell'Agricoltura*, available at: http://censimentoagricoltura.istat.it/

Jounin, N. (2008). *Chantier interdit au public. Enquête parmi les travailleurs du bâtiment*, Paris: Editions La Découverte.

Lindner, K. and Kathmann, T. (2014). 'Mobility partnerships and circular migration: managing seasonal migration to Spain' in Gertel, J. and Sippel, S.R. (eds), *op. cit.*, pp. 121–129.

Mannon, S.E., Petrzelka, P., Glass, C.M., and Radel, C. (2011). 'Keeping them in their place: migrant women workers in Spain's strawberry industry', *International Journal of Agriculture and Food*, 19, 1, pp. 83–101.

Marzano, M. (2012). 'Infromed consent' in Gubrium, F.J., Holstein, J.A., Marvasti, A.B. and McKinney, K.D. (eds). *The Sage Handbook of Interview Research: The Complexity of the Craft,* 2nd editon. Thousand Oaks, CA: Sage, pp. 443–457.

Morice, A. (2008). 'Quelques repères sur les contrats OMI et ANAEM'. *Etudes rurales*, 182, pp. 61–67.

Morice, A. and Michalon, B. (2008). 'Introduction. Les migrants dans l'agriculture: vers un crise de main d'œuvre?'. *Etudes rurales*, 182, pp. 9–28.

Morice, A. and Potot, S. (eds). (2010). *De l'ouvrier sans-papiers au travailleur déthaché: les migrants dans la 'modernisation' du salariat*. Paris: Karthala.

Ngai, P., Huilin, L., Yuhua, G. and Shen, Y. (2015). *Nella fabbrica globale. Vite a lavoro e resistenze operaie nei laboratori della Foxconn*. Verona: Ombre Corte.

Ong, A. (1987). *Spirits of Resistance and Capitalist Discipline: Factory Women in Malaysia*. New York: State University of New York Press.

Perrotta, D. (2011). *Vite in cantiere. Migrazione e lavoro dei rumeni in Italia*. Bologna: Il Mulino.

Piore, M.J. (1979). *Birds of Passage: Migrant Labor and Industrial Societies*. Cambridge: Cambridge University Press.

Piro, V. (2015). 'What is deemed to be 'fake'? The case of 'fake agricultural workers' in South Eastern Sicily'. *Mondi Migranti*, 1, pp. 65–83.

Preibisch, K. and Binford, L. (2007). 'Interrogating racialized global labour supply: an exploration of the racial/National replacement of foreign agricultural workers in Canada'. *The Canadian Review of Sociology and Anthropology*, 44, 1, pp. 5–34.

Pugliese, E. (2009). 'Il lavoro degli immigrati' in Corti, P. and Sanfilippo, M. (eds). *Storia d'Italia. Migrazioni*. Torino: Einaudi, pp. 573–592.

Roy, D. (1952). 'Quota restriction and goldbricking in a machine shop'. *The American Journal of Sociology*, 57, 5, pp. 427–422.

Roy, D. (1953). 'Work satisfaction and social reward in quota achievement: An analysis of piecework incentive'. *The American Sociological Review*, XVIII, pp. 507–514.

Salzman, P.C. (1994). 'The lone stranger in the heart of darkness' in Borofski, R. (ed.). *Assessing Cultural Anthropology*. New York: McGraw-Hill, pp. 29–39.

Schneider, J. and Schneider, P. (1976). *Culture and Political Economy in Western Sicily*. New York: Academic Press.

Theodore, N., Valenzuela, Jr A. and Meléndez, E. (2006). 'La esquina (the corner): Day laborers on the margins of New York's formal economy'. *The Journal of Labor & Society*, 9, pp. 407–423.

Toscano, F. (2013). 'Effetto serra. Lavoro migrante nel settore agricolo della Provincia di Ragusa', Master thesis, Università di Bologna, unpublished.

# Conclusion

# 19 Agrarian change and migrations in the Mediterranean from a food regime perspective

*Alessandra Corrado*

## 19.1 Introduction

A reading of migration and agricultural change in the Mediterranean area – where the case studies in this volume are situated – should be placed in a broader historical frame that includes the socio-economic and political dynamics under which the conditions of mobility and the valorization of labour and capital are defined. The application of food regime theory serves this end. Since the publication of the seminal article by Harriet Friedmann and Philip McMichael at the end of the 1980s (Friedmann and McMichael, 1989), this theory has been developed to interpret changes in agri-food systems across space and time, by identifying different periods of capital accumulation and their corresponding transitions, interconnections and contradictions. What was once termed the 'food system project' has since been developed by scholars into a 'political geography of the global food system', which analyses changes in agri-food relations in different contexts (McMichael, 2013a).

The present chapter aims to bring the Mediterranean into critical conversation with the food regime approach and with broader debates in rural sociology and agrarian studies, in order to grasp the specific development and dynamics of the agrarian question in this region within the historically specific forms of global value relations.

One could object that the Mediterranean is not a homogeneous area. It obviously includes countries from the global North and global South, former colonies and colonial empires, 'developed' countries, members of the European Union (EU), and 'less-developed' or 'developing' states in the Middle East and North Africa (MENA). Nonetheless, I believe that a number of elements justify the choice of analysing the Mediterranean basin as a whole. First, Mediterranean countries share a similar natural environment and agriculture (Braudel, 1985). Second, social, political, economic and trade relations are intense across the region. Third, migration processes are extremely important. It is precisely its role as a (multiple) border (Mezzadra and Nielsen, 2013) that makes the Mediterranean extremely interesting to analyse from a food regime perspective. The Mediterranean is a key border zone of Fortress Europe where the politics of mobility and the differential inclusion of migrants are enacted, but it is also a site that challenges territorially bounded spaces of citizenship and their associated labour markets. As well as a space reshaped by physical capitalization, the Mediterranean region has come to be characterized by new territorial divisions of labour, the opening up of cheaper resource complexes and by the penetration of capitalist social relations and institutional arrangements (Harvey, 2003, p. 115).

Attention will be paid hence to comprehending the specific dynamics of accumulation in what, according to Arrighi (1985), can be defined as 'peripheral capitalism'. In such a context, local profit-driven actors participate in the world division of labour – through their market power and thanks to the support of their states (which are less powerful than those states at the 'core'). At the same time, they are progressively deprived of the benefits of such participation, to the advantage of other, more powerful, actors, located instead at the 'core' (see also Arrighi and Piselli, 1987).[1]

If, on the one hand, food regime theory can contribute to a deeper understanding of Mediterranean agriculture, on the other, a study of the Mediterranean can broaden the food regime approach. In particular, as this volume clearly demonstrates, it is not possible to understand the history of Mediterranean agriculture, and especially the current processes of neoliberalization, without highlighting the roles of migration and migrant labour. As such, my aim here is to bring labour and migration into the food regime framework and, more broadly, into rural studies debates. Since the 1990s, in fact, longstanding discussions about the agrarian question and the condition of workers and farmers have diminished, as analysts have focused on other topics, such as consumption, sustainability and governance. In recent years, acknowledging this significant void, some scholars have started to turn their attention to working conditions and changes in the organization of labour in globalized agri-food systems. However, according to Bonanno and Cavalcanti (2014), although labour relations are 'a primary area of resistance', they still appear to occupy a marginal position in agri-food studies (2014, p. xiv). For the two authors,

> the many works that look at agri-food immigration, gender, race, and labor flexibility focus predominantly on the personal experience of these members of the working class. Their biographies and personal cases often constitute the core of the analysis. These 'invisible' workers, producers of the 'food from nowhere', are removed from the context of the system that generates their exploitation.
>
> (Ibid., p. 283)

I argue that it is necessary to appreciate the specific conditions in which the exploitation and resistance of small-scale (peasant) producers and labourers are determined in the context of neoliberal globalization.

The chapter is organized in three sections. The first section presents a brief overview of food regime theory. The second section analyses three phases in Mediterranean agrarian history, drawing upon the three global food regimes identified by McMichael and Friedmann: liberal-mercantile, Fordist and neoliberal.

The last section highlights the role of migration and labour in contemporary Mediterranean agrarian change and in food regime theory.

If it is possible to talk of a common 'Mediterranean' framework in relation to agricultural and economic policies and structural dimensions, of course there exist different trajectories of change and idiosyncrasies in each country and sub-region. Although the following discussion is based primarily on knowledge of the situations in southern European countries, the chapter aims to develop an approach to thinking about the Mediterranean basin as a whole.

## 19.2 An overview of food regimes

By situating the analysis of agriculture within the geopolitical history of capitalism, food regime analysis, from the outset, sought to link the 'international relations of food production and consumption to forms of accumulation, broadly distinguishing periods of capitalist transformation since 1870' (Friedmann and McMichael, 1989: p. 95).[2] As McMichael has recently written, food regime theory was a product of the times:

> it arose in the late 1980s in a 'de-nationalizing' context in which states faced the prospect of transformation from within by agri-food restructuring on a world scale, and from without as new multilateral principles were under debate in the General Agreement on Tariffs and Trade (GATT) Uruguay Round (1986–1994).
>
> (McMichael, 2013a, p. 2)

These transformations pushed the author to analyse how each food regime has reformulated the state–market relationship within a specific time and space in order to make capital accumulation possible and stable in agriculture. Every food regime and transitional period has redefined development policy and has revisited the purpose and significance of agriculture and food technologies, with implications for natural resources, food security/sovereignty, and rural livelihoods. In this sense, the food regime concept provides an original and historically comparative perspective on the ecological and political relations of modern capitalism (ibid., pp. 7–9).

As is well known, the first formulation of food regime theory defined two food regimes. The first (1870–1914) was identified as the 'settler-colonial' or 'colonial-diasporic' food regime (Friedmann, 2005), which was characterized by the hegemony of the British Empire and the rhetoric of free trade. It combined colonial tropical imports to Europe with imports of basic cereal and meat from the settlement colonies supplying the emergent European industrial working classes with cheap food, and so ensuring that Britain maintained its status as the 'workshop of the world'.

The second food regime (1945–1973) was defined as the 'surplus' or 'mercantile-industrial' food regime (Friedmann, 1993) and was dominated by the United States of America (US). It emerged from a period of transition and from two world wars, and lasted until the international crisis of the 1970s. It was based on the national integration of agricultural and industrial sectors and the modern paradigm of intensive industrial agriculture. The US combined state intervention with the 'development project' ideology in international relations during the Cold War (McMichael, 1996). The food surplus, which originated from state subsidies to the agricultural sector, supplied low-cost food aid programmes (in post-war Europe through Marshall Aid and then to the Third World under Public Law 480 of 1953), ensuring anti-communist loyalty and the control of international markets. Western European and developing countries internalized the US model of agricultural industrialization nationwide, adopting the technologies of the Green Revolution. Agrarian reforms aimed at calming peasant unrest and expanding market relations to the countryside. In the meantime, agribusiness corporations elaborated on the transnational reach of domestic agriculture sectors, which were subdivided into a number of specialized agricultural products connected by global supply chains – i.e. wheat, durable foods and livestock complexes (Friedmann, 1993). A new international division of labour thus emerged around the complex of transnational foods (Raynolds *et al.*, 1993).

Friedmann and McMichael have since identified a third food regime. For McMichael (2005) this is part of a 'globalization project' originating out of the crisis of Fordism and the strategy to further develop capital accumulation on a global scale. Defining it a 'corporate food regime', McMichael argues that agri-food corporations have incorporated new regions within food commodity chains and established a new international division of labour through the 'supermarket revolution' (Reardon *et al.*, 2003) and new consumption styles. The WTO and structural adjustment policies were instrumental to the restructuring of world agriculture and trade relations. On her part, Friedmann has argued that a 'green environmental regime', namely 'green capitalism', arose in response to the pressures of social movements (Friedmann, 2005). What should be called a 'corporate-environmental' food regime thus represents a 'convergence of environmental politics' and corporate repositioning, especially through 'retail-led reorganization of food supply chains' aimed at 'increasingly transnational classes of rich and poor consumers' (ibid., pp. 251–252).

Some scholars disagree on both the existence of this third food regime and its characteristics. They stress that states continue to play an important role in promoting 'neoregulation', international agreements and national legislations that impose the neoliberal agenda (Prichard, 2009; Magnan, 2014; Otero, 2014; Lawrence and Campbell, 2014). Some prefer to call the current era a 'neoliberal' food regime (Pechlaner and Otero, 2008, 2010). This definition highlights the increasing integration of transnational agri-food capital, global sourcing and challenges to the national regulation of agriculture through corporate economic strategies. According to McMichael (2013a), financialization plays a key part in the restructuring of the corporate food regime, with 'a state-finance capital nexus dedicated to constructing new frontiers of accumulation' (p. 130). This is evident in retail diversification and equity investment by supermarkets as well as land grabbing for the purposes of agro-exports or financial speculation.

In what follows, I apply the food regime perspective to the analysis of Mediterranean agrarian change. The first food regime in the region was characterized by the development of agriculture oriented to foreign markets and the coexistence of family farms and large estates that exploited poor rural labourers, both in southern European countries as well as in European colonies. The second food regime coincided with the enactment of the Marshall Plan in postwar Europe, the subsequent implementation of the CAP, the strengthening of the relationship between national industry and agriculture, and the rise of trans-Mediterranean and intra-European labour mobility. The third moment has been characterized by post-Fordist restructuring, the debt crisis in the South, the 'Mediterranean model of migration' (King, 2002) and the progressive autonomization of transnational mobility (Castles and Miller, 2003; Mezzadra, 2011), as well as the reorganization of food chains in the light of the oligopolistic concentration of the agri-food sector and neoliberalization (trade agreements, labour flexibility and global sourcing).

## 19.3 Food regimes in the Mediterranean

### *19.3.1 The liberal-mercantile phase: peasantization, forced commercialization and internal colonialism*

The agrarian crisis in the last quarter of the nineteenth century was the upshot of long-term international changes, the first agricultural revolution and the grain crisis caused by the flooding of European markets by Russian, American and Argentinean grain. Britain dominated both in Europe and at a global level. In fact, already in the eighteenth century, the British model of mixed farming (based on cereals, fodder and livestock) saw the agricultural dominance – that had been centred in the Mediterranean for millennia-shifting to the North. Through a focus on technological changes, Garrabou (1993) has spoken of Mediterranean countries' 'delay' in the industrialization process, which can be illustrated by their much lower agricultural growth in comparison with Atlantic Europe. Technological innovations gave rise to increased grain production in the latter case, while Mediterranean agriculture sought to respond to the crisis by exploiting the rich environment and deploying agronomics to maximize production. Monoculture planting, functional specializations and the mass production of crops became the new modes of agricultural production. The criterion of labour productivity was vigorously introduced in the countryside of the Old World, which resulted in both the bulk of farm produce and the cost of labour being estimated with much greater care. Olive and almond trees, vines and citrus groves were planted, and this production was oriented towards the processing industries of northern Europe and international trade. During the nineteenth century and early decades of the twentieth century, small family farms and large estates of the agrarian bourgeoisie became the protagonists of Mediterranean agriculture (Bevilacqua, 1989; Garrabau, 1993; Lupo, 1990; Petrusewicz 1996; Pinilla and Ayuda 2006).

Different views have been expressed regarding the effects of attempted liberal land reform in southern Europe during the mid- to late nineteenth century. As is well known, Gramsci (1977) criticized liberal reform in Italy as a 'failed revolution' and denounced the internal colonialism[3] that disadvantaged the South. More recently, some scholars have highlighted the impact of land liberalization, the sale of church and national properties in Spain, France and Italy, and agrarian reform in Greece, and have analysed these processes in terms of *peasantization*. These reforms favoured the urban middle class and descendants of oligarchies of property owners as well as small farmers, although nearly all individually owned properties were reduced in size. Changes in other Mediterranean countries were also influenced by exogenous factors, such as independence from the Ottoman Empire in the case of Greece and Egypt and the colonial administration of the Maghreb (Perez Picazo, 1994; Dertilis, 1995; Petmezas, 2006).

In Spain, Italy and southern France the strengthening of peasant property was modest; nonetheless, in some regions family farming was able to reign supreme until the mid-twentieth century for other reasons: the accelerated commodification of the sector arising from the pressure of internal/external markets, institutional change and modern means of transport; increasing tax burdens which led to forced commercialization and the growing monetization of the rural economy; an expansion of new and highly profitable crops, such as vines and olive and almond trees, that continuously responded to changes in demand. Small farmers retained capital by avoiding the employment of non-family labourers, and by adopting indirect management strategies such as tenant farming or sharecropping. The accumulation of significant amounts of capital interested small and family units, mainly in vineyard areas and irrigation perimeters (such as the Spanish Levante), and excluded other regions such as Western Andalusia, Sicily, Calabria, Puglia and parts of Egypt, where the latifundium continued to be a structural factor in agrarian relations (Perez Picazo, 1995).

Among key features of many Mediterranean regions was an economic and social structure that favoured land revenue and commercial speculation, and the fragility of comparative advantage, which was continuously threatened by international competition from new producers, due to the expansion of the market and changes in consumption. At the turn of the century, for example, agriculture in California expanded and increasingly competed with Mediterranean production, both in European and North American markets at the same time as the United States progressively introduced protectionist tariffs (Rhode and Olmstead, 1995).

In Europe, an increase in population and the lack of investment in agriculture and other sectors put pressure on land. In some areas, such as the Italian region of Emilia-Romagna, this pressure led to collective mobilizations against poor social and economic conditions (Crainz, 1994), but more often, as in other parts of Italy, it resulted in emigration abroad.

In this first food regime, relations across the Mediterranean were characterized by colonial relations. The administrations of France, Britain and, to a lesser extent, Italy transformed the agrarian situation in the colonies and protectorates along the Mediterranean shore, by carrying out expropriation and land privatization, and inducing the intensification of agriculture and proletarianization. In turn, these processes led to increased migration that would continue after the Second World War. In North Africa, the colonial rulers oversaw the forced expansion of commercial specialized agriculture oriented towards overseas markets, in particular France and Britain, which contemporaneously exacerbated the vulnerability of local peasants and food insecurity. In this model of agriculture, foreign settlers were cast as protagonists, who established mainly small and medium-sized farms and in some cases large estates, which led to a significant increase in agricultural operators, tenants and sharecroppers. In Algeria, European settlers occupied 2.7 million hectares at the start of the War of Independence in 1954, which was equivalent to over 40 per cent of the total cultivated area. In Morocco, the presence of settlers was much lower but they still controlled more than one million hectares, nearly 12 per cent of the total cultivated area. Between 1917 and 1931 around 1,500 mainly French settlers established themselves on 245,000 hectares of land. The average size of property in Morocco was just over 160 hectares, which was larger than the farms of colonial Algeria. From the 1930s, following the demise of the idea of turning Morocco into a North African 'granary', attention switched to pursuing the 'California dream', a new model of specialization based on the expansion of commercial agriculture through the production of early harvest fruit and vegetables and a comprehensive programme of irrigation that would concern one million hectares of converted land (Sánchez Picón, 2005; Sebti, 2013; Swearingen, 1987).

In Egypt, under British colonial rule, the cotton boom years during the nineteenth and twentieth centuries coincided with the consolidation of large estates for intensive production, controlled by private investors and their political allies, which in turn provoked the dispossession of peasants, famine and the 'relative exhaustion' of socio-ecological spaces in the Nile Delta and Valley (Dixon, 2013).

### *19.3.2 The Fordist phase: modernization, proletarization and path dependency*

From the mid-twentieth century, in the wake of the Great Depression and two World Wars, European countries developed protectionist policies. This shift was influenced by both the internal production structure and contemporary international relations. According to some scholars, key postwar events – the Cold War, decolonization and European integration – played fundamental roles in region building in southern Europe. Indeed, it was during this period that 'Southern Europe' emerged as a geographical and political area, at roughly the same time as the categories 'Western Europe' and 'Eastern Europe' acquired political currency. However, the term has been used regularly only since the 1970s to indicate Portugal, Spain, Italy and Greece (Pedaliu, 2013). The idea of a 'southern agriculture' also developed during the same decade, when 'structural and political elements contribute more than natural features to the character of agriculture in the countries of southern Europe' (Cruz, 1993, p. 517).

In 1947 the Marshall Plan (European Recovery Program) was launched, with the explicit intention of supporting NATO's southern flank, in line with US President Harry Truman's doctrine of containment. Among other things, it sought to remove communist groups from government positions; to influence reform processes (as in the case of the Italian agrarian reform in 1950, which aimed at halting the peasant movement and securing the dominance of anti-communist groups); to promote the postwar reconstruction of the productive base of countries; and to develop agriculture along the lines of the Western bloc.[4] Post-conflict reconstruction in Western Europe adhered to the US model of intensive cropping with stock farming in complex transnational agri-food chains dominated by large conglomerates. Marshall Aid to Europe simultaneously established the basis for Atlantic agri-food relations, and 'invented' the mechanisms of foreign aid that were later adapted for application in the Third World (Friedmann, 1993).

The mechanization of agriculture, new and high-yielding varieties of crops, chemical fertilizers, pesticides and herbicides together transformed rural European landscapes, and increased agricultural productivity, but also led to a dramatic decline in the number of individuals employed in agriculture. A large army of previously non-proletarianized workers was thus made available for expanding industries during the period of Fordist development. This new mass of workers was largely composed of migrants who originated from the Mediterranean countryside. The rural exodus from southern Italy towards northern Italy, Germany and other northern European countries was later followed by movement from other southern European countries, such as Spain, Portugal and Greece, and from former colonies in the Maghreb and Turkey towards northern Europe (Bevilacqua, 1989; King, 2002; Noiriel, 2006; Bourdieu and Sayad, 1964; Sayad, 1999).

The CAP officially came into effect in January 1958 as a part of the Treaty of Rome signed the previous year. It had five main goals: increase agricultural productivity; develop a fair standard of living for farming communities; stabilize food markets; guarantee the security of supplies for European Economic Community (EEC) countries; and assure reasonable consumer prices. The CAP was determined by the agricultural policies of the six founding EEC countries, and took into account the priorities of production and income as well as the requirements of the Marshall Plan. During the postwar period, the principal type of European farm consisted in a fairly small-scale family-owned farm. Increased production through increased productivity was seen as a solution to farmers' income problems, and in all six countries a price and market policy, combined with various structural policy measures, was chosen as the means to achieve this goal as along with food security.[5]

Nonetheless, from its inception, the EEC was characterized by significant structural differences in terms of its agriculture, particularly in parts of Italy that were marked by low productivity and 'underdevelopment'. The domestic economic dualism and internal colonial dynamics characterizing Italy since unification, continued to endure in the postwar period. The country was substantially incapable of negotiating a CAP that was more suited to the agricultural specificities of southern Europe. The expansion of the livestock sector in northern Italy, based on imported grains (in accordance with the deal with the US), linked its interests to those of northern European countries, which subsequently allowed Italy to maintain imports of feedstuffs at a lower tariff than northern countries. Between the 1960s and 1980s the CAP dedicated 90 per cent of the EEC budget to guarantee prices for producers of grain, beef, dairy products, and oils, to the ultimate advantage of northern European agriculture.

In the 1960s and 1970s the EEC achieved self-sufficiency in terms of mass consumer goods, while experiencing dramatic structural changes. From 1958 to 1980, employment in the primary sector fell from 18.2 per cent to 7.8 per cent, while income from agriculture fell from 11 per cent of total income to 3.4 per cent. At the same time, the levels of mechanization and part-time employment in agriculture doubled. The total number of farms decreased from 7.3 million to 4.7 million, while the percentage of farms with more than 20 hectares grew from 14.7 per cent to 25 per cent. About 5 million hectares were removed from production completely and specialization was accentuated. As Dulce Freire and Shawn Pankhurst have argued:

> Agriculture became much more integrated in the overall European economy as its growth was accompanied by greater dependency on external credit, labor markets, and production inputs. Individuals working in agriculture increased their standard of living and consumed a wider range of goods. The EC achieved a strong position in the world agricultural market.
>
> (Freire and Parkhurst 2002, p. 7)[6]

A number of structural measures between 1972 and 1985 targeted two areas for specific intervention: on the one hand, regions with problems arising from their overall economic situation, and on the other, those where agricultural efficiency criteria imposed by the 'green revolution' were deemed to be reachable: Languedoc in France, the Mezzogiorno in Italy, and later Portugal and Spain.[7] Although limited by a small budget, these measures aimed to support farms that were able to modernize at the same time as encouraging agricultural restructuring, for example through the unification of dispersed holdings, the expansion of irrigated areas, support for farmers associations, the retirement of farmers over 55 years old, and the development of information systems for the rural population (Freire and Parkhurst, 2002).

Over the following years, other southern European countries entered the EU: first Greece in 1981, and later Portugal and Spain in 1986. In particular, the issue of the entry of Spanish farm products into the EU stimulated an important political debate in Italy and France, as well as in North Africa (Josling, 2009). Freire and Parkhurst's query about the effects of European integration upon southern European countries found a shorthand response in the Report of the European Commission for 2000:

> The member states with higher average revenues are generally those with large farm enterprises specializing either in field crops or in the more competitive sectors (pork and/or poultry, dairy products, or truck gardening). With a high number of enterprises based in mixed agriculture, or in 'other permanent crops' the southern member countries have average revenues below the mean for the EU as a whole.
>
> (Commission Européenne, 2002, p. 21)

During the same years, in non-European Mediterranean countries such as Egypt and Turkey (but also further afield in India, Pakistan, the Philippines, Indonesia and Mexico), the Green Revolution was promoted as a tool 'not only for the rebuffing of Communism, but staunchly for the advance of capitalism' (Patel, 2012, p. 26). It naturalized markets and the commodification of agriculture (McMichael, 2005, p. 141). Since the 1950s, the 'wheat complex' had facilitated food import dependency in the Third World (Friedmann, 1982): countries like Egypt, Tunisia, Algeria and Morocco produced significant amounts of wheat, but production levels were not able to keep pace with population growth and increased consumption per capita (Mitchell, 1991; McMichael, 2013a).[8] The combination of US food aid and the decline of international markets for colonial crops depressed agricultural wages and crop prices in contrast to industrial wages, which generated a process of depeasantization. When food and oil prices soared in the 1970s, states with little or no oil (such as Egypt) became heavily indebted, while the newly rich oil states of the Arabian peninsula began to rapidly industrialize and urbanize. This conjuncture of political crisis was wrongly interpreted as a 'world food shortage' (Friedmann, 1993).

### *19.3.3 The neoliberal regime: post-productivism, supermarketization and ecological imperialism*

The third Mediterranean food regime was shaped by new factors: the European integration process and the reform of the CAP on the northern shore and the debt crisis and structural adjustment policies on the southern shore. These processes ushered in a phase of neoliberal, post-Fordist development (Bonanno *et al.*, 1994; Marsden, 2006), which produced new conditions of accumulation, new social relationships, new global governance structures (WTO) and the 'denationalisation' strategy of neoliberal class fractions (Tilzey, 2006). EU regulations on agri-food production and trade, as well as on transnational mobility, strongly affected the Mediterranean region's transition to the neoliberal food regime. The expansion of migrant wage labour in agriculture is also a relevant aspect of this phase, and should indeed incite greater attention to the question of migrant labour in food regime analysis more generally.

The previous productivist regime, with its focus on the production of meat, grains and dairy products, by the 1980s, had led to both inequitable income distributions among farmers (80 per cent of CAP subsidies went to the richest 20 per cent of Europe's farmers) and massive overproduction (Knudsen, 2007). Some of the surplus was exported at subsidized prices, while other products were destroyed. Overproduction, environmental problems and consumer concerns for health and quality (Commission of the European Communities, 1988) were key motivations for reforming the CAP. The transition to a post-productivist regime – in an increasingly competitive international market – has been characterized by a reduction of food output and state subsidies, while the 'environmental' regulation of agriculture has increased. Agrarian priorities shifted from food production to more careful consideration of rural development and environmental issues

(Marsden *et al.*, 1996). This resulted in, *inter alia*, a move from quantity-driven to quality-driven production of organic and locally embedded foods, a growth in alternative farming and state efforts to promote sustainable agriculture (Murdoch *et al.*, 2000), which fits with Friedmann's definition of an environmental food regime. In this phase, the CAP has adopted a new approach towards family farming, abandoning the goal of 'professionalization' in recognition of the need for agricultural diversification and an expansion of non-agricultural activities alongside more varied inputs ensuring adequate living standards for rural families. Attention has thus switched to supporting rural areas and communities and territorial development, also in recognition of the countryside's increasing attraction to society at large in terms of offering different lifestyles and leisure spaces (Etxezarreta, 2006, p. 142).

The role of consumption has increased relative to that of production within the industrial production chain, while consumers have become more sensitive to the negative effects of the industrial model of production. As a consequence, food production is increasingly regulated in terms of labelling and legislation, which has been reinforced by retailers as they pressure producers into adopting private regulations to their advantage (Hennis, 2001, p. 842; Bain *et al.*, 2013).

The tension between regulation and liberal trade for European agriculture (Friedmann, 1993) has been resolved by an 'embedded neoliberalism', reflecting the domestic balance of class and class fractional interests (Potter and Tilzey, 2005; Tilzey, 2006; Tilzey and Potter, 2006). The CAP is thus becoming progressively more market oriented, which affirms the primacy of global markets and transnational capital, but admits the limits of *laissez-faire* through selective market protection and support, social welfare legislation, labour standards and the preservation of social consensus. Market-based forms of regulation (or, better, market deregulation), therefore, have been accompanied by re-regulation, in the form of exemptions, safeguards and sideline measures in order to protect domestic commodity interests and to support strong agricultural sectors. These changes obviously reflect international pressures, but also structural transformations and power shifts in Europe (Hennis, 2001).

The CAP has hence become a 'mega-policy' by incorporating environmental concerns, wider social and economic demands as well as territorial adjustments. The 'exceptionalist' European model of agriculture is the result of the transition from a 'classic interventionist' paradigm to a free-market or liberalist paradigm coupled with 'rural development interventionism'. If neoliberal productivism concerns the 'rural core', such as the intensive and specialized agriculture in south European countries, 'post-productivist enclaves' exist to supply products to regional markets and middle-class reflexive consumers and to provide spaces for leisure activities that support the rural periphery (Tilzey, 2009).

Structural differentiation characterizes the four principal countries of southern Europe. As in the case for the rest of Europe, a growing polarization of interests at the agricultural level is emerging between the larger, more capitalized businesses, which are able to respond to the demands of processors, distributors and retailers, and those labour-intensive family-run holdings that depend on state assistance (if to a lesser extent than in the past) or other non-agricultural sources of income in order to continue operating. Within the relative policy security of Fordist productivism, the upper stratum of farmers has been progressively subsumed within corporate agri-food networks, as buyers of inputs and as suppliers of unprocessed products for food manufacturing and retailers (Tilzey, 2006).

Significant differences exist within the EU with regards to the land consolidation process, the diminishing number of small-farm holdings, the decline of agricultural employment, the substitution of family by non-family labour, and the increasing role of migrant labour. The four main southern European member states (Greece, Italy, Portugal and Spain) account for two-thirds of the holdings of the EU-15; but, more significantly, they possess the vast majority (88.5 per cent) of holdings with a low economic size, and only one-third of holdings with a large economic size. Large farms predominate in the north-western member states but they are also progressively becoming a prominent feature in southern member states. This indicates that the CAP has probably accentuated pre-existing inequalities and peripheralities within the EU, rather than leading the way to the increased resilience of farm holdings and rural economies. According to Papadopoulos (2015) the CAP has not overcome many of the pitfalls related to the uneven agricultural and socio-economic conditions of EU member states: 'there are different 'peripheralities' within Europe [. . .] these peripheralities lead to the consolidation of an economic hierarchy between the rural regions that struggle to survive, seeking ways to increase their resilience against the expansion of market mechanisms' (p. 2). Since the austerity turn after 2008, the new CAP budget has been significantly reduced in terms of its share of the total EU budget, although it remains the most important policy in terms of funding resources.[9] The effects of this change, especially upon small to medium farms and labour, will need to be analysed.

Southern European rural populations and farms have responded to the growing integration of agriculture into global markets in a number of ways, including: off-farm employment, the use of migrant labour, the flexible use of the labour force, as well as the utilization of forms of non-waged, contract labour, self-employment, untaxed and undeclared activities. Informality, income diversification and labour flexibility may be considered survival and/or resistance strategies for rural households, particularly in the agricultural sector (Pugliese, 1998; Papadopoulos, 1998; Kasimis and Papadopoulos, 2013). During the neoliberal food regime, family or small/medium-scale farming has developed in two different directions: first, towards *repeasantization*, through endogenous strategies of innovation and resistance, and along the post-productivist turn in agriculture; and second, towards further intensification and modernization and full incorporation within corporate agri-food networks (Ploeg, 2009). However, productivist and post-productivist dynamics are more interconnected than would immediately appear (Moreno-Pérez *et al.*, 2015). For instance, quality production is closely bound up with the intensification of agriculture and the growth of medium/large farms supplying northern European markets such as Germany, the UK and France (Arnalte-Alegre and Ortiz-Miranda, 2013; De Devitiis and Maietta, 2013), and, it is also often based upon the over-exploitation of migrant workers on irregular contracts or casually employed (Laurent, 2013).

Some areas are still characterized by productivism and intensive agriculture. This is the case of certain regions in southern Italy (De Filippis and Henke, 2014) and Southern Spain, which are characterized by the 'mobile production of fruit and vegetables factories' (Pedreño, 1999, 2001; Aznar-Sánchez *et al.*, 2014), and the artificialization and degradation of environment by greenhouses and chemicals. In such contexts, migrant labour not only represents a survival strategy for farms: it also provides leverage for innovation and resilience in coping with the upstream and downstream pressures along global value chains. The strategic role of transnational mobility plays out across race, gender and legal divisions and through differential inclusion, under conditions of discrimination and exploitation within territorially bound spaces of citizenship and their associated labour markets (Mezzadra and Nielsen, 2013).

In the meantime, value-chain agriculture across the Mediterranean region is built on 'an inter-hemispheric "switch" in agri-food exchange' (Pritchard, 2009), where wheat and durable foods from the global North are exchanged for air-freighted food originating from the global South. In North Africa, private foreign investors and local élites extend their control to crucial nodes in export oriented fruit-horticulture commodity chains, agricultural policies promote intensification and agrarian counter-reforms, while migration policy regimes work to control the flexible labour supply. These processes are produced through the CAP and bilateral trade and investment agreements between the EU and MENA for the creation of a Euro-Mediterranean Free Trade Area, which had as its premise the structural adjustment programmes imposed by international institutions within a 'system of debt relations'. Ecological imperialism expands the frontier of capitalist accumulation, through transforming some areas of the global South into modern and highly productive agro-industrial enclaves, transferring technologies and organizational models, grabbing resources and subordinating agriculture to price relations. These transformations are further proletarianizing marginalized farmers and peasants (McMichael, 2013b, p. 674), and creating dependency and food insecurity by way of wheat imports and supermarkets, thus, in the process, turning countries into hostages of transnational corporations (Ghada *et al.*, 2014).

As a consequence of long-term transformations, in the third food regime, food dependency and food crises have progressively affected MENA as well as European countries. The supermarket revolution has been connected to dietary changes and food insecurity on both sides of the Mediterranean (Akesbi, 2014; Gertel and Sippel, 2014; Fort, 2012; Fritz, 2011). The renowned Mediterranean diet is increasingly hard to distinguish from the average EU food consumption pattern. These dietary changes have evolved in relation to the CAP.[10]

## 19.4 Conclusions: labour and mobility in food regimes

In this chapter, I have proposed a reading of the historical transformation of Mediterranean agriculture through the perspective of the three food regimes described by McMichael and Friedmann. In doing so, I have argued that the food regime perspective is helpful in identifying and understanding agricultural transformations – as well as political and economic relations – on both sides of the Mediterranean. While this analytical framework has sought to highlight the general trajectories of agrarian change in the Mediterranean region, further analysis of southern European countries and especially MENA countries, also in a comparative perspective, is required to fully understand ongoing developments and relevant issues, such as the transformations of peasant and family farming, mobility, food security/sovereignty and forms of social resistance.

In this concluding section, I want to stress the fundamental need of analysing labour and migration in order to understand agrarian change in the Mediterranean. As Bonanno and Cavalcanti (2014) have noted, the issue of labour has not been sufficiently considered by recent agri-food studies. The history of the Mediterranean shows that topics such as the creation of wage labour, the reproduction of labour (through migration) and its inclusion into the dynamics of accumulation should be incorporated into the food regime approach; in particular, these issues are especially relevant to understand the current food regime.

Labour mobility can be considered an essential element for understanding the agricultural processes in each of the three food regimes that I have analysed in this chapter. In the first colonial-diasporic food regime, the agriculture of North African colonies was deeply transformed by colonial settlers, while in southern European countries transoceanic migration provided a release to the 'pressure on land' due to overpopulation and poor social and economic conditions in rural areas. In the Fordist food regime, intra-European migration and the recruitment of workers from former colonies developed in parallel with the industrialization of agriculture in Europe. In the third food regime, the competitive strategies inside agri-food chains, on both sides of the Mediterranean, revolve around a continuous deterritorialization and reterritorialization of labour relations. On the one hand, this occurs through the differential inclusion of migrants in the agricultural labour markets on the basis of race, gender and legal status; on the other hand, trade and investment between the EU and MENA countries alongside the intensification of agriculture, agrarian counter-reforms and dispossession (Ayeb, 2010, 2012; Bush, 2007a, 2007b) have strengthened the competitive position of large companies and corporate networks to the detriment of peasant and small farming, with the result of displacing or exploiting agricultural workers on both sides of the Mediterranean. These processes have spurred internal and transnational mobility, with some of the migrants crossing the Mediterranean ending up employed in southern European agriculture, and thus becoming an essential factor in the neoliberal restructuring of agriculture in these regions.

In sum, mobility regimes and agricultural/trade policies have both contributed to regulate the incorporation of labour into Mediterranean agriculture. By viewing the development of food regimes in the Mediterranean, over time and space, it is clear that the dual processes of peasantization/depeasantization and emigration/immigration have continually taken place in relation to changes in land control and capital flows and regulation. Small to medium-scale family farms have become increasingly entrepreneurial or have closed down due to modernization and dispossession, or else have resisted through pluriactivity and integrating export-oriented monocropping and mixed farming. At different moments in history, mobility – mostly from rural areas and the agricultural sector towards manufacturing, urban service economies and ultimately the agri-food sector – has coincided with agricultural restructuring and proletarization.

Focusing in particular on the current era, my analysis has demonstrated that neoliberal transition in the Mediterranean appears to fit with the features of the third corporate/environmental food regime theorized by McMichael and Friedmann. This is especially due to the CAP reforms, which have decoupled subsidies from production quantities, and have sustained the post-productivist, environmental turn and competitiveness. On the other hand, I argue that transnational mobility should be considered as one of the most relevant elements to be integrated into a wider analysis of neoliberal transition. Indeed, migrant labourers – and in general wage labourers as well as farmers – represent 'disposable commodities' within the 'new' agriculture dominated by food retailers and finance (Arrighi, 2007, p. 172).

Migrant labour has been fundamental both for the reorganization and competitiveness in the agri-food system and for the resilience of small-scale and family farming. In addition, it generally contributes to household reproduction and peasant agriculture in the country of origin. Migrant labour in southern European agriculture is often extremely vulnerable due to a host of reasons including legal-administrative status and limits on mobility. This weakness is emblematic of the current agri-food regime in which value creation and the accumulation of capital are dependent precisely upon differentiation, precariousness, intensification, flexibility and mobility.

In response to the contemporary situation, food justice movements, alternative food networks and new farmers' movements have emerged over the last decade across the Mediterranean region, often with global connections, as in the case of La Via Campesina. These initiatives have paid particular attention to food quality, environmental sustainability and the plight of small and peasant farmers, and have addressed a range of issues from agricultural policies and food governance to models of production and consumption. It is often the case that working conditions, especially those of migrants, and related questions of labour precariousness and flexibility are instead taken less into consideration. Nevertheless as I have argued here, serious engagement with these aspects also requires a deeper understanding of food production and agricultural change.

## Acknowledgements

I would like to thank Apostolos Papadopoulos, Antonio Onorati, Dionisio Miranda Ortiz, Isabella Giunta, Mauro Conti, Carlos de Castro and Domenico Perrotta for their comments and the discussions I have had with them on earlier drafts of this chapter. I am grateful to Philip McMichael for his inspiring work and suggestions.

## Notes

1 As a consequence, countries that entered the perimeter of the core, as in the case of Italy in the 1970s or Spain in the 1990s, tend to be limited in their capacity to remain in such a position. Portugal and Greece are in an even worse situation, having partially failed to upgrade (i.e. strengthening supply). Arrighi (1985) described south European countries as 'semi-peripheral', which is a notion that could also be applied to look comparatively at MENA countries.

2 The establishment of 'a world price for staple foods' is the distinguishing and world-historical feature of food regimes (McMichael, 2013a, pp. 22–24).

3 The category of internal colonialism was borrowed from the analysis of the relations of socio-economic domination in Europe (Halperi, 1997) and Latin America.

4 Agrarian reforms were introduced after dictatorships in Portugal in 1976 and in Spain in 1982.

5 The CAP's market price policy is based on the idea that producers should receive their income according to the price of their products. In this way, the CAP transfers income from consumers to producers through higher prices for agricultural products. This mechanism of income support encouraged member states to increase domestic production, either by maximizing net recipients or by minimizing their net contribution to the EC budget (Hennis, 2005, p. 42). With the MacSharry CAP reform in 1992, market price support was reduced and direct payments were introduced. Subsequently, 2009 reforms decoupled subsidies from production, and consolidated measures for competitiveness, environmental issues and for the improvement of quality of life in rural areas (OECD, 2011).

6 On the role of banks and agricultural debt, see Hennis (2001).

7 See the Communications by EU Commission from the middle of the 1970s onwards in the Archive of European Integration: http://aei.pitt.edu.

8 The same can be said for other countries in Latin America, Asia and Sub-Saharan Africa (McMahon, 2013; González, 2015).

9 For the period 2014–2020, the CAP has been allocated 37.8 per cent of the EU budget, against 43.5 per cent for 2007–2013. This reduction is significant if compared to previous decades, with the CAP accounting for 60 per cent of the budget in the 1990s and 70 per cent in the 1970s (Papadopoulos, 2015, p. 7).

10 The EU has provided – through various trade and association agreements – preferential access to its relatively lucrative (i.e. highly priced) market, particularly for off-season shipments of nutritionally valuable products. In turn, it has supplied commodities in surplus at high EU prices, which are subsidized down to the price levels of recipient countries (such as those of the MENA region). Where, instead, proceeds from oil and gas exports have been insufficient, domestic affordability has often been fostered through an 'urban bias' in agricultural policies, by which farmers are taxed and staple foods for consumers in urban areas are subsidized. The incentive structure of food policies was thus quite the opposite of what the CAP provided (Schmidhuber, 2007).

## References

Akesbi, N. (2014). 'Which agricultural policy for which food security?' in Gertel, J. and Sippel, S.R. (2014). *Seasonal workers in Mediterranean Agriculture. The Social Costs of Eating Fresh*. London: Routledge, pp. 167–174.

Arnalte-Alegre, E. and Ortiz-Miranda, D. (2013). 'The 'Southern Model' of European agriculture revisited: Continuities and dynamics' in Ortiz, D., Arnalte, E. and Moragues, A.M. (eds). *Agriculture in Mediterranean Europe between Old and New Paradigms*. Bingley: Emerald, pp. 37–74.

Arrighi, G. (1985). *Semiperipheral Development. The Politics of Southern Europe in the Twentieth Century*. London: Sage.

Arrighi, G. (2007), *Adam Smith in Beijing*. London-New York: Verso.
Arrighi, G. and Piselli, F. (1987). 'Capitalist development in hostile environments: Feuds, class struggles, and migrations in a peripheral region of southern Italy'. *Review*, 10(4), pp. 649–751.
Ayeb, H. (2010). *La crise de la société rurale en Egypte*. Paris: Karthala.
Ayeb, H. (2012). 'Agricultural policies in Tunisia, Egypt, and Morocco: Between food dependency and social marginalization' in *Reversing the Vicious Circle in North Africa's Political Economy, Confronting Rural, Urban, and Youth-Related Challenges*. Mediterranean Paper Series, pp. 5–11. Washington, DC: The German Marshall Fund of the United States (GMF).
Aznar-Sánchez, J.Á., Belmonte-Ureña, J. and Tapia-León, J. (2014). 'The industrial agriculture: A 'model for modernization' from Almería?' in Gertel, J. and Sippel, S.R. (2014). *Seasonal Workers in Mediterranean Agriculture. The Social Costs of Eating Fresh*. London: Routledge, pp. 175–199.
Bain, C., Ransom, E. and Higgins, V. (eds) (2013). 'Private agri-food standards'. Special issue. *International Journal of Sociology of Agriculture and Food*, 20, pp. 1–2.
Bevilacqua, P. (1989). 'Tra Europa e Mediterraneo. L'organizzazione degli spazi e i sistemi agrari dell'Italia contemporanea' in Bevilacqua, P. (ed.). *Storia dell'agricoltura italiana in età contemporanea, vol. I, Spazi e paesaggi.* Venezia: Marsilio.
Bonanno, A. and Cavalcanti, J.S.B. (2014). 'Introduction' in Bonanno, A. and Cavalcanti, J.S.B. (eds). *Labor Relations in Globalized Food.* Bingley: Emerald. pp. xiii–xlix.
Bonanno, A., Friedland, W.H., Llambi, L., Marsden, T., Belo, M. and Schaeffer, R. (1994). 'Global post-Fordism and the concept of the State'. *International Journal of Sociology of Agriculture and Food,* 4, pp. 11–29.
Bourdieu, P. and Sayad, A. (1964). *Le déracinement. La crise de l'agriculture traditionnelle en Algérie*. Paris: Le Minuit.
Braudel, F. (1985). *La Méditerranée*. Paris: Flammarion.
Bush, R. (2007a). 'Politics, power and poverty: Twenty years of agricultural reform and market liberalisation in Egypt'. *Third World Quarterly*, 28(8), pp. 1599–1615.
Bush, R. (2007b). 'Mubarak's legacy for Egypt's rural poor: Returning land to the landlords.' in Borras, S.M., Kay, C. and Akram-Lodhi, A.H. (eds). *Land, Poverty and Livelihoods in an Era of Globalization: Perspectives from Developing and Transition Countries*. London and New York: Routledge, pp. 254–283.
Castles, S. and Miller, M.J. (2003). *The Age of Migration. International Population Movements in the Modern World.* New York and London: Guilford Press.
Commission of the European Communities (1988). Green paper, *The Future of Rural Society,* Com (88) 371 final, Brussels.
Commission Européenne (2002). *La situation de l'agriculture dans l'union européenne.* Rapport 2000, Bruxelles/Luxembourg.
Crainz (1994). *Padania. Il mondo dei braccianti dalla fine dell'Ottocento alla fuga delle campagne*. Roma: Donzelli.
Cruz, J. (1993). 'El futuro de las agriculturas del sur de Europa' in Ministerio de Agricultura, Pesca y Alimentación (ed.). *Agriculturas y políticas agrarias en el sur de Europa*. Madrid: Ministerio de Agricultura, Pesca y Alimentación, pp. 517–537.
De Devitiis, B. and Maietta, O.W. (2013). 'Regional patterns of structural change in Italian agriculture' in Ortiz, D., Arnalte, E. and Moragues, A.M. (eds). *Agriculture in Mediterranean Europe Between Old and New Paradigms*. Bingley: Emerald, pp. 173–205.
De Filippis, F. and Henke, R. (2014). 'Modernizzazione e multifunzionalità nell'agricoltura del mezzogiorno'. *QA Rivista dell'Associazione Rossi-Doria*, 3, pp. 27–58.

Dertilis, G.B. (1995). 'Grecia, siglos XVIII–XX: la tierra, los campesinos y el poder' in Morilla, J. (eds). *California y el mediterráneo: estudios de la historia de dos agriculturas competidoras*. Madrid: Ministerio de Agricultura, Alimentación y Medio Ambiente, pp. 371–400.
Dixon, M. (2013). 'The land grab, finance capital, and food regime restructuring: The case of Egypt'. *Review of African Political Economy*, 41(140), pp. 232–248.
Extezarreta, M. (2006). *La agricultura espanola en la era de la globalizacion*. Madrid: Ministerio de Agricultura Pesca y Alimentacion.
Fort, F. (2012). 'Traditional Mediterranean products: Markets and large-scale retail trade' in Mombiela, F. and Abis, S. (eds). *Mediterra 2: The Mediterranean Diet for Sustainable Regional Development*. Paris: Presses de Sciences Po, pp. 305–324.
Freire, D. and Parkhurst, S. (2002). 'Where is Portuguese agriculture headed? An analysis of the common agricultural policy'. Working paper PRI-5, Institute of European Studies. Berkeley: University of California.
Friedmann, W.H. (1982). 'The political economy of food: The rise and fall of the post-war international food order'. *American Journal of Sociology*, 88, pp. 248–86.
Friedmann, W.H. (1993). 'The political economy of food: A global crisis'. *New Left Review*, 197, pp. 29–57.
Friedmann, H. (2005) 'From colonialism to green capitalism: Social movements and the emergence of food regimes' in Buttel, F.H. and McMichael, P. (eds). *New Directions in the Sociology of Global Development*. Oxford: Elsevier, pp. 229–67.
Friedmann, H. and McMichael, P. (1989). 'Agriculture and the state system: the rise and fall of national agricultures, 1870 to the present'. *Sociologia Ruralis* 29(2), pp. 93–117.
Fritz, T. (2011). *Globalising Hunger: Food Security and the EU's Common Agricultural Policy*, Berlin: FDCL-Verlag.
Garrabou, R. (1993). 'Revolución o revoluciones agrarias en el siglo XIX: su difusión en el mundo Mediterráneo' in *Agriculturas mediterráneas y mundo campesino: cambios históricos y retos actuales: Actas de las Jornadas de Historia Agraria*. Almería, 19–23 April, pp. 95–109.
Gertel, J. and Sippel, S. (2014). 'Super/markets: Beyond buyer-drivenness in southern France' in Gertel, J. and Sippel, S.R. (eds). *Seasonal Workers in Mediterranean Agriculture. The Social Costs of Eating Fresh*. London: Routledge, pp. 58–72.
Ghada, A., Hamrick, D. and Gereffi, G. (2014). 'Shifting governance structures in the wheat value chain: Implications for food security in the Middle East and North Africa'. Duke University Center on Globalization, Governance and Competitiveness, Durham, NC.
González, A. (2015). 'The long hangover from the 2nd Food Regime: wheat dependence in poor and insecure countries'. Paper presented at *Rural History Conference*, Girona, September.
Gramsci, A. (1977). *Quaderni del carcere*, Vol. I. Torino: Einaudi.
Halperi, S. (1997). *In the Mirror of the Third World: Capitalist Development in Modern Europe*. Ithaca, NY: Cornell University Press.
Harvey, D. (2003). *The New Imperialism*. Oxford: Oxford University Press.
Hennis, M. (2001). 'Europeanization and globalization: The missing link'. *Journal of Common Market Studies*, 39(5), pp. 829–850.
Hennis, M. (2005). *Globalization and European Integration: The Changing Role of Farmers in the Common Agricultural Policy*. Lanham, MD: Rowman and Littlefield Publishers.
Josling, T. (2009). 'Western Europe' in Anderson, K. (ed.). *Distortions to Agricultural Incentives: A Global Perspective, 1955 to 2007*. London and Washington, DC: Palgrave Macmillan and World Bank.

Kasimis, C., and Papadopoulos, A.G. (2013). 'Rural transformations and family farming in contemporary Greece' in Ortiz, D., Arnalte, E. and Moragues, A.M. (eds). *Agriculture in Mediterranean Europe Between Old and New Paradigms*. Bingley: Emerald, pp. 263–293.

King, R. (2002). 'Towards a new map of European migration'. *International Journal of Population Geography*, 8, pp. 89–106.

Knudsen, D.C. (2007). 'Post-productivism in question: European agriculture, 1975–1997'. *The Industrial Geographer*, 5(1), pp. 21–43.

Laurent, C. (2013). 'The ambiguities of French Mediterranean agriculture: Images of the multifunctional agriculture to mask social dumping?' in Ortiz, D., Arnalte, E. and Moragues, A.M. (eds). *Agriculture in Mediterranean Europe Between Old and New Paradigms*. Bingley: Emerald, pp. 149–171.

Lawrence, G. and Campbell, H. (2014). 'Neoliberalism in the antipodes: Understanding the influence and limits of the neoliberal political project' in Wolf, S. and Bonanno, A. (eds). *The Neoliberal Regime in the Agri-Food Sector: Crisis, Resilience and Restructuring*. New York: Routledge, pp. 263–283.

Lupo, S. (1990). *Il giardino degli aranci. Il mondo degli agrumi nella storia del Mezzogiorno*. Venezia: Marsilio.

Magnan, A. (2014). 'The rise and fall of a prairie giant: The Canadian Wheat Board in food regime history' in Wolf, S. and Bonanno, A. (eds). *The Neoliberal Regime in the Agri-Food Sector: Crisis, Resilience and Restructuring*. New York: Routledge, pp. 73–90.

Marsden, T. (2006). 'Pathways in the sociology of rural knowledge' in Cloke, P. Marsden, T. and Mooney, P. (eds). *Handbook of Rural Studies*. London: Sage, pp. 3–17.

Marsden, T., Munton, R., Ward, N. and Whatmore, S. (1996). 'Agricultural geography and the political economy approach: A review'. *Economic Geography*, 72(4), pp. 361–375.

McMahon, P. (2013). *Feeding Frenzy: The New Politics of Food. London:* Profile Books.

McMichael, P. (1996). *Development and Social Change: A Global Perspective*. Thousand Oaks, CA: Pine Forge Press.

McMichael, P. (2005). 'Global development and the corporate food regime' in Buttel, F.H. and McMichael, P. (eds). *New Directions in the Sociology of Global Development*. Oxford: Elsevier, pp. 229–267.

McMichael, P. (2013a). *Food Regimes and Agrarian Questions*. Halifax and Winnipeg: Fernwood Publishing.

McMichael, P. (2013b). 'Value-chain agriculture and debt relations: Contradictory outcomes'. *Third World Quarterly*, 34(4), pp. 671–690.

Mezzadra, S. (2011). 'The gaze of autonomy. Capitalism, migration and social struggles' in Squire, V. (ed.). *The Contested Politics of Mobility: Borderzones and Irregularity*. London: Routledge, pp. 121–143.

Mezzadra, S. and Nielsen, B. (2013). *Border as Method or the Multiplication of Labor*. Durham, NC and London: Duke University Press.

Mitchell, T. (1991). 'American's Egypt: Discourse of the development industry.' *Middle East Report*, 169, pp. 18–34.

Moreno-Pérez, O., Gallardo-Cobos, R., Sanchez-Zamora, P. and Ceña-Delgado, F. (2015). 'La agricultura familiar en España: pautas de cambio y visibilidad institucional'. *Agriregionieuropa*, 11(43). Available at http://agriregionieuropa.univpm.it/it

Murdoch, J., Marsden, T. and Banks, J. (2000). 'Quality, nature, and embeddedness: Some theoretical considerations in the context of the food sector'. *Economic Geography* 76(2), pp. 107–125.

Noiriel, G. (2006). *Le Creuset Français. Histoire de l'immigration XIXème XXème siècle*. Paris: Seuil.

OECD (2011). *Evaluation of Agricultural Policy Reforms in the European Union.* Paris: OECD.

Ortiz Miranda, D., Arnalte-Alegre, E.V. and Moragues-Faus, A.M. (eds). (2013). *Agriculture in Mediterranean Europe Between Old and New Paradigms.* Bingley: Emerald.

Otero, G. (2014). 'The neoliberal food regime and its crisis: State, agribusiness transnational corporations, and biotechnology' in Wolf, S. and Bonanno, A. (eds). *The Neoliberal Regime in the Agri-Food Sector: Crisis, Resilience and Restructuring.* New York: Routledge, pp. 225–244.

Papadopoulos, A.G. (1998). 'Revisiting the rural: A southern response to European integration and globalization' in Kasimis, C. and Papadopoulos, A.G. (eds). *Local Responses to Global Integration, Rural Transformations and Family Farming In Contemporary Greece.* Aldershot: Ashgate, pp. 245–271.

Papadopoulos, A.G. (2015). 'The impact of the CAP on agriculture and rural areas of EU Member States'. *Agrarian South: Journal of Political Economy* 4(1), pp. 1–32.

Patel, R. (2012). 'The long green revolution'. *The Journal of Peasant Studies* 40(1), pp. 1–6.

Pechlaner, G. and Otero, G. (2008). 'The third food regime: Neoliberal globalism and agricultural biotechnology in North America'. *Sociologia Ruralis* 48(4), pp. 351–371.

Pechlaner, G. and Otero, G. (2010). 'The neoliberal food regime: Neoregulation and the new division of labor in North America'. *Rural Sociology* 75(2), pp. 179–208.

Pedaliu, E. (2013). 'The making of southern Europe: A historical overview' in *A Strategy for Southern Europe.* LSE Ideas Special Report SR017. London: London School of Economics and Political Science (LSE), pp. 8–14.

Pedreño, A. (1999). *Del Jornalero Agrícola al Obrero de las Factorías Vegetables: Estrategias Familiares y Nomadismo Laboral en la Ruralidad Murciana.* Madrid: Ministerio de Agricultura, Pesca y Alimentación.

Pedreño, A. (2001). 'Efectos territoriales de la globalización: el caso de la ruralidad agroindustrial murciana'. *Revista de Estudios Regionales,* no. 59, pp. 69–96.

Perez Picazo, M.T. (1994). 'La disolucion de las sociedades campesinas tradicional en el mundo mediterraneo' in Sánchez Picón, A. (ed.). *Agriculturas mediterráneas y mundo campesino: cambios históricos y retos actuals.* Almería: Instituto de Estudios Almerienses, pp. 15–43.

Perez Picazo, M.T. (1995). 'Pequena explotacion y consolidacion del capitalismo en las agriculturas mediterraneas, 1856–1939' in Morilla, J. (ed.). *California y el mediterráneo: estudios de la historia de dos agriculturas competidoras*, Madrid: Ministerio de Agricultura, Alimentación y Medio Ambiente, pp. 335–337.

Petmezas, S.D. (2006). 'Agriculture and economic growth in Greece'. *XIV International Economic History Congress,* Helsinki, Finland.

Petrusewicz, M. (1996). *Latifundium. Moral Economy and Material Life in a European Periphery.* Ann Arbor: University of Michigan Press.

Pinilla, V. and Ayuda, M.I. (2006). 'Horn of plenty' revisited: The globalization of Mediterranean horticulture and the economic development of Spain, 1850–1935' Documentos de trabajo, DT-AEHE No. 0606.

Ploeg, J.D. van der (2009). *The New Peasantries. Struggles for Autonomy and Sustainability in an Era of Empire and Globalization.* London: Earthscan.

Potter, C. and Tilzey, M. (2005). 'Agricultural policy discourses in the European postFordist transition: Neo-liberalism, neo-mercantilism and multifunctionality'. *Progress in Human Geography,* 29(5), pp. 581–601.

Pritchard, B. (2009). 'The long hangover from the second food regime: A world historical interpretation of the collapse of the WTO Doha Round'. *Agriculture and Human Values*, 26, pp. 297–307.

Pugliese, E. (1998). 'Labour market and employment structure in the Mezzogiorno'. *Journal of Regional Policy*, 13, pp. 147–157.

Raynolds, L.T., Myhre, D., McMichael, P., Carro-Figueroa, V. and Buttel, F.H. (1993). 'The "new" internationalisation of agriculture: a reformulation'. *World Development*, 21(7), pp. 1101–1121.

Reardon, T., Timmer, C.P., Barrett, C.B., and Berdegue, J. (2003). 'The rise of supermarkets in Africa, Asia and Latin America'. *American Journal of Agricultural Economics*, 85(5), pp. 1140–1146.

Rhode, P. and Olmstead, A. (1995). 'La competencia internacional en productos mediterráneos y el auge de la industria frutícola californiana, 1880–1930' in Morilla, J. (ed.). *California y el mediterráneo: estudios de la historia de dos agriculturas competidoras.* Madrid: Ministerio de Agricultura, Alimentación y Medio Ambiente, pp. 173–232.

Sánchez Picón, A. (2005). 'Vecinos ignorados: brechas y encuentros en la historia económica desde las dos orillas (el Magreb y España)' in Nadal, J. and Parejo, A. (eds). *Mediterráneo e Historia Económica*, Alicante: Caja Rural Intermediterránea, Cajamar.

Sayad, A. (1999). *La double absence: des illusions de l'émigré aux souffrances de l'immigré.* Paris: Editions du Seuil.

Schmidhuber, J. (2007). 'The EU diet – evolution, evaluation and impacts of the CAP'. Paper presented at the WHO Forum on Trade and Healthy Food and Diets, Montreal, 7–13 November.

Sebti, A. (2013). 'Colonial experience and territorial practices' in Maghraoui, D. (ed.). *Revisiting the Colonial Past in Morocco.* London: Routledge, pp. 38–56.

Sippel, S. and Gertel, J. (2014). 'Shared insecurities? Farmers and workers in Bouches-du-Rhône' in Gertel, J. and Sippel, S.R. (2014). *Seasonal workers in Mediterranean Agriculture. The Social Costs of Eating Fresh.* London: Routledge, pp. 31–49.

Swearingen, W.D. (1987). *Moroccan Mirages: Agrarian Dreams and Deceptions, 1912–1986.* Princeton, NJ: Princeton University Press.

Tilzey, M. (2006). 'Neo-liberalism, The WTO and new modes of agrienvironmental governance in the European Union, the USA and Australia'. *International Journal of Sociology of Food and Agriculture*, 14(1), pp. 1–28.

Tilzey, M. (2009). 'Neoliberalising Global agriculture: The food crisis and the 'first' and 'second' contradictions of capitalism'. Paper prepared for RC-40 Mini-Plenary: Theoretical Perspectives on the Food Crisis.

Tilzey, M and Potter, C. (2006). 'Productivism versus post-productivism? Neo-liberalism and agri-environmental governance in Post-Fordist agricultural transitions' in Robinson, G. (ed.). *Sustainable Rural Systems: Sustainable Agriculture and Rural Communities.* Aldershot: Ashgate.

# Index

Note: Page numbers in **bold** indicate figures, tables or maps.

For Product Safety Concerns and Information please contact our EU representative GPSR@taylorandfrancis.com
Taylor & Francis Verlag GmbH, Kaufingerstraße 24, 80331 München, Germany

www.ingramcontent.com/pod-product-compliance
Ingram Content Group UK Ltd.
Pitfield, Milton Keynes, MK11 3LW, UK
UKHW021623240425
457818UK00018B/702
*9780367200121*